Pioneering a Global Vision

Pioneering a Global Vision

The Story of Baker & McKenzie

Jon R. Bauman

Designed by Pivot Design, Inc. (Chicago)
Typeset by Desktop Miracles, Inc. (Dallas)

Published by Harcourt Professional Education Group (Chicago)
1-800-787-8717

ISBN 0-15-900433-0

Printed in the United States of America.

Table of Contents

Acknowledgments & Apologia

I want to thank the one hundred eighty-plus persons who granted interviews to me. Of the persons I asked for interviews, only two refused to talk to me. These interviews, and the minutes of Baker & McKenzie meetings going back to 1961, formed the primary basis for my research.

Firm staffers, including Judy Herreweyers, Julie James, Janet Lai, Suzanne Meyers, Debbie Plucinski, Teresa Townsend, Robert Velcich, and Dolores Villa were kind and patient enough to take time from their busy schedules to respond to my questions and requests for information. Lindy Ruggiero reviewed and corrected technological material that was beyond my grasp.

I also want to thank my very excellent editor, Charlotte Wright. Trying to organize material related to hundreds of lawyers and over fifty offices was mind boggling. Ms. Wright unboggled my mind—and the text—to help produce a coherent manuscript.

A number of transcribers, including Donna Curtis, Linda Enloe, and Terry DeLeon, worked long hours, carefully listening to the tapes of persons from all over the world with dozens of accents. They put my sometimes rambling conversations with interviewees into readable form.

A special thanks goes to my editorial board, Thomas Bridgman, John Connor, Robert Cox, Wulf Döser, and Thomas Haderlein. I am sure that, when they were asked to review the text, they were flattered. However, after wading through a 1,407-page rough draft and a later draft that exceeded six hundred pages, they undoubtedly felt their task was a mixed blessing. These partners, four of whom were Chairmen, gave me invaluable guidance as to whether I had under- or over-emphasized an issue or whether I had simply missed the mark. Equally important, they insisted that I write an honest history of the stresses and successes the partners encountered as they glued together a truly cosmopolitan institution.

My last acknowledgment is to current Chairman of the Executive Committee John Klotsche, who approached me with the idea of writing the history of Baker & McKenzie's first fifty years. He understood that, because of the Firm's global sweep and the paucity of written records, the book was difficult to write, and he was unfailingly supportive.

A few apologies. To my English and Commonwealth friends for the use of American spelling and references. To the rest of the world for the use of American (English) weights and measures and references to U.S. dollars, unless otherwise indicated. To the female gender for the use of the masculine. To avoid constant explanations or the use of substantial space, I elected to follow these guidelines. I also apologize to the offices and practice groups that are not discussed in detail, but we would have had six volumes if I had dealt with them all. In addition, there were many partners and staff not mentioned in the text who contributed to the Firm's development, but time and cost limited the number of persons I could deal with.

One of my objectives was to make the book readable and interesting. To bring the story alive, I described the human dynamics that underlay Baker & McKenzie's emergence as the premier international law firm. In part, this was a reaction to the ten or so histories of other law firms that I read in order to prepare for this book. With few exceptions, they were boring descriptions of long-forgotten lawsuits and/or Martindale-Hubbell-style biographies of long-forgotten partners. Instead of that approach, I wanted to tell the story of people who were continually faced with new issues and to describe how they handled them. I also wanted to tell the story of a truly extraordinary man, Russell Baker, who lived a Horatio Alger life, starting as a dirt-poor farm boy and winding up as the founder and senior partner of the world's largest law firm.

Foreword

They were headed for Vienna. From six continents, they funneled through the Frankfurt airport on their way to Baker & McKenzie's 1991 Annual Partners Meeting. As they milled around the crowded terminal waiting for their flights to Austria's ancient capital, the partners searched for colleagues from other Firm offices. When they met, they spoke in a symphony of sounds: flat Midwestern American tones mingled with Australian brogues, and soft, slurry Brazilian Portuguese blended with guttural German.

The partners were genuinely happy to see one another after a year of separation. They had talked on the phone or exchanged telefaxes, but it wasn't the same as seeing one another in person. Some of the friendships dated back more than thirty years, and in Vienna they hoped to duplicate the good times they had had at Annual Meetings in Chicago, Madrid, Rio de Janeiro, Singapore, and other cities. Many partners remembered the 1974 Mexico City gathering, when the Firm rented a small bullring for its informal party. After downing wine and tequila, several partners entered the ring to fight the brave bulls, actually calves that got bigger as they got closer. They also recalled the "lovely tradition" of the Baker & McKenzie World Cup soccer matches, with teams of U.S., Latin American, European, and Asian partners who "were fanatic to win." These, and many other, common memories were important hardening agents in the glue that bound them together.

As the airport loudspeakers announced departure information, the partners and their families filed into the boarding lines. Most of the Baker & McKenzie fraternity looked haggard, with the men badly needing shaves and the women needing coifs after lolling in airline seats during the long flights. Those who had come from North and South America had flown all night, and the Australians and Asians had been on planes for up to twenty-four hours. Still, there was a cheerfulness, a camaraderie, a pleasure in being part of a vibrant law firm that was a pioneer in opening new offices around the world.

It was also fun to think of themselves as being what some called "the United Nations of law firms"; a partnership without nationality, where partners viewed their colleagues as partners first and only then as Chinese, Hungarian, or Venezuelan. They were particularly proud of the fact that Baker & McKenzie had eradicated the accident of nationality as a factor in determining their roles in the partnership, even though that had not always been true. Until the 1970s,

American influence had been strong. As the network of global offices grew, however, that predominance quickly faded to the point that everybody in Baker & McKenzie became a minority.

When their planes arrived in Vienna, the partners fanned out to the four hotels the Firm needed to house them and their families. Some stayed at two modern facilities, while others chose the venerable Imperial and Bristol Hotels that resonated the Austro-Hungarian Empire's nineteenth-century charm. The doormen ushered the partners into lobbies that had welcomed the world's royalty and celebrities for more than a century. When they checked in, many partners, long accustomed to handling jet lag after crossing multiple time zones, took naps. That evening, they went to dinner with their friends from London, Moscow, or elsewhere. Some went to Figmüllers, which serves the world's best wiener schnitzel, and others to the Sacher to sample its famous torte.

The next day, many partners walked along the Ringstrasse on a crisp October morning, passing the cafe where Sigmund Freud had often taken his coffee. A few yards farther on, they arrived at the Annual Meeting site, the Hofburg Palace. The Hofburg had been the seat of the Habsburg dynasty that had ruled the Empire for seven hundred years until its collapse in 1918. The Austrian government had turned the Palace into an international conference center, and, in an anteroom, the partners sipped coffee and snacked on pastries.

Knots of partners burst out laughing as they told "war stories" about deals they had worked on in Saudi Arabia or Buenos Aires. Some paired off in quiet corners to review the status of client requests for reports on discrimination laws in seventeen countries or environmental laws in the Asian and African nations. Others discussed cutting-edge business transactions in which one client was bartering French computer chips for Hungarian lambs and another was selling its stock on Asian, European, and American exchanges. In addition to mulling over the legal issues, the partners considered the cross-cultural elements that might spell the success or failure of a client's venture. Still other partners headed to the office the Firm had set up, complete with eight telefaxes, thirty computers, and fifty telephones to give them instant access to their clients around the globe.

At 9:00 A.M., the partners entered the Hofburg's former ballroom, and gazed up at its elegantly gilded and frescoed ceiling. The setting was vastly different from that of the Annual Meetings in the early 1950s—a partner's office in a Chicago office building. As late as the mid-1960s, the Firm was still small enough for the partners to sit at a square of tables where they were eye-to-eye with their colleagues. By 1991, however, Baker & McKenzie required the spacious Imperial ballroom, outfitted with a sea of tables and chairs, to seat its two hundred-eighty partners from the twenty-seven countries whose national flags decorated the dais. To keep track of who was speaking, three television cameras flashed the partners' images on huge screens as they spoke into ultra-sensitive microphones that caught each nuance of the many accents.

The meeting came to order as partners flipped through the four-inch-thick Annual Meeting books that described the agenda items. With well over ninety percent of the partners present, the Firm's chief executive, the Chairman of the Executive Committee, delivered the traditional State of the Firm address. In it, he outlined the past year's developments, mentioning the settlement of an intra-partner dispute in São Paulo and the adverse effect of the Persian Gulf War on the Firm. The next topic was most pleasing: average partner incomes had increased by twenty percent.

After the morning session ended, the partners adjourned to the Habsburg's former throne room for lunch. Surrounded by its majestic white walls decorated with ornate molding, they were gratified by the fact that Baker & McKenzie's success had surpassed the wildest imaginings of its early partners. At the end of the Firm's first year, June 30, 1950, there were five lawyers and $89,000 in gross income. By 1991, those numbers had soared to 1,576 and $478 million.

That evening, partners and their spouses attended the first of the social events. At an informal party in a former casino located in the Stadtpark, the Japanese partners bowed politely to their colleagues and the Latin Americans bear-hugged their comrades. As the partners wandered outside through the park's lush green lawn, they gossiped about the Sydney office and groused that the Executive Committee was spending too much money. While they sampled foods from the old Austro-Hungarian provinces and listened to a gypsy orchestra, they asked how their friends' children were doing at university and about their plans for hiking through the Australian outback.

The next morning, and during the rest of the meeting sessions, the partners voted on a number of routine matters, but tempers flared over several controversial issues. Passionate arguments were not new to Baker & McKenzie veterans. In the Firm's formative years, quarrels over policy and—occasionally—personality punctuated many Annual Meetings. Looking back, however, most partners felt that the open debates served as a catharsis, allowing everyone to vent their feelings and to participate in important Firm decisions. Things seldom got out of hand in the early years because the Firm's founder was always there to steady the ship, sometimes with quiet persuasion and sometimes with "arm twisting."

There were many reasons for the squabbling during the early years, but the primary one was that Baker & McKenzie was *sui generis*. Law firms had existed for centuries, but they were very localized and insular. The Firm had no blueprint to show it how to patch together a mélange of partners from every major culture, religion, race, and language group on earth. It had no formula for how to allocate costs to partners in Bogotá and Brussels or how to compensate them. And it had no model for whether to give local offices autonomy or to weld them together in a tight hierarchical structure. Compounding the problem of facing totally new issues, the personalities of the early partners sometimes created stumbling blocks. Many were highly individualistic and entrepreneurial men who rankled at any attempt to control the way they practiced law. However, they were always united on one issue: their determination to prove to the hidebound legal establishments around the world that they deserved to be counted in the first rank of lawyers.

To overcome the obstacles, Baker & McKenzie developed a unique culture under the umbrella of an "Athenian democracy." It created an objective compensation system that virtually eliminated fights over money. And it fostered the concept of one universal firm that still allowed its offices to retain their local flavor and identity.

On Friday night in Vienna, the partners donned tuxedos and many wives slipped into floor-length Biedermeier-era dresses to attend the formal dinner dance at the Gothic-style Rathaus (City Hall). During the evening, spotlights played on a troupe of professional dancers in tails and white ball gowns who recreated an 1890s Viennese gala as they swirled to Strauss waltzes and mazurkas. Later, the Chairman gave an emotional speech evoking the Firm founder's memory, the strength of the Firm's culture, and the global friendships that knitted them together. Most partners felt that the talk reinforced the Firm's spirit of adventure and renewed their sense of belonging to a unified global community.

On Saturday night, many families saw Mozart's *La Nozze de Figaro* from boxes at the famed Vienna State Opera House. Others strolled through the city's old center, admiring the brilliantly lit St. Stephan's Cathedral and chatting about their tours of the Schönbrunn and Belvedere Palaces. After a snack at one of Vienna's historic coffeehouses, they browsed gallery windows displaying works by Austria's famed artists Gustav Klimt and Egon Schiele.

Baker & McKenzie partners would never have enjoyed the glamour and excitement of strolling through Vienna unless one man had had a vision of a globe-straddling law firm. To help him cobble his dream into a firm that would break the bonds of the parochial legal profession, Russell Baker recruited a talented cadre of lawyers. Understanding that a firm's lawyers are its machines, he mined a mother lode of clients to keep them working. He also crafted a cultural superstructure that gave Baker & McKenzie the flexibility to adjust to changing world conditions, and that permitted it to carry out its mission of providing quality legal services to its clients.

Chapter One

Absorbing Frontier Cultures: Russell Baker, 1901–1919

In the early 1900s, the American West was an uncomplicated place, a world with dew on it, a world largely rural and isolationist. Its rustic inhabitants were only a generation away from the frontier, the Wild West. They had rough manners and used earthy language. With Jeffersonian independence, they operated their own farms and ranches and rejected the corrosive traditions of aristocracy and hierarchy. Westerners saw themselves as new men with new hope in a new world. They were convinced that their democracy, coupled with their spirit of entrepreneurship and individualism, had allowed them to complete their century-long march across the continent.

To win life's battles, Westerners believed, a man had to be self-reliant, competitive, and pragmatic. He could not waste time pondering theoretical possibilities, but needed to get directly to the main point of an issue. To build something out of nothing, a man had to rely on his own effort and be willing to take risks. He had to work, and he had to stand ready to fight to protect his interests. That, mixed with a dollop of luck, was the way a man made his mark, the way he built something of lasting value.

Most turn-of-the-century Americans, protected by the Atlantic and Pacific Oceans from Europe's squabbling royal families and Asia's struggles, looked inward, defining their lives by the nation's borders. The only reason Americans looked across those oceans was to track the wars, pogroms, and famines that sent millions of immigrants fleeing to their country. Although the country was insular and isolationist, a few Americans sensed that the twentieth century might be their time in history. It was into this uniquely American framework that Mary Day Baker gave birth to Thomas Russell Baker,[1] the fourth of her five sons, on April 28, 1901. Russell's four brothers would be uncomplicated and ordinary. He would not.

His father, George Baker, was a farmer in Portage County, Wisconsin, laboring to make a living for his wife and sons. Sometime in 1912, however, George became interested in moving his family away from Wisconsin's snows to West Texas's flat, dry plains. He made several trips to Crosby County, Texas, checking out land deals being offered by a group of Chicago land promoters calling themselves the C.B. Livestock Company.

Europeans had first seen this land in 1541 when Francisco Vásquez de Coronado and his Spanish conquistadors crossed the Llano Estacado in search of the jewels, gold, and silver that the Indians had told them were theirs for the taking. Until the Americans pushed into West Texas after the Civil War, Comanche, Kiowa, and Cheyenne warriors ruled the Llano Estacado. Men not much older than George Baker remembered that the Plains Indians were so fierce that only a few Hispanic Comancheros were brave enough to venture out on the Llano Estacado to trade guns and liquor for horses and long-horned cattle.

In the 1870s, the U.S. Cavalry subdued the Indians and forced them to live on reservations. The first permanent settler, a cattleman, came to Crosby Country in 1876 to take advantage of the free grass on the open range. Later, a group of Kentucky whiskey makers founded the first large ranch in Crosby County. Later, slumping cattle prices forced the Two Buckle Ranch's owners to sell the land to C.B. Livestock. Around 1912, George Baker read the company's glossy brochure extolling the wonders and riches of Crosby County. The land promoters downplayed the area's quixotic weather and rainfall, and touted the richness of the chocolate loam soil as perfect for growing abundant crops.

After he bounced around the county's dirt roads in a land salesman's auto, George Baker decided to buy a flat piece of land three miles south of the county seat. He closed on the purchase of his four hundred eighty acres in March 1913, paying $31.70 per acre. Evidently, he had gotten a good price from the sale of his Wisconsin farm, because he paid eighty percent of the $15,216 purchase price in cash. C.B. Livestock took a promissory note for part of the balance and Baker assumed an existing note for the rest.

The exact date that Russell Baker and his family moved to Crosby County is not known. But, when the twelve-year-old boy got off the train in the county seat, Crosbyton, he saw a neatly surveyed and divided town. It had a volunteer fire department and a horse-drawn fire engine, which was a set of buggy wheels with a barrel mounted on it. Crosbyton boasted a courthouse, railroad station, school, churches, three hotels, and a steam-powered cotton gin. The town had no saloons or bars because the straight-laced Protestants would not tolerate the sale of alcohol. There were a few lawyers, but, in a C.B. Livestock publicity pamphlet, the County Judge attested: "Litigation has not been heavy . . . and I see no indications of its growing very much . . . [because] our people love peace, and if any difficulties arise, they are usually settled out of court."

Even though Crosby County had many civilizing amenities, when the Baker family moved there the land was still virgin. Native buffalo and gamma grasses still covered much of the soil, providing food and home to pronghorned antelope, quail, rabbits, and mustang horses, the descendants of Spanish horses that had escaped into the wild centuries before.

George Baker broke the ground with his plow, planting thirty acres in cotton, one hundred thirty acres in maize, and thirty acres in corn. The rest he left in grass for the twenty-three Holstein dairy cattle he brought with him from Wisconsin and the fifty cows he bought in Crosbyton. He loved his new home. In a testimonial letter he wrote to C.B. Livestock, he proclaimed that "this country can be made to produce as much butter and cheese per acre as can be produced on the high-priced lands in the dairy district of Wisconsin. Fruits of all kinds do well here. [There is a] fine class of people, splendid school and church . . . climate ideal . . . an abundance of rainfall . . . ."

Despite the senior Baker's Eden-like description of life in Crosby County, Russell Baker and his father and brothers worked hard, plowing with mules to raise their crops and working cattle on horseback. Russell liked working the cattle, but he hated the farm work. He later told a friend that "looking at a mule's ass" from behind a plow made him start thinking about a career off the farm. It was sometime during this period that Baker decided that he wanted to be a lawyer. Why he chose that path was a mystery, even to himself. He once said that he "had never had any contact with lawyers or with the law. There were no lawyers in my family. Why or how the idea became a fixed purpose with me, I am unable to say. But it did."

As a teenager, Russell understood that the thing that would get him off the farm was an education. A few musty school books with his name in them testify that he got part of his schooling in West Texas. He attended Crosbyton High School, where he struck a solemn pose in a starched white collar and tie for a photo on the school's front steps. Probably, Baker's early schooling was not of the highest quality. All his life, he had trouble with mathematics, "and he couldn't spell worth a damn either," his son Wallace says.

At school, Baker undoubtedly heard stories of how mounted Indians drove panicked buffalo over the sides of the steep cliffs of Blanco Canyon, about two miles east of his father's farm. The wild frontier was a vivid image for a boy his age, and the tales of Comanche massacres and Cavalry charges must have been passed around the schoolyard. More immediately, Baker and his schoolmates gossiped about the cattle rustlers who still prowled the ranges in Crosby County. In addition to the dangers of cattle thieves, West Texas's unpredictable weather was a constant hazard. Crosby County is in the heart of the tornado belt, and Baker always remembered the loss he suffered when a "twister" swooped away his pet eagle.

The Bakers' first three years in Crosbyton were good years for moisture. Between 1913 and 1915, over twenty inches of rain doused the Baker farm every year. But, in 1916, the clouds spawned only ten inches of rain, half the area's average. During the spring growing months, the rainfall was so paltry that only weak sprigs came out of the ground. May was the worst month, with only .02 inches of rain. One bad year followed another. In 1917, Crosby County got a meager 12.5 inches of rain.

Even though George Baker didn't owe much for his land, he, like all other farmers, had undoubtedly borrowed money to buy seed, build his house and barns, and cover other farm expenses. For many farmers, one dry year forced them into bankruptcy. George Baker struggled for two years to save his farm. Then, in the winter of 1917, he decided to move to New Mexico to try his luck.

———

Russell Baker never discussed the reasons his family left West Texas, but he never forgot the bitter winter cold when they traveled to the eastern slope of the Sangre de Cristo Mountains in a horse-drawn wagon. "We practically froze to death on the way because we were camping out with primitive equipment," he said. The Bakers shivered on their wagon trip across the flat, arid country between Texas and New Mexico. When they arrived at their new home at the foot of the eleven-thousand-foot Sangre de Cristo Mountains, it must have seemed like a deliverance.

In the tiny community of Sapello, George Baker acquired one hundred thirty-three acres of land bordering the swift-flowing Sapello River. Included on the home place were a classic Spanish adobe house that dated back to the 1840s, corrals, barns, and sheds. Baker also bought 1,435 acres of "dry land" just to the east, where he could graze horses and cattle and grow corn to feed pigs and chickens.

When the Baker family went to Sapello in 1917, they moved into a Hispanic town, where the ninety families who lived there did almost all their business in Spanish. Even though New Mexico had been part of the United States since 1848, the habits and customs in Sapello were Spanish. The women baked bread in beehive-shaped adobe *hornos* (ovens) that sat in the back yard. In the Catholic Church, the priests performed baptisms, weddings, and funerals for the village's faithful. One of the most revered saints in Our Lady of Guadalupe Church was San Isidro, the patron saint of farmers. Each year, the villagers took San Isidro's statue out of the Church and paraded him under the cloudless blue sky in the hope that his magic would bring about a good harvest. Although they were not Catholic, the Bakers dropped money in the Church's offering box so that San Isidro would look favorably on them. Years later, when Russell Baker owned the family ranch, he continued the tradition in the hope that San Isidro would bring him luck.

In 1917, few automobiles stirred the dust of Sapello's roads, and most farmers relied on wagons and carts to transport their supplies. The only light came from kerosene lanterns and wood fires, and telephones would not arrive in the remote hamlet for years. In the village's six saloons and small plaza, men repeated the legends and stories that were part of Sapello's fabric. Russell Baker no doubt heard the tales from the children of parents or grandparents who had been alive when macabre or mysterious events occurred.

One story involved a strange Italian mystic who walked down the Santa Fe Trail in 1864, and took up residence in Sapello. With his flowing white hair and beard, he looked like a nineteenth-century artist's version of the Almighty. Many people believed the Italian, who they called *El Ermitano* (the Hermit), had miraculous healing powers. He left Sapello and moved to a cave on a nearby mountain, which is still called Hermit's Peak.

Teen-aged boys like Baker would also have relished the story of Paula Angel's crime of passion and gruesome death. A jury sentenced her to be executed for stabbing her lover in the Sapello cemetery. Paula rode to the hanging in a wagon, sitting on her coffin. When the first attempt to hang her failed because she grabbed the rope with her untied hands, the sheriff cut the gasping woman down. This time, he tied her hands behind her back, and hanged her again. Baker probably heard Paula's tale in Spanish. The preceding three centuries of Spanish and Mexican rule continued to set the village's tone and tempo. He learned to love the Hispanic culture, and, years later, he told a Hispanic friend: "You know, everything good that has happened to me has had a little Latino in it."

While he was learning to speak Spanish and was absorbing the Hispanic culture, Russell Baker and his brothers worked on the farm. They slopped the hogs in pens behind the house; hoed the weeds so they wouldn't choke the corn, beans, squash, beets, and lettuce in their kitchen garden; cleaned irrigation ditches; and slouched in their saddles as they rode horseback over the "dry land" to herd their cattle. To bring in the cattle, Russell learned to call them with a trumpet blast shout that strained his lungs and vocal cords. When the animals bunched up, the Baker men drove them into a rock corral close to the house for branding, dehorning, and castration. Some of the cows were dairy breeds. When they produced surplus milk, Russell loaded the cans on a horse-drawn wagon and took it to Las Vegas, New Mexico to sell. In 1917, a one-way trip from Sapello to Las Vegas took almost half a day. In dry weather, a choking layer of yellow dust covered the road. In the wet, the thoroughfare turned into a deeply rutted bog that sucked at horses' hoofs and wagon wheels.

Because the road to the county seat was so bad, when Russell Baker decided to further his schooling, he probably moved into a Las Vegas boarding house that catered to country children who wanted to get a high school education. His insistence on continuing his studies led to quarrels with his parents, who argued that going to school was a waste of time. What a strapping young man needed to do, the parents said, was to stay on the farm and work. Years later, Baker still resented the clashes with his parents over whether he should work or study. "There was lots of squabbling. Lots of fighting," his son Donald says. "It was not a happy, close-knit family."

Despite his parents' disapproval, Russell Baker went down the winding road to Las Vegas, a town still under the influence of the Wild West and its frontier values. From its beginning some eighty years earlier, Las Vegas had been a tough way station on the Santa Fe trail. Comancheros, travelers, and settlers came and went, but the Santa Fe Railroad put Las Vegas on the map. The Santa Fe's steel rails arrived in 1879, linking the isolated little town with Chicago, and making a three-day journey of what had previously taken weeks.

Just as gold discoveries elsewhere in the West had lured seamy gamblers, whores, and reprobates, Las Vegas's new prosperity attracted many of the most notorious outlaws. "[N]o town . . . harbored a more disreputable gang of gangsters, desperadoes, and outlaws than did Las Vegas. [Near the railroad depot] were located some of the most disreputable saloons, dance halls, and resorts [bordellos] ever seen in frontier days. The gambling houses never closed . . . ."[2] Jesse James, Billy the Kid, Doc Holliday, and Wyatt Earp all spent time in Las Vegas. Lesser known characters included the Pock-Marked Kid and Bull Shit Jack.

Despite the town's raucous past, in 1917 Russell Baker entered the civilizing world of New Mexico Normal University. Although the school's name proclaimed it a university, it also offered high school courses and gave secondary school degrees. New Mexico Normal's catalogue described the school as having excellent teachers and Las Vegas as a place with a delightful climate that had "no mosquitoes, fleas or other annoying insects." Tuition was $3.75 per semester, plus a $5.00 book deposit.

To pay for his schooling, Baker worked as a busboy and janitor in a cafe near the railroad station. During his two years in Las Vegas, the town was a major stop on the Santa Fe Railroad's Chicago to Los Angeles route. When the passenger trains steamed into Las Vegas, the travelers jumped off to grab a quick meal in the cafe. As he worked his way between the tables picking up dirty dishes and soiled napkins, Baker no doubt heard the passengers talking about the bustling city of Chicago. After the diners finished their meals, Baker performed one of his other duties, beating on a large iron triangle with a metal bar to signal that the engines were stoking their boilers.

Before Baker got his high school degree from New Mexico Normal, he may have visited some of the sights around Las Vegas, where the cinema's first cowboy hero, Tom Mix, had made four movies in 1915. But Baker didn't need to see a Tom Mix film to tell him what the West was like. He was so close to the frontier that he could feel it. Las Vegas might have had electric streetcars rather than stagecoaches when Baker was there, but the frontier spirit was still alive and well.

The strong anti-German sentiment during and after World War I also influenced Baker. The university's newspaper, *The Trigonian News*, reported on a speech that Baker made to his classmates. In it, he accused Germany of stealing all its World War I weapons technology from other countries. But he painted a bright post-war future for Germany, one in which "workingmen [would be] paid a living wage and [there would be] a newer, better type of womanhood." The newspaper reporter gushed that, "We can see in the canvas of the future a great American lawyer and statesman who will honor the N.M.N.U. by his great deeds, for, if Russell Baker continues his promising speeches, he will surely be known to the annals of history as the greatest American statesman since Daniel Webster."

A later edition of the university newspaper jokingly predicted that Baker would become President of the United States, fulfilling his class's motto of "Over the Top." And, just before he graduated on May 28, 1919, an article making fun of the graduates listed Baker's chief occupation as "foolishness." At Baker's graduation ceremonies, a professor delivered a surprisingly international commencement address, "Pan-Americanism and the League of Nations," to his provincial audience.

———————

All his life, Baker would love New Mexico's beauty. But he was eighteen years old, and he had made the decision that he would go to a university and become a lawyer. He received no encouragement from his parents, but he knew that he did not want to spend his life scratching out a living from what he called a "dirt poor ranch." Why Baker chose to go to Chicago is not clear. Perhaps a fierce ambition spurred him to go to America's largest city outside the East Coast. Perhaps he was caught up in America's infectious optimism of the early 1900s: the idea that a man, with enough hard work and a little luck, could better his lot. Or, as Baker's eldest son Wallace says, his father went to Chicago for no other reason than "that was the end of the Santa Fe line."

Whatever the motivation, Russell Baker made his first train trip to Chicago in 1920. He often told how he could not afford a train ticket, so for part of the trip he "rode the rails" on a cattle train. Recalling the journey, Baker said it "was colder than hell . . . but I could sit on the backs of those fat steers. They were nice and warm."[3] Baker's traveling companions, the cattle, were on their way to end their lives in Chicago's great slaughterhouses. But Russell Baker, who first saw Chicago from a boxcar door, was on his way to start a new life.

Chapter Two

Life Before the Firm:
Russell Baker, 1920–1949

The University of Chicago accepted Russell Baker as an undergraduate student in 1920, even though he himself said that he had only had a "fragmentary and undistinguished secondary education" from schools on the Western frontier. He took general humanities courses, including political science, Spanish, and geology. He also probed the intricacies of logic and learned to twist and turn syllogisms to win an argument. His undergraduate efforts at Chicago produced a lackluster "C" average.

Baker found a number of jobs, including work as a janitor at the Del Prado Hotel, where he mopped floors and washed dishes. In addition to his salary, the hotel gave him his meals and a room heavily populated by cockroaches. "It was menial work," his son James says. "He was doing that and getting through his studies at the same time, which made those years difficult for him." Russell Baker was more sanguine when talking about the experience years later. "It was a good job," he said. "It was warm. There was food. And a little bit of money. I stayed there seven [sic] years [during undergraduate and law schools]."

To pick up extra money, Baker put to practical use the boxing lessons he took for his physical education requirements. At county fairs, he stood in the ring and offered to fight all comers. At about five feet, ten inches tall and rather slight, Baker undoubtedly took on a number of hulking farm boys who were out to impress their sweethearts. He must have been a better-than-average boxer, because he carried no scars from his days in the ring. "It was the easiest way I knew to make $25 a night—even though I had to get knocked out to do it," he said years later.

Although he had to work to pay for his schooling, the energetic young man found time to belong to the Delta Chi fraternity. Baker was also active in the Western Club and was on the track team. He improved his dramatic skills by acting in Shakespearean and other plays with a campus theatrical group called the Blackfriars. Baker's thespian talents were not limited to the classics. He played the part of a cowboy in a Wild West show produced by the Western Club. For a publicity photo, a grinning Baker posed in familiar clothing: a cowboy's wide-brimmed hat, neckerchief, and work shirt.

Baker found time not only for recreation, but also for courting a young woman who had transferred from Stanford University to the University of Chicago. During a University of Chicago football game, Baker was working as part of the crowd control crew. "Stagg Field was surrounded by low brick walls," his son Donald says, "and he was standing on the wall with a megaphone directing the crowd. Mother was part of the crowd, and that's the first time they saw one another."

When they met on a more formal basis, Elizabeth Wallace was attracted to the young man with light brown, wavy hair and penetrating blue eyes. They soon found that they had a mutual interest in the Spanish language and culture, as well as ice-skating on the frozen ponds near the University of Chicago campus. Although the young couple had many interests in common, there was a large gap between their backgrounds. Baker's parents had grubbed out a living farming and ranching, and Elizabeth's parents had spent most of their careers as Presbyterian missionaries in Mexico attempting to woo Mexicans away from the Catholic Church's baroque finery to the austerity of Scotland's contribution to religion. The Wallace family had little money, but both parents were well educated and well respected. William Wallace had been a brilliant student, winning a Phi Beta Kappa key from his college. And he could read the Bible in Greek, Latin, Hebrew, and Spanish.

While the Wallaces were working and living on the high desert plateau of central Mexico, they awaited Elizabeth's birth, which came only five months after Russell Baker was born in Wisconsin. When the Wallaces' first child was born in Saltillo on September 22, 1901, President Porfirio Diaz ruled Mexico with an iron hand. Nine years later, Mexico's disenfranchised peons rebelled against the vestiges of the Creole aristocracy and the new industrial class that Diaz favored.

In the Mexico City suburb where the Wallaces lived, they heard Emiliano Zapata's peasant troops firing their rifles. Later, Elizabeth watched from her roof as General Victoriano Huerta bombarded Mexico City for ten days. After the shelling stopped, Elizabeth heard boots tramping down the cobblestone street in front of her house, and then a knock on the door. Huerta's troops demanded that Elizabeth's mother turn over the house to them for use as a barracks, but Mary

Wallace refused to leave. When the troops left, Ms. Wallace took her family into hiding with a neighbor, fearful that her brashness might cause the soldiers to return to seek retribution.

After a few days in hiding, Elizabeth, carrying her doll Martha, moved with her family to a location in another part of Mexico City. During the trip through the capital, Elizabeth passed through the Zocalo, Mexico City's main square, and saw "dead bodies lying in the street, the shade trees charred and burnt, and the walls of the Cathedral, [and] the National Palace . . . pock-marked with bullet holes."[1] As the killing reached a frightening level, William Wallace and his family boarded a train for Vera Cruz, Mexico's chief port on the Gulf of Mexico. The train crept along, and, during one stretch of the journey, Elizabeth looked out the open windows and saw the bodies of hanged men swinging from telephone poles only a few feet away. In Vera Cruz, Wallace arranged passage on a steamer headed for America. From New Orleans, the family made their way to Palo Alto, California.

Even though Elizabeth had left Mexico as a child, she took with her a fluency in Spanish and a bicultural upbringing that would serve her well. When she was old enough, Elizabeth enrolled in Stanford University. Mid-way through her college career, her aunt, also named Elizabeth Wallace, invited her niece-namesake to transfer to the University of Chicago, where she taught Romance languages. Elizabeth accepted her aunt's invitation, and transferred to Chicago, where she would meet her future husband. She never listed the reasons why a well brought-up missionaries' daughter was interested in someone like Russell Baker, but her sister Janet says that, out of all the boys she dated, the most attractive was "a handsome ex-cowboy, Russ Baker, who at age 16 [sic] had taken his $60 savings and ridden a freight train from his parents' dirt-poor ranch in New Mexico to Chicago to get a college education."

Even though the ambitious young man was appealing in many ways, he didn't have the same pedigree that Elizabeth did. Two of her uncles were successful businessmen in Minnesota. And there was the immediate presence of Aunt Elizabeth, a Wellesley graduate whose photographs reflect a formidable Victorian grande dame. "She felt that my father was not a worthy partner for my mother, and that my mother was making a big mistake," Donald Baker says. "My father felt inferior from a social point of view." For one of the few times in his life, Russell Baker was intimidated. Years later, he told Elizabeth's sister, "I was scared to death of your Aunt Elizabeth, until one night when I brought your sister home and came into the hallway to say good night to her. Your aunt's bedroom door was open, and the snores that came out of there were shaking the walls. Then, I knew she was human. I wasn't afraid any more." Over the years, the older woman's feelings toward Baker mellowed, and she came to appreciate "his Will Rogers, earthy sense of humor."

Still, Baker remained self-conscious about his lack of family background. Regarding his wife, Baker wrote, "Dibsie [his pet name for Elizabeth] married me out of innocent recklessness. What a chance she took! Careful, calculating girls look for a guy from a good family, backed up with as much dough as possible."

———

Baker came under the influence of a small group of University of Chicago professors who looked at the world beyond America's borders. From them, he developed an interest in internationalism. "There was a Professor Good at the University of Chicago," Baker said, "a geographer, and he published a monograph called 'Chicago, the City of Destiny.' He described Chicago's future from a geographer's point of view, putting it right in the center of the universe."[2] Baker's attachment to the internationalist scholars was so strong that, even after he graduated, he remained friends with several of his old professors and had lunch with them at the University of Chicago's Quadrangle Club.

But Baker and this handful of globally inclined professors were a minority. In reaction to World War I's horrors, many Americans had turned even more inward. They proudly labeled themselves isolationists, and vowed that America would never again involve itself in foreign wars. The isolationists believed that America had been suckered into World War I, a war between aristocrats, kaisers, and kings fighting over issues and territories that had no impact on, or importance to, the United States. Americans were quite content to remove themselves from the international community, and to devote their energies to the "flapper" era of the 1920s. The nation's largest interior city, Chicago, was a hotbed of isolationism. Many of its prominent citizens fully agreed with the U.S.'s withdrawal from world affairs. *The Chicago Tribune* trumpeted the doctrine of "America First," and told its readers to heed George Washington's warning to avoid entangling foreign alliances. The 1920s fervor to quarantine America led to the Smoot-Hawley Tariff Act of 1930. That new law raised import duties to an average of sixty percent, virtually cutting off the country from world trade.

Despite the nation's powerful isolationist bias, Baker was fascinated by the University of Chicago internationalists' claims that the United States would play an important global role. "The world was growing smaller by the day," Baker wrote, "and . . . the peoples and nations of the world were becoming increasingly interdependent. Realization was growing that the frontier for American business for the rest of the century would be as much outside this country as within it." He sometimes participated in a bit of boosterism, saying that Chicago had assumed "a dominant position as the center for air travel, domestic and international, [because it was] the traditional center of transportation for the North American Continent, be the vehicle a birch-bark canoe, a river raft, steamboat, railroad or motor vehicle."

Although the internationalists' vision of America's future captured Baker's imagination, the young man stayed focused on his first priority—doing the academic work that would make him a lawyer. He began his law studies in 1922,[3] but his marks were as undistinguished as his undergraduate grades had been. During his law school career, he earned two As, twelve Bs, ten Cs, one D, and two Es. A partial excuse for the twenty-four-year-old Baker's marks was that he was juggling his studies with his courtship of Elizabeth and his work schedule.

In the summers, Baker worked for the Chicago Motor Club ("CMC"), selling road maps to farmers in the rural towns surrounding Chicago. Because his own farm background made it easy for him to tailor his sales pitch to the Illinois farmers, he made good money peddling the maps. He also learned some of the art of salesmanship. Later, Baker worked nights and weekends as a clerk for the CMC, handling members' calls for assistance if their cars broke down. After regular hours he moonlighted as a trial lawyer. In the first court appearances of his career, Baker tried traffic ticket cases in Justice of the Peace courts.[4] Later, he remembered that the money his clients had paid him was "a welcome supplement to a meager salary." In these lowest level courts, where the judges were often not lawyers, the trials could be "rough or hilarious or sometimes both," Baker recalled. For the ex-prize fighter, the rough and tumble of slugging it out orally in court must have been exciting, even though it was on the bottom rung of the legal profession.

After Elizabeth graduated in 1923, she moved to San Francisco to find a job near her family. Baker followed her to press his courtship, spending some of his hard-earned money on a three-day train journey to California. During that trip, Baker asked Elizabeth to marry him, and she agreed. He returned to Chicago, and finished his third year of law school in 1925. Although he lacked one course to earn his law degree, he took and passed the Illinois Bar Examination, and was duly enrolled as a licensed lawyer.

In the early summer of that year, Baker went to Mexico City, where Elizabeth's parents had returned to live after the Revolution's violence had subsided. Before the wedding day, Russell and Elizabeth strolled through the woods around Chapultepec Castle, and boated through the floating gardens of Xochimilco. The Revolution had had such a strong anti-clerical element that

Mexican law required the couple to have a civil ceremony in addition to a religious one.

On the day before the religious wedding, a *Juez Civil* (Civil Judge) came to the Wallace house in San Angel. The Judge read the prescribed Articles of the Mexican Constitution related to marriage, and watched as Elizabeth and Russell signed the *Acta de Matrimonio* (Marriage Contract) to solemnize the marriage. Elizabeth's father noted that the Judge, the witnesses, and the newlyweds drank sherry and ate wedding cake, "adjourning in a delightful state of mind. Not, however, before the Judge handed me a receipt for thirty pesos to cover the dignity of the marriage in one's own house."

On the day of the religious wedding, June 5, 1925, Russell and Elizabeth went to Christ Church, where William Wallace and two other Protestant ministers conducted the nuptials. The bride and groom, Wallace recalled, wore their "going away costume—Russell a soft white collar and shirt, with blue tie, and light woolen suit of soft tannish gray and brown tan shoes. With his broad face, square shoulders and height, he made a very good match physically for the bride. Elizabeth wore an ensemble designed by herself . . . ." Wallace was pleased with his new son-in-law. "The fact is that, during the whole week of wedding festivities, we have not had a single incident to regret, and Russell has endeared himself to us all. He says very little, but his personality is so clean and deep and solid, that we congratulate Elizabeth on bringing him into the family. Mumsey and I have returned home feeling very happy over the whole affair, especially glad we have had the privilege of knowing Russell."

Baker had scraped together enough money to pay for a wedding lunch at one of Mexico City's finest restaurants, near the Chapultepec Castle. As the wedding party was leaving, the Mexican President, Plutarco Calles, was entering, and nodded politely to the newlyweds. Afterwards, Elizabeth and Russell Baker drove through the mountains to Cuernavaca. There, they spent their honeymoon weekend in a well-appointed country house owned by a friend of the Wallaces. Shortly before or after the wedding, Baker took Elizabeth to Sapello, New Mexico, to introduce her to his family. "I think he was a little bit leery about introducing his family to [Elizabeth because her family] was so highly educated, and his family wasn't," Janet Ullmann says. "I think he was embarrassed by them. They hadn't climbed out of it."

After the newlyweds returned to Chicago, Baker occupied himself with plotting his career course. Because of his undergraduate interest in geology, he considered going back to the Southwest and becoming a mining lawyer. "But I discovered that mining law is practiced where the money is and not where the mines are," Baker said. "I was so damn poor I couldn't leave town. Besides, we liked Chicago very much."

Even before he had married, Baker had begun sorting through the alternative ways to practice law. Small-town law practice had no appeal. During his trips to rural counties selling maps to farmers, he had met some of the local lawyers and decided, he said, that "the practice of law in a county seat was a rather dismal experience and held very little attraction. The typical pattern was for individual lawyers to operate from a one- or two-room office, in drab one-story buildings clustered side by side around the Court House Square. They were not much concerned with the affairs of the world."

Having ruled out a country practice, he had to decide whether to become a sole practitioner, along with seventy-five percent of Chicago's lawyers. Or he could work on salary for a company or become a partner with one or two other lawyers. The other choice was to join a large law firm, which, at the time, would have had ten or twelve lawyers. Some of the larger firms had been built on the reputation of a single man, such as Clarence Darrow, who was renowned for his defense of the evolution theory in the Scopes Monkey Trial. To Baker, "that type of practice had a limited appeal. It lacked the element of continuity. The practice died or disintegrated with the man."

Another reason he wanted to avoid large law firms, he said, was that he was "without antecedents, connections, money, or influence." In the 1920s, many traditional law firms expected junior attorneys to spend several years working for minimal pay. One of Baker's law school friends, a Phi Beta Kappa in undergraduate school, had graduated number one in the University of Chicago Law School's 1925 class. He then took a job with one of Chicago's top law firms at a $100 per month salary. "It was thought that a period of apprenticeship was necessary," Baker said. "I noted, however, that the period of apprenticeship was often extended for as long as the victim would take it—all under the transparent pretext that what the young lawyer needed was experience rather than adequate compensation. That system was exploitive." And, as a practical matter, "it was not possible for a married man to live on what the traditional law firms were willing to pay a beginning lawyer."

Baker never got over his distaste for the financial exploitation of young lawyers by their elders. Nor did he get over his resentment of the old-line law firms that hired the well-connected young men, regardless of their skills, who had the right social graces and who belonged to the right clubs. The rough-hewn young man from the frontier had none of this to offer.

With the establishment law firms eliminated from consideration, Baker still had the urgent need to make a living for himself and his new wife. At first, he stayed with the CMC, where the steady income was comforting. But, after some six months, he quit, even though his CMC income was, he said, "four times more than what I could have earned as a starting lawyer in a law office. But defending speeders and reckless drivers was not the kind of law I was interested in spending my life practicing."

Baker entered into private practice with a law school friend, Dana Simpson, and they named their firm Simpson & Baker. Even though Baker had few clients and little money, he bought a Model T Ford with a fabric top and no side curtains. "It was real fresh breezing around Chicago in that outfit in below-zero weather," he said. "The total emphasis was finding enough income to pay the rent and to support our families. We had to take what we could get, and what we got ranged pretty well over the whole spectrum of the problems of the poor and the unimportant people."

Baker says he dedicated himself "to the primary task of generating enough fee income to stay alive. That was no easy task, considering that the Depression began in earnest in 1929. Those years were interesting and exciting, but not remunerative. As a training ground, those first ten years of practice were worthwhile. It was a litigation practice in the areas of bankruptcy, immigration, criminal, and tort law. The clients were individuals, generally without means, except for their earnings at hard labor."

In his search for clients, Baker utilized his understanding of Hispanic culture. In the mid-1920s, some 125,000 Hispanics lived in Chicago, and many of them needed legal representation. But, even with his fluency in Spanish, he knew he couldn't sit on his hands and expect to get clients. "I made contact with the Mexican Consulate General here," Baker recalled, "and began getting 'denial of justice cases'—cases decided against Mexican nationals on the basis of prejudice, not on evidence."

In the 1920s, the bigotry against Mexicans was not limited to Cook County's courts. It also showed up on the streets. Most Americans remembered that Mexico's revolutionary government had expropriated American property, and that Pancho Villa had invaded Columbus, New Mexico, killing seventeen Americans in a 1916 raid. Those events, and the fact that many Mexicans were poor, created a situation where "prejudice against Mexicans was severe," Baker said. "You had to be a good trial lawyer to get a verdict for a Mexican. And you had to be lucky."

Chicago's police sometimes abused Mexican nationals so badly that their government issued official protests. Although Baker detested the injustices, in court he was usually even-tempered and under control. In one case, however, Baker's temper flared. He thought the judge had shown bias against his Mexican client, and shouted that the judge was "off base." That outburst brought him a night in jail for contempt of court. Baker snorted privately that his black-robed adversary was a "roughneck judge."

That story may have helped him become better known in the Mexican community. The Consul fed him a steady stream of his citizens. "Russell became sort of like their public defender," James Baker says. In addition to representing Mexicans in court, Baker soon discovered that their poverty could produce another revenue stream for his fledgling law practice. He developed a substantial bankruptcy practice for what he called "economic refugees." Instinctively, Baker took the side of the underdog Mexicans who, he said, were exploited by "loan sharks and the fast-talking merchants who sold on extended credit terms at very high prices and at elevated interest rates. Those bastards shouldn't have sold them so much."

In what he believed to be an innovation, Baker proudly took credit for being one of the first lawyers to use the bankruptcy laws to protect ordinary laborers. "We gave many hundreds of Mexicans a new financial start by restoring them to solvency with a discharge in bankruptcy," he wrote. To handle the "vigorous increase" of work and to keep the fees low, Baker set up an assembly line of standard form bankruptcy court documents, which only required him to fill in blank spaces. Although he sympathized with his underdog clients, Baker was equally interested in the business side of his practice. Referring to some of his less-grateful bankruptcy clients, he said, "By the time the client had been restored to solvency, he often had developed a flexible conscience in the matter of paying our fees."

Baker did some legal work for free, betting that the client, or one of his relatives, would come back with a personal injury or criminal case that would produce fees. The strategy worked. In addition to the routine criminal cases, he represented several Hispanics accused of murder. The State of Illinois paid lawyers $200, a large sum at the time, to represent accused murderers. He defended at least twenty-one murder cases, and none of his clients was electrocuted. "You should have seen [Baker] in criminal cases, defending stabbing murders," a former Baker clerk said.[5] "He was a whirlwind, and so logical and dramatic. He swung around the courtroom in a most convincing manner, and convinced juries . . . that these unfortunate men were victims of circumstances and their environment. [T]hey all wound up in Joliet [the Illinois State Prison], fortunately with life sentences instead of capital punishment."

During his first murder trial, Baker had an epiphany. As the jury was filing back into the courtroom to deliver its verdict, his client clamped his hand so tightly on Baker's arm that he feared it would injure him. The thought flashed through Baker's mind that he was the only thing separating the accused from the electric chair. "You know," Baker said, "once you do that, nothing in your life ever again frightens you. When that jury came in and acquitted him, from that day forward, nothing ever frightened me again. Once you face up to that, if you're going to be a lawyer and put yourself in that position consciously, then everything else is easier."

In addition to criminal cases, Baker and his partner "became, under the stern hand of necessity, quite successful personal injury lawyers. Verdicts were small, but they were numerous, and we eked out a poor living for several years." As Baker's reputation as a plaintiff's lawyer grew, the insurance companies began noticing him, and started hiring him to defend, rather than sue, them. At the same time, Baker was tiring of the plaintiff's practice and wanted a more reliable income to support his growing family. "The insurance companies paid our fees whether we won the case or lost it," he said. Eventually, Baker assembled an impressive stable of insurance company clients, including Insurance Company of North America, Aetna Casualty, and Fireman's Fund. He also defended several self-insured corporate clients, such as Standard Oil of Indiana and Montgomery Ward.

"He won those cases," his son Wallace says, "because he was so intense. He worked like crazy. He worked about four times as hard as the other guy. He just prepared the hell out of all of those cases. He had an attractive personality, and was handsome. And he had a good touch with the common people on the juries." Baker firmly believed in the frontiersman's credo that sheer hard work could overcome any obstacle. "Russell never thought that he was particularly brilliant," his son James says. "He always laid his success to hard work. He felt he had to keep working all of the time." Baker used preparation and hard work as his first line of defense—and attack. He seemed to feel that he was always starting from behind, beginning with his rural primary and secondary education and his mediocre college and law school records. Although he had gaps in his background, he did have a pragmatic intelligence, a dogged tenacity, a love of battle, and a profound distaste for losing.

———

The income from his law practice allowed the Bakers to live comfortably, but modestly. By 1927, they had an apartment on South Lake Shore Drive, where their three sons were born: Wallace in 1927; Donald in 1929; and James in 1931. By the mid–1930s, Baker's income had improved to the point that he could afford to move to the north Chicago suburb of Lake Bluff, at that time a village of about 1,500 residents. They leased a house at first, and in 1939 the family moved into the house that Baker would live in for the rest of his life. An architect for whom Baker did legal work designed his house near the edge of a deep ravine. The trees around it were so dense that no curtains were needed on the windows. At meals, the Bakers watched the birds flitting about the feeder outside the dining room window or caught glimpses of the deer. "You could feel nature all around you," Dolores Villa, Baker's former secretary, says.

When the Bakers gave large parties, guests could flow from the living room onto an adjacent screened porch. Behind the home, the twenty-foot-deep ravine channeled run-off water into Lake Michigan. Baker scooped out a twelve-by-sixteen-foot space by the ravine and lined it with railroad ties and stone. He called it a kiva, the word New Mexico's Pueblo Indians use for the place where they hold their most serious tribal councils and perform religious rituals. In the middle of his kiva, Baker built a barbecue pit with a spit to roast meat. To one side of the home, he constructed a two-room house he called the *casita* for his retired missionary father-in-law. The modest $25,000 house was unpretentious. Years later, when he was the senior partner of his global law firm, many of his partners were shocked to find that he lived so simply. But Baker loved the house so much that, when Elizabeth painted a picture of it, he hung it on his office wall.

———

Baker overtly and unselfconsciously loved his wife. Their relationship exhibited "an extraordinary feeling of love," Wallace Baker says. "It was a good marriage that they had—intellectual stimulation in addition to the physical and spiritual." Throughout their lives, Elizabeth's interest in music and books helped divert Russell's intense concentration on work. They went to classical music concerts at Ravinia in the summer, and often attended Great Books lectures at the University of Chicago.

Elizabeth was typical of American wives and mothers of her generation: her first duty was to her husband and children. In her spare time, she did volunteer work for charities, and she eventually became President of the Lake Bluff chapter of the League of Women Voters. In her private habits, Elizabeth wasn't a teetotaler, but she looked askance at excessive drinking. "She was from a Presbyterian missionary background," James Baker says. "Drunkenness was getting close to sin. And Russell never would have drunk much because my mother wouldn't stand for it." Although Elizabeth allowed moderate drinking, she absolutely forbid Baker's smoking in her house. Once, when she caught him at it, she shouted, "Don't stink up my house!" James Baker recalls "my mother going around the house in a huff, and my father looking like a whipped puppy."

Baker's ties to his family were strong, and his affection for his three sons was almost as fierce as that he had for Elizabeth. A former law clerk remembers taking the three boys to Marshall Field's Department Store to buy presents for their father at Christmas time. When the law clerk later commented to Baker that his sons had picked out "terrible colors for your neckties," Baker answered, "I would wear any color they chose." He wanted to be a friend as well as a father to his three children. To break down the authoritarian father barrier, he told his sons to call him Russell, Russ, or Wuzzy, a nickname that probably came from one of the children trying to mimic Elizabeth saying "Russell." "He was a friend," Wallace Baker says. "We did things together. He was interesting. He retained a child-like curiosity and interest in the world."

Baker wanted his children to know about his life at work. In the 1930s, he worked at least a half-day on Saturdays, and often brought one or more of his sons to the office. The boys rifled through their father's desk, finding the usual bric-a-brac, paper clips and used pencils. In addition, they found two items that few men kept in their desks, a blackjack and a pistol. When one son asked why he had the pistol, Baker told him that he needed it because of the criminals who visited his office.

Baker often reminisced about how hard he worked during the 1930s, but he always set aside time for family vacations. On most of the trips, they went to the West to camp, in part because it was a cheap vacation for five during the Depression. Baker built his own camping trailer on the chassis of an old Model T Ford, and hitched it to his elegant, but secondhand, Franklin automobile. His homemade rig carried a large tent that accommodated all of the family, the blackened pots and pans they used for cooking over open fires, and a barbecue spit made out of an automobile brake rod.

On their driving tours, Baker lectured to his boys on the ages of the rocks and the curious fossils embedded in them. If he saw an interesting rock formation, he stopped the car, pulled rock picks out of the trailer, and the whole family chipped away. If one of their geology picks split open a rock that revealed a beautifully preserved leaf or twig, the family regarded it as a triumph.

World War II's gasoline rationing cramped their ability to travel by car. In 1942, Baker took his family on the Santa Fe Railroad to Las Vegas, New Mexico. In the same wagon that the George Baker family had used to go from Crosbyton to Sapello in 1917, Baker's brother George met them at the railroad station and took Russell and his family to Sapello. There, he hired a local Hispanic cowboy to wrangle the horses and to guide them on a camping trip into the Sangre de Cristo Mountains. Around the campfire at night, Baker and the cowboy often sang songs in Spanish that he had learned as a boy.

The camping trips and his intellectual pursuits with his wife were almost Baker's sole recreations. He joined a country club during World War II, and tried to play golf. But he played poorly, and gave it up after a few months. Except for watching boxing on television, he had almost no interest in spectator sports. "I don't think he could tell you who was ahead in baseball, football, or basketball," James Baker says. "That was not his thing, to spend a lot of time watching or following sports."

———

Although Baker was intensely interested in his family, he was equally devoted to his law practice. In the Depression's early days, his partner Dana Simpson became ill, leading to his retirement in 1932. After his first partner's departure, Baker formed Freyberger, Baker & Rice with Corrine Rice and Walter Freyberger. Freyberger, a tax lawyer, struggled to make a living during the Depression, when paying taxes on almost non-existent profits was a low priority for most people. Because Freyberger's income was so paltry, Baker often gave him more of the office's profits than he was entitled to under their agreement. "I would have starved during the Depression if Russell Baker had not helped me," Freyberger said later. In 1935, Freyberger left to take a job with the Internal Revenue Service in Washington, D.C. When he left, Baker formed his third law firm, Hubbard, Baker & Rice, with Alvin Hubbard and Rice as partners.

Baker had brought Corrine Rice into Simpson & Baker in 1928, a time when most American men had strong prejudices against women in the work place. Rice, one of the handful of female lawyers in Chicago, was a thorough and diligent researcher, and excelled as an appellate lawyer. Because of the bias against women attorneys, she signed her appellate briefs "C. L. Rice." "I am confident," Baker said, "that the appellate judges never knew they were reading a brief prepared by a woman member of the Bar. Her position was, 'If we have done what we were supposed to do in the brief, there is nothing more to say, and to appear before the judges and argue the same points tends more to confuse them than to clarify their thinking.'"

Rice was often successful in overturning criminal verdicts on appeal because, Baker said, the "Chicago police were uninstructed in what constitutes due process of law." During the seventeen years that Baker and Rice worked together, her appellate briefs, he said, "pried a good many characters out of the 'pokey.' I hope they were all innocent. I have my doubts. As fast as I lost cases in the Trial Courts, she would reverse them on appeal. Her success was what built our reputation as trial lawyers who never quit." Rice died in 1944, but Baker kept her name in his firm until 1949.

———

At a time when many lawyers felt that actively developing clients was ungentlemanly, Baker took a very realistic stance. To bring in clients, at least once a year Baker invited some two hundred fifty Hispanics to his Lake Bluff house. There, they strolled on Baker's heavily wooded lawn with their wives and children, eating barbecue and drinking beer and listening to Latin music. When Chicago played host to the 1933 World's Fair, Baker brought in several new clients, including a midget, Bimbo the King of the Gypsies, and a skydiver. He also met a Costa Rican coffee farmer who was marketing his products at the Fair. After it closed, the farmer opened the Costa Rican Coffee House Restaurant on Randolph Street, not far from Baker's office at One North LaSalle. The man was not only a client, he and Baker became friends, so much so that he left Baker $15,000 when he died.

To raise his profile in the community, in 1938 Baker became a member of the Chicago Crime Commission, an organization dedicated to studying the causes of crime and its suppression. To help the Commission's efforts, Baker wrote a handbook for peace officers entitled *Manual on the Law of Arrest, Search and Seizure*. In the forty-nine-page document, he spelled out the proper procedures for policemen to use when collecting evidence so that it would meet the Constitutional tests to make it admissible in court.

Through his work defending underprivileged Hispanics, Baker met a wealthy widow who had a similar interest. In addition to helping the downtrodden, Henrietta Heinzen was the controlling shareholder of a Chicago company that made barley malt. As a result of their friendship, Mrs. Heinzen hired Baker to represent her company, Albert Schwill & Company. "That was the first corporate client of any consequence that had come to us," Baker said. "Representing that company gave us confidence, courage, cash and, above everything else, standing in the community." Shortly after Baker became Schwill's general counsel, the Justice Department charged it, along with sixteen other barley malt manufacturers, with Sherman Act civil and criminal antitrust violations. Baker defended the criminal case to a not-guilty verdict. Over time, the level of trust between Ms. Heinzen and Baker increased to the point that she asked him to vote her Schwill stock.

In the mid-1930s, Baker had also begun doing some of his first international work. His brother-in-law had acquired the right to harvest timber from a large tract of rain forest in Mexico's Isthmus of Tehuantepec. Baker invested in the venture and became its general counsel, making several trips to Mexico to inspect the project. Family connections helped him get the timber client, but pure luck brought Baker the most important client that he would ever attract. As Russell and Elizabeth were walking down Ravine Drive in Lake Bluff, another couple was walking toward them from the opposite direction. When they got closer, Elizabeth recognized an old friend from her Mexico City days, Bantita Nielson. Bantita introduced her husband, Carl Nielson, beginning a friendship that lasted the rest of their lives. Nielson was a Danish pharmacologist and biologist who had gone to Mexico to work for President Porfirio Diaz's government. He left Mexico in the 1920s, and joined Abbott Laboratories, a leading pharmaceutical company, headquartered in Chicago. Eventually, Nielson became Abbott's chief of pharmaceutical research.

At almost the same time that Baker met Nielson, Abbott was starting to dabble in international markets. In 1933, Abbott's international sales were a mere $62,000. But, inside the company, three executives were pushing Abbott to expand globally. At their insistence, the company stepped up its efforts to sell abroad, first in Mexico, and then in Brazil and Argentina. After the successes in those countries (Mexican sales jumped from $5,000 to $100,000 in the first year), Abbott allocated a $200,000 budget to organize foreign subsidiaries, hire salesmen, and pay for advertising. Baker, evidently with Nielson's help, and perhaps because he spoke Spanish, convinced Abbott that he could do the legal work.

The only way he could learn was on the job. In the 1930s, international corporate law practice did not exist. A few New York law firms represented foreign governments that were selling their bonds in the U.S., and, on rare occasions, lawyers handled cross-border transactions. But, with America locked in its isolationism, few, if any, attorneys could hold themselves out as international law specialists. It was a fortuitous time for Baker to master a new legal skill. Abbott's executives had almost no background in doing business abroad, and, if their novice international lawyer made mistakes, the company's executives would be none the wiser.

Baker started out working on relatively minor assignments for Abbott, but they were his first real taste of international business law—and he liked it. The company's overseas expansion confirmed Baker's long-held conviction that American corporations could, and would, operate on a global scale. Even with war looming in Europe and the Far East, in the late 1930s Abbott made itself a multinational corporation some thirty years before the term came into being. It opened sales offices in Bogotá, Bombay, Havana, Johannesburg, Manila, and Wellington, and built a new plant just outside London. In short order, Abbott's non-U.S. sales rose to $1.6 million, ten percent of total sales.

After World War II, Baker began doing even meatier work for the pharmaceutical company. Abbott gave him a retainer of $40,000 per year, a large fee in the mid-1940s, to help it negotiate contracts, acquire companies, organize subsidiaries, and protect intellectual property. Baker traveled all over Europe and Latin America for Abbott. He had launched a career as an international lawyer, and, in less than thirty years, he would be the senior partner of the world's largest law firm.

Chapter Three

The World's First Multinational Law Firm

After World War II, European plants were in ruins, Latin America was primarily a supplier of agricultural products and raw materials, and Asia had little industry. Untouched by the War, the U.S. reigned as the world's most powerful nation. Still, there was a threat.

Winston Churchill saw the Iron Curtain coming down as early as 1946. During the next few years, the Soviet Union, the West's ally against Nazi Germany, was brazenly asserting its hegemony over Eastern Europe. Soviet forces blocked access to Berlin. Communist parties in France and Italy were gaining strength, and Mao Zedong's forces were rolling up victories in China. To many Westerners, it appeared that Communism would fulfill its self-proclaimed destiny of crushing capitalism.

The Western allies reacted to the Soviet threat economically, militarily, and politically. President Harry Truman proclaimed his containment policy to keep the USSR from extending its reach, and the Western countries organized the North Atlantic Treaty Organization, which obligated them to fight jointly against outside aggression.

Although the political and military deterrents to Communism garnered most Cold War headlines, the West's economic steps to corral Soviet aggression had a major impact. Based on the theory that healthy, wealthy economies would not succumb to Communism, the U.S. adopted the Marshall Plan. During the Plan's first four years, America pumped some $40 billion into sixteen European nations to help resuscitate their economies. The U.S. Export-Import Bank increased its loan activities, often in support of foreign policy goals. And America imposed stringent controls on the export of strategic products to the Communist bloc. Forty-four nations organized the World Bank for the express purpose of reconstructing the war-torn countries. To promote world trade, most of the major powers signed the General Agreement on Tariffs and Trade, and the West European nations began moving toward cooperation. First, they established the Council of Europe, and then, in 1951, they adopted measures calling for integration of their coal and steel resources. These initial steps eventually evolved into the European Community.[1]

While the Western nations were cooperating economically, improved transportation was also drawing them closer together. Commercial flights, with propeller-driven planes, from London's Heathrow Airport were arriving in New York in an astonishingly short twenty hours. By 1947, the airlines inaugurated regular flights from the U.S. to Japan. The next year, the first jet aircraft crossed the Atlantic Ocean. Along with easier travel, innovations that would speed other types of communication were in the budding stage. ENIAC, the world's first electronic digital computer, began operating in 1946, and American researchers at Bell Laboratories perfected the transistor, which would eventually permit the miniaturization of electronic devices.

All of those developments propelled U.S. companies into the global marketplace. With virtually no competition, U.S. businessmen raced to fill the economic void, and American factories strained to turn out goods they could market around the world. One lawyer foresaw that those U.S. companies would want—and need—quality international legal services. During the post-World War II period, Russell Baker began germinating his ideas for an international law firm. It was a radical departure from tradition, which mandated that law was localized and should be practiced in a single city. Concluding that the predictions his Chicago University professors had made in the 1920s were coming true, Baker's mind hurdled the parochialism of his fellow attorneys to envision a law firm that reached not only beyond a single city but to other nations.

Even before he started Baker & McKenzie,[2] Baker had seized on a new law that would prove to be a signal event in his future law firm's development. In 1942, the U.S. shed part of its isolationist baggage, and supplemented President Franklin Roosevelt's Good Neighbor Policy. It adopted the Western Hemisphere Trade Corporation ("WHTC") provisions as part of the Internal Revenue Code ("Tax Code").

WHTCs gave American companies a tax incentive to help their good neighbors to the south develop their economies.[3] Congress approved the WHTC legislation based on the rationale that the measure would encourage American companies to invest in manufacturing, mining, and other on-the-ground projects in Latin America. When Baker read the WHTC law, however, he discovered a way to broaden its scope. "The thing that helped make Baker & McKenzie,"

James Baker says, "is that a non-tax lawyer [Russell Baker] started to fiddle around with tax concepts. He came up with a fairly simple but brilliant idea." Baker found a way that American exporters could use the WHTC provisions in selling their products in Latin America.

His structure was easy to implement: a U.S. parent company simply organized a separate WHTC subsidiary in any American state and then channeled its export sales to Latin America through the subsidiary. If the parent company sold an item for $200 to the WHTC subsidiary, and the WHTC sold it in Latin America for $300, the new law substantially lowered the tax burden. On the WHTC's $100 profit, it received a fourteen-point tax reduction. If, for example, the U.S. corporate tax rate was fifty percent, then the tax bite on the $100 WHTC profit would only be $36, a savings of $14. However, there were restrictions. A WHTC could only do business in the Western Hemisphere, and it had to earn ninety percent of its gross income from the active conduct of a trade or business. Since selling goods was an active business, that rule presented no problem. But the requirement that ninety-five percent of the WHTC's income had to come from foreign sources was an obstacle. A U.S. company wanting to manufacture in Latin America could easily meet the test, but it was a ticklish issue for a U.S. company that only wanted to sell its products there. Baker solved the problem by grafting onto the WHTC legislation the English common law rule that says that sales are consensual contracts. This left contracting parties free to agree that title to products would pass at the place where the contract said it would pass. Therefore, if the parties agreed that title would not pass until the products reach the docks in Colombia or Peru, the sale was consummated outside the U.S., and the WHTC met the foreign source income test.

Baker rushed to Abbott Laboratories with his innovation, and persuaded his major client to organize a WHTC using his new ideas. Both the Internal Revenue Service ("IRS") and some law professors, however, took exception to Baker's interpretation. They viewed his stitching together of the WHTC rules with contract law as a triumph of form over substance, and branded it little more than a tax avoidance gimmick. The critics carped that Congress had intended the WHTC law to apply only to a U.S. company that had actual operations in Latin America, and that Baker was distorting that intent. He brushed aside the naysayers' claim that his scheme was a tax avoidance device, arguing that the law was placed on the books to be used. He also noted that Congress wanted to stimulate trade between the U.S. and Latin America, and that his application of the law merely furthered that purpose. The WHTC law, he said, was "part of a growing pattern in our tax philosophy. . . . to encourage international commerce. Good international political relations necessarily rest on a firm base of profitable two-way trade."[4]

Baker's controversial use of the WHTC concept was his first major stroke. But a far more important tax stratagem waited to be exploited. Before World War II, few American companies had done business abroad, and there was little reason for the Tax Code to address how the government should deal with overseas operations. But, after the War, Americans saw that they could use their undamaged industrial plants to reap large returns from beyond the country's borders. International business was surging, and creative tax planners found that the Tax Code left a huge opening for American companies to escape domestic taxes.

As with the WHTCs, the scheme's beauty was in its simplicity. All an American company had to do was to organize a foreign subsidiary, a foreign base company ("FBC"), in a country that had either low or no taxes.[5] The U.S. parent corporation then conducted its overseas operations through the FBC. When Baker test-marketed the concept, he found that American companies were delighted with a plan that kept their offshore profits out of the U.S. tax collectors' hands.

"The idea was," William Gibbons says, "that, if you could earn a million dollars, you could take that tax-free million and build a factory in Brazil so that you could make even more money."[6] FBCs offered two advantages over WHTCs. American companies were not limited to the Western Hemisphere and could use the FBC concept all over the world, and, rather than being limited to only a fourteen-point tax reduction, with the right FBC structure a clever planner could reduce taxes to zero.

Armed with two tax strategies that could save companies millions, Baker was ready to redirect his career.

Besides envisioning an opportunity from a macro standpoint, personal reasons drove Baker towards changing his practice midway through his life. His travels to Europe and Latin America for Abbott had taken the Texas/New Mexico farm boy away from the tedium of court procedure and evidentiary rules. For a man who never lost his boy-like curiosity, exploring Amsterdam and Caracas was more fun than wending his way through the Cook County Courthouse. And Baker's ego drove him to try to build a monument—the world's first multinational law firm.

By most standards, leaving what he knew best seemed foolish. He had an excellent practice defending some of America's top insurance and industrial companies against tort claims. He had a nice house, in a nice neighborhood, with a nice wife, and nice children. He wasn't rich, but he was doing well. When Baker decided to launch his new venture in 1949, he was forty-eight. If his international odyssey failed, he might be too old to make up lost financial ground. "But he had the courage, strength, and vision to embark on an adventure with an unknown future at an age when most people have been satisfied with, or resigned to, what they have achieved in life," one of his partners, Wulf Döser, said years later.

Baker always believed that luck played a large part in achieving success. As luck would have it, the elements he needed to make his then-bizarre idea work were in place. Chicago was America's industrial and transportation capital. The Midwest's companies were primed to expand around the world. Thanks to Abbott, Baker had been dabbling in international law for almost fifteen years, and probably knew more about it than any other lawyer in the country. Along with the sizable retainer Abbott paid him, his representation of the well-known pharmaceutical company enhanced his credibility and prestige. And his successful experiments with U.S. tax law gave him something to sell that set him apart from almost all of his competitors. The establishment U.S. law firms were so busy with their traditional domestic practice areas that they were blind to international possibilities. Baker saw the gap, and laid his plans to exploit what he believed was an enormous opportunity.

He took his idea for creating an international law firm to his partners at Hubbard, Baker & Rice. He told them that lawyers should prepare themselves to serve their clients' needs, and that hundreds of U.S. businessmen were already stalking the globe looking for new possibilities. Those American businessmen, Baker argued, wanted U.S.-style legal services: they wanted their attorneys to assess a fact situation, decide how the law applied, and recommend a course of action. To meet that need, Baker sketched the outline of a law firm that could serve American companies doing business overseas. He wanted an international law firm with lawyers who spoke more than one language and who understood both the English-derived common law and the Continental European civil law. Eventually, he believed, this new firm should have offices in the world's major business centers.

All these notions excited Baker. But what his Chicago partners saw was that Baker's successful litigation practice would suffer if he was roaming around foreign capitals instead of trying lawsuits at home. They had no interest in what appeared to them to be Baker's dreamy notions of blazing new legal trails in the international arena. It was a practice that didn't even have a name, a practice that nobody in Chicago had ever heard of. Too risky. Too new. Two of his partners, Alvin and Reece Hubbard, rejected his peculiar idea. "The Hubbards were fine men and fine lawyers," Baker said later. "But neither of them could see the possibilities for an international practice, particularly one located in the middle of the country. The firm was prospering. Everybody was eating regularly. Why chase what appeared to them to be a will-of-the-wisp, especially in view of the cost? That was their point of view. It had much to recommend it." Baker and the Hubbards agreed to disagree, and terminated their fourteen-year partnership.

On July 1, 1949, Baker opened his new firm. When word spread through the Chicago legal community that Baker was starting an international law firm, "everybody in town told him he was crazy. That it would never work," Thomas Bridgman says.

Even before the Hubbard break-up, Baker had been on the lookout for an experienced trial lawyer who could take over the litigation and free him to develop an international practice. By chance, Baker ran across John McKenzie.[7] Both Baker and McKenzie had worked late one evening, and caught the train home. When they got off the train, four miles away from their homes in Lake Bluff, there was only one taxi. McKenzie didn't know Baker, and introduced himself. They discovered that they both lived in Lake Bluff, and agreed to share the cab.

As they drove along, the two men chatted about their work, discussing strategies for trying lawsuits. When the taxi got to Lake Bluff, it delivered Baker to his home and McKenzie to his Frank Lloyd Wright-designed house nearby. The two men met again later, and Baker laid out his plan. He told McKenzie that he wanted someone to handle his trial docket, and that he was willing to turn over a full plate of prestigious clients. Ever since McKenzie had started practicing law, he had made his living as in-house counsel defending taxi companies. He was thirty-six years old, and was primed to try his hand at private practice. He jumped at the chance to take over Baker's clients.

"John McKenzie was the perfect partner for Russell," Thomas Bridgman says. Baker's new partner was an imposing figure. He stood just over six feet, three inches tall, and had a shock of silver hair to set off a handsome face. "He could have been the Marlboro man," Francis Morrissey says. A former secretary, Elizabeth Challenger, recalls that "he was a man of very good physical appearance. He was good-looking and very smart."

McKenzie had been born into a middle-class Irish Catholic family in 1913 in Chicago. During most of his undergraduate and law school career at Loyola University of Chicago, McKenzie went to night school. Days, he worked as a foundry laborer. He also found a job at the Chicago Motor Club, where Baker had worked some fifteen years before. When World War II began, McKenzie joined the Coast Guard, continuing his love affair with the sea. "He was a sailor," his Swiss partner Peter Achermann remembers.

The lanky trial lawyer enjoyed a few beers after a day in court, and he enjoyed getting together with his friends—mostly judges, lawyers, and clients—to tell jokes and stories. One story the gregarious McKenzie loved to tell involved the 1959 World Series. He had bought tickets for himself and his son Johnny to go to the baseball game between the Chicago White Sox and the Los Angeles Dodgers. On the morning of the game, he sent Francis Morrissey to the courthouse to see which of the Firm's cases were called for trial that day. When Morrissey, who knew about the baseball tickets, saw that one of McKenzie's most important cases was scheduled for trial, he asked for a postponement. The judge denied the request, and set the case for immediate trial. Morrissey called McKenzie to give him the bad news. "Look, don't worry about this. I'll take care of it," McKenzie told Morrissey. McKenzie took his son by the hand and walked to the courthouse to see the judge. "You have one of the most difficult tasks any judge has faced in this building," he said. "You have to explain to Johnny McKenzie why he can't go to the World Series." The judge postponed the case.

Although McKenzie could be casual about some things, he was deadly serious about his litigation practice. He and Baker both knew that the Firm's success depended in large measure on the trial department. From the outset, Baker had designed the litigation department to be the Firm's bread-and-butter fee earner until the international practice could carry itself. If McKenzie had fallen down on the job in those early years, the Firm might have collapsed. Fortunately, he was a prodigious worker. If he had an urgent matter, secretaries couldn't turn out his work fast enough to suit him. In the courtroom, McKenzie could try a case without notes, relying on his memory when questioning witnesses. Having learned his trade defending errant cab drivers in Chicago's courthouses, he was a tough litigator who was more than willing to fight. In the right situations, he used his large frame to intimidate opposing counsel and hostile witnesses.

To McKenzie, a lawyer won or lost a case in the courtroom. Rather than poring over mounds of documents before a trial, or spending hours questioning witnesses, McKenzie's abundant self-confidence led him to rely on his memory and quick wit. Baker, on the other hand, spent hours preparing and rehearsing for trials. "It drove Russell crazy when John tried a case. John did it by the gift of gab, and he was damned good because he won a lot of cases," Gibbons says.

Despite their different trial styles, Baker admired McKenzie's creativity as a litigator. Baker often told the story of a case in which an employee of one of the Firm's clients looted a subsidiary company with the help of a confederate at the Nicaraguan branch of a London bank. Instead of pursuing the employee, McKenzie sued the English bank in Chicago. He got a judgment and attached the bank's funds on deposit in another Chicago bank. "The surprise and rage of the London bankers," Baker crowed, "were such that their protest could be heard from London to Chicago without the benefit of long-distance telephone. John collected every dime that the client lost."

During his trials, McKenzie pushed himself to the limit. When he was only forty-one, he had his first heart attack. Six years later, McKenzie was trying a case in Chicago when he was told that he had to appear in a crucial trial in Evanston immediately. He left the Chicago trial for a younger lawyer to finish, and went to Evanston. During the Evanston trial, he suffered another, more severe, heart attack that kept him away from the office for several months. His doctors told him that, if he continued trying his normal fifty lawsuits a year, the stress would kill him. With only the slightest deference to the medical advice, McKenzie put a couch in his office and tried to take naps each day. He also took up knitting to relax himself, but he treated the therapy as a joke. On the commuter train to Lake Bluff, he chortled at the startled expressions on the businessmen's faces when he pulled out his knitting needles and yarn.

Baker and other partners pleaded with McKenzie to take better care of himself. "Rightly or wrongly," McKenzie told Bridgman, "I have never been a spectator. I will always be a participant, and that is the way I look at life." On a Friday evening, September 28, 1962, McKenzie died of a massive heart attack. He was forty-nine. When Morrissey went to Baker's office the next morning, he found him crying. "The toughest man I have ever known," Morrissey says, "was crying over the death of his friend and colleague."

McKenzie had done his job. From the Firm's beginning in 1949 until about 1955, the Chicago trial department supplied a substantial amount of the cash flow needed to fund the Firm's promotional efforts in the international area. In addition, McKenzie recruited and trained the two men who ran the trial section for the next thirty years—Michel Coccia and Thomas Bridgman, both of whom eventually served as Chairman of the Firm.

As the Chicago trial department grew steadily, Baker and Dwight Hightower worked to build the Firm's international law reputation. Hightower graduated cum laude from Northwestern University in 1940, and attended one year of law school there before dropping out to join the diplomatic service as a Vice Consul at the U.S. Embassy in Bogotá, Colombia. He enlisted in the Army during World War II, and landed on Omaha Beach on D-Day, June 6, 1944. After the War, Hightower returned to Northwestern Law School.

He got his law degree in 1947, and then joined Hubbard, Baker & Rice. Early in his career, Hightower's colleagues regarded him as a good technical lawyer. But, after he married a wealthy Chicago socialite, his interest in digging through musty law books and drafting complicated legal documents seemed to dwindle. Instead, the outgoing Hightower devoted himself to meeting people and developing new business for the Firm. And he was good at it. Gibbons says, "He was on the phone all day long with clients. He had card files on card files on card files of clients."

Hightower lived in one of Chicago's more elegant suburbs, Winnetka, in a home that was described as "really regal." Many of his neighbors were corporate executives who had enough seniority to pick their companies' lawyers, making them prime prospects for the young man who was constantly on the lookout for new clients. Hightower also played golf at his country club, which he used as a venue to promote business. By the mid-1960s, his client list covered twenty-four pages and included a number of America's best-known corporate names.

Hightower's partners enjoyed his affability, but his sometimes lax approach to the minutia of law practice began to sour the relationship. Baker genuinely appreciated the younger man's client development abilities as being a prime Firm asset, but one event shook Baker's feelings about his partner. In the early 1950s, Hightower brought in a new client who instructed him to set up an insurance company in the Dominican Republic. Before long, the company was exposed as a fraud. After it went broke, the investors began looking for someone to blame, and, seeing "deep pockets" in Baker & McKenzie, they sued, claiming damages of over $1 million. "Russell was terribly worried about this case, which threatened the existence of our Firm," Wallace Baker says. When it finally went to trial, however, the judge directed a verdict in the Firm's favor.

Hightower also became involved in a major real estate project, borrowing from several banks to develop property in downtown Chicago. It soon became apparent that the project was in trouble and that Hightower had serious financial problems. Several banks asked the Firm to pay its partner's debts. The banks' unspoken threat was that failing to do so would sever relationships for both loans and client referrals. At first, Baker didn't want to let Hightower go, but, as the stories about his financial affairs became increasingly tangled, Baker changed his mind. When he stopped arguing to save Hightower, it sent a signal to the partners that it was time for Hightower to leave. He withdrew in late September 1966.

———

With four lawyers and a rough sketch of an operating philosophy, the fledgling law firm began its first year. As its fiscal year neared its end on June 30, 1950, "we danced in the aisles and hallways when fees reached $75,000 in June," Dolores Boyle, Baker's secretary when the Firm began and later the Firm's chief administrator, wrote. The final count for the year was $89,000 in fee collections. After deducting $18,000 for secretarial salaries, $7,000 for rent, and other expenses (including a $20 write-off of uncollectible fees), the lawyers divided $51,000 in net profit.

In the Firm's second year, fee income increased twenty percent to $107,000. Baker's two most important corporate clients, Albert Schwill & Company and

Abbott, contributed almost forty percent of the fees. During the June 30, 1951 fiscal year, the Firm paid out $14.36 for the Christmas party, Baker spent $80 entertaining guests at his home, and Hightower charged $35 worth of football tickets for client promotion.

Although the Firm was spending money to develop new clients, Abbott was still the underpinning of the Firm's international practice. Baker later said that the Firm was "formed on the back of Abbott Laboratories." Sometimes he was gone for weeks, flying to Abbott's European and Latin American outposts around the world to organize subsidiaries and to put out legal fires, including the settlement of a bitter strike by Abbott's Cuban employees. Most of the trips, however, related to more sober tax and corporate issues. During his travels, Baker was on the lookout for good lawyers in the countries he visited. To help him handle work for Abbott and other clients, he developed working relationships with attorneys in Amsterdam, Caracas, London, Mexico City, and Zürich.

Although he focused on making contacts and developing an international practice in the early 1950s, he continued to handle a few lawsuits. Michel Coccia saw Baker try several tort cases: "He didn't waste time on side issues, and he always got right to the important point. Also, Russell had a unique ability to communicate a simplified, concise story to the jury. He simply stood up and asked great questions. No theatrics, just simple warmth, honesty, and credibility in his presentation."

Baker had little time, and even less interest, in handling the Firm's administrative tasks. He delegated that job to the junior men, who hired staff, oversaw accounting, and nagged delinquent lawyers to collect their fees.

Baker & McKenzie collected $157,000 in gross fees during its third year. Baker's monthly draw was $1,166, and McKenzie's was $833. Even in 1952, these were modest incomes, but the partners ended fiscal year 1952 with an additional $46,000 in profits to divide. By 1953, the partnership structure had become more stratified, and the Firm called full partners Administrative Partners and junior lawyers Associate Partners.

In addition to doing client work and recruiting new lawyers, Baker spent hours developing business, making speeches throughout the Midwest and writing numerous articles on international law and business. During those early days, he established ties with accounting firms and with many of Chicago's largest banks, and convinced many of them to refer their customers to Baker & McKenzie. The banking contacts had a multiplier effect. When the Chicago bank officers made trips throughout the Midwest to solicit international business, they also touted Baker and the Firm. In effect, Baker developed a corps of traveling salesmen who spread the word that Baker & McKenzie was the only law firm in the region with international expertise.

By the end of the Firm's fifth fiscal year, June 30, 1954, the incessant promotional efforts were yielding returns. Gross fees were up two hundred fifty percent over the Firm's first year—to $224,000. After five years of watering and fertilizing its international image, Baker & McKenzie had gained recognition as a law firm that had bilingual lawyers, understood foreign law, and could structure multinational transactions.

As Baker's reputation as an international law expert grew, the fact that he had not gotten his law degree in 1925 became increasingly awkward. Even though he was working hard to build the Firm, he decided to go back to law school and pick up the needed credits. Baker wrote to the Chicago University Law School Dean, "I am almost forced to get my degree because people are constantly crediting me with a J.D. when in fact I do not possess one. I will be deeply grateful if you will advise me what will be required of me to fulfill the requirements for a J.D." In June of 1955, Baker put on cap and gown and marched in the academic processional with the other students, most of whom were thirty years younger, to receive his law degree.

In between studying and working at the Firm, Baker squeezed in Portuguese lessons. "I learned Portuguese," he said, "simply by setting aside the time required to travel to and from Chicago on the commuter train. It was a long process. I kept at it for five or six years." He also had a tutor come to his office most afternoons, and he practiced speaking Portuguese with a Brazilian secretary in the office. Baker's study of Portuguese was not an idle intellectual exercise. He had long thought that Brazil would be an economic giant, and, in time, would become an industrial country where the Firm would want to open offices.

In addition to devoting long hours to tangible activities that produced financial results, Baker paid close attention to the psychological—to the morale of his lawyers. "It wasn't a master-servant situation," Coccia says. "He was so supportive and so helpful that he made you feel that you were really a part of this Firm. Russell was in charge. We always listened to Russell. Russell also always listened to all of us. He wanted to know what our ideas were. He was always asking: 'What should we do about the future? How can we make this into something?'"

Chapter Four

Going International:
The First Offshore Offices

In 1954, Baker & McKenzie completed its first five years. It had had steady, but not dramatic, growth. The letterhead listed eight lawyers, and there was talk of opening its first international office in Caracas. The business community had begun to notice Baker & McKenzie, and it listed more than forty of America's best-known multinational companies as clients.

Baker & McKenzie had also been noticed in other quarters. In America, Red-baiting politicians had whipped up an anti-Communist frenzy. Senator Joseph McCarthy was charging that "pinko" subversives had penetrated the U.S. Army and the State Department. During that period, the Central Intelligence Agency approached Baker to enlist the Firm to feed it information. Knowing that the slightest hint that the Firm was spying for the U.S. would destroy all chance of creating an international law firm, he declined.

Instead of fronting for the CIA, Baker directed his efforts toward developing business. He wrote nearly a dozen articles on the U.S. tax treatment of foreign operations. He and other Firm attorneys also gave speeches to proselytize the tax-sheltering benefits of WHTCs and FBCs. Before Baker gave his speeches, he did his homework. He got the list of attendees and researched their companies. If he found that a company was doing business in France or Peru, he would be sure to let the corporate executive know that the Firm was familiar with French and Peruvian law. He also collected the participants' business cards, and then bombarded them with literature describing the tax benefits of WHTCs and FBCs.

"Russell and Hightower would be giving speeches every week to groups," William Gibbons recalls. "Every damned week, they would come to the office with ten new clients." As part of his business development strategy, Baker taught his colleagues to sell the tax concepts and "the legal work that went into it. We had a 'Standard Operating Procedure' that you would sell as a package," James Baker says. "It was profitable and easy to sell. It was beautiful."

In the early 1950s, the drumfire of speech-making, article writing, and personal contacts began to pay off. American corporations were getting the message that Baker & McKenzie could show them how to run their foreign operations, tax free at best or with healthy tax reductions at least. "It was like a gold rush," Wallace Baker says, and his brother James remembers: "Big-name clients were almost beating down our doors." The Firm was no longer tied to just one major international client. The loyalty to Abbott would always remain, but a bevy of impressive new clients began to light up the Firm's scoreboard. On golf courses and at business meetings, Baker & McKenzie became known in the U.S. as the legal expert on the taxation of American companies doing business abroad.

When Firm attorneys met with clients to describe FBCs, they began by asking questions. The first decision was which non-U.S. country to use. Depending on the client's needs, it could choose a country like the Bahamas, which had no income tax, or Switzerland, which had low tax rates, or Venezuela, which didn't tax offshore profits made by a Venezuelan company.

After choosing the country and organizing an FBC, the parent company elected one of two ways of doing business abroad. The U.S. corporation could sell its products to the FBC for $200. The FBC then increased the price to customers to $300. The FBC got to keep the $100 profit outside the U.S. with little or no tax. Other companies wanted to do more than merely export their American-made goods. Those corporations would set up headquarters companies and manufacturing plants, principally in Europe and Latin America. Many U.S. companies with older machinery sent it abroad to produce products that were outmoded in the U.S., but were considered top-of-the-line in some other nations.[1] These companies enabled the Firm's lawyers to augment their skills in handling exchange control issues, corporate law, and intellectual property matters. The lawyers also delved into transactions involving distributorships, manufacturing, technology licensing, and the full panoply of international legal issues.

To implement the FBC structure for clients in Latin America, Baker first looked for the right country. He ruled out the traditional tax havens, such as Panama and the Bahamas. To some in the international business community, those countries had a "bad odor" because they were not serious business centers and because there were rumors that criminals were laundering dirty money through them.

Baker decided on Venezuela. With its booming petroleum industry, the nation had a vibrant economy and was moving toward industrialization. More importantly, its tax law operated on the territorial principle, whereby Venezuelan companies only paid taxes on profits made in the country, not on profits made outside its territory. This meant that a U.S. company could organize a Venezuelan subsidiary, then sell its products to the subsidiary, which could, in turn, sell the merchandise to other countries around the world. Because the sales were not made on Venezuelan territory, the subsidiary paid no Venezuelan income tax.

To help organize the Venezuelan companies, the Firm needed a local lawyer. Baker discovered Ramon Diaz almost by accident. In the mid-1950s, Diaz, who had attended Harvard Law School and spoke impeccable English, made a trip to New York to try to establish a correspondent relationship with an American law firm. The Brahman Wall Street firms had no interest in the Venezuelan. Diaz next went to Chicago, where he met with the same resistance from the establishment firms, until someone steered him to Russell Baker.

Baker & McKenzie began sending work to Diaz's law firm, and, in short order, many of the Venezuelan FBCs had millions of dollars flowing through them. As the FBC business grew, and as the IRS became increasingly interested in it, the Firm decided that it would be prudent to have its own lawyer in Venezuela to insure full compliance with U.S. tax law. In 1955, Baker & McKenzie established its first non-Chicago office. Baker arranged for his son Donald to work out of Diaz's office to make sure that the FBC subsidiaries' account books and corporate records were "in apple-pie order. We knew that many of these companies would be heading into tax litigation in the U.S.," Donald Baker says, "and we wanted to make sure that we couldn't be criticized by our legions of enemies in the legal profession."

When Donald Baker went to Caracas, it was understood that his assignment would be temporary, so Russell Baker began a search for his son's replacement. Baker had met a possible candidate who spoke fluent Spanish and who wanted to work in Latin America. William Gibbons, a young man with a craggy, Lincolnesque face, impressed Baker. He had served in General George Patton's Third Army as it raced across Europe during World War II. After the War, Gibbons earned his undergraduate degree from Harvard University. From there, he became a "Cold Warrior" with the CIA, and soon found himself in Spain working as a spy. Gibbons left his undercover assignment after two years, and transferred to the CIA's Washington headquarters. Rather than accepting an assignment to go to Korea as part of a CIA paramilitary group, Gibbons went to Harvard Law School.

He graduated in 1955, and took a job with one of New York's blue-ribbon law firms, but the more Gibbons saw of the traditional firm, the less he liked it. Paying unproductive older partners for doing nothing was a particular irritant. One of the name partners was ninety-three, and "they used to wheel the old son-of-a-bitch down in a wheelchair every two weeks to pick up his paycheck," he recalls. He also disliked the hierarchical firm's requirement that he serve an eight-to-ten-year apprenticeship before becoming a partner.

One cold, gray afternoon, Gibbons got a call from his Harvard undergraduate classmate, Wallace Baker, asking him whether he would be interested in going to Baker & McKenzie's new Caracas office. When he looked out the window at the New York winter, going to Caracas—which bills itself as the City of Eternal Spring—sounded like a deliverance. He went to Chicago and met with Russell Baker, who told him more about the Venezuelan office and dangled the possibility of an almost immediate partnership. Gibbons was interested. He liked the idea of going back to the Hispanic culture he loved, but he wanted to mull over the offer. Back in his New York office, Gibbons called his uncle, a lawyer, and told him about the opportunity to go to Caracas with Baker & McKenzie.

"You're crazy," the uncle said. "You have a job with one of the best law firms in New York. But Baker & McKenzie? No one has ever heard of them. Why would you do a dumb thing like that?"

"I did it anyway," Gibbons says, "because the Firm was doing what I wanted to do. I wanted to go to Latin America, and I thought it was an exciting thing to do, being a pioneer. It was an adventure. I've made a lot of mistakes in my life, but joining Baker & McKenzie wasn't one of them."

Gibbons resigned from his New York firm, and started to work at Baker & McKenzie in Chicago around Christmas of 1955. He began in the litigation department, and won three cases before he caught a ship bound for Caracas in July 1956.

Russell Baker was furiously promoting FBCs and sending new U.S. clients to Venezuela. On his end, Gibbons developed a contact with a large New York bank, which sent him a number of clients. "So our practice took off immediately," Gibbons says. "I was so busy I didn't know what to do." The office was so successful that, in 1957, Diaz became a Baker & McKenzie partner, and the other lawyers in his office joined the Firm as associates.

To help with the crush of work, Gibbons hired Malcolm Caplan, an American lawyer who was studying in Venezuela. Later, Diaz brought in a Cuban exile who was scraping out a living selling sodas and magazines door-to-door. When Fidel Castro first marched triumphantly into Havana in 1959, Miguel Zaldívar had cheered. But the young lawyer's joy soon soured, and he began representing political prisoners who Castro had thrown in jail. An old friend in the Public Prosecutor's office told Zaldívar that he had a choice: he could either stop representing the anti-Castro agitators, or he could go to jail. Zaldívar chose a third alternative—exile. He took asylum in the Spanish embassy, where friends shuttled him to the Havana airport and put him on a plane for Miami. From there, the twenty-nine-year-old lawyer went to Caracas. Luckily, he met Diaz, who liked him and offered him a job. In 1962, Zaldívar started to work at the Firm. Shortly before Zaldívar joined the six-lawyer Caracas office, Gibbons returned to Chicago, leaving behind a model for how a new office could be successfully opened and operated.

With the Firm's first test case having proved that a non-U.S. office would work, it opened a Zürich office in 1958. When U.S. companies were searching for a European site to organize an overseas subsidiary, Switzerland was often the first place they looked. The mountain nation had a stable currency, good banking system, multi-lingual population, and political stability. Plus, it was a good place to live.

While American executives stationed in Zürich enjoyed most of the comforts of home, their companies enjoyed Switzerland's low taxes. In addition, the tiny country had an extensive tax treaty network with most of its European neighbors. The treaties allowed a U.S. company's Swiss subsidiary to get total or partial tax reductions from, for example, the Italian or German tax man on dividends, interest, royalties, and sales proceeds that flowed back to Switzerland.

For these reasons, the inflow of American investment into Switzerland in the 1950s and 1960s was tremendous. With taxes that totaled only ten percent, the Swiss Canton of Zug was a prime location for organizing subsidiaries. Given these attractions, within two years after the Zürich office opened, it was representing some fifty foreign subsidiaries. By 1965, that number had swelled to about three hundred. To get the new corporations organized and registered under Swiss law, the Zürich lawyers "worked like hell," Johannes Müller says. Müller remembers stuffing several briefcases with incorporation documents, and then lugging the heavy cases to the railroad station for the half-hour train ride from Zürich to Zug.

The growing success and reputation of Baker & McKenzie's Zürich, Caracas, and other offices attracted favorable attention from the business community. But the Firm's rising profile drew criticism from the establishment law firms and their spiritual mentors at Ivy League law schools. When they got wind of an upstart law firm from Chicago having success with WHTCs and FBCs, they almost unanimously predicted that the tax devices wouldn't work. "The preeminent lawyers in the tax bar throughout the United States felt that the Firm's interpretation of the law was wrong," Roger Quinnan says. "They thought that the Firm was playing fast and loose with the rules."

The tax intelligentsia labeled Baker's ideas preposterous. How, they asked, could a company escape or reduce taxes by merely signing a piece of paper saying that title passed outside of the U.S.? "Russell defended it tooth and nail against all the establishment legal opinion. It was a new law firm giving out fairly novel advice, and most of the established firms reacted against it," James Baker says.

When the white-shoe lawyers looked at the Midwestern law firm, they did not take it seriously. Who was this Russell Baker, a middle-aged tort lawyer turned tax lawyer? Even worse, the establishment thought that the Firm's aggressive promotion of business was ungentlemanly. Their own clients came to them because of their names, reputations, and family and social ties; Baker had none of these. To compensate, he worked as hard at business development as he had done when he walked behind a mule in New Mexico.

There were other reasons why the blue-chip law firms tweaked their rising Chicago competitor. To most of them, the Firm was an enigma. Rather than sitting around polished conference tables with attorneys from New York or Chicago, the Firm's business lawyers spent most of their time cobbling together ventures with lawyers in other countries. Perhaps the primary reason they scoffed at Baker & McKenzie was that it was becoming a competitive factor to reckon with. "It was because we were the new kid on the block, and we were taking clients away from them," Michael Waris says.

Partners in traditional firms gleefully picked away at the parvenu Chicago firm headed by a man who used earthy language and wore a Western hat and a shabby raincoat. Part of it was snobbery. "If you were from an Eastern establishment law school like Harvard, Yale, or Columbia," Robert Cox says, "and if you were a member of a major New York law firm, there was a bit of arrogance about you. We were not Ivy League as a firm." Some competitors sneered that the Firm's real name should be the "Butchers and the Bakers" or the "McDonald's law firm," insinuating that it was a franchise operation. "Russell always tried to help the underdog," Donald Etienne says. "He considered himself the leader of a big underdog—and the underdog was Baker & McKenzie."

———

The chorus of derision did not come just from law firms. Officials at the U.S. Treasury Department and the IRS entered the fray by attacking Baker's WHTC structure. The courts decided two landmark WHTC cases in 1960,[2] and the big question, Gibbons says, "was whether you could pass title abroad. Russell was advising clients before the seminal cases were decided that, by passing title in Latin America to goods sold there, income would be produced from Latin American sources. The Treasury lost, and Russell was the big winner."

On the question of whether WHTCs could be used for export sales, one court[3] said unequivocally, "We are satisfied that the Congress did not intend to limit [WHTCs] to railroads, mines, public utilities and other businesses requiring foreign investment." The court also soundly thrashed the government for its argument that it wasn't fair for a company to set up a WHTC to avoid taxes. The opinion upheld Baker's premise by quoting one of America's most respected jurists, Learned Hand: "[A] transaction, otherwise within an exception of the tax law, does not lose its immunity because it is actuated by a desire to avoid, or . . . to evade, taxation."[4]

From the beginning, Baker had known that the Firm's application of the WHTC law was a gamble, but he had been convinced that he was right. His reaction to the attacks was instinctive. He labeled his detractors "the enemy." And the best way to fight the enemy, he decided, was to concentrate on building a first-rate international law firm. To shore up Baker & McKenzie's tax expertise in the 1950s, Baker brought in several partners who were well known in New York and Washington tax circles. Along with recruiting new talent to deal with the untested tax concepts, Baker concluded that clients needed precise instructions on how to comply with the WHTC requirements. Following the system he had used in the 1930s to standardize bankruptcy documents for his Hispanic clients, Baker developed a four-inch-thick *Manual on the Organization and Operation of Western Hemisphere Trade Corporations.*

Even with the *Manual* as a guide, Baker worried that clients would not follow the guidelines. The Firm instituted a policing system to make sure that its clients met all technical requirements and used the right documents. Baker & McKenzie lawyers checked invoices and sales contracts to make sure that they contained the carefully crafted provisions that made the export sales take place outside the U.S. Baker also insisted that the WHTCs and FBCs have as much substance as possible, including leasing offices and hiring employees whenever possible.

Even though the Firm was taking great pains to assure that clients met all requirements, there was one academic who so disliked what Baker & McKenzie was doing that he decided to take action. Stanley Surrey, a Harvard law professor, was the best-known American scholar in the international tax field. Among his other credentials, he had been the Assistant Secretary of Treasury for Tax Policy in the 1940s.

When Surrey discovered what Baker and his partners[5] were doing with FBCs, he instituted a crusade to plug the escape hatches Baker had found in the tax law. "Surrey was basically a Puritan at heart," says Waris, who had worked with him in the Treasury Department. Surrey doggedly pushed his belief that it wasn't fair for an American company to sell its products through an offshore FBC company and not pay U.S. taxes. The fact that other industrial nations permitted their companies to trap profits offshore without domestic tax didn't interest Surrey. He rejected Baker's argument that FBCs merely allowed American companies to compete abroad on an even field.

Donald Etienne, who took Surrey's Harvard tax course in 1959, recalls that the professor told the class that "Russell Baker thinks FBCs and WHTCs will work, and that is nonsense." Surrey also told his students that the Firm's use of the tax vehicles was not what the law intended, and, when tested in court, Baker's concepts would fail. Roger Quinnan says that, "Stanley Surrey was the archenemy of Baker & McKenzie. He criticized any evaluation that anybody from Baker & McKenzie came up with."

During President John F. Kennedy's administration, Surrey became the champion of righting the wrongs that he thought the Firm was perpetuating. From his Treasury Department post in the Kennedy Administration in the early 1960s, Surrey battled to stop what he saw as U.S. businesses unfairly siphoning off enormous untaxed profits. Because the courts had blunted most IRS attempts to corral the alleged abuses, the only way to combat the "unfairness" was to get Congress to change the law.

Baker viewed Surrey's assault as a genuine threat to a bedrock practice area. "So much of our work still revolved around FBCs," James Baker says, "that there was grave concern that the Kennedy legislation would be very destructive to our practice and to our Firm." FBCs had been the great engine that helped propel the Firm's growth, brought it a degree of prestige and recognition, and put pre-mier companies on the Firm's client list. Baker & McKenzie actively lobbied against any changes in the law. Walter Slowinski of the Washington office, who was also the U.S. Chamber of Commerce's international tax counsel, testified against the Surrey-inspired legislation. Other Firm lawyers attempted to derail the proposed changes by giving testimony to Congressional committees. Despite their efforts, Surrey convinced the government that American corporations were dodging taxes.

Seizing on FBCs as their primary target, the Treasury Department began moving a bill through Congress that was designed to stamp out the perceived evil. In 1962, Congress adopted new sections of the Tax Code that it grouped together in Subpart F. Subpart F made the income earned by a foreign subsidiary of a U.S. corporation taxable in the year the subsidiary earned the income. There were exceptions, but, in general, an American company could no longer set up a subsidiary in a tax-haven country, do business in another foreign country, and shelter its subsidiary's profits from U.S. tax.

Shortly after Subpart F crimped the use of FBCs, Baker wrote to his Swiss partner, Eric Homburger: "I am working frantically to keep up the flow of business [to Zürich] in spite of the Revenue Act of 1962." Baker also worried that the Firm had relied too heavily on "gimmicks in the tax area. . . . [We must] re-orient ourselves . . . [to work on] contract manufacturing . . . joint ventures, and, above everything else, a two-way flow of business." Baker also wrote to Homburger that he had discovered a "secret weapon" that would get around Subpart F's restraints. Although Baker's secret weapon proved impractical in most cases, Baker & McKenzie's tax partners continued to sift through every sentence and paragraph of Subpart F. After painstaking study, they understood the new rules as well or better than partners in any other law or accounting firm. Initially, some Firm tax partners had been fearful that Subpart F would bring their careers to a halt. But, because the new law was so complex, it created even more tax work for Baker & McKenzie.

Chapter Five

A Radical Democracy

Was Russell Baker a true democrat or a closet autocrat? Was he a brilliant strategist or merely a person who worked harder than most? Baker's partners have differing views of him, but they all agree that he was a visionary. He correctly foresaw a new frontier for American businessmen; that American companies would fill the void left by World War II's disruption of the old order. "Russell conceived of a firm that would find its way around the world in a democratic, multicultural environment," Robert Cox says. "His ability to conceptualize a way to do that, to bring in bright people from around the world, and to make it work, was phenomenal."

Baker understood that, with communications shrinking the world, lawyers would be forced to accommodate themselves to their clients' needs. "The world around us was internationalizing at a frantic rate," he said. "The profession should serve the community. To do that, the changes in business patterns and the ways of doing business could not be ignored." Although he recognized the need for a multinational law firm, there was no model for him to follow anywhere in the world. Because customs and cultures were so different, lawyers around the globe saw legal practice as a localized profession that did not travel well. To overcome that bias, Baker needed the proper mixture of original thought, idealism, pragmatism, and luck.

During the Firm's early days, he handled client work and business promotion. He also spent substantial time refining cultural values and creating an institutional framework that would transcend national boundaries. It appears that Baker had not formulated his entire set of principles before he started the Firm in 1949, and that they evolved over time. "I doubt that he had a vision that he was going to create a law firm that would be the largest in the world," his son James says. "The 'vision thing' came pragmatically—little by little.

Venezuela was the first step. Then, the business of branching out and forming offices and making people partners who were not located in Chicago came very quickly."

Irrespective of whether Baker began the Firm with a comprehensive plan, he pursued his goal with an extraordinary single-mindedness. He dedicated himself totally to the idea of an international law firm, and was willing to devote whatever time and energy was required to achieve his objective. For Baker, the Firm's interests came before anything else. Norman Miller, a partner who often disagreed with Baker, says that "Russell was a very complicated individual. He wasn't an ordinary man. He was an exceptional man." Miller also says that Baker had the ability "to concentrate all his energies on building a firm in the image he had conceived, and the ability to eat, sleep, and breathe the Firm twenty-four hours a day and 365 days a year." Peter Bentley, a Baker loyalist, says simply, "Without him, there wouldn't be this Firm."

––––––––––

To implement his then-revolutionary idea of building a multinational law firm, Baker developed a set of guiding principles. The major premise was that American businessmen wanted, and needed, a single law firm with multiple offices throughout the world that would provide clients with seamless service in all its offices. To service multinational companies, Baker gave high priority to recruiting the right people. He wanted, he said, "to bring together people of a like mind, people who intuitively would act decently without the controls that are associated with a proprietorship."

In the 1950s, the few U.S. law firms having outposts abroad staffed them mostly with American attorneys sent over for three- or five-year tours of duty. Since the posting was only temporary, they had little incentive to master the language or burrow into the culture. With no roots in the local society or its legal traditions, those transplants found it difficult to deal with French tax collectors or British customs agents. A few U.S. firms did hire local lawyers for their overseas branches, but they usually treated them as second-class citizens, giving them little hope of ever sharing in profits or becoming a partner.

Early on, Baker mandated that the Firm would hire non-U.S. lawyers and would treat them with full dignity. They would share profits and become partners on an equal footing with their American counterparts. He believed that bringing in lawyers from diverse countries and cultures was the only way for the Firm to become a truly international partnership—"a partnership without nationality." Baker understood that a long-term relationship couldn't survive in a master-servant atmosphere. "You can't clone U.S. lawyers all around the world," Cox says. "People become lawyers to have control over their lives. As a Baker &

McKenzie partner, you're an individual and a profit center—but you're also part of the team."

After traveling extensively in Latin America and Europe for Abbott Laboratories, Baker knew that giving good legal advice wasn't simply a matter of looking at a book and telling the client what the law said. He knew that legal advice also had to include a practical solution to the client's problem. Only a native of the country, he believed, who understood the cultural backdrop, could give that kind of advice. In Baker's view, each office should be the equivalent of a local law firm, and should be populated with locally licensed attorneys: *bengoshi* in Tokyo, *rechtsanwälte* in Frankfurt, and *licenciados* in Mexico City.

In the Firm's early days, Baker worked hard at recruiting the right people, choosing those who were bilingual wherever possible. "It got to be like Noah's Ark—he wanted every species," one partner says. Thomas Haderlein adds that "Russell Baker was color blind, race blind, nationality blind. Russell used to ask, 'Why hasn't Wall Street ever figured that out? We will know when Wall Street has figured it out the day they are willing to make a Venezuelan a full partner.'"

Before Baker & McKenzie developed its office network, U.S. companies needing a foreign lawyer relied on paging through legal directories or getting a list of lawyers from the U.S. embassy. Often, American executives flew to a foreign country and spent days interviewing local lawyers. When they made their hiring decision, they could only hope that the local attorney was competent and would be able to find a creative solution to their problem. Baker's idea for clearing that hurdle was to create a single, worldwide law firm that would provide consistently good advice, all under one banner. "The capstone of our convictions as to the kind of firm we were going to build," Baker said, "was that it was to be a single firm with no pretense or make-believe in it. We did not visualize exactly how it could be done. So far as we knew, no one had done it. But it would be one firm or no firm. We committed ourselves to establishing a multi-office practice based on the single-firm concept."

Skeptics thought Baker's one-firm concept would never work. They chortled even more when they heard Baker's fanciful idea that law practice should be fun and that it should be an interesting, stimulating way of making a living. To Baker, making money was not the primary goal. Rather, how one made a living was paramount. The Firm, he said, should have a family atmosphere, where the partners were friends as well as business colleagues. He felt strongly about his own family, and he wanted his partners to feel the same way about Baker & McKenzie.

To create a collegial ambiance, Baker incorporated his frontiersman's belief in independence and democracy into the Firm's culture. In his most radical break with the hierarchical law firms around the world, he insisted that Baker & McKenzie would operate on the democratic principle of one man, one vote. If

Baker had had dictatorial tendencies, he could have set himself up as an autocrat with a central command in Chicago. He was the Firm's founder and senior partner. More importantly, he controlled the majority of the Firm's clients, the lifeblood of any law firm. But, Baker said, each partner, regardless of age, earnings, or political clout in the Firm, should have as "much individual freedom as possible, compatible with the practical operation of the business." He set up Baker & McKenzie to be governed by Articles of Partnership "which allow the maximum freedom to a Partner to extend himself to the limit of his energies, talents, and good fortune."

He recognized that democracy in a law firm was often a messy, inefficient way to run a business, but he also felt that democracy was the only way a multinational law firm would survive over the long term and would attract the entrepreneurial personalities he wanted. Baker was shrewd enough to understand that neither he nor a small committee could dictate how lawyers in Argentina or Belgium ran their practices. A democratic structure, on the other hand, would bond together lawyers from a grid of nationalities, cultures, and languages, while allowing them to retain control of their personal and professional lives. "Once Baker had set out on the democratic road, I think it would have been impossible to reverse," says Terence Lane, a former London partner who had bitter disagreements with Baker. "I was an equal partner with all the rest. We distributed our profits in accordance with the amount of work we did and the amount of clients we attracted. We didn't want Russell Baker sitting in Chicago and sending marching orders for the next day at work."

"Russell was a funny mix of idealism in some respects," John Connor says. "Very egalitarian. Very democratic." But some partners believe that, on occasion, Baker paid only lip service to democracy. "As Russell got an increasing number of capable and strong-willed people in, it was more difficult for his wishes to be automatically followed. He didn't much like that, but that's understandable," Peter Lederer says.

Baker sometimes bucked when the independent-minded attorneys he brought into the Firm did not support him on crucial Firm issues, but he never gave up on his egalitarian principles. When a group of younger lawyers challenged his power in the early 1970s, he discussed the democracy issue with the Firm's librarian, Frank Lukes. After Lukes opined that it was impossible to combine business and a democracy, Baker shot back that he had started the Firm with the democratic principle, and that he wasn't going to become a dictator. "That's what we have to live with," Baker said. "We'll see what will develop." Robert Dilworth adds that democracy was a format "that would send other senior partners up the wall screaming. But Russell was able to live with the lack of controls."

Baker went a step further to assure his colleagues that they were full members of the club. The Firm made all financial information available. Every partner knew exactly how much money every other partner made, and every partner could comb through the Firm's financial data to see how it was spending money. With this full disclosure policy, Baker eliminated the suspicion and rumor that spring from the secretiveness practiced by some law firms.

By introducing these cultural elements to the Firm, Baker created an organization that allowed Asians, Europeans, Latin Americans, Middle Easterners, and Americans to live and work together as equal partners who were free to operate their local offices within their own cultural context. To complete the institutional equation, Baker searched for a device that would provide his partners with economic freedom.

———

As a law student in the 1920s, Baker was repelled by the traditional ways of compensating junior lawyers. Years later, he often spoke to his partners about the evils of one individual reaping the fruits of another person's efforts. He also understood that, whether there are five or five hundred partners, the most difficult problem that a law firm faces is deciding how to divide profits.

Although law firms have existed for centuries, none of them has found the perfect way to compensate partners. In many firms, determining incomes is easy. The firm's owner takes what he wants and doles out to the other lawyers what's left over. If they don't like what they get—they leave. In some law firms, the senior partner or a committee of partners determine which partner is paid how much. Frequently, the most powerful partners populate the compensation committee, which is supposed to consider objective criteria such as hours worked, fees collected, and new clients brought in. Inevitably, subjective criteria creep into the decision-making process. Then, such matters as personality and social connections come into play. The subjective approach often creates a highly politicized culture, where lawyers are in direct competition with their contemporaries and waste time currying favor with partners on the compensation committee.

To avoid the harmful effects of a subjective compensation scheme, the Firm adopted an objective formula system. In order to create the collegial, family atmosphere that he envisioned, Baker determined that the system had to treat Japanese, Brazilian, and English lawyers equally. It had to eliminate infighting and back-biting over money, which would sap the lawyers' enthusiasm. Further, he wanted the new approach to attract entrepreneurial young lawyers, and, if they were successful, to allow them to earn good incomes early in their careers. It also had to give properly proportioned incentives to attorneys who performed the tasks necessary to build a law firm.

Baker cast about for a compensation system that fit his parameters. Exactly where or when Baker got the idea for what eventually developed into "the

Formula" is not clear. But, at some point in the 1950s, he read about a formulaic partner compensation procedure that a Boston law firm was using. He gave two young lawyers, Wallace Baker and Donald Donovan, a copy of an article describing the Boston firm's objective formula, and asked them to rough out a proposal that Baker & McKenzie could consider. They came up with a draft that contained most of the modern Formula's basic elements, but it was much cruder.[1]

Work Credit is the Formula's single most important element. Calculating Work Credit is a simple matter. The International Financial Department in Chicago adds up the amount of cash fees collected for a partner's work before the end of the Firm's June 30 fiscal year, and multiplies that number by seventy-five percent.

Determining Client Credit is more difficult. Technically, a partner who brings in a new client is allocated twelve percent of the gross fees collected from that client. But, "in recognition of the role that the Firm plays in the attraction of clients," fifteen percent of the twelve percent of gross fees goes into the Firm's Fund A. This translates into a partner receiving just over ten percent of gross fees collected from a client for which he has Client Credit. For partners who are more adroit at bringing in new business, Client Credit provides a healthy supplement to their incomes. A partner whose clients pay $2 million in fees during a year gets $200,000 credited to his account, even if the work is done by other lawyers. Baker, the Firm's most prolific client generator, received a handsome income each year from the Client Credit dollars allocated to him. Determining how to award Client Credit to a particular attorney can be complex because clients come to the Firm by many different avenues. To decide which partner gets Client Credit, Baker & McKenzie developed a ten-page set of intricate rules to help sort out Client Credit entitlement.

Before 1984, a committee of partners, which met almost weekly, handled the Client Credit decisions. As Baker & McKenzie grew and the number of Client Credit claims became a deluge, it became impractical to tie up hundreds of hours of partner time. To solve the problem, the Firm established the Client Credit Administration, and appointed a non-lawyer as the Administrator to process the several thousand New Business Reports that lawyers filed annually during the mid-1980s. The Administrator decides which fact situations fit into which one of the Client Credit rules. If a situation does not clearly fall under one of the rules, the partners involved usually agree on how to divide the Client Credit allocation. An aggrieved partner, however, has the right to have murkier situations decided by an appeals process. The Client Credit Director, a partner, reviews more complicated Client Credit claims. If a partner disagrees with the Director's conclusion, he can appeal to the Client Credit Appeals Committee, which is composed of partners from around the world. If a partner is still dissatisfied, the

Articles of Partnership permit him to appeal to the Policy Committee, although, in practice, this is rarely done.

Client Credit is an important part of many partners' incomes, but a third element is also significant. Associate Profit reflects how well each office manages its business at the local level. Computing Associate Profit is relatively easy. Each office totals its associates' gross fees collected and deducts the associates' share of expenses and the ten percent of associate fees that go to Fund A. The partners in the office then divide the resulting profit or loss.

The last major element of the Formula is Fund A, which does two things. It recognizes a partner's seniority, and it gives each partner a stake in the Firm's global profitability. "Without Fund A," William Gibbons says, "the Firm wouldn't have any commonalty. There would be no common sharing in what the Firm did."

For each year of partnership, partners receive one Fund A point. Money flows into Fund A from several sources, including twenty-five percent of partner fees, ten percent of associate fees, and Client Credit that is allocated to the Firm rather than to a partner. Money flows out of Fund A to pay costs, including compensation for partners working on Firm matters, subsidies to partners and offices, currency exchange losses, and retirement benefits to partners. The resulting balance is divided by the number of Fund A points issued. Each partner receives an amount equal to the number of Fund A points he owns. In the late 1980s and early 1990s, each Fund A point had a value of about $5,000.

The Firm computes, on a cash-actually-received basis, each partner's Work Credit, Client Credit, Associate Profit, and Fund A for the June 30 fiscal year. To determine a partner's annual income, which Baker & McKenzie calls "a participation," local office and global expenses are deducted.

The Formula's basic principles are easy to understand, but fathoming its subtleties can be mind-boggling. "The Formula produces wonderful Pavlovian behavior in a number of directions," Peter Lederer says. "But it is unbelievable how arcane it is to most people. Probably, in the history of Baker & McKenzie, there have been only twenty partners who understood it intimately." A former Firm financial officer, Charles Kessler, adds that "the Formula is the key to dividing the pie. And, when you read the Articles of Partnership, it sounds very simple. When you have to apply it, it's very complex."

Although the Formula has been a central element in the Firm's institutional culture since the mid-1950s, it has its detractors. Perhaps the two sharpest criticisms are: that the Formula forces each partner to be an individual profit center, which focuses his attention on his selfish interests; and that it is a "here and now" system that produces immediate penalties or rewards, giving no inducement for partners to look to the future. One example of a vice that stems from the Formula is that it causes some partners to hoard work. If, for instance, a partner has $10,000 of work to be done, but gives that work to another lawyer, he loses $7,500 in Work Credit. "There is a tendency, if there isn't enough work," Wulf Döser says, "for the partners to keep the work for themselves rather than have it done by the guy who does it better or has more time."

Although some partners feel an ambivalence towards the Formula, Claudio Camilli says that, when he served on the Executive Committee in the late 1970s, he "came to the conclusion that the Formula was the most imperfect thing you could put together. But it was an irreplaceable thing, and thank God that we have it." David Macdonald thinks that, in the Firm's first few decades, "without the structured freedom of the Formula, I don't think you could have set up a multi-office, multi-jurisdictional partnership with people trained in different fields of law without the Formula. It got rid of all subjectivity. Everybody could see why everybody else was making the money they were making. The Formula sucks the venom out of what otherwise is a poisonous battle for control of the distribution of money to the partners." Wulf Döser adds that, "We don't spend fifteen minutes discussing compensation at the Annual Partner Meetings. For the type of law firm that Russell envisioned, it is the only way to create an automatic adjustment for different social, cultural, business, economic, and monetary environments."

Chapter Six

Forging the Firm

Everyone—his sons, his partners, his friends, and his enemies—uses one word to describe Russell Baker: complex. When riled, he could harry his enemies with relentless determination. Or he could coo over the telephone to his wife like a youthful lover. Depending on the situation, he could muster character traits that covered most of the spectrum in between those two extremes. He alternated, Wulf Döser says, between "being kindly, soft-spoken, democratic, and being very powerful, autocratic, blunt."

One of his bête noire, Terence Lane, viewed Baker as a "highly complex man" who enjoyed being "involved in intrigues. He needed to have a fight with someone all the time." Peter Achermann, who had a fondness for Baker, agrees that "he always seemed to have the need of having at least one enemy who he fought with." William Gibbons adds that, "Beneath that facade of a preacher beat a heart of total steel. He was tougher than nails. He was a street and alley fighter." Baker never shied from combat. He had "duked it out" at county fairs to help pay his way through school, and, as a trial lawyer, he became an accomplished verbal pugilist. One reason he battled so hard, Hubert Stitt says, is that "Russell couldn't stand to be a loser. He was driven to win."

"Russell didn't mind fighting for his ideas about the Firm," Thomas Bridgman says. "But there was nothing he respected more than a guy hitting him right back in the forehead. He admired a guy he was trying to intimidate who would say, 'No, here is my view, and here is why.' Russell would not like it too well, but he would respect it."

Some partners who received the brunt of Baker's anger suspected that personal feelings clouded his judgment. But others believe that only Firm-related issues fully ignited his passion. "Russell was one of the world's ultimate pragmatists," Peter Lederer says. "He had as his overwhelming interest building a successful

Firm. And I don't think he cared whether you had two heads or not, if he viewed you as a positive contributing force to that goal. I don't know of a time when I saw Russell's personal feelings about anybody get in the way of his dealing with them regarding the Firm."

He sometimes criticized partners for not being self-starters, or for having too much "lead in their fannies." He also included womanizers and sycophants on his list of undesirables. But he reserved a special place in his pantheon of miscreants for "Firm politicians" who had self-serving personal agendas. "That angered him," his longtime secretary Elizabeth Challenger says. "The Firm meant every-thing to him. He wanted to build something special. When he felt that some-thing was good for the Firm, and they would buck him, he would get really mad." When irritated, Challenger says, he would bring himself under control by writing "nasty memos over and over again to get it out of his system. Then, what came out at the end was just telling them the way he felt, but in very mild words." Baker's son Wallace, however, recalls that "he wrote some pretty strong memos. Very straightforward and to the point. He told them, 'That's not the way. You can't operate like that. We won't have a Firm if you are not playing according to the rules.'"

Baker had definite ideas about how to organize and operate the Firm, but, before he made up his mind on an issue, he would listen to other partners' opin-ions. After he took a position, however, it was hard to sway him. "Baker's view was straight ahead," Michel Coccia says, "and there was not too much side view regarding specific areas of administration or management of the Firm. He would take advice before he jumped, but sometimes he was dogmatic in his conclusions."

In addition to being guilty of occasional tunnel vision, Baker sometimes rationalized that his decisions were in the Firm's best interests. "He was forging the Firm," Robert Cox says. "And the end justified the means." When Baker made up his mind that the Firm should move from Point A to Point B, he was relentless in his determination to get it there. If anybody got in his way, he invited them to move. If his invitation went unheeded, he took stronger mea-sures. Carlos Grimm says that, "Russell could be pretty intolerant when he thought you were interfering with the way he wanted to run things. These guys ran into a buzz saw when they ran into Russell."

Some partners still have disquieting memories of the signal that Baker was immovable. His "Santa-Claus eyebrows" would go rigid, and his eyes would glint through his metal-rimmed glasses. Hans-Georg Feick remembers that, "If you looked into his eyes, you knew you were talking with someone who knew what he was doing. You had the feeling that you shouldn't cross him too many times."

Although friends, enemies, and family members saw different sides of Baker, they all agree that he was not interested in glorifying himself. "Russell was not power driven in the general sense," an old adversary, Norman Miller, says, "only in terms of Baker & McKenzie."

Theoretically, he had no control over the Firm because its democracy and the Formula freed people to do as they wished. In practice, "Russell did as much as he could to keep running the Firm out of his back pocket," David Macdonald recalls. Baker seldom exercised his power overtly, however, correctly judging that letting his more vocal opponents vent their dissent was therapeutic. At partners' meetings, he didn't cut off debate, even if he knew that he had the votes to win a controversial issue. "It was not Russell's way to stand up and say, 'Look, I've got the votes and this is the way we are going to do it.' That was not his style," Peter Bentley says. "He let people have their say, and, when the vote came, he walked out with a win." Another reason "Russell generally got his way," Miller says, "was that he knew the Firm infinitely better than anybody else."

Baker employed a number of techniques to assure victory. If he needed a recalcitrant partner's vote at a meeting, he reminded the partner that he had brought him into the Firm and had helped make him financially and profession-ally successful. Jorge Sánchez recollects that, at Annual Meeting sessions, Baker "would walk slowly around the room, pausing now and then to talk to individual partners. He was like a tiger stalking his prey. He'd say something like, 'This seems good. You should vote for it.'" Donald Baker says that his father "didn't beat up on people. His control was not through *en terrorem* measures. He would call in chits. He would develop longstanding friendships and would do favors for them, and would supply them with clients and work."

To get his way, Baker relied primarily on his persuasive powers and force of personality. As he got older, and as the younger men began challenging him more openly, he sometimes resorted to more heavy-handed techniques, and, when he did, those stuck in partners' minds. "Russell did what it took to get your vote," John J. Byrne says. "He could cajole and make you feel good if that's what it took, or play a little hardball if that's what it took." When critical issues came up, Baker would lean heavily on even his closest friends and allies. At one Annual Meeting, Michael Waris voted against Baker on important amendments to the Articles of Partnership. "He came down from the head table and walked beside me and said in quiet voice, 'You son of a bitch, you change your vote,'" Waris vividly remembers.

After an Executive Committee meeting, Andrew Joanes got a strong dose of Baker's pressure. At the Rio de Janeiro meeting, Joanes had voted against Baker. When the Committee adjourned that evening with the matter still unresolved, Baker suggested that they take a stroll along Rio's famed beach. Despite the spectacular setting, "it wasn't all that pleasant," Joanes says. "That walk taught me that, if you produced an opposite view from Russell, you were liable to be attacked by him." Still, after Joanes told Baker that he would continue casting a negative vote, "I didn't detect any resentment from him."

If persuasion didn't work, Baker sometimes adopted the British gambit of co-opting his opposition by inviting them onto the Policy Committee, which, during the 1960s and early-1970s, was the Firm's governing body. Over the years, he gave Ira Wender, Norman Miller, Terence Lane, and other disaffected partners treasured seats on the Policy Committee. As the Executive Committee increased its influence, Baker included the discontented among its membership. "Russell valued the contributions that a lot of his adversaries made," Lederer says. "He wanted to bring them into the leadership of the Firm. We may have been bastards, but we were *his* bastards."

Baker was an enigma to many of his colleagues, who saw only one or two facets of his often contradictory personality. The partners who did battle with him saw facets that sparkled brilliantly, but also cut. The partners who stayed in the *casita* at his Lake Bluff home saw the warm side, and carried fond memories of a benevolent patriarch. Those who observed his relationship with his wife, Dibsie, were often surprised by his deep affection for her. Even into his seventies, when Baker spoke to his wife on the telephone, Challenger says, he "would talk to her like she was his high school sweetheart in a way that was extremely touching. It was almost poetry." He was also an "American puritan" who was scrupulously faithful to Elizabeth. Connor recalls Baker's "intense feeling for his family. He once said about a partner who had been divorced, 'Well, if a man's own wife can't trust him, who can?'"

Russell and Elizabeth Baker established a fund to enable minority students to attend college in the Chicago area, and they helped several young people in New Mexico further their educations. In 1960, Baker's Cuban-born secretary, Dolores Villa, told him that she was getting married. But, she said, her parents were trapped in Castro's Cuba and couldn't attend the wedding. Baker immediately volunteered to stand in for her father. On her wedding day, he picked Villa up in his Bentley, and, wearing tails, he walked her down the aisle.

Some observers think Baker never completely threw off his southwestern background. "He had a very low-key, sincere way about him that brought you along with whatever it was that he was advocating," Macdonald says. "He sounded like he was straight off the New Mexico range." Grimm says that, even though Baker lived most of his life in Chicago, "he had a lot of the western, southwestern personality. I always identified him with those old movies of the West with Spencer Tracy as a western patriarch who watched over things."

Baker genuinely wanted his partners to think well of him. "He was interested in building the Firm as something very special," Challenger says. "That is the reason the Firm was built on friendship." He had a few friends outside the Firm, including his Unitarian minister and a University of Chicago geography professor, "but his friends in the Firm were perhaps closer than those people," Wallace Baker says. "The friends in business were not just business relationships. This was an enterprise. We were all together making this funny little thing—the Firm—go."

Although he was close to most of his partners, some of those who liked him the least claim that Baker's agrarian upbringing left him intellectually flawed. Robert Dilworth disagrees, arguing that Baker's occasional lapses into backwoods aphorisms were "an affectation. He was a well-read guy. I remember several literary discussions with him." When Connor was living in Baker's *casita*, on weekends he invited the young Australian into the main house to listen to tapes of Shakespeare's plays. After he launched the Firm, much of his leisure reading dealt with practical subjects, such as trade with China or economic developments in Spain. Connor says that "until the day he died, he had an enormous intellectual curiosity. Allied with that was a tremendous amount of street shrewdness about people."

Between his intellectual interests and his intense work schedule, Baker had little time for pure recreation. The only spectator sport he enjoyed was the one that had partially paid his way through school. "He had an affinity for boxing all his life," James Baker says. "He just loved it." Besides boxing, the Firm, and Elizabeth, Baker had another great passion in his life—his ranch at Sapello, New Mexico. He bought the ranch where he grew up from relatives, and spent some $60,000 renovating the classic Spanish U-shaped ranch house. Despite the restoration, as late as 1968, Baker and his guests still used an outdoor privy. The conditions were primitive, but Baker liked it that way. And he liked his horses and cattle. James Baker says, "You could see he knew horses, not from an English gentleman's point of view, but how to run them and how to make them behave."

On one trip to New Mexico in the early 1970s, Baker was so anxious to ride his favorite horse, Stevie, up the canyons into the Sangre de Cristo Mountains that he told his ranch foreman, Susano Ortiz, to forget about elaborate preparations for the expedition. After two days of camping in the mountains, they had eaten everything. "I kept saying we were going to run out of groceries," Ortiz recalls. "But, when he made up his mind to do something, he'd do it. So we spent an extra day up there, and we got back home almost half-starved. He was a tough old man."

Every summer during his later years, the ranch served as a meeting place for his far-flung family. From Paris, Madrid, and Chicago,[1] his three sons and their families gathered in the sprawling adobe ranch house. Baker had several grandchildren, but he made sure that he spent time with each one of them alone. "I remember rides with him," his granddaughter, Beatriz Pessoa de Araujo, says. "You were left with the impression that you were very special because he gave you his time and his completely undivided attention." Some evenings, he loaded his family on a horse-drawn hay wagon, took them up on a high mesa, and built a fire to barbecue their dinner. To help him with the horses and the cooking, Baker brought along a Hispanic cowboy, and the two men entertained the children with Mexican campfire songs.

Baker usually voted Republican, but Elizabeth, a staunch Democrat, canceled out his vote. Although he normally had little interest in politics, there was one issue that he did feel strongly about—America's use of its international trade laws as a political weapon against the USSR, China, and their allies. Baker delivered many speeches denouncing the American government's policy. At a 1965 meeting in Portland, Oregon, he championed increasing East-West trade and eliminating U.S. restrictions on trading with Communist countries. "I wouldn't bellyache so much," Baker said, "if I thought there was the slightest indication the controls had been effective." The American restraints, he said, were a mockery that only succeeded in keeping U.S. companies from developing business in the Communist countries, while their European and Japanese competitors were making millions there.

Baker had almost as little interest in religion as he did in politics. When he registered as a student at the University of Chicago in 1919, he indicated that he was a Methodist. As he approached middle age, Baker found that the Unitarian Church's toleration of all religious faiths appealed to him, as did its freedom from dogma and its pragmatic approach to the spiritual side of life. Hubert Stitt speculates that Baker liked the Unitarians because "it was like his internationalization of the Firm. He thought of the Unitarian church as a group of different religions coming together within a non-dogmatic framework. There is a similarity between the concepts of the church and what he tried to accomplish by forming the Firm."

Baker was intellectually curious about religion, but few partners remember him discussing it. Instead, they remember his dry, understated humor. They also recall another side to his humor, which they describe as "salty" and "earthy," that was rooted in his Texas and New Mexico youth. The frontier also taught him disdain for phoniness. "Russell had no pretensions, and was not attracted to the glitzy or the gaudy," Robert Berner says. "He was not attracted to titles, or to the trappings of status." Baker often wore a battered western hat and an old, tattered raincoat, and carried a well-used briefcase that "looked like it had been run over by a train." One partner recalls that Baker was "totally unassuming. If you saw him walking on the street, you would never say that he was a senior partner of the largest law firm in the world."

Baker didn't insist that his subordinates treat him with deference. In 1972, Paul Slocomb, a fresh Harvard graduate, gave his new secretary a stack of papers to have copied. At the time, the Chicago office had two older men who served as messengers. As an elderly gentleman ambled down the hall one morning, the secretary shouted: "Oh, sir, Mr. Slocomb has to have three copies of this. Take them down and copy them." A few minutes later, Slocomb heard Russell Baker saying: "Here are your copies, young lady. Now, if there is anything else you need, you just let us know and we'll take care of it." When Slocomb's secretary went into his office, she asked him who the silver-haired man was. "Until ten minutes ago, that was my employer," the associate answered. Baker never mentioned the incident.

He had a keen sense of the value of money. As the son of a poor farm family, and a man who had spent much of his early career struggling to make a living during the Depression, he was frugal. Even after his income soared in the 1960s and 1970s, he never considered moving from his modest Lake Bluff house. Patricia Beal says, "He was very proud of the fact that he graduated from law school with no money and had to hustle to eat." Baker was parsimonious with his own funds, and was equally so with the Firm's money. In his later years, he often complained that Baker & McKenzie spent too much money on computers and other equipment, and he constantly grumbled about partners who flew first class and stayed in expensive hotels.

His distaste for what he regarded as profligacy was so well known that his partners went to extra lengths to hide their free-spending ways from him. Once, when he and a young partner were scheduled to fly tourist class from Chicago to Tokyo to meet with a client, Baker canceled. His partner immediately upgraded himself to first class, but, as he was standing in line at the airport to pick up his ticket, he saw Baker bustling towards him shouting, "I can make it." The partner broke out of line, grabbed Baker, sat him down, and told him that he would get the tickets for them both. He switched back to tourist class. Despite Baker's economical instincts, on occasion he could be extravagant. His most lavish possession was his automobile. In 1959, when a client and business partner died and left him $15,000, Baker used the money to buy a Bentley, but he justified his purchase by saying that it would last him the rest of his life.

More frequent than the spurts of prodigality were acts of generosity. A Baker antagonist, Terence Lane, when asked if he liked Baker, responds with a blunt

"No! But I admired him. He was a very farsighted man. He was extremely generous." If a partner was financially strained, Lane says, "Russell would simply take a slice of his share of profit and put it back into the Firm for distribution wherever the need arose." It wasn't unusual for Baker to make interest-free loans to partners caught in a financial pinch, but "if you borrowed money from him, and you told him you were going to pay it back in September, you darn well better keep your word," Challenger says. "If you didn't pay when that time came, that angered him. It was the principle of the thing—you had to keep your word."

––––––

Baker's colleagues recall that he had a large measure of the Protestant work ethic. Rather than regarding work as drudgery, to him it was fun. "He was like a kid who wants to build a box. He might not know why, but he just wanted to make it," Wallace Baker says. His sister-in-law, Janet Ullmann, recalls that "work was his passion." He once told her that "a man without his work is nothing," and he constantly urged young lawyers to work hard. At Alejandro Alfonzo-Larrain's first Annual Meeting in 1969, Baker told him, "I want you to work in this Firm as if you were starving."

Baker often got up at 5:30 in the morning to work. If the task required it, he worked Saturdays and Sundays. On many Monday mornings, Baker came to town with dictation tapes full of letters and memos that he had done over the weekend in his tiny office over his garage. Once, when he was crushed with work and was in a hurry to get out of town on a business trip, he had his secretary ride with him to O'Hare Airport. As they rode along, he dictated a stream of correspondence up until the moment he jumped out of the taxi. Michael Waris speculates that Baker's compulsion to work came from his being "a poor boy and being driven. He remembered how it was to have nothing. In addition, he had a lot of energy—animal energy—and he was just competitive by nature."

At an age when many men are in their dotage, Baker could work as hard as he did because "he was blessed with a lot of stamina," Wallace Baker says. "But he had the ability to relax. He was always well balanced when the pressure was high." One former secretary, Elizabeth Challenger, says he worked constantly, but "he was a calm, not a hyper person. He was an easy-tempo type of person."

Baker brought the same concentration he gave to client work to bringing in new business. The Firm had several good rainmakers, Thomas Haderlein says, "but Russell was head and shoulders and hips and everything else above all of them." In the late 1950s and early 1960s, Baker spent half his time promoting new business. Later, that figure jumped to sixty-five percent. Some of the other Firm lawyers promoted clients at country clubs or parties, schmoozing with executives who could channel them business. "But Russell was totally ill at ease in that setting," Wallace Baker says. "It didn't interest him. Going out to society parties was not his thing. He would rather write articles or give speeches."

"The way he promoted was by keeping his name in front of everybody," Challenger says. "And that's why it was a lot of work for us [his secretaries]. He made a job of promoting." Following the advertising industry's maxim that repetition eventually generates business, Baker used almost any excuse to keep the Firm's name flowing across an executive's desk. If he discovered that a client was thinking about opening an office in Ireland, he searched his own files for relevant materials and sent them to the client. Baker also wrote to clients to announce that he had hired a new lawyer who brought fresh expertise to the Firm. If a Firm attorney wrote a legal article that applied to a particular client's business, Baker sent him a copy. If a client hadn't used the Firm's services for some time, he called or made a personal visit. "He was very big on writing letters," Dolores Villa says. "He always kept an eye on what a company did, and how Baker & McKenzie could serve that company." When he came back to the office after a seminar or meeting, he wrote follow-up letters, sometimes as many as three hundred, to the people he met.

Baker delighted in his promotional efforts. Donald Baker says his father "got enormous pleasure in bringing in a new client. It was like a hunting expedition. He was bagging clients." What seemed to attract them was Baker's strong character, sense of humor, and interesting line of talk. "He'd been raised in a rustic culture in which the main form of entertainment was talk," Donald says. "People talking and telling stories, swapping stories, and making conversation."

Baker often drew on vignettes from his boyhood background to flavor one of his favorite business development techniques—making speeches. In college theatricals and during his twenty-five years in the courtroom, he had made himself into an excellent speaker. Challenger says, "His speeches were more personal in nature. You felt like he was talking to you." Eugene Theroux adds that Baker made his audience "think that they were in the presence of someone who could see around the corner into the future. The person he most closely resembled was Will Rogers, with one hand in a pocket, slouched, head kind of tilted to one side. But looking at you in a respectful and disarmingly informal way—the way someone would talk to you as if they were leaning against a fence post."

Baker's speeches were not extemporaneous. Like everything else he did, he prepared them carefully, sometimes polishing them through five or more drafts. "He was always trying to make it better," Villa says. "He was very critical of himself." After he wrote his speeches, he spent hours studying the list of attendees and their companies so that he could strike exactly the right chord when he met them. At each speech-making event, Baker attended to every detail. "I invariably see to it," he wrote, "that the introducer emphasizes the name [Baker & McKenzie] and the things which distinguish our firm from any other firm in the world, *i.e.*, dual training of its personnel, multiple offices, single firm idea, the presence if not the predominance of non-U.S. partners in the partnership, the truly international character of our organization and of our practice."

When his promotional efforts brought results, Baker was delighted. "He did not care how small the client was. What mattered was that he got a new client for Baker & McKenzie, even if it was something for a $100 fee," Villa says. Baker worked hard at attracting smaller companies, but he also took pains to get his message across to the general counsels of large corporations. Before the 1980s, many establishment law firms regarded in-house attorneys as second-rate lawyers who couldn't succeed in their firms. Baker, who had none of the establishment lawyers' snobbism, went out of his way to court the in-house lawyers.

In the early 1970s, an American in-house attorney asked Baker to advise his company on which country to use for its European headquarters. The company lawyer made it clear that his management had given him a short deadline. He also told Baker that some top executives were pressuring the legal department to stop using Baker & McKenzie. He quickly contacted several European partners, and finished the opinion by the deadline. In a memorandum to the partners who had worked on the project, Baker quoted the in-house counsel as saying "'your material arrived on time and was very well received here.' [The company lawyer] did not say that the battle had been won. And we know that such battles are never won. They go on forever."

Baker mastered the art of the care and feeding of clients, and he often coached his partners on business development techniques. He told a young Brazilian lawyer, "Never give up on a client. Persistence. Perseverance. You may be turned down once, twice. Don't get upset. Bombard him with written stuff. Call him up once in a while. Eventually, you will get more clients that way than if you give up. When you least expect it, the client will commit."

Baker awed most partners with his ability to attract clients, but some belittled his efforts, at times making him unsure of himself. He sent Eric Homburger a memo asking, "Is it advisable for me to keep on doing what I have been doing [attracting legal work to the Firm]?" He went on to describe a "slight incident" in the Chicago office. "One of the partners made reference to me as a salesman, implying that I am less than a lawyer. The way he said it, and the context in which it was said, made me feel that he was simply reflecting an attitude, if not a conversation that he had previously had with some others of the partners."

The issue was still on Baker's mind a year later when Peter Lederer returned to the U.S. from Zürich. Lederer was making the rounds of the Chicago office to greet his friends, and one of the first things Baker said to him was: "You know, I'm getting back and really working like a lawyer again. I'm off this promoting business bandwagon. I'm working as a lawyer in the library, doing my own research. If there's one thing I can't stand, it's my partners thinking I'm too damned dumb to practice law any more."

———————

Baker paid particular attention to the younger lawyers and their progress in the Firm. Almost all of them were middle-class, with no connections in their local power structures. Rather than target young people from establishment families, John Klotsche says, Baker searched for "the best and the brightest. His idea was to get them at an early stage, and to have them very much committed to the Firm. He was a very, very complex individual, but a very caring individual. Not only about his partners, but about all of the lawyers."

The "common man" who grew up on Texas and New Mexico ranches had the knack of making young lawyers from Tokyo, Mexico City, and Milan comfortable. John Connor recalls that he "liked being around young people. He liked listening to them, and seeing them develop. Russell enjoyed bringing them into important Firm roles early in their careers because that was not what conventional law firms did. Russell was very driven by being an outsider. He was very anti-establishment. He thought that most people who came from privileged backgrounds were pompous idiots."

Canadian Edward Kowal, the son of a Ukrainian immigrant farmer, remembers going from Toronto to Chicago for his first job interview with Baker. Kowal was nervous that he wouldn't pass the "rabies test," but Baker calmed the associate candidate by asking him about his personal interests, his career goals, and political events in Canada. For Monique Nion, Baker arranged a scholarship at the University of Chicago Law School. When she arrived in Chicago, she stayed in the Bakers' *casita* for a month. Baker, Nion says, treated her almost like a daughter, driving her to church on Sundays and advising her on her career.

He worked hard to make the lawyers' spouses feel that they had a stake in the Firm. He encouraged the partners to bring their wives and children to Annual Meetings. When he went to his colleagues' offices to chat, he almost always asked about their families. "He went out of his way to be very warm," Challenger says. "He made the lawyers feel that they were part of something very important. He became very close to the families of the earlier partners."

Baker always made himself available to those who wanted to talk to him. Carlos Rossi recalls Baker speaking "with a low voice, very calm, but with bright eyes, always picking up things very quickly." In private conversation, Bruce Porter says, Baker was a "surprisingly impressive person. When I looked in his eyes, there was always a vitality there. He looked very directly at you, and spoke with strong sincerity." If a partner hadn't been in Chicago for some time, he telephoned him "just to ask what was new and to pump him up a bit," and he wrote to encourage them regarding their careers. "He tried to develop a sense of, 'If you have a problem any time, come to me and we will try to solve it,'" Challenger recalls.

When out-of-town partners visited Chicago, they always went to Baker's office to give him the latest news about their families, their practices, and their offices. "Russell was a friend of his partners and associates," Rossi says. "He generated a kind of personality glue. He would make someone feel so comfortable and so rewarded by working with him that you wanted to be there with the Firm. You wanted to share in his dreams. Not on account of money, but for the reward of working with a nice, intelligent group of people."

Baker believed that a family atmosphere strengthened the Firm, and he believed that luck played a large part in success. He often told his colleagues that "in life it is better to be lucky than smart. When Lady Luck puts her hand on your shoulder, she seldom takes it off." Just four months before he died, the theme of luck crossed his mind. "The best in life is the fortuitous and the unexpected," he wrote Michael Waris. "The fun consists of identifying the breaks and exploiting them."

On rare occasions, the struggle to find the right combination of economic and management techniques for the Firm made him quiet and morose. Despite the few down periods, Baker's overriding optimism always righted his internal compass. He had an unshakable faith that a well-trained, well-disciplined, well-prepared lawyer could achieve almost anything. No matter how difficult it was to find the right prescription, he believed that he could achieve his goals. "Maybe not the first time," Wallace Baker says. "But, when you add willpower and preparation behind it, he could do a lot of things."

Baker had a strong streak of loyalty. In a 1961 memorandum to a Swiss partner, he set out his philosophy: "Loyalty to a friend in my book is the most important of all virtues. In fact, without loyalty, there can be no friendship. A Partnership should be a bond of friends." Those who knew Baker well learned to use his sense of loyalty to their advantage. In the early 1970s, Francis Morrissey was campaigning for election as the Chairman of the Chicago Office Committee. When he heard a rumor that Baker was supporting another candidate, he was furious. Morrissey decided to confront him. "I started swinging right from the beginning. I immediately went on the attack very aggressively, and kept emphasizing loyalty. I told him that I was a loyal partner of Baker & McKenzie. That I deserved loyalty from him. That I was just shocked that he would not be loyal to a partner who had been loyal to him over all the years." The postscript, Morrissey says, is that "I did become Chairman."

On occasion, his tendency to be overly loyal led him to select the wrong man for the wrong job. "But Russell regarded a partner as a very special person. And, if you were his partner, he would support you with all his energy and all his strength," Morrissey adds. "He was very, very loyal to anybody in the Firm against third parties on the outside." In the early 1960s, Connor, who was in his mid-twenties, got a clear signal that an older client thought he was too young to be handling his legal affairs. Connor went to Baker.

"Do you know the difference between an old fool and a young fool?" Baker asked him. Then he answered his own question: "Thirty years."

"There was a message there to forget all that stuff and just do the work," Connor says. "I did."

In addition to loyalty, Baker was instinctively drawn to the underdog. If he felt that older lawyers were taking advantage of a young lawyer, he supported the junior man. When William J. Linklater was being considered for election to partner, he shared with Baker his worry that some of the Chicago partners would kill his chances because they considered him a "boat rocker."

"The way I see it, Joe Boy, we could use a few more boat rockers around this place," Baker said. Linklater became a partner.

———

Until 1955, Chicago had been the Firm's sole office. But, between then and 1963, offices sprouted in Caracas, Amsterdam, Brussels, Washington, Zürich, New York, São Paulo, London, Mexico City, Frankfurt, Milan, Toronto, Paris, Manila, and Tokyo. "All of us got excited about that," Coccia recalls. "Not only was the grand plan working, it was working well. The joy of seeing things develop from mere ideas into reality, and being the leaders in the international field, drove us all the harder. The lawyers understood Russell Baker's idea, and believed in it, and wanted to break their butts to get the job done."

Even though the Firm was growing geometrically, Chicago was still the hub around which the other offices turned. Partners from around the world were constantly coming to "headquarters" to meet with the Firm's blue ribbon clients that included Caterpillar, Chrysler, DuPont, Westinghouse, American Home Products, Eli Lilly, Morton Salt, and United Fruit. As each new client came in, Baker prepared what he called an "opus" that described the legal aspects of a client's international business. An opus had to be perfect, with no spelling or typographical errors. One of Baker's early secretaries, Villa, still remembers the opus she worked on for Pittsburgh Plate Glass. "We typed this monster thing. We typed it and typed it and typed it."

Even though Baker was churning out opuses almost weekly, the Chicago office was still small in the mid-1950s. One person ran the accounting department, doing the books by hand. Chicago's meager law library took up only a few shelves, and a part-time librarian came twice a week to shelve the books and add new items. A telephone operator sat at the old-fashioned switchboard, plugging wires into the proper extension when clients called. The copy machine used wet paper, and it took more than thirty minutes for the copies to dry.

Meanwhile, Baker was spending substantial time working on an Illinois Bar Association issue that was blocking his "one firm" concept. The rules barred Illinois lawyers from being partners with non-Illinois attorneys. As a stopgap measure, the Firm had two partnerships: the formal, written Illinois Articles of Partnership, and an informal international partnership that included partners from around the world. But Baker wanted a permanent and fully recognized solution. He lobbied his friends on the Illinois Supreme Court, who, in the early 1960s, ruled that non-Illinois lawyers could be members of an Illinois partnership so long as they were admitted in their own jurisdictions and they did not practice law in Illinois. In addition, Baker convinced the Supreme Court to allow non-U.S. citizens to be admitted to the Illinois Bar.

Although Baker worked hard on what he believed was important to the Firm's success, with his frugality and his disinterest in administrative details, he overlooked the office's decor. When David Macdonald moved into his new office in the One North LaSalle Building in 1962, it was "a lousy building. Very rundown, very dirty," he recalls. "The windows were all seeping soot. The Firm had not done much to refurbish the space." Since the floors were small, the shape of some offices was bizarre. Macdonald's first office was about thirty feet long, but very narrow. Not only did the configuration make his office seem like a bowling alley, but the noise level was similar to one. Because it backed up to the elevators, whirring cables and clanking doors disturbed his work. Robert Dilworth recalls that, "The reception room carpet was worn all the way down to the concrete. But Russell Baker was a genius at image building. He had arranged to have Japanese law books surrounding the reception area so that the Firm would look very international— just in case anybody wondered what line of work Baker & McKenzie was in."

Even in these ordinary surroundings, the Chicago office's international atmosphere was exhilarating. When an overseas call came in, the lawyers gathered around the phone because it was a "major event." Despite the air of excitement, the office had some serious problems. Tension arose between McKenzie and Coccia over their different approaches to operating the Chicago trial department. McKenzie, the swashbuckling litigator, hated what he considered to be administrative trivia. Coccia believed that the litigation department was "drifting," and that it "was not expanding into other disciplines, including the business and international litigation fields."

To McKenzie's annoyance, Coccia pushed his agenda for bringing a more formal structure to the litigation section. He prodded his senior to expand the client base, set up form files, catalogue opinions, and adopt other organizational techniques. But McKenzie resented the younger man's insistence, and refused to make substantive changes. There was no shouting or screaming, but they deadlocked over how to run the trial section. When Coccia finally concluded that they could not coexist in the litigation department, he volunteered to go abroad, and begged Baker to get him involved in international law practice. Baker arranged for Coccia to transfer to the Brussels office in the early 1960s, but McKenzie died of a heart attack in 1962. Although Coccia was happy in Belgium, Baker talked him into coming back to Chicago. "Coccia was the man who saved our litigation practice in Chicago," Gibbons says. "Mike built it up and made it a department that, after four or five years, could have survived his exit. He built an institution."

After McKenzie's funeral, Coccia and two young trial partners, Francis Morrissey and Thomas Bridgman, met to discuss the litigation section's future without McKenzie. Fearing that the insurance clients who had relied on McKenzie to try their major cases would find other lawyers, Coccia went to the litigation group's largest client and persuaded it to give the Firm a chance to prove that it could handle their work. "Partly because the Lord was looking over my shoulder," Coccia says, he got favorable verdicts back to back in significant cases.

Nevertheless, McKenzie had clearly been the star of Baker & McKenzie's trial practice, and the remaining litigation partners knew that they would have to mount an intensive campaign to keep their clients. Coccia, Morrissey, and Bridgman had myriad lunches and dinners with insurance company executives to convince them that they could pick up where McKenzie had left off. Even with the remaining trial lawyers pulling together, trying "to preserve the existing business and to become identified as a viable unit without McKenzie's presence was difficult," Coccia says. "That was done by the loss of a great deal of sleep and with a great deal of stress."

The litigation partners also mapped a new strategy for the Chicago trial section. First, they abolished the "star system," explaining to clients that the litigation department would be working as a team, and that any attorney in the group with comparable experience could do a first-class job of trying a lawsuit. They also insisted that a client would no longer be treated as a client of an individual lawyer, but as clients of the department. And they agreed to make decisions on a consensus basis. These changes proved to be "the beginnings of a family operation that kept us tight, close, and supportive of each other," Coccia says.

In their most radical step, the three trial partners opted out of the Formula. Instead of having individual Work Credit, they agreed to pool their income and to divide it equally among all litigation partners.[2] The idea behind their special compensation system was to keep the trial lawyers from competing to get Work Credit, and to encourage a system that put the best man on a particular case.

They didn't want "competition within the house," Morrissey says. "The competition was outside the house. You never used the words, 'My file.' It was always, 'Our file.' The whole idea was to take a group and get them all working together."

———————

Russell Baker's 1949 game plan had called for the Chicago litigation section to provide a steady income that kept the Firm afloat while he developed an international law practice. Within a few years, however, the Chicago Foreign Trade and Tax Departments[3] emerged as core contributors to the Firm's growth. Until the 1960s, few American lawyers had specialized in tax. They scoffed that only the dreary accounting profession should handle boring numbers and tax returns. But, kindled by the U.S. tax law that permitted WHTCs and FBCs, Baker & McKenzie managed to build an international tax practice that became a drive wheel of the Firm's development. Indeed, the Firm's first five non-Chicago offices—Caracas, Washington, Brussels, Amsterdam, and Zürich—opened for the primary purpose of servicing clients' tax law needs.

To help American clients get in on the tax bonanza, the Firm's U.S. tax lawyers spent hours carefully planning and implementing WHTC and FBC structures. Part of the reason for the Firm's caution was that the large accounting firms were its chief competition for international tax work in the 1950s and early 1960s. "The accounting firms were particularly rough because they were in the tax field, and they had contact with all of the Firm's clients," Macdonald says. "They were looking over our shoulders on the tax actions we were recommending. They attacked us for being too risky, and told their clients that Baker & McKenzie would get its comeuppance."

When Congress adopted Subpart F of the 1962 Tax Reform Act, which curbed the use of FBCs, some competitors chortled that Subpart F spelled Baker & McKenzie's doom. Instead of an early demise, however, Subpart F spurred the Firm's growth because it was so complicated that it forced the amateurs out. Baker & McKenzie had another advantage. Because Subpart F effectively denied American companies the old tax benefits of manufacturing in the U.S. and selling abroad, many corporations decided to manufacture overseas. With its network of European, Asian, and Latin American offices, the Firm was positioned to help clients with their tax and corporate work when they set up operations abroad. Further work came via other U.S. tax law requirements related to transferring assets abroad and reorganizing foreign operations.

"We were handling transactions that no one had really handled before. So, we were in an area where nobody knew whether they were right or wrong," Macdonald says. "The tax lawyers had to make judgment calls in a lot of areas."

Because the Firm's clients were receiving advice based on complex tax provisions for which there were no clear answers, they sometimes found themselves in litigation with the IRS or the Justice Department. Prior to the early 1960s, the IRS had had so little experience in international tax matters that it hired Washington partner Walter Slowinski to teach the subject to its senior officials. As many American companies began doing business abroad, however, the government became more sophisticated in cross-border tax issues. With increasing frequency, the IRS assailed international tax structures in court. This, in turn, allowed Baker & McKenzie to become the first U.S. law firm to develop in-depth expertise in handling international tax controversies. From the 1960s on, Firm lawyers were continuously working on several pieces of tax litigation involving millions of dollars.

The government consistently lost its WHTC allegations and stopped bringing cases in that area, but it continued its efforts under Subpart F, Section 482, and many other tax provisions. Between 1970 and 1993, Firm tax lawyers went to court in one hundred three cases, and settled many times that number. Controversy work represented some thirty percent of the U.S. tax assignments by 1970, and the remaining seventy percent was devoted to planning. By the 1980s, the labor was about equally divided between planning and controversy work.

As the U.S. tax practice grew, the Firm brought more young lawyers into the system. Robert Dilworth had gone to law school because, while he was writing his senior thesis on *Kant and the Natural Law*, he decided that he wanted "to establish the intellectual connection between the natural law and the common law." During the scholarly young man's last year at Harvard Law School, both the Firm and another prestigious Chicago law firm were recruiting him. Dilworth made his decision, and told a partner in the establishment law firm that he was going to Baker & McKenzie.

"This very nice partner looked at me as if I had defecated right there on the floor. He said, 'You know, there are a lot of firms besides ours. But, really, Baker & McKenzie is just not the kind of place you go to without really being aware of what you are doing. They're sort of pirates.'"

Dilworth thanked the partner for the advice and joined the Chicago office in 1966. His first assignment confirmed that he had, indeed, signed on to work for an exotic law firm. The case involved a Rumanian who had immigrated to Colombia, where he set up a textile factory. His company prospered, and he invested his money in Canadian real estate, the U.S. stock market, and Israeli bonds. The Rumanian met an American woman, fell in love, and the couple were married in Miami in an Orthodox Jewish ceremony. Then, they went to Caracas and lived there until the man died. Dilworth had to figure out whether Colombian, Venezuelan, Canadian, Florida, New York, Israeli, Rumanian, or Talmudic law applied to the estate.

Shortly after Dilworth started with the Firm, a tall young man who had played football at the University of Wisconsin joined the Chicago office. What interested John Klotsche about the Firm was that it was headquartered in the Midwest rather than New York, whose law firms he viewed as having a "sweat-shop environment. The Firm was exciting, and it offered the prospects of travel and all the trappings that go with an international practice," he says. "I wanted to get into the international area in Baker & McKenzie, and tax was the best opportunity for me to get involved because I didn't have the language capability they required for the foreign trade work."

The U.S. offices were not the only ones where tax law made up a large part of the work. In Amsterdam and Zürich, Johannis Caron and Eric Homburger, both of whom had been general civil lawyers, studied tax law so that they could wed American and local tax concepts. In the Toronto office, founder Hubert Stitt was primarily a tax specialist. "In Canada, we were able to win cases and do tax planning," Edward Kowal says. Each year, on the night the Canadian government issued its changes to the tax law, "the entire office would stay at work. You worked through the night to produce a pamphlet on the new tax law. By the time the sun shone the next day, there would be a publication out to our clients," Kowal recalls.

In the U.S., Baker & McKenzie's international tax law reputation reached the point that, by the 1970s, "If you had an international tax question or controversy problem, we were it," Robert Cunningham says. "We were doing very sophisticated projects for the multinational corporations." Upon graduation from New York University Law School, Cunningham taught at NYU for two years before deciding to leave academia for law practice. When he began interviewing, a friend at the Law School told him, "'Bob, there's a guy here who you should meet. He's a very interesting person, a special individual.'"

"I went up, and it was Russell Baker," Cunningham says. "We talked for half an hour. It was fascinating. He talked about it being a young, dynamic Firm that was truly international and a true democracy. About how it had interesting people and that it was the United Nations of law firms."

Even though Baker's charisma fired Cunningham, he had heard the establishment firms' derision of Baker & McKenzie. Worried, Cunningham called a tax law professor at the University of Chicago, who assured him that the Firm was "doing some of the best, most exciting things in the world." Lured by the chance to work on cutting-edge transactions, he joined the Chicago office's tax group in 1969.

As Cunningham and others increased the roster of tax practitioners, they saw a need to organize their practice area. In the late 1970s, the tax lawyers formed the North American Tax Practice Group. Its purposes include sharing technical information, developing new business, and establishing common standards for opinion letters. The tax partners share the Group's costs, and designate a lawyer from each office to serve on a Steering Committee that organizes meetings and sets the agendas. Because the Group was the first to formally organize, it has served as a model for other Firm practice groups.

———

Baker implemented one of his basic concepts through the Chicago Foreign Trade Department. Early on, he conceived the idea of locating a corps of bicultural attorneys in Chicago who spoke two languages and who had training in both the civil and common law systems. In addition to having non-U.S. lawyers permanently on staff in Chicago, he wanted the Foreign Trade Department to serve as a melting pot where young attorneys from around the world would come to train for a few months or for several years. During their tenures, they would be exposed to the workings of an American law firm and to the quirks of American clients. At the same time, the Firm would inoculate the expatriates with its culture. The Foreign Trade Department's primary purpose, however, was to provide global legal services to clients at a single location. From Chicago, Friedrich Weinkopf could advise a client about German law and Peter Bentley about English law.[4] Bentley had left his London law firm in the mid-1960s to join the Chicago office. At that time, he says, "you didn't expect to see a foreign lawyer in a U.S. law firm. Law was pretty much a provincial skill."

A young Spaniard, Marcel Molins, also staffed the Foreign Trade Department. He was born near Barcelona at the height of the Spanish Civil War in 1936, and received his university training in his native country. Through a series of scholarships, he studied in London, Strasbourg, Hamburg, Trieste, Helsinki, and, finally, Chicago. While he was a student at Northwestern University, a professor put him in touch with Baker. By the time Molins became a partner in 1970, he was known as the Chicago office's expert in Spanish and Latin American law. It wasn't unusual for him to work simultaneously on projects in Brazil, Argentina, Peru, and Chile. Since all Spanish- and Portuguese-speaking Latin American countries follow the Napoleonic Code's civil law system, switching from one country to another was not too difficult. But, as the laws of those countries became more complex, and as the amount of Latin American work began to mount, Molins began building a staff. By the mid-1990s, the Chicago Latin American staff had risen to twenty-five, and it was working closely with four other specialists in New York.

Over the long term, the Latin American Group has been successful, but political and economic events have sometimes hurt its practice. In the late 1960s, Molins spent several years making himself a Chilean law expert. Then, in 1970, Salvador Allende became president, vowing to nationalize the nation's industry and recognizing Fidel Castro's socialist government. "Investment in Chile dropped to zero," Molins ruefully recalls.

That same year, in a show of defiance against perceived foreign economic domination, five South American countries adopted Decision 24 of the Andean Common Market.[5] That "drastic change" in the law created a hostile investment climate by severely limiting the amount of profits that foreign companies could take back to their home countries, and by making it extremely difficult for foreigners to own a majority interest in local operations. In 1982, Argentine work almost disappeared when that country's armed forces invaded the Falkland (Malvinas) Islands. In the early and mid-1980s, most major Latin American nations collapsed into technical bankruptcy. Foreign investment plummeted, as did the Chicago Latin American group's work. "Our work dropped by at least fifty percent," Molins says. With so much free time, his income dipped sharply under the Formula, but he used the slack period to develop new clients.

The Foreign Trade Department gave Baker & McKenzie a significant competitive advantage that no other law firm had—one-stop shopping for legal questions in multiple countries. But the Firm's advice on Latin American, Asian, and European law had to be current and it had to be right. To supply the necessary research materials, Baker laid plans to create what eventually became the world's largest private international law library. To head the effort, he chose Frank Lukes, who was born in 1923 and grew up in western Czechoslovakia (now the Czech Republic) near the German border. Shortly after Prime Minister Neville Chamberlain announced that he had secured "peace with honor" under the Munich Agreement in 1938, the Nazis took over the Sudetenland and made it a German protectorate.

During World War II, Lukes joined the Czech underground, reporting on German troop movements. When tanks and trucks rolled through his town, he relayed the information to students in Prague, who, in turn, radioed the information to the Allied Forces in London. After the War, Lukes entered the Charles University Law School and planned to graduate in late 1948, but political turmoil almost kept that from happening. Earlier that year, the Communists had deposed the democratically elected government. At the university, a Communist-controlled Action Committee began rooting out students who were not partisans. Lukes did not meet their loyalty test, in part because he had marched in the front row of a student protest against the Communist takeover.

An unrelenting anti-Communist, Lukes nevertheless kept his feelings to himself. When the Action Committee's agents tried to persuade him to join their ranks, he refused. The Action Committee branded him a "lost cause" and threatened to block his graduation from law school. Luckily, a close friend who was a strong Communist stood up for him, and the Action Committee allowed him to graduate in December 1948. Three days later, the Communists purged all non-Communist students. In 1953, Lukes escaped to West Berlin. "I spent six years under Hitler and six years under Stalin," he says of his youth.

After two years in West Germany, Lukes came to the U.S., where he eventually met Baker, who gave him a job as the Firm's chief librarian. At the time, the international law library consisted of about one hundred books. Baker told the Czech that he wanted him to build it into a first-class research facility. Lukes assembled a collection of tax materials, and then built up the intellectual property collection, buying books on patent, trademark, and copyright laws from around the world. He also gathered extensive materials on exchange control, corporate, labor, and other laws. "Every country where we had any interest was there," Lukes says.

By 1965, the library had swelled from one small room to an entire floor, and was serving not just the Chicago office, but the entire Firm. By 1979, Lukes had built the international law library to more than ten thousand volumes in twenty-seven languages.

Because of Russell Baker's presence, Chicago was the center of the Baker & McKenzie universe until the early 1980s. From the office near Lake Michigan, Baker's gravity pulled the rest of the Firm into its orbit. Chicago also housed some of the Firm's most influential partners. "From the standpoint of the Articles of Partnership, it was one man-one vote," Patricia Beal says. "But from a standpoint of practical application, it was run by a handful of partners, and that handful resided in Chicago."

Until 1969, the Washington and New York offices were appendages of Chicago, and were governed as if they were part of the Chicago office. In 1965, the three U.S. offices accounted for almost fifty percent of the Firm's gross income. As late as 1975, the Chicago office alone accounted for some twenty-five percent of the global gross income. During the glory days of American economic expansion abroad, the Chicago office generally, and Russell Baker in particular, generated much of the legal work that flowed to the Firm's office network.

From Baker's office, with its copy of a Charles Russell painting of the American West, he would finger his worry beads while he and his Chicago partners discussed Firm matters. "People went into Russell's office," Thomas Haderlein says. "They talked to him, counseled with him, and pleaded with him. But, when the day came for the Policy Committee to say what kind of Executive Committee we would have, and who would be on it, the only person who knew what that was going to be was Russell Baker."

Chapter Seven

The Boys of '60 in Chicago

In the 1950s and 1960s, America pressed its goal of fostering economically strong trading partners who would side with it against the Communist Bloc. As part of the plan to develop free enterprise and market economies, the U.S. and other nations agreed on significant tariff reductions under the General Agreement on Tariffs and Trade. But the Cold War continued. In rapid succession, the East Germans built the Berlin Wall. The USSR shot down an American U-2 spy plane. And Britain's war minister scandalized his nation by consorting with Christine Keeler, a twenty-one-year-old call girl who was also sleeping with a Soviet spy code-named "Honeybear."

Despite the uncertainties created by the Cold War, world trade was expanding. Germany's "economic miracle" allowed Volkswagen to flood the market with its Beetles. France was producing four times more electricity than it had only thirty years earlier, and Japanese automobile companies manufactured 79,000 cars in 1958, up from 110 in 1948. High-tech was in its infancy in the early 1960s, but U.S. manufacturers were selling an increasing number of computers. Xerox revolutionized the copying industry with its new Model 914, and IBM brought out its Selectric typewriter.

———

Even with the marked increase in the flow of international trade in the 1950s and early 1960s, to many Americans, doing business abroad was only a vague notion. The vagaries of unfamiliar international commerce, they thought, were not worth the risk when they could make fat profits in the burgeoning and predictable U.S. market. While American businessmen were just beginning to hone their international skills, a group of young men who would play a key role in

Baker & McKenzie's future percolated through the Chicago office. Some five years on either side of 1960, lawyers from the U.S., Asia, Europe, and Latin America worked at the Firm's "home plate." During the coming decades, this cadre of lawyers, "the Boys of '60," and Russell Baker would spearhead Baker & McKenzie's growth and provide its moral and intellectual leadership.

Baker assumed the role of world-wide talent scout. With "luck, clairvoyance, guesswork, and shrewdness," he found a group of lawyers who were flexible enough to operate in a multicultural setting. In Chicago, the Boys of '60 picked up an American Midwestern flavor. In Baker, they could see many of those Midwestern values: informality, optimism, frankness, pragmatism, and a certain naiveté. Some critics felt that his American naiveté was a defect, but for the Boys of '60 that trait made the Firm an easy place to be.

Under Baker's tutelage, the Chicago office became a training camp. "It was a summer camp of sorts," Robert Cox says. "They developed a sense of camaraderie and adventure, knowing that they were going to do something very special. It was a magical time." Partners and future partners learned to appreciate one another's cultural differences. At the same time, they accepted Baker's innovative institutional guidelines. His notions of democracy—of not exploiting young lawyers and of being able to create their own futures—were unconventional and exciting. He indoctrinated his recruits with the enthusiasm that spurred them to implement his concept of an international fraternity of friends and business partners.

Even at that embryonic stage, one writer notes, "Baker's master plan called for a cross-pollination between the American lawyers and the visitors, whereby all participants in the melting pot would absorb through cultural osmosis bits and pieces of each other's customs, languages, and legal principles. As all learned more about their colleagues . . . the 'law firm without nationality' would rise from dream to reality."[1]

Baker brought in a corps of highly individualistic lawyers who, nevertheless, shared several common characteristics. They were a little hungry, a little pushy, and a little ambitious—traits that people in some countries thought to be "ungentlemanly." They also had a sense of adventure, and were risk takers who were not afraid to stake their careers on an upstart law firm.

Almost all of the Boys of '60 had little or no connection to the establishments that controlled the legal profession in many countries. Baker, the son of lower-middle-class farmers, did not care who their families were. The non-American Boys of '60 in particular were "non-establishment," Amsterdam's Willem Stevens says. "None of the establishment would have joined the Firm. We were the new kids on the block, renegades to a certain extent. Our lawyers had a sense of fighting against the establishment, and of showing them that we were at least as good as, if not better than, them. We had to fight in all our countries against bar rules and against the prejudice of being associated with Americans, who many Europeans viewed as tough, rough, and vulgar."

In most nations, going to the right schools, knowing the right people, and having a wealthy family to supplement the meager income of a junior lawyer were requirements for success in law. Typically, fresh law school graduates served an apprenticeship for three or four years. Based on the theory that the experienced lawyers were teaching the junior men to become real lawyers, some apprentices received no salary. In a few countries, law clerks actually paid their employers for the learning experience.

Middle-class young men who chose to work at law firms also faced a conservative tradition that included a rigid hierarchy and stiff formalities. In some cases, family law firms were a barrier to budding lawyers. Often, a father or grandfather who had started a law practice would hire his sons, nephews, and sons-in-law. The firm might hire one or two outsiders, but it was understood that, barring some extraordinary event, the outsiders would never become partners. In Italian family firms, for example, a non-family member who wanted to stay in the profession worked for six or eight years, then left to practice on his own. If he didn't leave, he became a perpetual employee. Alejandro Alfonzo-Larrain says that, in Venezuela, "If you are the founder, you get fifty percent of all of the income. The co-founder gets twenty-five or thirty percent. Then you split the rest among all the other lawyers. Baker & McKenzie was something brand new. If you were good, and you became a partner, you were a full-fledged partner."

Another Firm principle appealed to the non-American Boys of '60—there was no discrimination. "Putting together people from various countries was unknown, unheard of, among law firms," Wulf Döser says. "Those Wall Street firms would never have dreamed of letting a German or an Englishman get anywhere near the partner level."[2] Baker & McKenzie looked at them as prized plums. "We could attract top guys outside the U.S. because those few American firms that had overseas offices would never make a non-U.S. lawyer a partner. It just wasn't in the cards," Robert Berner says.

To train the non-U.S. recruits, Baker brought them together in Chicago. He insisted that the Firm's civil law attorneys be well schooled in the common law system. Training at a U.S. law school and working for a U.S. law firm, Baker said, would give his recruits three competitive advantages: they would speak fluent English; by understanding both the civil and common law they could mesh those sometimes conflicting systems; and, perhaps more importantly, they would understand how American businessmen thought and what kind of legal service they expected. One civil law tradition that Baker knew American clients would not tolerate was the aloof attitude that some non-U.S. lawyers affected. It was not uncommon for a civil lawyer to make it clear that his client was privileged to receive a dollop of his legal wisdom. Many European lawyers, Brussels partner

Jacques Ghysbrecht says, felt that "it was a favor for them to see clients and to communicate their great knowledge." That patrician approach, Baker understood, would have no appeal to those U.S. executives who were the sons of Detroit auto workers or Nebraska farmers.

He faced two obstacles to his staffing strategy, however. On the whole, lawyers are not entrepreneurial. Their conservative profession teaches them to be cautious whenever they confront a new situation, such as working for an untested Chicago law firm. The second obstacle was that only the U.S. and the former British colonies use England's common law legal system. Most other countries follow the civil law tradition. Napoleon began the modern civil law system by instructing his French scholars to prepare legal codes covering civil, commercial, and other laws.[3] Eventually, most Latin American, European, and Asian nations adopted the civil law system.

Under the common law system used in America, England, and other former British colonies, the law is derived from precedents. Instead of looking at an organized legal code to find the law, a common lawyer looks at court decisions.[4] The common law system tends to produce lawyers who get quickly to the point. They are trained to take their client's problem, strip away the unimportant facts, apply the law, and recommend a solution. If a transaction can't be done in one way, they try to find another way to achieve a satisfactory result. Civil law training, on the other hand, tempts lawyers to merely tell their clients what the law is, and to write lengthy memoranda describing the theoretical basis for the law. That approach often leaves a client with the difficult task of deciding how to apply the law to his fact situation.[5]

One of the primary conduits for non-U.S. lawyers into the Firm was through a University of Chicago law professor. By the 1950s, Dr. Max Rheinstein and Baker had become friends. Rheinstein, previously a distinguished law professor at the University of Munich, had escaped the Nazi regime and come to America. "He became one of the towering figures of that era in comparative law," Peter Lederer says. "Max had an extraordinary passion and love for learning. He could work in ten or twelve languages." When the world-class scholar found a promising student from Europe or Latin America who wanted to work for a U.S. law firm, he called Baker to tell him that he had a good prospect.

Wulf Döser was one of the Boys of '60 who came to the Firm through the Rheinstein connection. The son of a German civil servant, Döser earned his law degree and a doctorate from one of Germany's ancient universities, Tübingen. He practiced law for a while, then, in 1961, he read a newspaper article that set his career on another course. In the article, the Foreign Minister criticized

German students for being too provincial, and for not using all the scholarships available for foreign study. Döser decided that he didn't "want to end up in a little industrial town in southern Germany doing family law and landlord-tenant law." He applied for a scholarship to study in the U.S., and got it.

When Döser asked a German law professor which American law school he should attend, the professor told him to go to the University of Chicago. There, the professor said, an outstanding international and comparative law scholar was running a program for non-U.S. students who wanted to study the common law system. When Döser arrived at Chicago and met Rheinstein, he agreed that the professor "was a master of all legal systems. His teaching was brilliant, and he could lead civil trained lawyers into the workings of the common law." At first, Döser's mediocre English made law school hard, and having to read reports of ancient legal cases in old English made it doubly difficult. Thirty-five years later, Döser still recalls a case report from the 1400s that covered only two and one-half pages in the textbook, but took him three days to comprehend.

Rheinstein taught Döser how to analyze cases and to write legal briefs, something that wasn't done in German universities. He also described the difference between the civil and common law approaches. The professor liked the German, and referred him to Baker & McKenzie. Döser started working at the Firm part-time in January 1962, taking classes in the morning, working in the afternoon, and studying at night. After he graduated with a Masters in Comparative Law, he went to work full-time in Chicago. In 1963, he returned to Frankfurt as the second lawyer in the newly opened office.

A Swiss lawyer was one of the first of the Boys of '60 to work in the Chicago office. Peter Achermann got his law degree from the University of Geneva, and went to the University of Chicago to study under Rheinstein. When the Swiss lawyer told his professor that he wanted to work for an American law firm, Rheinstein called Baker to see if there was any interest. Foreign Based Company ("FBC") business was booming, and the Firm had just opened a Zürich office. Baker was indeed interested; he told Rheinstein to send Achermann over for an interview. As the two chatted, Baker mentioned that several U.S. companies had called him with questions about Swiss law. Then he asked Achermann if he could translate the Swiss Corporation Law into English within two days to meet a client's deadline. Achermann did, and began work in 1958 in the Chicago office, where he dealt with the flood of client requests to set up Swiss FBCs.

Rheinstein furnished another candidate, this time an Englishman. Andrew Joanes's father had been gassed while fighting in the British Army during World War I. The gassing affected his heart, limiting the father to only sporadic work. With little money, Joanes couldn't afford expensive English public schools,[6] but the boy's quick intelligence got him into a school that had been set up for promising youngsters from middle-class families, Christ Hospital. Joanes did well at Christ Hospital, and received a scholarship to Oxford University. At Queen's College, he studied law, receiving first class honors. In 1957, Joanes began his studies for a masters in law at the University of Chicago. Through Rheinstein, Joanes joined the Firm in 1960.

The University of Chicago was not the only pipeline into the Firm. Through their programs for non-American students, Harvard, Northwestern, Southern Methodist, Yale, Texas, Columbia, and other universities supplied lawyers to Baker & McKenzie. Modesto Aparicio came to the Firm through Columbia University. Aparicio, a Panamanian, caught the eye of Professor Henry de Vries, who later became a Firm partner. Through de Vries, Aparicio met Baker, and spent some three years in the Chicago and Washington offices before transferring to Caracas.

Another Latin American lawyer, Jorge Sánchez, found his way to the Firm by a different route. He had law degrees from Harvard and the University of San Carlos in Guatemala. After he finished school, Sánchez took a job with a Venezuelan company that went broke shortly after he came. Casting about for a job in Caracas, Sánchez met William Gibbons, who put him to work at half the salary he had been making. Even worse, his first office consisted of a desk in the bathroom. "When someone had to use the facilities," he says, he had to "move out and then come back in afterwards. After a few weeks, I said to Bill, 'Forget it, this is ridiculous.' So he put me in the library, with fresh air from an open window."

In 1961, Sánchez transferred to Chicago, where he joined the other Boys of '60. "We were all young, and we all had the same problems. Later on, when we discussed Firm problems, it was very easy to deal with them because we knew each other. There was a great rapport," Sánchez says. A year after the Mexico City office opened, Sánchez became one of its first associates.

From Asia, Juan Collas went to Yale University to do graduate work. There, the young Filipino shared a suite with a European student, Johannes Müller, a Swiss lawyer who would later become his partner. When Collas graduated from Yale, he joined the Chicago office, and then returned to Manila to open a new office there. The Boys of '60 "thought about opening offices for the Firm because that was where the growth would be," Collas says. "That was what we were dreaming about. You could do your own thing, and be your own boss."

With young lawyers coming into the Firm through U.S. universities, and Baker's keeping a constant eye out for talent as he traveled the globe, by 1962 the Firm had some eighty-five lawyers. Worldwide, they collected some $2.5 million in fees. Baker's hourly rate was the highest of any partner's—$60. Younger men commanded $25 per hour. The Firm had grown to thirteen offices in the U.S., Canada, Latin America, and Europe. Although Chicago, with some thirty lawyers, was the Firm's largest office, it was small enough for the lawyers to become a close-knit group.

In the early 1960s, the thirty-eighth floor at One North LaSalle was Chicago's main reception area. The trial department occupied the thirty-seventh floor, and, later, the Firm added offices on the thirty-ninth floor. Although the facilities were not grand, the Chicago office paced itself at a high level. "All of the lawyers at Baker & McKenzie," Roger Quinnan says, "were running faster than lawyers in other firms. I can remember following a group of partners to lunch and literally running to keep up with them. They were highly driven people, which you would expect to find among people performing on the cutting edge of things."

Baker worked hard to add lawyers and offices to the Firm. He worked equally as hard to build the culture that he knew the Firm would need in order to flourish. He conceived of Baker & McKenzie as a congenial family of good friends. "He wanted to have a family," Gibbons says, "with a camaraderie where everyone helped each other." Creating a family atmosphere also had a practical aspect—it developed a sense of loyalty to the Firm. Baker seemed to know, Dolores Villa says, that "if you have a family that likes not only what they are doing, but who they are doing it with, it is going to be much better. He not only created a sense of loyalty to him and to the Firm, but also among the young associates, who became brothers and best friends."

To encourage the family feeling, Baker and his wife opened their home to the Boys of '60. He had spent enough time traveling abroad to realize that, to non-Americans in particular, inviting a person to your home had a special significance. It meant that the person was a close and trusted friend. Baker and his wife gave countless dinner parties in Lake Bluff, usually for only a few couples because Baker did not like large crowds. Baker often barbecued the meat, and Elizabeth did the rest of the cooking. Some of the young lawyers were shocked that the Firm's senior partner and his wife prepared the meals themselves. Even more startling, the Bakers had no staff of servants, and everybody pitched in to wash the dishes after dinner.

Baker cooked enormous slabs of meat over an open fire in the kiva that he had carved out of the ravine running behind his house. Sitting in the kiva, Baker shared with the Boys of '60 his vision of where the Firm was headed and how it was going to get there. "It was very comfortable," John Connor recalls. "You did not feel in any way alien or strange, or that you were in the presence of a senior partner." Baker took them into his confidence, making it clear that they would be the advance guard to carry out the Firm's pioneering mission. Although he used the dinners to size up the young men and to decide whether they could be entrusted with becoming caretakers of the Firm's culture, his main purpose was to make them feel that they were an integral part of Baker & McKenzie. It worked.

In addition to Baker's dinners, the Boys of '60 did a lot of socializing, which helped weave the Firm's essential fabric. The non-U.S. lawyers in particular came in without knowing anyone in Chicago. "Our social contacts were all Firm related," Sánchez recalls. "There was a great loyalty to the Firm because we liked each other. We liked what we were doing." The social interaction was a collection of small, often forgettable, incidents. But the parties, the fun, and the involvement of families all created a glue that bound the Boys of '60 together during the coming decades.

They got together almost every weekend. At Irecê Trench's apartment, they dined on Brazilian *feijoada*. On winter nights at Donald Etienne's, they scooped Swiss fondue out of a common pot. When Achermann's wife gave birth to twins, a group of lawyers immediately organized a party, and spent half the night drinking and singing to welcome his babies. After German partner Karsten Schmidt's second daughter was born, complications required that she have blood transfusions. The word spread through the Chicago office, and twelve lawyers donated blood. The baby survived, and became known as the "Girl with Thirteen Fathers."

Everyone, partners and associates, went to the parties, where they played parlor games like charades. Years later, one attorney remembers John Creed, a partner and former West Pointer, getting on his knees and running around the floor in a vain attempt to act out Caroline Kennedy. And another lawyer acted out "peas porridge hot, peas porridge cold" with appropriate vulgarity.

Most days, groups of the Boys of '60 lunched together. On occasion, the partners took them to lunch at the University Club or the Mid Day Club, where they enjoyed downing a dry martini. On many Friday and Saturday nights, groups of young lawyers went to the Boom Boom Room or Butch McGuire's bar to drink beer and talk. In addition to nights spent in smoky bars, the Boys of '60 went to baseball games, bowled, and organized a soccer team to play in an amateur league. The Firm librarian, Frank Lukes, acted as an informal travel agent for those who wanted to go on canoe trips to the forests of northern Wisconsin or Michigan. Lukes also played another important role. He wasn't a partner or an associate, but he was close to Baker and had an insider's understanding of the Firm and its partners. With those credentials, Lukes served as a father confessor for the young men when they had problems with partners.

Although Baker was a generation older than the Boys of '60, and was the Firm's founder and chief business generator, he had no pretense. "[Baker] was so down-to-earth that he attracted people who were down-to-earth," Sánchez recalls. "There was no stuffiness about it. Everybody was on a first-name basis. Russell was 'Russ' or 'Wuzzy.'" Sometimes, it was Baker's earthy humor that put the younger men at ease.

Shortly after Thomas Bridgman joined the Chicago trial department, Baker invited him to lunch. Bridgman, thinking that senior partners were dry and humorless, made excuses for why he couldn't go. Baker persisted, and cornered the twenty-five-year-old Bridgman into the dreaded lunch. During the meal, Baker asked him whether a certain plaintiff's lawyer was still practicing. When Bridgman told him that the lawyer was, indeed, active, Baker said, "That no-good son of a bitch. Is he still as big a pain in the ass as he always was?"

"As soon as he said that, I settled down," Bridgman says. "I knew this guy was going to be all right, and that he and I were going to get along fine. We did."

Johannes Müller remembers that "Russell Baker just made you feel good to be there. Somehow you had the feeling that, if you had a serious problem, you could go to him. He would help you." Gibbons says, "They were sort of Russell's kids." To the non-U.S. Boys of '60 in particular, the fact that Baker was thirty-five years older than most of them served to increase their respect. Wulf Döser summarizes the impression Baker made: "It was always taken for granted that the Firm was Russell Baker. Even though he didn't make a fuss about it, he kept an eye on everybody, and saw to it that they developed." Although he kept a paternalistic eye on the young men, at the same time he made sure that they were moving down the path he wanted them to follow. "Russell saw very clearly what he wanted to do and how it should be done," Döser adds. "If anybody did something that he thought endangered his vision, or the way he thought things should be done to achieve those goals, he could be very tough."

The Boys of '60 sensed Baker's underlying toughness, but he could be surprisingly forgiving. Shortly before the 1962 Annual Meeting, Bridgman and Karsten Schmidt were having lunch at a Greek restaurant in Chicago. There were two rows of booths, divided by a planter box that screened the booth on the other side. A rumor had gone around the Firm that the partners might create a second class of partner who would have no vote. The two young men, who were being considered for partnership that year, were worried about their status.

Bridgman recalls Schmidt asking, "What happens if the partners create a second tier of partners? What do you think we should do?"

"Tell them 'screw you,'" Bridgman answered.

"What about Russell?" Schmidt said.

"Screw Russell," Bridgman replied.

"All of a sudden," Bridgman remembers, "I hear, 'Hi, Tommy, how are you doing?' I looked over the planter box and there was Russell in the booth on the other side. I know he heard us. But nothing happened to our partnership election six weeks later."

Baker was very cognizant of the impression he made on the Boys of '60. He wanted them to trust him and to like him, not to boost his ego, but so that he could indoctrinate them with his conception of how to build the world's first broad-based international law firm. "The idea was," Gibbons says, "that we were going to bring people to Chicago and kind of brainwash them. The consequence of having all those people here was that they developed personal relationships. You can put up with a lot of guff from a good friend that you would not put up with from someone you didn't know or who didn't share your values."

Baker hammered home the Firm mantra that they were building a truly international Firm with partners of all nationalities. He also had other lessons to impart to the Boys of '60. While he and Modesto Aparicio were riding the commuter train from Lake Bluff to Chicago one morning, Baker folded his newspaper and told the Panamanian, "If you want to get anywhere, open a new path. Don't walk down the path that already exists. Everybody does that."

Although Baker could be a fatherly advisor, when a Boy of '60 made a mistake, he heard from Baker. In the early 1960s, he asked Jorge Sánchez to research a point of Panamanian law. Sánchez looked and looked, but couldn't find a clear answer. Frustrated, he asked another lawyer who was familiar with Panamanian law. The other lawyer told Sánchez not what the law was, but what the accepted practice was. Based on this off-the-cuff advice, Sánchez prepared a memorandum and gave it to Baker.

"Where did you find this information?" Baker asked. When Sánchez told him, Baker replied in a steely tone: "That's a hell of a way to practice law. You have to have knowledge of the answers yourself. You can't rely on something just because somebody told you that."

The Firm pushed the Boys of '60 hard. New WHTC, FBC, and other work was coming into the Chicago office. The young lawyers were "prepared to work preposterous hours," Peter Lederer says, "simply because the work was there and it was fun to do it. On any given evening, there would be five or six of us who were still at work around 10:00 or 10:30 at night. And we'd usually wind up the evening gathered in somebody's office just shooting the breeze for another hour."

———

During informal conferences and in client meetings, the Boys of '60 learned from Baker and from the other senior lawyers. "We had an educational institution," Wallace Baker says. "You learned a lot from just being in the Firm and listening." For the non-Americans, living and working in a foreign country taught them to see law practice from a different angle, and the Americans learned how lawyers solve problems in other countries. By working on legal issues from all over the world, they discovered that the problems they thought were so unique in their jurisdictions were not unique. They also learned that the ways of doing things in their home countries were not necessarily the best solutions.

Part of the training process involved exposing the Boys of '60 to clients. The Firm literally heaped clients and assignments on them. The non-American attorneys learned to deal with Americans on a hands-on basis. As the Firm's talent pool of young lawyers who were skilled in handling international clients and transactions grew, Baker had a group of bilingual and bicultural lawyers in Chicago who could service a client's worldwide legal needs. If an American client wanted information from abroad, time zone differences were a problem. In some countries in the 1950s and 1960s, it took one or two days to book a long-distance telephone call, and mail was extremely slow. By using the Firm's Chicago-based country experts, a client could get answers to its questions almost immediately.

While Baker shouldered a major portion of the client development load, he also saw to it that the Boys of '60 learned to promote business. They absorbed part of their training by simply watching, but Baker did not leave the crucial art of bringing in new clients to happenstance. Some of the Boys of '60 took to his training and others didn't, but he prodded all of them to try. Baker frequently handed young lawyers a list of names and addresses of companies in one part of the U.S., gave them plane tickets, and told them to "go visiting." While Connor and Sánchez were working in Chicago, Baker arranged for them to make a swing through New England. "He called up a number of clients and prospective clients, and told them that we were going to be in their area, and asked them if we could drop by," Connor recalls.

At meetings with clients, Sánchez would talk about the latest developments in Latin America. When he finished, Connor would start his discussion of British Commonwealth countries. "You almost always found a hook," Connor says. "You would get some work out of it. Not that minute, but it created a little spark that would lead to work. It was very good training. I learned how to sell the Firm's services and my services."

"He was relentless on the promotion trail," Johannes Müller says. When Baker took young lawyers to a social function, he told them, "Go work the crowd. Don't just stand there." On occasion, Baker introduced a young lawyer as being "highly trained," even though he might have been a recent law school graduate. Although he sometimes took liberties with the breadth of a lawyer's expertise, it stemmed from his conviction that an intelligent, well-trained lawyer could handle any situation. During Müller's stay in Chicago, Baker anointed him the Belgian and North African law expert. When the cautious Swiss told Baker that he was not comfortable being presented as an expert in Belgian and North African law, Baker responded, "Heck, you know the civil law, and you know the corporate laws of Switzerland. It's not that different in Belgium. It's not that different in Morocco."

Baker used a number of techniques to make the statement that his international law firm was one of a kind. When clients came to the office with legal problems in four or five countries, he surrounded them with country experts who could answer their questions. "Russell tried to find out what the clients were interested in, and then he tried to get the equipment in place," Wallace Baker says. "Clients had problems to solve, and we put the country law experts and the overseas offices in place to get them the answers better and faster than anybody else."

"Russell would stand us up in a row, like a reception line, and the client would come in and go down the line. It was very effective, because here were all these people from one firm who could give the client advice from all these countries," Sánchez says. "Russell would say, 'This is André Saltoun, he was born in Baghdad, and he is an expert in this. And this is Modesto Aparicio, he is a Panamanian lawyer, and he's involved in Latin America. And this is John Connor, and he's from Australia.'"

The combination of energetic young men from around the world who were thrown together in close proximity, and the feeling that they were entrepreneurial pioneers who were building something unique, produced an atmosphere of excitement and common purpose among the Boys of '60. "We were interested in building this thing worldwide," Gibbons says. "We thought we were the wave of the future."

Roger Quinnan says the Boys of '60 felt like they were "going to blow the world apart. We knew there was no other law firm in the world that was involved in international transactions on the same scale that we were." Quinnan, who joined the Chicago office in 1960, remembers that, "There were lawyers from all over the world, working together to resolve clients' problems and to come up with solutions that fit within the civil and common law systems. It was exciting to see someone come running in the front door from Venezuela, then somebody from Germany, and the next person from England."

"There was kind of a gunslinging atmosphere," David Macdonald says of the early 1960s in Chicago. "We were in an area where no one could compete with us. We were the only ones who knew what the law was in most foreign jurisdictions." And, as Baker had predicted from the outset, the work was interesting. The Firm's client list included some of the best known industrial companies in America, who brought with them what was probably the world's most sophisticated international trade and tax work.

Another bonding agent that cemented the closeness among the Boys of '60 was a lack of sharp elbows or jealousy. There were no battles for a limited number of partnership positions. Unlike some U.S. law firms, which pitted six or more young lawyers against each other in a struggle for one partnership slot, in the fast-growing Firm there was room for all of the young men to become partners. Alberto Di Libero and Wulf Döser knew that they were going back to Milan and Frankfurt, where they would have the opportunity to build new offices. Once they became partners, there was no cause for divisive clashes over money because the Formula eliminated economic competition. And Baker saw to it that there was little competition for clients. "Russell had gotten the pump primed until the water was flowing," Wallace Baker says. "When I got to Paris, it was like opening a faucet. You had to scramble like hell to take care of the clients."

"We were temporary sojourners who met in Chicago and had a rather intense and close friendship for a short period of time," Mexico City partner Grimm says. "And then we each went our separate ways. I don't think we competed against each other in the sense of trying to nudge anybody out. It was not the typical atmosphere found in a Wall Street law firm. We knew that we would remain friends even though we might have gone to the four corners of the earth." From their time in Chicago, the Boys of '60 "developed a special relationship. You really learned to love the Firm as a firm, as an international community. It was the environment, the culture," Aparicio says.

Chapter Eight

The Boys of '60 Branch Out:
Frankfurt, Milan, Toronto, Sydney & Paris

When the non-U.S. Boys of '60 completed their indoctrinations in Chicago, most of them returned to their home countries. As they fanned out around the globe, they opened thirteen new offices for Baker & McKenzie, and were among the very first lawyers in nine more offices.

In Asia, Baker & McKenzie started the Manila and Tokyo offices in 1963, but Pacific Rim expansion slacked off as the Vietnam War heated up. In the Middle East, the Israeli-Egyptian Six Day War and the closing of the Suez Canal in 1967 frightened foreign capital away from that region. With war stifling economic growth east of Suez, the Firm concentrated on opening new offices in Europe and Latin America during the late 1950s and early 1960s.

———

As West Germany continued its rapid climb out of World War II's destruction, the Firm sent Lajos Schmidt to scout a possible office location. After looking at several possibilities, Schmidt predicted that Frankfurt was going to be the place of the future. Even though Allied bombs had flattened the city during the War, it was rebuilding at a fast clip. Located on the Main River at the hub of the European transportation system, Frankfurt had Germany's only international airport in 1962. Its central location allowed lawyers to fly to any part of West Germany in the morning, work with a client, and return home that night.

Schmidt, who prides himself on frugality, oversaw the purchase of second-hand furniture and typewriters from a bankrupt estate for $1,500. He found inexpensive office space, which was located on the fringe of Frankfurt's red-light district. The location may have offended some clients, but, one German partner says, the nearby strip bars and prostitutes may have caused "a few clients to use the office *because* of its location."

Karsten Schmidt,[1] one of the Boys of '60, was the first full-time lawyer in Frankfurt. Problems soon developed. He "liked to be seen as the boss of the office," an early Frankfurt partner, Horst Amereller, says. Karsten Schmidt introduced the custom of requiring that all incoming mail be opened by his secretary and placed on his desk for review. This accomplished two things. It let him know what everyone was doing, and it gave him the power to parcel out work to whomever he wanted. Many Frankfurt partners objected to Schmidt's acting as "the founding father, king, and emperor of the office," and began agitating for change. Wulf Döser, another of the Boys of '60, "got really mad," Amereller recalls. "He went into Karsten's office, took the mail from his desk, and brought it into the conference room," where each lawyer could pick up his mail himself. "Karsten tried to stop that, but lost." Today, the Frankfurt office still puts all lawyers' correspondence on the conference room table for them or their secretaries to pick up.

In the 1960s and 1970s, the "German miracle" made the country Europe's economic engine, and U.S. corporations scrambled to acquire companies or to organize subsidiaries in Germany. Many of the American companies selected Baker & McKenzie to be their legal advisor. With this influx of business, in quick succession the Frankfurt office added a string of lawyers who would become long-term partners, several of whom spent time in the Chicago office. After two years in Frankfurt, Hilmar Noack transferred to Chicago for a year of study and work. He still remembers a Chicago partner strolling into his office on a Friday afternoon and asking him to prepare a complicated opinion on German law by the next Monday morning. "I worked all weekend, and asked my secretary to stay so that we could have the opinion ready. We did, and the client later gave us assignments for all of Europe."

Peter Ficht and Hans-Georg Feick, who met while doing graduate work at the University of California at Berkeley, also spent time in Chicago. When Feick transferred to Germany in 1972, he joined some ten lawyers in the office. At that time, over ninety percent of the Frankfurt office's work came from American companies doing business in Germany. This gave it a high profile in the U.S. business community, but the German legal community saw it as "a foreign firm. There was a bad taste. They felt that the Frankfurt office was riding in from the Wild West on horses," Feick recalls.

From the outset, the relationship between the Firm and the German Bar Association was hostile.[2] "We were attacked as aggressive foreigners," Amereller says. Bound up by the conservative legal tradition, the German Bar fought to keep what it viewed as American interlopers off its turf. "When we came to Frankfurt, we were outlaws, because the local lawyers were afraid that we would take business away from them," Döser says. Although the German Bar was primarily interested in protecting its members from foreign intervention, it fought the battle on a number of technical issues.

When the office opened in 1962, it operated under the Baker & McKenzie name, and used it on office letterhead, business cards, and the office building. In addition, the receptionist answered the telephone "Baker & McKenzie." Seven months after the Frankfurt office opened, it received a letter from Dr. Heinz Brangsch, Secretary of the German Bar, pointing out that German law prohibited foreigners from practicing law in Germany. Then Brangsch demanded that the Firm "immediately stop giving . . . any legal advice in your Frankfurt branch . . . and that you . . . close your Frankfurt branch without delay." If the Firm didn't comply, he said, the German Bar would go to court.

Russell Baker was in his element. He loved a good fight, and took personal charge of defending the Firm against the "enemy"—the German Bar—personified by Brangsch. The many memoranda that he wrote on the subject make it clear that he relished his role in defending his underdog David against the Teutonic Goliath. Baker devised several hair-splitting legal arguments, but his strongest point was that all of the Frankfurt office's lawyers were German and had German law licenses. Firm lawyers went to the U.S. Embassy and the German Ministry of Justice to protest what they felt was discriminatory treatment.

Despite his combative instincts, Baker decided not to litigate. Instead, he negotiated a settlement with Brangsch, agreeing that the Firm would stop using "Baker & McKenzie" in Frankfurt. Down came the name, and the Frankfurt office began operating under the names of its German partners. This arrangement satisfied Brangsch until 1966, when he fired another shot, claiming that the Firm had breached its earlier agreement. He cited as evidence the facts that Baker & McKenzie belonged to the American Chamber of Commerce in Germany and that the Chicago office's letterhead listed Frankfurt as being part of Baker & McKenzie. Also, the Firm had telephone, telex, and cable listings for Baker & McKenzie in Frankfurt that were the same as those of the office that used the German partners' names.

The sparring began again. But it turned into a slugging match at a meeting of the International Bar Association in Lausanne, Switzerland, in the summer of 1966. Baker and Brangsch both attended the meeting, but avoided direct contact. On the third day, however, Baker "ran smack into Dr. Brangsch" on a marble staircase at the convention center. As Baker recalled later, "It was, so to speak, a head-on collision." The angry German leaped to the attack. "Two years ago you agreed to stop practicing law in Frankfurt. You have violated the agreement."

After thirty years in the courtroom, Baker was not one to be taken by surprise. "I felt that I had nothing to lose," he wrote. "I also felt that a conciliatory, or even respectful, attitude would be misinterpreted as weakness. So, in a literal sense, I 'let him have it.' I told Dr. Brangsch that he did not know what he was talking about. That he either did not know what the facts were or, if he did, he was misrepresenting them, which was worse." Baker also told Brangsch that his claim that the Firm was practicing law in Germany because it belonged to the American Chamber of Commerce was "stupid."

The two men orally pummeled one another for some time. "I felt a good deal of heat and no doubt showed it," Baker wrote. "Perhaps the high point of heat was reached when I told Dr. Brangsch that he was a bureaucrat in a bureaucratic job, with nothing constructive to do; consequently he was busy nit-picking and pestering us. I said that he was acting in the spirit of . . . a Business Agent of a Bricklayers' Union . . . . As you would expect, Dr. Brangsch did not take this news with a very happy countenance." When the two calmed down, they adjourned to a coffee shop and continued their discussion "in a much lower key."

Baker and Brangsch agreed to resume their dialogue after Brangsch returned from his summer holidays. At a lunch in Essen in September, each man stated his side of the legal issues, then they discussed practicalities. Brangsch revealed that three American law firms had indicated that they wanted to open offices in Germany. As the protector of the profession, he was afraid that, if the Baker & McKenzie case went to trial and he lost, hordes of foreigners would open German offices. For his part, Baker didn't relish the adverse publicity a lawsuit would bring, even though he felt he could win. They compromised, and reached a final agreement in early 1967.

The solution, the two agreed, would be for Baker & McKenzie to transfer the ownership of the furniture and the office lease to the individual German partners. Baker & McKenzie would be able to use its name in Frankfurt, but it would get new telephone, telex, and cable addresses, and would lease separate quarters. In addition, on all correspondence with Germany, the Firm would not use a letterhead that referred to the Frankfurt office. In return for these concessions, the Frankfurt partners could continue their association with Baker & McKenzie and could practice law under their own names without further harassment from the German Bar.

After the mid-1960s flare-up, the German Bar took no further action to force the Firm out of business, but the Frankfurt legal establishment continued to treat the office as a pariah. "We responded by keeping a low profile," Döser says. "We found out that we could do very well without our peers, and we stayed in that withdrawn state until the early 1990s." In the office's first years, it was easy for the German partners to ignore the other Frankfurt lawyers who scoffed that they were "foreigners in German cloaks." With a steady stream of overseas clients, the Frankfurt partners had no need to attract German clients. "We had new assignments on the telex or in the mail every day," Feick recalls. "So it was just a matter of distributing the work and getting it done. Almost nobody actively promoted German clients."

The Frankfurt office existed in semi-isolation, but it unloaded one burden in 1976. The partners moved the office from the red-light district to a staid, gray building in the financial district. Criticism of the Frankfurt office eased further when the German Bar, responding to European unification, lifted most of its restrictions on foreign law firms. Since then, the sneers that Baker & McKenzie was "just a bunch of Americans" have disappeared. "We're now considered one of the well-known and respected law firms in Frankfurt," Döser says.

Although relations with local lawyers improved in the late 1970s and early 1980s, new American investment in Germany slowed. The slowdown triggered a debate among the partners. They began discussing whether the office should grow or remain small. Some Frankfurt partners argued that the office did not need to grow, and that it shouldn't spend the money to attract new clients. They were happy, they said, with the small, close-knit group of lawyers, many of whom had been working together for close to twenty years. But the majority of the partners "recognized that to be just a boutique firm wasn't sufficient any more," Feick says. "In order to attract top young people, you need to have a certain size and to play a certain role in the German legal community."

Changes in the German Bar's rules in 1989 made implementing the decision easier. After it amended its rules to permit law firms to have offices in more than one city, merger fever broke out, and small German law firms suddenly became large organizations with offices in several cities. Almost overnight, the Frankfurt office fell from being one of Germany's largest international law firms to being near the bottom of the list. The Frankfurt partners had previously developed a detailed business plan in which they predicted that the office's lifeblood—foreign investment—would continue to dwindle. To offset that trend, the plan called for an increased effort to bring in German companies as clients. The plan also placed heavy emphasis on the need to recruit more lawyers, enhance lawyer training, and expand into new practice areas, including telecommunications, banking, and finance.

The growth strategy worked. Between 1985 and 1995, Frankfurt office revenues jumped from $3.8 million to $34 million. During that ten-year span, the number of lawyers grew to sixty-four. Although the office expanded rapidly on its own initiative, political events played a dramatic role in its growth.

As the Soviet Union was crumbling in 1989, East Germans demonstrated against President Erich Honecker's Stalinist dictatorship. Honecker, meaning to gun down his protesting citizens, issued live ammunition to his forces. Just before the slaughter began, however, he resigned. As the East German state wobbled, millions of people flocked across the border into the West. And, during the winter of 1989/90, East and West Berliners joyfully joined together to demolish the twenty-eight-year-old Berlin Wall and to throw open the Brandenburg Gate.

While the sledgehammers and pickaxes were smashing holes in the Berlin Wall, the Frankfurt partners jumped at the chance to open a Berlin office. At a December 1989 meeting, substantial emotion affected their decision making. But it was apparent that this was also an opportunity to be on the ground floor of the enormous business opportunities that would arise out of the upgrading of East Germany to Western standards. The Berlin strategy called for it to be part of the Frankfurt office under the Formula. If Berlin lost money, Frankfurt would have to pay, and if it made money, Frankfurt would share in the profit. Despite the financial risk, the normally deliberative Germans decided to move immediately. Hilmar Noack, a native Berliner, says, "We never had fears or were negative about Berlin. We didn't think about the costs. We were willing to pay all the costs necessary to build something."

The Frankfurt partners decided to open both East and West Berlin offices because West Berlin had existing communications and other infrastructure, but East Berlin did not. More importantly, the Frankfurt partners wanted to have a presence in East Germany. "We felt that we needed to have a symbol that we were going there immediately, not after everything was nice and tidy," Döser says. "We wanted to be there early so that we couldn't be accused of being carpetbaggers. And we wanted to be there first—which we managed to do."

Two young partners, Wilhelm Hebing and Carl Andres, volunteered to move to Germany's former capital. With a business plan and the partners to implement it, the Frankfurt office asked the Executive Committee for provisional approval, although the Articles of Partnership required a full partner vote for a new office. The Executive Committee gave its blessing, and the East and West Berlin offices commenced business on March 1, 1990. When Germans voted for reunification in October 1990, the partners closed the East Berlin office and merged it into the West Berlin facility. With financial and administrative backup from Frankfurt, and a rush of business activity, the Berlin office has operated at a profit from its inception.

————

In the same year the Frankfurt office opened, 1962, the Firm started the Milan office. Lajos Schmidt spent time in Milan early on, but Alberto de Libero was the first permanent, on-site lawyer in Italy. De Libero had graduated from the University of Rome Law School in 1954, and worked for a few years before receiving a scholarship to study at the University of Texas Law School. Hoping to work in the U.S. before returning home, de Libero wrote to several American companies that had Italian operations. When he got no job offers, he returned to Italy.

Meanwhile, unbeknownst to de Libero, Abbott Laboratories had passed the young Italian's letter on to Russell Baker, who wrote to de Libero in 1960, saying that he would be visiting Italy, and that he would like to meet him. At their first meeting, de Libero was somewhat surprised by the Firm's senior partner, who wore a western hat and a shabby beige overcoat. Nevertheless, Baker's description of the Firm's plans to open a Milan office aroused the Italian's curiosity. In addition, the American's portrayal of a democratically run law firm that didn't exploit its young lawyers was attractive. Practicing in Italy, de Libero had concluded, offered him little future because it was usually done by an individual "prima donna who had a small law firm with two or three slaves. And maybe the son or the daughter would inherit the law office."

Of Baker, de Libero says, "I liked him immediately. He had a very good idea of what he wanted to do and where he wanted to go." Baker also liked the tall Italian who spoke excellent English. He commenced a correspondent relationship with de Libero, and began sending him clients. As discussions of a full Milan office became more serious, the Firm invited de Libero to Chicago, where he spent a year with the other Boys of '60. Impressed with the Italian lawyer's work, the partners decided to send him back to Milan to open an office.

As more work came in, de Libero needed assistance. He had met Claudio Camilli, a young trial lawyer from his hometown of Pescara who, like him, had migrated north to try his luck in Milan's booming economy. With no family or connections in Milan, Camilli was struggling to make a living teaching at the Catholic University of Milan for very little pay. Camilli also worked *pro bono* as a public prosecutor in misdemeanor courts. After four years with a marginal income, Camilli was delighted by de Libero's offer to work for a law firm.

A part-time job quickly became full-time. Until the mid-1970s, the office grew steadily. Communist and Socialist gains in the 1975 elections, however, blunted the office's growth. "Foreign investments stopped totally. Companies liquidated and left the country," Camilli says. "The old work of forming new companies and buying businesses dried up." Just as Italy was tilting back toward more conservative government, another political shock rocked the nation. A terrorist group, the Italian Red Brigade, kidnapped former Prime Minister Aldo Moro in 1978, and dumped his bullet-riddled body in a parked car in Rome. Despite the political setbacks, the Milan office, which began with two lawyers in 1962, grew to twenty-five by the mid-1990s, and ranked as one of the top three international firms in Milan.

Another of the Boys of '60 opened the Toronto office in 1962. Hubert Stitt started working for the Canadian Department of National Revenue after being called to the bar. In his early career, he traveled across the vast nation arguing tax cases for the government. Through a Canadian lawyer, the Firm got Stitt's name and invited him to Chicago to interview.

"I was fascinated by the letterhead that included Caracas, Amsterdam, London, Mexico City, and Chicago," Stitt says. He flew from Ottawa to Chicago to meet that office's lawyers. Russell Baker impressed him. "He was exciting—a homey, down-to-earth, nice guy. He wasn't the staid conservative lawyer type. He liked to give the impression of being right off the farm. He intentionally nurtured the image of a naive rural rancher, but he could socialize with and impress the most sophisticated business executives."

The Firm partners told the young Canadian that they planned to open a Toronto office. But they wanted someone who would move to Chicago to get to know the Firm before moving back to Canada. They also said that the person who opened the Toronto office would be made partner without the five-to-seven-year wait that was common at the time. As an additional part of the courtship, Baker outlined the Formula. "Russell was very proud of the Formula," Stitt says. He told the Canadian that it "was designed so that a partner in his second year could end up earning more than someone who had been in the Firm for a long period of time." Convinced, Stitt left his government job and moved to Chicago in 1961.

Because of his tax background, Stitt spent much of his time on work involving tax-saving structures that employed Canadian non-resident companies. Under Canadian tax law, a company qualified as a non-resident if the company's "mind and management" (*i.e.*, its board of directors) made decisions outside Canada. The several thousand miles of border with the U.S. made it easy to arrange board meetings in America. The payoff was that, for non-resident companies that earned their incomes abroad, Canada did not tax their profits.

Although Canada was lenient in the tax area, the Ontario Law Society was inflexible when it came to using the Baker & McKenzie name. "Other than the Firm," Toronto partner Edward Kowal says, "there was no such thing in Canada as an international law firm. The concept was foreign, and the Law Society rules never contemplated such a firm." The rules required that a law firm could only use the names of its partners, and that those partners had to be qualified to practice law in Ontario.

To meet the Law Society's tests, Stitt began looking for Ontario lawyers named "Baker" and "McKenzie." He found a Canadian lawyer by the name of Samuel Baker, and persuaded him to join the Firm in 1966. The Toronto office's name then changed to Stitt & Baker. To fill in the other half of the name, Stitt identified a lawyer named McKenzie, who lived in a rural Ontario community. Stitt commissioned Samuel Baker to contact McKenzie at his home to see whether he would lend his name to the Firm. "Sam went to the farm, and

McKenzie, after hearing the story, ordered Sam off the property," Stitt says. "McKenzie said there were certain things that were for sale, but his name wasn't one of them." Although that attempt failed, Stitt was able to hire another lawyer named McKenzie, and changed the office's name to Stitt, Baker & McKenzie.

As the Law Society relaxed its rules regarding law firm names in the 1980s, several partners felt that Stitt should remove his name from the Toronto office. But the office's founder and senior partner was reluctant. "Bert Stitt was a good friend of mine," Robert Cox, who was then Chairman, says. "I went to him privately, as a friend, and said that the day would come when I would ask him to change their name. I also told Bert that our friendship would buy him one or two years before I pressed the name change issue. But, after that, I said, 'I was coming at him.'" The Toronto office changed its name to Baker & McKenzie in 1989.

Over the years, the Toronto office added lawyers. During the office's early years, tax and commercial law constituted the bulk of their work. In 1972, the Canadian Parliament adopted two pieces of legislation that became a gold mine for the Toronto office. One was a revised tax code that was so complicated that tax work continued to be an office mainstay. The second statute addressed Canada's fear of being bought up by American economic interests. Parliament adopted the Foreign Investment Review Act ("FIRA"), which required government approval before a foreign company could acquire control of a Canadian company. A steady stream of foreigners who wanted to invest in Canada created a bonanza for the Toronto office until Parliament revoked FIRA in 1984.

While FIRA and tax work kept several lawyers busy, the office broadened its base of legal expertise to include finance, real estate, customs, labor, intellectual property, and mergers and acquisitions. A treaty between Canada, Mexico, and the U.S. played to another Toronto office strong suit—international trade. The North American Free Trade Agreement helped the office that Stitt started by himself in 1962 grow to some forty-five lawyers by 1993.

———

Yet another Boy of '60, John Connor, leased a two-room office and started practicing law in Sydney in 1964. Before that, he had graduated from the University of Melbourne in 1958, where his friends assumed that he would become a barrister in an old-line Melbourne firm. But Melbourne, according to Connor, was an "establishment sort of city. There were major law firms that wouldn't hire Catholics or Jews. I was very intolerant of intolerance."

Rather than signing on with a law firm, Connor approached his law school dean to see if he could get a scholarship to study abroad. The dean told him that, if he went to Oxford or Cambridge, he "would learn to be a gentleman, which, in my case, he thought would be an admirable objective." Instead, Connor went to the University of Chicago Law School, and then returned to Melbourne and qualified as a solicitor. But he didn't want to follow the traditional Australian lawyer's career path. To escape the doldrums of a strictly domestic practice, Connor wrote to Andrew Joanes, an English lawyer he had met at the University of Chicago, saying: "I do not want to be stuck in the normal sort of Solicitor's practice dealing with Mrs. Bloggs' tenants and Mr. Bloggs' motor-car accidents, let alone their matrimonial disputes and real estate transactions."

Connor also badgered the Chicago Law School placement office, which put him in touch with Russell Baker. He interviewed Connor by long-distance telephone and offered him a job in Chicago. In 1964, Connor moved back to Australia to implement a plan that he and Baker had discussed three years earlier. The twenty-six-year-old Australian opened a Sydney office, and, the next year, he hired Michael Ahrens as the office's first associate. Born in Fiji, where his father was a Methodist missionary, Ahrens had worked his way through Sydney University Law School, graduated with honors, and won a scholarship to Harvard Law School. After returning home, he joined an old-line Sydney law firm that he soon found to be "stuffy and claustrophobic," Connor says, "and he wanted to get in on the ground floor of something that was international."

When Ahrens moved into the Sydney office, he recalls, "there were two of us and an aspidistra plant." But the two lawyers had plenty to do. During those first years, the U.S. offices were sending Sydney more than ninety percent of its work, mostly tax, trademark, and corporate matters. One of the clients was an American advertising agency that had opened an Australian office. Working closely with that client, Connor became fascinated with the dynamics of marketing. When the Sydney office got an insurance company client, the gangly Australian went door-to-door with experienced insurance salesmen to learn how they plied their trade. "That taught me how to sell," Connor recalls.

He liked selling, and he liked traveling. His roaming took him to Tokyo, Manila, and other Asian cities. Those short visits led him to an epiphany. "Some exciting things were happening in the Orient," Connor says. "And Baker & McKenzie needed to be there." Connor, who was easily bored by minutia, had the restless temperament of an entrepreneur. "He was in a hurry," David Shannon says. "John wanted to have everything all at once, and he could never get enough. When he was still a pretty young man, he was running his own office in Sydney and making a great reputation for himself. Having achieved all that, he wasn't content. He still needed the adventure."

With his penchant for traveling, Connor left the Sydney office "in great stretches," sometimes to work on Firm business as a member of the Executive Committee, and sometimes to explore the feasibility of opening new Pacific Basin offices. His partners teased him about his long absences, and Connor poked fun at himself, joking that his body was shaped like an airplane fuselage.

At one of his birthday parties, the Sydney partners had waitresses dress up in air-line stewardess uniforms to serve Connor his dinner on a plastic tray.

In addition to learning marketing and sales tactics from clients, Connor learned another lesson from the multinational companies that were migrating to Asia. "Baker & McKenzie needed to have lawyers who could deal with the clients throughout the Far East because the clients were organized on a regional basis. We needed to handle tax planning, intellectual property, etc., regionally. By looking at the representation this way, we would have all of our offices representing a client for all of its needs in the Pacific Basin."

Connor pushed his vision of a regionally integrated group of Firm offices, but it wasn't the right time. "It didn't work because of the Firm's tradition of separate, autonomous offices," he says. "And Hong Kong and the other offices grew so rapidly that they didn't want to spend time worrying about regionalism." Nevertheless, Connor became the pied piper of the Firm's expansion in the Orient. He left Sydney in 1974 to open Hong Kong, and he later opened Bangkok and Singapore. Connor also helped develop Taipei, and spent substantial time counseling regarding Tokyo and Manila.

Before Connor began implementing his grand design for Asia, however, he concentrated on building the Sydney office. In the late 1960s and early 1970s, the office improved its litigation and real estate capabilities, and began edging into the practice area, mining, that laid a foundation for its later growth. In the late 1960s, companies from all over the world were scrambling to find lodes of coal, iron, bauxite, and other minerals in Australia.

Seeing a huge legal market in the mining business, Connor recruited two Canadian mining law experts. With this capacity, the Sydney office entered the top ranks of mining law firms in Australia. As that word spread, many foreign and small Australian companies came to the Firm for their mining law needs. The Australian companies needed large amounts of capital to exploit their mineral discoveries, and the Sydney lawyers handled several public share issues, sometimes representing the company and sometimes the financial companies that sponsored the public offerings. Work in the mining and securities businesses, Connor says, "gave us more of a public profile, although not at the top end of the market. It gave some of us a lot more experience in business and a broader view of business, including familiarity with an extraordinary number of crooks. Learning how to spot and weed out the less savory clients was valuable. But acquiring that experience was dangerous."

The Sydney office broke with the traditional pattern of representing, almost exclusively, American companies sent by Chicago, New York, and Washington. Instead, the Sydney lawyers set their course to represent the Australian merchant banks and mining companies that, over time, became a core part of their practice. They began recruiting young lawyers from across the country and from other Firm offices. Bruce Porter transferred from London to Sydney in 1967 and stayed for five years. From the University of Adelaide, Connor recruited James Beatty. Keith McConnell left a job with an oil company to join the office. And David Shannon came on board to help handle the burgeoning antitrust and intellectual property work.

In the 1970s, the Australian partners were working hard at leveraging off the mining and publicly traded companies they were representing, expanding their securities and merger and acquisition work, and establishing even closer ties to the foreign and domestic financial communities. To attract—and keep—clients, the Sydney lawyers concentrated on providing quality legal services, which included being attuned to the clients' needs and getting work done promptly. In contrast, many traditional law firms "were very sleepy hollows, where it had been nice and cozy for a hundred years," Paul McSweeney says. "It was cozy in the sense of being an old gentleman's profession. You sat in your office and waited till the client called on you, and you gave your opinion and sent the client the bill." Many of the Firm's Sydney lawyers had U.S. training, and "they would come back and apply American style initiative to problems," Paul Davis says. "The business community generally found it refreshing to have a law firm that was more interested in using the law to solve their problems, rather than sitting on the other side of a desk giving academic answers to questions."

By the mid-1970s, there was a clear consensus among the fifteen or so lawyers that they wanted the Firm to become a substantial force in the Australian legal market, and that they wanted the office to grow as quickly as possible. To carry out their growth plan, they accelerated their client promotional efforts, and the legal establishment responded as expected. "Those law firms were quite happy to describe us as being a brash, pushy outfit, and we became a target for sniping and snide remarks," McSweeney says. Davis adds that "we weren't a member of the old club, and were regarded as a young upstart in Australia. There was a lot of sour grapes because we took clients away from other firms."

One of the office's newest lawyers, John McGuigan, helped it develop its tax and mining business. He had gone to Sydney University on a scholarship, and, in between "playing rugby and learning how to drink vast quantities of beer," he earned a degree in economics and accounting. He went to work for an international accounting firm, and, at the same time, studied law at Sydney University, where he earned a degree in 1973. McGuigan recalls that, during his interview with Baker & McKenzie, "What intrigued me was that the lawyers in the Sydney office had a vision of creating an organization that was going to be more client oriented, more business oriented. And they believed that they were doing something different, and were doing something special. There was a lot of camaraderie, a lot of friendship. Quite a bit of socializing. It was a very exciting place to be." After he joined the Firm, McGuigan kept in touch with mining clients he had worked for at his old accounting firm, and brought some of them with him to Baker & McKenzie.

Meanwhile, Paul Davis helped the Sydney office take advantage of another business trend. Britain's 1971 decision to enter the European Community, and to substantially reduce its centuries-old commercial relationships with the Commonwealth countries, forced Australia to find new trading partners. As the near-monopoly business relationship that the UK had enjoyed came to an end, the nation-continent opened its doors to foreign investment. Japan, which had no natural resources, began pumping billions into Australia's mining industry and many other businesses.

Davis's credentials made him a perfect candidate to seize on the influx of new Japanese business into Australia. After graduating from Canterbury University in his native New Zealand, he studied and worked in Japan for several years. In Sydney, Davis hired a Japanese secretary, bought Japanese green tea to serve his clients, and printed business cards in Japanese and English "as an indicia of my interest in Japan." Through contacts he had made in Tokyo, two banks and an industrial company were among his first clients. In addition to providing legal services, Davis brought other assets—he could switch from one language to another with ease. More importantly, he could translate between the cultures, explaining the Australians' ways of doing things to his Japanese clients, and vice versa.

With steady growth in Sydney, the Australian partners began discussing the possibility of a Melbourne branch. To implement the plan, Paul McSweeney volunteered to return to his home town to open an office in 1982. Along with the Sydney office, Melbourne grew rapidly as Australia's economy raced along in the 1980s. Baker & McKenzie's Australian offices rode the same roller coaster that most major law firms were on. Until the late 1980s, the coaster only went up, with some law firms growing five hundred percent. "A lot of this growth was based on a paper chase," Connor says. "People were buying or selling shares or floating companies or financing takeovers and mergers or real estate acquisitions. The banks were financing these follies."

Although the Firm's Australian offices were still doing work for foreign investors, they were also taking advantage of the financial expertise they had begun acquiring over a decade earlier. With many young Australian entrepreneurs coming to the fore who had no ties to the old-line Australian law firms, Baker & McKenzie had an equal chance to help these newcomers. Based in part on his close relationship with one of Australia's most prominent entrepreneurs, James Beatty had become the star partner in Sydney.

But the October 1987 stock market crash set off a chain reaction of grisly economic events that plunged Australia into a deep recession and exposed the entrepreneurs' wobbly corporate structures. Bankruptcies mounted. Several merchant banks tottered on the brink of bankruptcy, and commercial banks wrote off millions of bad loans. The press blamed the "corporate cowboys" who had been "financed to dizzy heights by greedy and reckless bankers." In addition to a number of corporate casualties, many Australian law firms had severe economic problems, and some went out of business when legal business shrank and some clients quit paying.

The downward spiral caught the Australian offices with high overhead costs. Their aggressive business plan had contemplated continuous growth, but when the recession hit, the offices had too much office space and too many staffers and lawyers. Compounding the expense crisis, the offices had invested huge amounts in computers and other high-tech equipment, which, one wag says, was so sophisticated that it could have "sent an Apollo rocket to the moon."

The Australian financial problems put Baker & McKenzie to its severest test. Did it truly believe in Russell Baker's one Firm concept? If the Firm was, indeed, *one*, then partners around the world would share in the Australians' financial woes. Actually, the Australian offices didn't show a loss, but the partners' incomes sagged to such low levels that Baker & McKenzie's Executive Committee worried that the most productive partners would be the first to leave. If they departed with their stables of fee-paying clients, income would nose-dive and the remaining partners' shares of overhead would go up.

The Australians took their problem to the 1990 Annual Partners Meeting in Bermuda, where several partners groused about their request for an $800,000 subsidy. The Executive Committee favored the underpinning, but, when the issue came to the floor, the Sydney partners were "vilified with comment after comment related to inadequate stewardship of the business."

Next, the frustrated partners turned their anger on the Firm's Chairman, Robert Cox, and on the Executive Committee for not detecting the problem before it got out of hand. From the podium, Cox pointed out that the Australian offices, like most offices, didn't collect the bulk of their fees until May and June, just before the Firm's fiscal year ends on June 30. Nobody, he said, knew the extent of the problem until August 1990, when the Firm computed its final financial results.

Despite Cox's personal support of the subsidy, the debate went on for hours. Some argued that the Australians had to suffer the full brunt of their own financial shortcomings. Others predicted that, without a Firm underwriting, Baker & McKenzie would suffer the humiliation of being forced to close major offices for the first time. When the vote came, the subsidy failed. Cox and other supporters cobbled together another solution that called for a repayable loan, rather than an outright subsidy. The loan version passed, and the partners adjourned for the day.

Still, Cox was troubled. "I woke up early Saturday morning, and realized that we had done ourselves great harm during our fighting and debating," he says. He called an Executive Committee meeting at six A.M. in his hotel suite. "I said I was going back for one more vote. So, when we went back to the meeting, I asked for a motion to reconsider. After a lot of bitching and moaning, it was approved. I said, 'Yes, the Australians were a bit cocky, but they have gone out and built something, and they have provided great profits for this Firm. Maybe franchise companies give loans, but partnerships don't. Baker & McKenzie is either one Firm, or it is not. By pushing the voting button for a subsidy instead of a loan, you are voting for one Firm.'" The partners adopted a subsidy measure. Another part of the compromise included a change in management. The "old guard" was out, and a group of mostly younger partners assumed the Sydney office's leadership.

As the effects of the October 1987 stock market crash worked their way through the business community, a number of high profile corporate groups began to unravel. The new breed of Australian entrepreneurs had built paper houses, that in some cases, would shudder and collapse under the economic stress.

One, the Spedley Group, was an important Sydney office client. When it went down, the business community was shocked. Spedley had been regarded as one of Australia's most respected financial houses. Brian Yuill had controlled Spedley, and had arranged for Sydney partner James Beatty to become the chairman of one of the Group's companies, GPI Leisure Corporation Ltd. As economic hard times worsened, Spedley began circulating funds to some of the financially needy members of the Group, including GPI. When Spedley's dealings came to light in 1989, a spate of litigation broke out. In some of the lawsuits, Beatty and Baker & McKenzie were named as defendants. Eventually, the lawsuits were favorably settled, but they placed substantial burdens on the Sydney office for several years.

While the Sydney office was still dealing with the adverse financial effect of Spedley's collapse, another problem arose. It stemmed from a seemingly innocuous tax break that the Australian government granted to thoroughbred horse owners. Major accounting firms were recommending the racehorse investment, and a host of prominent businessmen and attorneys jumped at the chance to shelter part of their incomes from the Australian tax collector.

In mid-1989, several Sydney partners invested in two joint venture syndicates. Soon after, the syndicate managers went bankrupt. Worse, the ventures were not generating enough income to repay the loans to Mortgage Acceptance Nominees, Ltd. ("MANL"), which the investors had made to make the racehorse investments. When the ventures tried to sell the horses to pay the debts, the thoroughbred bubble had burst, leaving the investors with debts of some A$1.5 million.

The Firm's investor-partners hired a prominent attorney, who advised them that they had a viable defense. The investor-partners decided to fight, and, at a 1993 trial, one of the key issues was whether they were justified on relying on the information the syndicate promoters had given them. The judge's written opinion was harsh. The press leaped on the story and focused on the judge's allegations that the investor-partners' testimony was not credible. In addition, the New South Wales Law Society launched an investigation of the partners' conduct.

A few days after the judge handed down his decision, the Firm's Chairman, John McGuigan, and Thomas Bridgman flew to Australia to assess the marketplace damage. They read the negative press clippings, and discussed the matter with several clients who were upset over the rash of bad publicity. They asked the investor-partners to resign or retire. "If we had not made a decision to act as decisively and quickly as we did, it would have led to the disintegration of the entire legal staff and the office," Bridgman says. The investor-partners who were still at the Firm at the time agreed to leave, except one, who moved to another office.

Some eighteen months after the furor, the Law Society concluded its investigation and wrote a letter to the investor-partners telling them that "having investigated . . . your conduct [in the MANL litigation, the Law Society] is of the opinion that . . . there are no matters in relation to your conduct . . . which in any way would constitute professional misconduct or unsatisfactory professional misconduct. . . ."

Despite the turmoil in the early 1990s, the Australian offices recouped. They attracted several new lawyers, and the Sydney and Melbourne offices' revenues jumped from $23 million in 1995 to over $33 million in 1998.

––––––––

Before 1963, the Firm had no Paris presence. "It is embarrassing for a well-known international law firm not to have a Paris office," Wallace Baker wrote his partners. There was logic to having a French office, but, in the late 1950s and early 1960s, the nation was still embroiled in a struggle over the independence of its African colony, Algeria. The political instability reached its height after President Charles de Gaulle began negotiations with the Algerian nationalists. The French colonists revolted, and a substantial French army group mutinied in their support. But de Gaulle loyalists crushed the rebellion, and France granted Algeria its independence in 1962.

Instead of worrying about dissident army officers, the French government began concentrating on currency stabilization, full employment, and trade balances. At almost the same time, Baker & McKenzie began studying the feasibility of opening a Paris office. To make its case, the Firm sent Wallace Baker from the Brussels office to determine whether a Paris location made sense. In an August 1962 memorandum to all partners, he concluded that a Paris office would increase the Firm's work from present clients and would attract new clients. He had also done his homework on the costs of starting the operation from scratch. A secretary's annual salary would be $3,500, rent "for the best premises in Paris" would be $5,000, and other costs would bring a year's total expenses to $12,000. His projections called for fees of $30,000, which would result in a generous $18,000 profit.

Wallace Baker, Russell's oldest son, had received his law degree from Harvard, spent seven years in Chicago, and then transferred to the Brussels office because, as he says, "Europe was the frontier in the late 1950s." In Belgium, he earned a law degree from the Free University of Brussels, and learned to speak fluent French. After the international partners reviewed and approved his memorandum, Wallace Baker opened the Paris office in 1963.

To provide a French connection, Wallace Baker interviewed seventeen lawyers. One of the most interesting was a mature French attorney who was among the country's most respected administrative law experts. Roger Pinto had studied in the U.S. and spoke excellent English. During his career, he had worked on several high-profile matters, including representing Cambodia, along with former U.S. Secretary of State Dean Acheson, in a case before the International Court of Justice.

Pinto agreed to join the firm as counsel, and set up his office in what had been the living room of a five-room apartment at 22 Avenue Victor Hugo. Their secretary worked at her typewriter in the former kitchen, and Baker sat behind a desk in the bedroom. The bathroom doubled as the copy room. "We had one telephone, and business was booming," Baker says. "Very quickly, we were overloaded. Our problem was handling all the clients that came out of the faucet when we opened it up. Another problem was to find qualified French lawyers who knew how to give U.S.-style advice to our clients."

When Baker reviewed Henry de Suremain's resume, the Frenchman's background fit the Firm's mold. As a young man in the 1950s, de Suremain had spent several months in the U.S. on the Experiment in International Living program. De Suremain returned to France and got his law degree from the University of Dijon, then obtained a scholarship for a year of study at the University of Michigan Law School. After returning to France in 1959, he spent the next few years in the French Army, including a year and a half fighting in Algeria as a tank commander. After President de Gaulle granted the Arab nation its independence, de Suremain mustered out of the army and went to Paris, where he worked for several French law firms.

Shortly after the Paris office opened in the summer of 1963, Wallace Baker called the Frenchman and invited him to lunch. There was a risk to signing on with a new office of a foreign law firm. But, de Suremain says, when he looked at his classmates who were toiling away in boring bank jobs or insular French firms, "I knew I didn't want to be limited or restricted to a national [French] firm," where "hierarchy is very, very strong."

Other lawyers joined the office, but it still lacked in-depth French tax expertise. To plug the hole, Wallace Baker ran an advertisement in *Le Figaro*. Jean-François Buisson answered. He had started his career with the French Tax Administration, but, Buisson says, he was not a very good civil servant. One day, his boss called him into his office and chewed him out, saying that he was working too hard and making his government colleagues look like slackers. Frustrated with the bureaucracy, Buisson quit to join a small French tax law and accounting firm. Still, he wanted to do international work, and his firm was "too dominated by one person. I wanted out." He joined the Baker & McKenzie office in 1965.

One of the Firm's first female lawyers, Monique Nion, started in the Brussels office in 1958. Later, she married a Frenchman and transferred to the Paris office, where she served for fifteen years as the Administrative Partner. Another female attorney also became active in management. As a teenager, Christine Lagarde had developed an interest in international affairs during the year she spent in the U.S. under the American Field Service program.

After she graduated from the University of Paris Law School in 1980, Lagarde began looking for a job. She interviewed with Wallace Baker in his office, which overlooked the French President's official residence, the Elysée Palace. Lagarde also interviewed with Nion. "That made a very strong impression on me," she recalls. "The fact that a woman could actually share the experience that she had with all these male partners was quite encouraging for a young woman my age. In those days, there were hardly any female partners in international law firms, and there were very few female partners doing business law."

Shortly after Lagarde started work, Wallace Baker asked her to research a complicated European antitrust law question. Knowing nothing about the subject, she spent an entire day in the library, but found no answers. Overwhelmed, she went to her mentor, Nion, and told her, "You've got to help me because I don't think I can produce anything that makes sense." Nion calmed Lagarde, and helped her complete the assignment. "I think Wallace gave tough assignments to new associates to test their reactions," Lagarde says. "To see whether they would panic. I survived." In the early 1990s, Lagarde served as the Paris office's Administrative Partner. Later, she was elected to the Firm's Executive Committee.

———————

The Boys of '60 successfully nurtured twenty-two offices, following the principles that they had learned during the time they had been in Chicago under Russell Baker's tutelage. There was, however, another group of early Firm offices founded by older, more mature lawyers who never went to Chicago for the indoctrination course.

Chapter Nine

Hiring from the Outside:
London & Zürich

In Paris, Sydney, and elsewhere, Russell Baker sent the Boys of '60 to open offices based on the principles that had been forged in Chicago. In other early offices, however, he recruited seasoned lawyers from the outside. They were "people of imagination, courage, and sizable egos, people who were extremely capable and aggressive individuals," Peter Bentley says. Unlike the youthful Boys of '60, however, these mature professionals had formed their own opinions on how to practice law, and had generally subscribed to the legal traditions of their home countries. Over the centuries, European lawyers had come to view themselves as independent professionals who did not answer to anyone, including their clients. Some countries' bar associations forbade their members from humbling themselves by going to a client's office. If clients wanted a lawyer's advice, they had to come to him.

In keeping with the European pattern of practicing solo or with a very small group, some of the newly minted Baker & McKenzie partners wanted to keep their offices small, to keep tight control over them, and to operate their offices without interference from Chicago. Many Firm partners dubbed this attitude "the founding-partner syndrome," while less charitable ones accused these founding partners of treating their offices like personal fiefdoms—barons independent of the king.

The founding-partner syndrome created friction between these partners and Russell Baker, but other barriers escalated the tensions. Post-World War II Americans were confident that their nation was the mightiest military and economic power on the globe. They felt that their technology, their dollars, and their way of doing business were superior to any other. Flashing their post-War wealth, Americans developed an arrogance that sometimes led them to treat their European cousins as inferiors. And the Europeans resented it. The Swiss, smug in their beautiful mountains, had been operating their precision society with orderly efficiency for centuries. And the English remembered when the sun never set on their empire. Who were these upstart Americans? Some Europeans called them naïve, *nouveau riche*, loud, brash, and pushy. To a degree, those mind-sets affected the relationships between Baker and the strong-willed individuals he enlisted to open the Zürich and London offices.

Just as World War I was ending, Terence Lane was born on the Northwest Frontier in India, where his father was serving as a British Army officer. In 1941, Lane himself entered military service, fighting in the jungles of Burma, Malaya, and Java. By the end of World War II, he was a major in the Royal Artillery.

After the War, Lane joined the Colonial Service in Tanganyika (today's Tanzania). There, he worked as a District Commissioner. While wielding the broad powers of an East African colonial official, Lane contacted tuberculosis, which, by the time he returned to England for treatment, was rampant. Surgeons removed parts of both lungs, and told him that he would never be able to work at a full pace. An acquaintance who later went to visit Lane found him seated on his fifteen-hand horse, defying the doctors. "Being Terry, he studied and pro-ceeded to become a solicitor," John Leaver says.

Lane started to work as a thirty-five-year-old junior attorney with one of London's most prestigious law firms in 1953. At the staid old City of London firm, Lane learned the protocol for partner treatment of junior attorneys. The juniors put on their coats before going into a partner's office, jumped to their feet if a partner entered the room, and called the partners "sir."

In the mid-1950s, English law prohibited firms from having more than twenty partners, and the quota at Lane's law firm was almost full. This, and the fact that most of the firm's partners came from just three families, left little room for his promotion to partnership. By the time he was thirty-nine, he felt he needed to be getting on with his career. Lane left the old-line institution to join a tiny two-partner firm. He managed to take a few clients with him, including an obscure Chicago law firm that had been sending him UK work for its American clients.

With his new firm, Lane continued to act as a correspondent for Baker & McKenzie. As the work flow from Chicago increased steadily, it appeared that a closer relationship with the Firm made sense. Even though Baker & McKenzie was only an inconsequential Midwestern law firm, Lane says that he was "intrigued by the thought of becoming part of a truly international partnership and of enjoying the benefit of having a lot of interesting and sound commercial work being sent to me by Baker & McKenzie." In 1961, he formally opened the London office.

For its first quarters, Lane took space on Norfolk Street, just a few yards outside the City of London. The rent was reasonable, but, to most English businessmen and lawyers, a law firm that did not headquarter in the City was not a major player—not a serious contender for the big-ticket legal work for English corporations, banks, and insurers. In the London office's early days, that wasn't important, because most of the fledgling office's work came from inbound investment by American clients.

The Norfolk Street office, Bruce Porter says, was "quaint." Andrew Joanes is less kind: "It was dreadful—dreadful." The unimposing Victorian building was so seedy that one potential client refused to enter it. The elevator, which an operator raised and lowered by pulling on a rope, was a creaking metal cage that made people feel in peril of their lives whenever they entered it. When new lawyers joined the London office, Lane sent them to a Dickensian garret on the top floor to perform their labor. In winter, a porter lighted the open coal fires that provided the office's heat, and the smoldering coal left a coat of black soot on everything. "The dust on the desks was unbelievable," Jeremy Sykes recalls. "I had to shake the papers, and blow the dust off before I started work." The restrooms were unhygienic, and put out foul odors. In the men's toilet, someone had placed a sign on one stall that said: "Partners Only."

Lane's personal code of conduct was rigid. "He drew lines. He was very black and white. He either approved of something or he didn't," Sykes remembers. Lane also subscribed to the military's chain of command system: he accepted total responsibility for taking care of his people, and he viewed actions that didn't comply with his rules as disloyalty. Richard Davidson recalls that Lane "was military in style. If you went into his room, he would not acknowledge your presence. You couldn't just go there and sit down. You would stand until he was ready to talk to you." Although Lane didn't formally line up his troops to issue orders of the day, "he was the guy who dished out the work and decided what you were going to do and what you weren't going to do," Sykes says. "He kept pretty tight control over what went on. He liked to run things his way."

Although opinion on Lane is divided, all agree that "Terry Lane was a formidable man," and that his dignity and bearing were imposing. Some of his partners, however, remember him as a man who loved jokes and enjoyed singing and carousing aboard a Venetian gondola. During one Annual Meeting, Lane and other partners stayed up very late drinking in a bar. Robert Berner recalls that "the next day at the partners' meeting, he sat at the table shading his eyes, looking down. I thought Terry was hung over and asleep. Then, I realized he was doing *The New York Times* crossword puzzle, not even using a pencil. It was a remarkable exhibition of concentration."

Lane was also "a brilliant lawyer. He had a strong personality, and he engendered an enormous confidence in clients," Sykes says. His colleagues admired his intelligence, his personal sense of fair play, and his desire to excel in everything that he did. But his inclination to dominate would be a problem in the future. In the London office's early days, however, the junior men toed the mark and the working environment was generally congenial. "We sometimes fell out with Terry Lane, but not seriously," Sykes says. "He was the senior partner, the founder. We recognized his strengths and his abilities, and we put up with some of the foibles. It was a small, intimate office. We enjoyed our work, and we enjoyed each other's company."

When Lane joined Baker & McKenzie, he brought with him another partner, John Leaver. Soon after, they hired Jeremy Sykes as their first articled clerk (now called a trainee). As the workload increased, Lane added another young lawyer to the office staff. Andrew Joanes was living in the U.S., and aching to return to England. In late 1959, he wrote to Lane, whom he had known earlier in London. "This is a shot in the dark," Joanes said, "but I wonder if you have a vacancy for an articled clerk, and whether you could pay some sort of wage. My wife and I have realized that we want to live in England, in part because of the dire prospect of rearing North American children."

Lane hired Joanes, and the two signed the solemn Articles of Clerkship that were customary at the time:

> "The Clerk [Joanes] HEREBY BINDS himself . . . [and] COVENANTS with the Principal [Lane] that he, the Clerk, will faithfully, cheerfully and diligently serve the Principal . . . and will at all times cheerfully and readily obey the . . . commands of the Principal."

The next year, Lane brought Bruce Porter into the London office. After spending almost two years in Australia on a scholarship, Porter returned to London in 1961. At an Old Boys' Dinner for his boarding school, Christ Hospital, he ran across a former schoolmate, Joanes, who described Baker & McKenzie "as being totally different from the image I had always had of solicitors—bent old men who spent their lives in rooms full of dusty books." When Porter showed an interest, Joanes suggested that he talk with his senior partner. As Lane and Porter chatted, the older man impressed Porter as being "very self-assured. A straight-shooter. You could talk directly to him, and he'd talk directly back to you."

In addition to being impressed with Lane's directness, Porter also noted that Baker & McKenzie wasn't populated with the upper-crust men from the traditional legal families that dominated London firms. Of his Oxford classmates who were headed for law practice, Porter estimates, some seventy percent had fathers or uncles in the legal profession. Since he came from a family with no ties to the City, the Firm's London office's interest in employing him showed that it "had a fresh approach to hiring lawyers, which, to me, was good."

Next, Lane decided that he needed a more experienced lawyer in the London office, and brought in Norman Miller. After completing his law studies at the London School of Economics in 1953, Miller won a fellowship to study at the University of Chicago, where he earned a master's of comparative law degree and worked as a researcher. He then left academia to join the other Boys of '60 in the Firm's Chicago office, where, at first, he was impressed by Russell Baker. Later, the relationship soured, and that, coupled with the opportunity to return home and be the second most senior commercial lawyer in London, caused him to leave Chicago in 1961.

With the office growing, it moved into larger quarters on Aldwych in 1963, still outside the City's borders. As time went on, the relationship between Baker and Lane became strained. Stylistically, Baker was a mix of rural Southwestern folksiness and Midwestern boosterism, which contrasted with Lane's hierarchical background. In private, Baker sometimes referred to Lane as "Lord Plushbottom." "They both irritated each other quite a lot," Sykes says. "They were not similar personalities, in any shape or form. Russell was not the formal English major, ex-army sort of character. Terry was constantly trying to do things that the old Chicago partners didn't want to do, like Formula and Articles of Partnership modifications."

Lane and his ally Miller viewed the Chicago office as "big brother." At the time, Peter Sturtevant says, "people talked about Chicago. Chicago says this, and Chicago says that. Chicago is doing this, and Chicago is doing that." Lane and Miller often railed against the "Chicago Bogeyman," derided the "Baker crowd," and talked of breaking the "Russell stranglehold."

Baker's ire rose when he heard that Lane was sniping at him and at the Chicago office's power in the Firm. They quarreled over Lane's insistence that he control the work flowing into London, and Baker became especially angry at what he perceived as attempts by Lane to undercut his influence with clients. Most companies that Baker sent to London looked to him for top-level decisions, but Baker suspected that Lane was trying to seal him off from knowledge of what the client was doing in the UK. On one occasion, Baker called Lane and "knocked the hell out of him," demanding to be kept in the loop.

"Deep down, Russell did not like Terence Lane very much. He thought Terry was too much like John Bull," Miller says. But most of the time Baker submerged his personal feelings in order to do what he felt was best for the Firm. Always a pragmatist, he saw Lane as a key factor in building the London office.

Problems in the London office didn't end with differences between Lane and Baker. As the young men Lane had brought in gained experience and became partners, they bridled at his power over their careers. At the Annual Partners Meetings, the freshly-made London partners heard the Firm's mantra about democracy and individual partner freedom, and felt that that wasn't happening in their home office.

Bruce Porter, who spent six years in the Sydney office, returned to London as a partner in 1972. There, he found that "Terry Lane was still trying to continue as he had when we were trainees. He and Norman Miller acted as a commanding officer and a second lieutenant." The two rarely consulted the younger partners, and they delegated little authority. "If we needed to change the color of the bog rolls [toilet paper], we would have had to ask Terry Lane," Sykes says. There were almost no partners' meetings. Lane made the decisions, Miller approved them, and the two implemented them. "As with all entrepreneurs, Terry saw the London office as his province," Leaver says. "Terry wanted to gather all the reins to himself."

The new partners also chafed at Lane's control over the office's work flow. To strengthen his grip on incoming business, Lane sent memos to other Firm offices, instructing them to refer all work to him, or, in his absence, to Miller, so that "it could be properly delegated within the office." When the lawyers were young and inexperienced, Lane's requirement made sense to them. As they began flexing their partner muscles, however, the senior partner's domination of the work pipeline became an increasingly sore point. In addition to affecting their incomes under the Formula, Lane wielded a powerful whip to discipline a partner who might think of stepping out of line.

In addition to the work-related issues, the junior partners were concerned because "there was no real organization—no central planning" in the London office. It lost money on its associates during some years in the late 1960s and early 1970s, because, Porter says, "We had superfluous people." After one year in which London had associate losses, Porter asked Lane whether the next year's budget would cure the problem. "Lane looked at me inquisitively, and said, 'Bruce, we don't have budgets.' It was ludicrous that a business of this size could just go off into the dark and not plan what it was going to do. We had to get our act together."

The young men Lane had recruited and trained grumbled, first in private and then openly. By the early 1970s their awe, and sometimes fear, of Lane was diminishing. They began pressuring him to let them participate in running the London office. Finally, he acceded to the junior men's demands for the creation of the post of Administrative Partner. He also agreed to holding weekly partners' lunches. At the lunches, the new partners lodged their complaints. Annoyed, Lane missed many of the meetings, even with fine food and wine at first-class restaurants as bait.

Until 1973, the younger partners' resentment merely simmered, but after that, three issues increased the heat. The first came about because of the London office's steady growth. Because the rent on new space was substantial, the Articles of Partnership required that the global partnership approve the lease. The Firm also had an informal policy of allowing the Executive Committee to review leases before they were sent to the entire partnership for a vote. When the London partners discussed sending the proposed lease to the Executive Committee, Lane and Miller were "adamantly opposed," arguing that kowtowing to the Committee reduced their independence as partners. Several younger partners countered that the policy was simply a prudent Firm procedure. When the issue came to a vote, only Lane and Miller were against an Executive Committee review.

In defiance, Lane sent a memorandum directly to the international partners asking for a favorable vote on the lease. "He had completely ignored the decision we had taken at the partners' meeting at lunchtime," Porter says. "Joanes, Malcolm Palmer, and I discussed it. We concluded that, if we just let it pass, then forever and a day, we were going to be his. Effectively, Lane was saying, 'I don't give a damn what your vote is, I call the shots.'" In retaliation, the junior partners sent a memo to all partners saying that Lane's request for a vote was "totally contrary to the vote of the London partners" and that they wanted the Executive Committee to review the lease.

At the 1973 Chicago Annual Meeting, a second issue flared. When Porter's elevation from Income to Capital Partner came up for a vote, Lane took the floor and denounced Porter as being intransigent. "We [Lane and Miller] considered that Porter had been a bad influence on the London partners," Lane said. "He wasn't constructive in his approach." The other London partners were outraged at Lane's public criticism of a partner who had his peers' support for election to Capital Partnership. After Joanes and Palmer rebutted Lane's assessment, those watching the duel knew that there was a much deeper-seated conflict in London. Sitting on the podium, Russell Baker listened to the debate. Then, in a speech favoring Porter's election, he gave the partners one of his rural aphorisms: "This whole fight reminds me of a tombstone inscription which said, 'I knew it was coming, but I didn't know when.'"

After the furor, the partners elected Porter a Capital Partner. Later, the third, and the most bitter, incident drove all London partners into two warring camps. Malcolm Palmer, a member of Lane's wife's family, had gone to his senior partner's office. On his secretary's desk, Palmer saw Lane's time sheets for a Friday, recording that Lane had done more work than Palmer thought was possible. Lane recalls bitterly that Palmer "wrote me a letter, saying 'Here is clear proof that you are falsifying your time sheets, because you have recorded eighteen hours of work in one day.' It was the day before I was going on holiday. I maybe put in twelve to fourteen hours that day. In addition, this was the end of the week—a Friday. It had always been my habit at the end of the week to take up all the scraps of notes on my desk and look through them to see if they should have been recorded in my time sheets. That is what I had done on that particular day."

Lane was also infuriated because, he says, "Palmer took it off my secretary's desk when she wasn't there. I had a feeling of considerable betrayal. Each one [of the younger lawyers] had come to me as an articled clerk. I had taken them on.

Malcolm Palmer was part of the family. Also, a group of people joined the London office who I felt were plotting against me." It was open combat from that point on, escalating from a mere domestic squabble to the level of a Firm-wide problem. With the controversy intensifying, the Executive Committee summoned all London partners to its Acapulco meeting. The young Turks recruited Sykes to present their case to the Committee. "I don't think I have ever felt so uptight in my life as I did then. I sat up all night trying to work up what I was going to say," Sykes recalls.

All they wanted, the rebel group said, was a broader democracy that would give them more control over their destinies. Lane said very little at the tense meeting, but he refused to compromise. "Russell Baker described my actions as being like one of the prophets of the Old Testament," Lane says. "I think he meant that I was being far too single-minded and stubborn in my approach. He may have very well been right."

At the Brussels Policy Committee Meeting in April 1974, the London issue was on the agenda. The discussion swayed back and forth as to who was to blame for the "blowup over the patrón syndrome." Some partners groused that Baker or the Executive Committee should have resolved the problem before it got out of hand, but, with the Firm's weak management structure, Baker's and the Committee's ability to intervene was limited.

The Policy Committee asked two partners, Thomas Bridgman from Chicago and Dennis Meyer from Washington, to mediate. When the mediators went to London, the dissident group agreed to meet with Lane, but he was not willing to meet with them. "Terry, being the true-blue Englishman," Sykes says, "wouldn't tolerate being accused of cheating. It was beneath him to discuss it." In private meetings with the two mediators, however, Lane and Miller didn't hide their feelings. They branded the dissenters "rebellious nuisances," and made it clear that they could not work with the disloyal opposition.

The rebels responded that, if the London office couldn't be run like a democratic Baker & McKenzie office, they wanted no part of it. With both sides adamant, the mediation team had to walk a delicate line to avoid destroying the office. One proposal called for the London partners to make decisions by unanimous consent, under which a single partner could paralyze the office by voting against everything. Porter recalls Lane's response to the idea: "To quote *Midsummer Night's Dream*, 'That way madness lies.'"

Baker himself attempted to head off a split, and pleaded with the dissidents to compromise. Porter attributes Baker's peacemaking efforts to his pragmatic view that "Terence Lane was tried and tested. His faults were known. Those of us who were leading the revolt were younger, and not as tried and tested. Lane had been a successful operator in London. He was a man with a strong personality, and he had a strong client attraction ability."

Because Lane was the figurehead of the London office, the situation posed a dilemma for many partners. At Annual Meetings, Lane, and occasionally Miller, had always represented the London office. As the office's founder and chief spokesman, Lane *was* the London office for many international partners, and few of them knew anything about the young Turks. Rather than taking sides, some non-London partners ignored the problem, and hoped that it would cure itself. As late as the spring of 1974, it still wasn't clear whether the Firm would support the office's founder or his upstart challengers. The young Turks were up against a formidable foe—a man whom even Russell Baker was chary of taking on. They realized that they might be risking their careers with the Firm, but "we had reached the stage where it would be very difficult to continue to work with Terry unless he was willing to change his ways. Those of us who knew his personality realized that that wasn't a real possibility," Sykes says.

There was no resolution. But, after months of discussion, Lane and Miller submitted their resignations in late 1974. Miller's friends begged him to stay and, after "a great deal of agonizing," he decided to remain with the Firm, although he later transferred to New York.

The two sides negotiated a separation agreement with surprisingly little rancor. "To the end, Lane was a gentleman," Porter says. "He wasn't somebody who would dirty his hands scrambling around engaging in devious tactics." After Lane left "there was a feeling of relief that it was over," Leaver says. "The London office had gotten to such a size, and the partners had reached such an age, that it had grown up and could carry on without Terry."

In reaction to Lane's tight grip, the London office tilted heavily towards democracy. So that no partner could build a power base, the partners rotated the Administrative Partner position each year. Decisions of any magnitude were made by all partners at weekly luncheon meetings, and a committee of partners distributed the work. As part of the reform package, the London partners also adopted a rule that they would elect as a partner only persons "who are congenial, who work harmoniously with each other, who cooperate, and who are willing to participate together."

Between 1975 and 1995, the number of partners in the London office grew from nine to thirty-nine, and its gross revenues soared from $1.6 million to over $50 million. To remedy the stigma of not being in the City of London, the office moved to a prime location on New Bridge Street in the early 1990s.

———

In Zürich, the Firm had to deal with a mature lawyer who was deeply immersed in his Swiss culture. Eric Homburger was an excellent law student who started his legal career in a highly prestigious post with the Zürich

Commercial Courts. After eight years at the courthouse, he left to get a masters degree at Harvard Law School. He worked for a New York law firm for a while, and then returned to Zürich in 1957 as a junior partner in a two-man law firm.

In the U.S. at the time, international tax and corporate work was cascading into the Firm's Washington and Chicago offices. Many American companies viewed Switzerland as a prime location to headquarter their European operations. To satisfy its clients' demands, the Firm began a search for a Swiss lawyer, and the thirty-eight-year-old Homburger's name made the short list.

With Baker & McKenzie being a primary exporter of American legal business, Homburger felt that a Firm affiliation would give him the opportunity to capture that business. In addition to the financial benefits, Baker's description of a proposed relationship gave Homburger something the Swiss treasure—autonomy and freedom from foreign entanglements. Homburger remembers Baker telling him that "he wanted to build an international firm which was not an American firm, but which had local offices headed by local people. It would not have the disadvantage of being considered American or foreign." Baker's statements fit in with Homburger's belief that "we should decide ourselves what we would be doing in Switzerland. And we should be autonomous within the Firm. I was of the strong opinion that we should be identified as a local Zürich office with a Swiss name," he says.

When Homburger opened the Zürich office in 1958, his character was fully formed. One partner says he was "conservative, slow to accept radical change, extremely thorough and scholarly." Another describes him as "a very calm, composed person. A man who tries to analyze things rationally, and a man who inspires confidence in clients." And a third says, "He was a typical Swiss in the sense that he was of the opinion that his Swiss law firm should remain independent and not be completely merged into Baker & McKenzie."

In keeping with his view that the office should blend into its Swiss backdrop, Homburger hired a former Swiss farm boy. Growing up, Johannes Müller had helped his father raise wheat, potatoes, and dairy cattle. Later, he studied law at the University of Fribourg, graduating in 1956. Müller then received scholarships to study at Yale and Stanford Universities. When he returned to Zürich, the young man interviewed with Homburger's office.

Eventually, Müller learned of the association with Baker & McKenzie, and, after three years in Zürich, he joined the Boys of '60 in the Chicago office in 1963. During his stay, Baker occasionally invited Müller to his Lake Bluff home, where they ate barbecue and talked about their mutual backgrounds as farmers' sons. They also discussed Müller's career. The young Swiss took his senior partner's advice about being trained in the common law system, and enrolled in night school at Chicago-Kent College of Law. He finished his course work, took a bar review course, and passed the Illinois bar examination in 1966, making him a fully qualified U.S. lawyer.

In that same year, the Zürich partners signaled that they wanted a U.S.-qualified lawyer in their office. Müller wasn't sure whether he wanted to go back to Switzerland, and once again sought Baker's advice. Believing that Müller was fully indoctrinated with the Firm ethos after four years in Chicago, Baker counseled him to return so that he could be a strong pro-Firm voice in the Zürich office when he got home.

Another Boy of '60 transferred from Chicago to Switzerland. Peter Lederer, whose Jewish parents escaped the Austrian Nazis in 1938 and immigrated to the U.S., had gotten his undergraduate and law degrees from the University of Chicago. There, he met Dr. Max Rheinstein, who introduced him to Baker & McKenzie. Lederer joined the Chicago office, and, after a few weeks, Baker invited the new lawyer to dinner in Lake Bluff. They finished supper, and Baker and Lederer walked to the beach on Lake Michigan. As they strolled, the older man asked him if he would consider moving to Zürich. "I reflected on that for a good ten or twelve seconds and said 'yes,'" he says.

When he arrived, Lederer found that Homburger's insistence on distancing himself from the Firm was not a mere personal preference. At the time, the Zürich Bar Association rules prohibited Swiss lawyers from being partners with foreigners. "Russell," Lederer says, "was prepared to push the envelope very, very hard, but somebody sitting on the ground and more exposed to the wrath of the local bar may have been less inclined to do so."

Baker regarded Homburger as one of the Firm's finest lawyers, and he respected his steadfast character. But the Swiss lawyer's reluctance to use the Baker & McKenzie name violated a basic Baker principle. "Russell had the one hundred percent accurate view that a brand name was of unbelievable importance in attracting and keeping work, and in projecting the image of the single Firm around the world," Lederer says. Despite Baker's pleas that Homburger go further to promote the Zürich office as being part of the Firm, Homburger dragged his feet. It wasn't unusual for clients to arrive in Zürich and not be able to find the office because it wasn't listed in the telephone book or on a name plate in its office building. "It was embarrassing," Wallace Baker says.

In a series of correspondence in 1959, Baker and Homburger jousted over the use of the Firm name. Baker told Homburger how important it was to have the Firm identified by name in Switzerland. He also insisted that Homburger use the cable address that offices around the world used, "ABOGADO," the Spanish word for lawyer. The prickly Swiss answered, "I gather that you are disappointed that I did not yet register the Firm in the telephone book and was late in placing its name plate on our office door. I object to these things being interpreted as symptoms of my reluctance to establish a close relationship with Baker & McKenzie."

Homburger agreed to put the Firm's name in the telephone book, and, although he said that a name plate was already on the front door, he promised to "replace it by a bigger one." He concluded his letter with an assurance: "I am in fact entirely on the Firm's side. There may be differences of opinion as to the best way to achieve our common goal; however, we are both driven by the same idea. I am prepared to carry the Firm's torch as high and as far as I can by working as hard and as well as possible."

Another factor that made it difficult for the cautious Swiss and the aggressive American to find common ground was that they had such disparate approaches to generating business. Among Swiss lawyers, asking for business was not done. It wasn't gentlemanly. "Our best means of promoting," Homburger told Baker, "is to do as good a job as we possibly can as lawyers, not as promoters." Baker, on the other hand, was adamant that the business of promoting clients should be faced head on. Just ask them for their business, he said.

If Homburger harbored an aversion to the Firm intruding on his fiefdom, then Lajos Schmidt personified his fears. Schmidt had made trips to Switzerland and worked directly with clients, never bothering to involve the Zürich office. Without Homburger's knowledge, he also met with Swiss government authorities. "You had somebody who was not practicing in the jurisdiction coming in and dealing directly with a government official with whom the local lawyers might have very carefully built a relationship over a period of time," Lederer says. "These frequent visits of Lajos Schmidt to Switzerland created tensions between Eric Homburger and Baker & McKenzie," Achermann says.[1] "Homburger felt that he was in charge of all legal activities of Baker & McKenzie in Switzerland, and strongly resented the visits of Lajos Schmidt to Cantonal tax commissioners."

Homburger recalls that "when we formed the Zürich office, I took the position that what was happening in Switzerland was our business—our concern." In letters to Baker, Homburger complained about Schmidt meddling in Swiss matters. In response, Baker wrote Homburger: "I am genuinely sorry that Lajos acted as he did in Switzerland. We have an agreement with you, and we intend to keep it. What Schmidt did is absolutely inconsistent with our agreement and it was a reckless thing."

Homburger also complained to the partners, who instructed Schmidt to stay out of Homburger's bailiwick. When the warnings didn't work, Homburger lobbied the global partners to stop Schmidt's trespassing. Finally, the partners adopted an amendment to the Articles of Partnership that required a traveling partner to take a local lawyer with him to meet clients or government officials in the country.

Several other irritants clouded the Baker-Homburger relationship, but a basic philosophical difference was the thorniest. Baker's most fundamental belief was that Baker & McKenzie should be "one single Firm." Homburger only wanted the offices to be loosely affiliated in a Swiss-like confederation. At partners meetings, Homburger continued to make his position clear—that local offices should be independent. "Eric's heart never flowed into the Firm," Wallace Baker says. "He never fully signed on for the dream. Russell was annoyed because he was breaking his ass to flow work to Europe, and he didn't think Homburger was properly appreciative of that fact. Russell pushed Eric hard to make this one Firm, even though there were substantial bar problems and different ethical rules that complicated these questions. Russell was not bashful in that respect."

Despite their differences, the Zürich office prospered. Much of its work was for non-Swiss companies. But Homburger began sensitizing his colleagues to developing business from Swiss clients so that they would not merely be "messenger boys of the U.S."

———

As new clients came into the Swiss offices in the late 1960s and the early 1970s, a second generation of Zürich partners joined the Firm. The group included Peter Widmer, described by his partners as the "most brilliant lawyer in this second generation," "excellent at handling clients," a man of "high ideals and high standards," and a man with "no sense of humor."

The son of a bicycle-shop owner, Widmer started out in the Zürich office handling litigation and commercial matters for banking and other clients. In the early 1980s, Widmer and other partners discussed leaving the Firm to set up their own law office. Homburger entertained thoughts of joining them because, as the global Firm grew larger, he felt that it was becoming more like a corporation. "Baker & McKenzie today is no longer a professional organization," he told Müller. "It is a business."

At Annual Meetings, Homburger expressed his concern that the Zürich office might lose its autonomy to a more powerful Executive Committee. Equally as damning to the frugal Swiss lawyer was the fact that "the bureaucracy and the expenses connected therewith were growing." Homburger also muttered that some Zürich partners "had the impression that, in certain offices, the quality was not up to standards, and we had the experience, in some places, that the clients were not well served." He also complained that the Firm was getting so large that it was impossible to know his new partners. The ever-increasing size, Widmer says, made Homburger "paranoid about liability issues." He feared that, because the Firm was a partnership, the "full fortune" of each partner was exposed to malpractice claims against other Firm lawyers around the world.

Sharing those concerns, several of the newer Zürich partners, including Widmer, were more insistent about leaving. But, when the older partners refused to leave, Homburger told the younger ones: "If everyone doesn't want to leave, then nobody leaves." He counseled them "to try to change the Firm, but not try to have a revolution."

Even though Homburger advised patience, the rest of the 1980s were what Achermann calls the "Unhappy Years" in the Zürich office. Zürich partners' meetings often turned into gripe sessions, and a cloud of pessimism enveloped the office. Some partners overlooked the good things that were happening, and concentrated on the Firm's perceived shortcomings.

The office had grown to occupy all four floors of a building in a wooded Zürich suburb, but the dissident partners continued to put out a constant stream of negativism. A partner, Anton Heini, brought distinction to the office when he was named a professor of law at Zürich University, but, as his client work dwindled to one day a week, he became a target of the dissidents' criticism. When Achermann and Müller served on the Executive Committee and were out of the office for long periods, the fault-finders argued that their absences cut into office revenues. And when Achermann spent a year trying to solve problems in the Rome office and then helped establish the new Moscow office, his disgruntled colleagues said that he was slacking off on his client work.

In 1986, the stabilizing force in the office stepped aside. Because his partners held Homburger in such high esteem, they persuaded him to allow them to continue to use his name. They also gave him an office and guaranteed him a handsome annual income in addition to his normal Firm retirement benefits. With Homburger semi-retired, the divisions between the Zürich partners became even wider.

When Executive Committee member Hans-Georg Feick attended a Zürich partners' meeting in the late 1980s, he found a very frosty atmosphere. The dissident Zürich partners peppered him with questions about global costs and the quality of other offices. After the outburst, Feick spoke with Widmer in private. Widmer told him that a group of young Turks felt that they might want to leave the Firm. Stunned, Feick reported to the Executive Committee that "something is going on in Zürich which may turn out to be very unpleasant," but the Committee took no action.

The Widmer group had developed a list of specific complaints, replaying the litany of criticisms that Homburger had been raising for years: that bureaucratic costs were soaring and that "big is bad." By 1990, the Firm had forty-three offices and over 1,500 lawyers spread around the globe. The dissidents argued that this growth, combined with a constitutionally diffused management structure, made it too unwieldy to manage.

The Widmer group had several cases to prove their point that the Firm was unmanageable. In addition to discrimination suits against the Firm in the U.S., one Zürich client refused to use certain other Firm offices that the client felt were weak. The Widmer group also argued that several of the twelve new offices that had opened between 1985 and 1990 were cash drains. One lateral partner in a money-losing new office remembers "the fish-eyed stares" he got from some Zürich partners at the Annual Meeting. "I thought I had some incurable disease," he says.

Although the Widmer group had adopted most of Homburger's grievances, they disagreed with their old mentor on one issue: they apparently saw law practice as a money-making business first, and as a profession second. The rebel group carefully calculated the net amount of money flowing out of their office into the Firm's central treasury, and figured that, if they left the Firm, the eight partners would each increase their already-healthy incomes by more than $125,000 per year.

The days when work flooded into the Zürich office from other Firm offices were over, and several Zürich partners had developed a large stable of well-known Swiss companies as clients. Even though the Baker & McKenzie network still supplied a sizable percentage of the office's total workload, the Widmer group viewed their Firm association as a hindrance because, as long as they flew the Firm flag, other law firms wouldn't send them business. In addition, as Baker & McKenzie and its client base grew larger, the Zürich partners were increasingly forced to turn down work from new clients because a Firm lawyer in another office halfway around the world was suing the same client. As a stand-alone Swiss law firm, the Widmer group said, the conflict of interest problems would be microscopic.

The buildup of discontent finally turned into action. During the summer of 1990, the Widmer group drew up a draft partnership agreement and compensation system for their proposed new firm. At the October Annual Meeting in Bermuda, the possibility of a split became well known. At one Meeting session, Robert Cox referred to the discontent in Zürich and expressed hope that they would find "the reasons and spirit to continue with the Firm."

Back home in Zürich after the Bermuda gathering, the separatists held closed-door meetings almost every day to refine their partnership and compensation structures. The defectors had carefully thought through the elements of their departure, but one major item remained to be settled—the use of Eric Homburger's name, which the office had used since its founding in 1958. That, and Homburger's prestige, caused most Zürichers to call the Zürich office the "Homburger Law Office." When the split appeared imminent, Homburger signed an agreement allowing the Widmer group to use his name.

On December 1, 1990, the Widmer group held a meeting of all Zürich partners to announce their decision to leave. Achermann glumly reported to the Firm's Chairman, Cox, that "it became crystal clear that all the Zürich partners except Johannes Müller, Max Wehrli, Anton Heini and myself have decided to form their own law firm. There is absolutely no point in trying to further talk to these partners; they have definitively made up their minds." Achermann also said that Müller and Wehrli were in the process of deciding whether to leave or stay. Because Wehrli would probably do what Müller did, Achermann reasoned, "it all depends on Johannes whether Baker & McKenzie will continue to have an office in Zürich." Achermann's message reached Cox at an Executive Committee meeting in Caracas: "Either you come to Zürich immediately, or you will no longer have an office in Zürich."

Cox recalls that "Achermann told me that matters had escalated very quickly in Zürich, and that all hell had broken loose. I decided to take the two Europeans on the Executive Committee, Richard Davidson from London and Hans-Georg Feick from Frankfurt, to Zürich with me." The three flew overnight from Caracas to Zürich, arriving groggy and jet-lagged.

Wehrli told the threesome that he had no interest in being in a one- or two-man Zürich office. Achermann said that he would not stay unless Müller stayed. This made Müller the pivotal figure. If he remained, the Zürich office could be rebuilt. If he left, the Firm's thirty-two-year history in the Swiss city would end. In addition, there was the hidden risk that the Widmer group's departure might start a chain reaction in other European offices.

Keeping Müller would not be easy. The defectors had agreed to put a substantial sum into a retirement fund and to guarantee him an income exceeding $800,000 per year. Müller was sixty, and the task of staying with Baker & McKenzie and rebuilding the office was daunting. He also felt a sense of loyalty towards Widmer and his cohorts, with whom he had worked for many years. And he was annoyed with the Firm's failure to act until the Zürich problem reached a crisis stage.

The Widmer group kept intense pressure on him to go with them. Meanwhile, the three Executive Committee members stepped up the tempo on the other side. "It was absolutely terrible," Müller recalls. Cox saw Müller's dilemma: "His colleagues of many years were people on both sides of the issue. He wasn't a young partner. You could see the emotional anguish he was going through."

As part of their courting strategy, the dissidents pointed out to Müller that he would be financially better off with them. If he stayed with Baker & McKenzie, the Formula would work against him because rebuilding the office would force him to spend substantial time on administrative matters, cutting into his Work Credit. And, they added, because most of the associates were going with the Widmer group, Associate Profit would be almost nonexistent.

To press their case, the three Executive Committee members arranged a dinner with Müller and the other non-Widmer partners. Cox offered to match the Widmer group's financial package. He also told Müller that it looked like two key associates would stay if he stayed. An instinctive salesman, Cox painted rebuilding the office as an exciting challenge to cap Müller's career with the Firm. His response was disheartening: "I helped build the Zürich office, and now you're asking me to do that again about three years before retirement. This is too much to ask me." Just before dessert, a frustrated Müller slammed his napkin on the table. "At half past eight, I told them, 'Gentlemen, I'm sorry, I have to leave.' I couldn't take it any more," Müller remembers.

At home, he mulled over the fact that, if he had not joined the Firm, he would not have met his wife while he was working in the Chicago office with the Boys of '60. He may have also remembered a memo Russell Baker wrote in 1965 supporting Müller's election to partnership: "Johannes . . . is an excellent man, and a very fine and talented lawyer. . . ." Müller also recalled that some fifteen partners around the world telephoned to encourage him to stay. Robert Berner called from Chicago to tell him, only half-jokingly: "Johannes, you are going to stay. I'll cry if you leave."

As he weighed his decision, Müller also remembered that the Widmer group had done something that offended him. "They told me 'Johannes, you are the senior partner in our office. If you do not come with us, and if we stay with Baker & McKenzie, you can forget about being the senior partner then. You will be nobody anymore. If you come with us, you will be Number One. You will be the head of this new firm.' I was appalled by that approach. I thought, my gosh, if they can go that far, to what extent can I rely on those fellows. It really came to this: If I went with the Widmer group, Baker & McKenzie in Zürich would shut down. It would be over and done with. I felt very much attached to my partners around the world. I was emotionally attached to Baker & McKenzie, and I didn't want to cut that."

He decided not to leave. Early the next morning, he went to Feick's hotel and told him of his decision. Knowing Müller's love for Bordeaux wine, Feick ordered a bottle of Chateaux Margaux, which they drank immediately. Then Feick called Cox to tell him that Müller would stay.

Cox, Müller, and other loyalists immediately began talks with two key senior associates to ensure that they remained with the Firm. Cox dangled promises of a fast track to partnership election, and pointed out that Achermann and Müller would be retiring in a few years, making them the senior men in the Zürich office. If they went with the dissidents, Cox said, they would have to wait fifteen or more years until Widmer and his peers retired. When the associates agreed to stay, the Firm had a core group of four partners and two associates.

In February 1991, Achermann went to the Western Hemisphere Partners Meeting in Acapulco and to the Chicago office to ask partners to help keep their clients in the Zürich office. He also visited a number of clients himself to explain the situation and to ask them to stay with the Firm. Many clients stayed, but some left. Within four years, however, the office had built back up to almost twenty lawyers, and, between 1992 and 1996, revenues leaped from $3.4 million to $7.1 million.

As Cox reflects on the Zürich episode, he concludes, "Even though we are a big Firm, there is a certain fragility. It is a business, but it is people. It is not a manufacturing facility with equipment. It is people whose faith and commitment to this Firm are measured each day; every time they come up and down the elevator."

Chapter Ten

The Search for Balance:
Firm Governance

With no blueprint for how to manage Baker & McKenzie, finding a way to govern a multi-office law firm was unsettling to the partners, who, like all attorneys, were uncomfortable when they had no precedent. Until the 1980s, few other law firms had an office in another city, let alone an office in another country. Making the problem even more difficult, Russell Baker wavered between his genuine romance with democracy and his conviction that he knew what was best for the Firm.

When Chicago was the only office, Baker consulted with his partners at meetings in his corner office, where they circled around his desk to "fight and scratch and get things done." For several years, the partnership was small enough for Baker to host the Annual Meeting dinner at his Lake Bluff house. As the Firm grew, however, there was a general sense that it needed some structure, and the Firm created a committee of Managing Partners in the late 1950s. The committee's makeup included the senior partners in each office and the heads of significant practice groups, such as John McKenzie from the Chicago litigation department. Even though the Managing Partners gave the Firm a semblance of organization, the partners had deliberately designed their governance system to be weak. The Articles of Partnership required a one hundred percent vote to eject a troublesome colleague, which left no mechanism for anyone, including Baker, to discipline a rogue partner.

Two of Baker's personal biases, which many partners shared, contributed to a feeble management structure. He treasured frugality, and viewed the creation of a manager class as a waste of money. He loathed administrative hierarchy, and often railed against what he called "a high priest caste" of professional administrators who spent their time building power bases. Rather than a complex management structure, he felt that, with the respect he commanded, his hand could steer the Firm's course. But Baker did not want to drown himself in ministerial details. William Gibbons says that Baker "hated the problems that came with daily administration. He wanted to be the Chairman of the Board who decided the big policy issues."

Although Baker wanted to direct the big issues, he agreed with the vast majority of his partners that it made no sense for administrators in Chicago to micro-manage the Firm by fixing secretaries' salaries in São Paulo or buying typewriters for Amsterdam. He understood that the local partners knew their legal markets better than any centralized management could, and that they could react more quickly and effectively to shifting local conditions. In addition, the mature partners in Europe and Latin America were "independent operators," Willem Stevens says, "and they had their own pride. Nobody would accept an American coming in and telling them how to practice or what to do. The strength of the Firm was what some people might call weak government. But the Firm would not have survived with a top-down governance system."

Baker & McKenzie's relaxed management approach was often inefficient, and by 1961 it had become apparent that something had to be done. New offices were popping up around the globe, and many new partners were signing on. With just over $2 million in revenues, the Firm needed more than the loosely structured Managing Partners committee. The partners began discussing two amendments to the Articles of Partnership. The first would relax the old require-ment of a unanimous partner vote for almost all major decisions. With some thirty partners, rounding up one hundred percent votes was almost impossible, and a tyranny of one or two people could paralyze the Firm. Although most partners wanted the decision-making process to be more workable, a small minority felt threatened. Fearing Baker's anger towards people who opposed him on major Firm issues, they lobbied for super majority votes on critical issues, the most important one being the vote required to throw out a partner. After spirited debate, the partners reached a compromise they called the "all save four" rule. Under that rule, the Firm could not force out a partner if that partner and four others voted against the expulsion. The minority group felt that, "no matter what," a partner could always find four allies to vote with him against his ouster.

The second Articles amendment would establish a Policy Committee as the Firm's chief governing body. That Committee would designate several subcommit-tees endowed with specific powers to administer certain areas. The sponsors of the new governance structure argued that it would admit more partners from around the world into the inner circle. It would afford the Policy Committee members a global perspective of the Firm. And, the supporters said, the Committee would provide a central forum for broader-based discussions of Firm problems.

At first, Baker opposed the Policy Committee idea. In a memorandum to Eric Homburger in Zürich, Baker blistered the proposed system: "Tell me,

Eric, do you know of one single business in Switzerland that is run by a bunch of committees? We have a complicated business. It earned more than $800,000 last year. Would anyone other than a status-conscious person or power seeker propose the running of such a business by a bunch of silly committees? We must have strong central management in a group that has continuity and which contains the staunchest, the most experienced and the natural leaders of the group. I am absolutely against annual election of the Policy Committee. Imagine the vote-collecting cliques forming. It would be a nightmare. The sole purpose of such a proposal is to break up present management rather than to strengthen it."

A few days later, a frustrated Baker wrote Homburger that he had discussed the management reforms with several partners. "My ideas are not welcome by a small group of partners, and I am tired. I am sick of being accused of fomenting a one-man rule. I could not care less. So committees it will be so far as I am concerned. The nub of the question is that some partners simply do not want central management. Each wants to decide every point which they think important for themselves. This is a perfectly proper point of view. The trouble is that not all partners support the things which they know to be good for the Firm. They are too closely occupied with work. For my part I feel abandoned by my friends and assailed by people who apparently want to do what I have been trying to do without cost to the group. I will not resist any more. I will get busy with my own affairs."

After heated debate at the 1961 Annual Meeting, the partners adopted the Policy Committee structure and the revised voting procedures. Although Baker had worried that the committee system would dissipate his ability to get things done, he dominated the Policy Committee. The partners elected him its permanent Chairman, and its members were "Russell's people, like his son, Lajos Schmidt, and Bill Gibbons," Thomas Haderlein says. Because the Articles didn't provide a way to remove Policy Committee members, they had lifetime tenures. With their seats guaranteed in perpetuity, some wags dubbed the Policy Committee the "House of Lords."

The Policy Committee met almost monthly, but the extensive travel requirements caused its non-U.S. members to miss many meetings. The Committee tried to bring some order to the developing Firm, but it was difficult because no one person had the responsibility to attend to the global enterprise's day-to-day affairs. To fill the void, the Policy Committee created the position of Secretary of the Firm, carefully choosing the title to make the point that the Secretary would not be a Managing Partner with power to give orders to the other partners. The Committee elected William Gibbons to the post, and gave him a list of twenty-four duties to fulfill, including settling inter-partner disputes and deciding conflict of interest questions. Still, worried about a concentration of power, the

Committee set up a grievance committee to which partners could appeal the Secretary's decisions.

Gibbons, then thirty-eight, had just returned from a successful five-year tour of duty in Caracas, and was one of Baker's most trusted lieutenants. In the future, there would be stormy scenes between the two, but in 1962 they were so close that some partners felt that Gibbons was Baker's heir apparent. Surprisingly, even the partners who thought that Baker had too much power supported Gibbons. Peter Lederer, who often disagreed with Gibbons, says that "as much as we screamed at each other, he had the interest of the Firm at heart—in a distorted fashion on occasion." Bridgman adds that "Bill was a person in whom all partners had confidence, and a person who could not be bulldozed by one partner or one group. He was someone in whom Russell had confidence, but he wasn't a pushover when it came to everything Russell wanted." Nevertheless, David Macdonald says, "when Russell wanted to weigh in on a topic, Gibbons had to put up with a lot that Russell gave to him in terms of what actions he wanted to take, who he wanted to hire, and who he wanted to transfer overseas."

The partners expected the new Secretary to manage their affairs on three continents, but they wanted Gibbons to sandwich it in between practicing law. "The idea of the Secretary's job being part-time was Russell's," Gibbons recalls. "He would say, 'What are you spending so much time on? There isn't anything to do here.'" Although the Secretary's job was supposed to be part-time, Gibbons made numerous trips outside the U.S. After one swing through the Far East, he routed himself back home through Frankfurt. Exhausted from the travel and multiple time-zone changes, Gibbons fell asleep during the main course of an elegant dinner with the German lawyers. "We woke him when dessert was served, and he sleepily finished the meal," Horst Amereller recalls.

Baker and his protégé had several traits in common. Neither was given to chit-chat. They were devout believers in the work ethic, and had little patience with slackers. The adventure of building the Firm enthralled them both. And they were energetic and overly intense, because, Gibbons says, "I don't want my tombstone to read, 'He sat on his ass all his life,'" a sentiment that Baker would have agreed with.

One trait that Gibbons's partners teased him about was his "Hamlet complex"—constantly weighing the pros and cons of an issue. "He was known for changing his mind within the same sentence," Hans-Georg Feick says. "He played devil's advocate with himself. It was very common for him to switch sides just to test his own opinion." For those partners who didn't understand this quirk, it could be annoying. In addition to abruptly changing his mind, Gibbons could be testy. Even with close friends, he would "fight like hell all the time. We called each other names. We would get into it, but we forgot it in five minutes," Bridgman says.

Even though Gibbons could be abrupt, to many young lawyers he was a "godfather," Irecê Trench says. "If you were depressed, Gibbons would buck up your morale. When you didn't have enough work to do, he gave it to you. If you had problems with clients, he helped you work them out."

———————

At the outset of Gibbons's tenure as Secretary, a major issue surfaced over the Firm's burgeoning size. In 1962, Baker & McKenzie added new offices in Frankfurt, Milan, and Toronto. The next year, it expanded to Paris, Manila, and Tokyo. Those partners who wanted continued expansion labeled the naysayers' attitude the "drawbridge syndrome," pulling up the bridge so that no newcomers could enter the partnership. The partners split into two camps—the consolidators, who wanted gradual growth that could be easily digested, and the expansionists, who championed the opening of offices in any city where quality lawyers could sustain a profitable operation.

Among the consolidators, there was a feeling of "stop the world, I want to get off." With a steady stream of new faces showing up at Annual and Regional Meetings, they fretted that the Firm's carefully nurtured culture would be destroyed and that its tradition of close personal friendships would be ruined. At Firm cocktail parties and dinners, the consolidators complained that there was no planning for growth, and that the weak management structure couldn't handle the avalanche of new lawyers and offices. More importantly, they said, under the Formula, money flowed out of their pockets to fund the expansion costs of the new offices. As a corollary, they pointed out that the Firm wouldn't be able to control the quality of work being produced and that incompetent lawyers might slip into the tent, creating potential liability for all partners.

The growth issue came to a head at the 1962 Annual Meeting, where the partners met from early morning until "ungodly late at night." Tempers were short when the subject of whether *any* new partners should be elected finally came to the floor. Michael Waris summarized how a number of partners viewed the squabbling: "Baker & McKenzie has found a very queer way to run a law firm. First, one guy gets up and makes an impassioned speech. Nobody listens to him. When he sits down, they all disagree."[1] To mollify those who complained that too many "new boys" endangered the Firm, the partners created a new class of partner—an Income Partner—who could hold himself out to the public as a partner and was treated equally under the Formula, but could not vote for four years. During that limbo period, its supporters claimed, the Income Partners would become familiar with the Firm's guidelines and culture.

———————

After two years, Gibbons was wearied by the long hours he was putting in as Secretary while practicing law at the same time. He announced his decision to resign as the Firm's chief administrator. In 1964, the Policy Committee agreed that one part-time person couldn't handle the job, and abolished the office of Secretary, creating instead a three-man Executive Committee and electing Chicago partners to fill all the slots. John Creed became the Firm's first Chairman of the Executive Committee, with Gibbons and Baker's son, Donald, rounding out the list.

Creed had graduated from West Point in 1948. He spent most of his Air Force career as a radarman/navigator/bombardier in B–36s loaded with atom bombs. When he left the service, he enrolled in Georgetown University Law School. After graduating in 1957, he became the second lawyer in the Washington office. Eventually, Creed moved to Chicago, where his partners regarded him as an expert on the Formula and Firm financial matters. A former financial officer, Patricia Beal, recalls that, "If I had a problem under the Articles or the Formula, the first person I called was John Creed."

To cure one of the Formula's vices, in the early 1960s he devised what became known as the "Creed Rule." The partners had little incentive to collect fees until near the end of the June 30 fiscal year. To pay the Firm's expenses during the rest of the year, it borrowed money and paid interest. In the few weeks before June 30, a riptide of money flowed in, allowing the Firm to pay off its bank debt. Then, the cycle of cash flow deficiencies began again. To motivate partners to collect their fees quarterly, the "Creed Rule" penalized partners who didn't collect throughout the year and rewarded those who did.

The partners gathered for the 1964 Annual Meeting in Chicago, where Meeting costs totaled some $30,000 and the forty-nine partners received $25 per day for food and hotel expenses. During his tenure as Chairman, Creed recalls, "Russell left me alone most of the time. But, when he really wanted something, he would push. If I disagreed with him, I would stand up to him. And, as long as he didn't think I was doing something that betrayed his trust, he wouldn't get mad."

In 1965, the Firm expanded the Executive Committee to five members and gave it additional powers. At the 1966 Annual Meeting in London, the first out-side the U.S., the partners again broadened the representation on the Executive Committee, approving a seven-man Executive Committee, with geographic seats reserved for each region. The partners also expanded the Policy Committee. Four of the five new Committee members were from outside the U.S., and all of them came from the ranks of the Boys of '60.

The 1966 Annual Meeting dragged on for six days, with sessions stretching late into the night. The most difficult issue the partners faced was the departure of Dwight Hightower, then a name partner. The partners also addressed the Firm's confusing system of capital contributions because its banks had refused to make loans unless it adopted a financially sound capital program. The old system was "the nuttiest thing you've ever seen," Haderlein says. Facing a tight cash situation and reluctant banks, Haderlein started working on a system of annual partner capital contributions that would provide a sound financial base for continued growth.

After focusing on financial matters, the partners turned to the issue of who would succeed Creed as Chairman. They floated the names of several candidates, but Baker engineered the election of his most loyal supporter, Lajos Schmidt. "Lajos was a larger-than-life character," Andrew Joanes says. "In any group of people, he was nearly always the dominant person." Born in 1920, Schmidt received his Hungarian law degree in 1941, then studied in Germany before returning to Hungary for further study and a job as a trainee with a Hungarian law firm.

During World War II's waning days, Schmidt refused to cooperate with the Nazis, who controlled Hungary at the time. They arrested him and clapped him in a Budapest prison. In the confusion of an American bomber raid, Schmidt escaped and remained in hiding until the Soviet army swept into Hungary in January 1945, when he was arrested again and forced to march eastward through freezing winter cold. After four days, the Communist guards herded their prisoners into an abandoned school building in a small village. Again, Schmidt escaped, and managed to make his way back to the Hungarian capital.

There, the Hungarian police, then backed by the Soviets, arrested him in April 1945, as an "enemy of the people." They put him in a Budapest prison camp, and assigned him to a squad that defused unexploded Allied bombs. After a few weeks of handling live explosives, Schmidt was released through the efforts of a highly placed Hungarian acquaintance.

Even though the experience made him a "virulent anti-Communist," he returned to law practice, gaining admission to the Hungarian bar in 1947. That fall, Schmidt obtained one of the few available exit visas and left Hungary. He went to northern Italy and found a job as a clerk in Genoa. In late 1948, Schmidt got a job that would take him out of war-wasted Europe. He left Genoa by ship, headed for the Dominican Republic, where he became the number-two executive at a government-owned small arms manufacturing company. At the time, Raphael Trujillo ruled the island nation. Trujillo was "one of the vicious-style Latin American dictators, and he didn't trust any of his countrymen to operate the arms factory," Donald Baker says. "So he hired foreigners who he thought would be less likely to plot against him."

Schmidt was living comfortably in the Dominican Republic in 1949 when he learned that an American lawyer, Russell Baker, would be visiting the country. Baker had helped Schmidt's sister with an immigration matter while she was a University of Chicago student. When she learned that Baker was going to the Dominican Republic, she told him to look up her brother. Only a few weeks after the Firm opened its doors on July 1, 1949, Baker met with Schmidt. The Hungarian spoke no English, so the two men conversed in Spanish. Baker liked the strapping six-foot, five-inch Hungarian, and they vowed to keep in contact.

Some two years later, Schmidt began to suspect that the dictator's brother, who oversaw the munitions factory, was stealing money from the company. He feared that the brother would blame the theft on him, so, in a preemptive strike, he went to the Ministry of War and accused "unknown perpetrators" of taking the money. "My assumption was that the discrepancy would be discovered," Schmidt says. "Since I was stateless, it was clear that I would be accused of having stolen the money, and that I would go to jail, be expelled, or disappear."

Rather than be a scapegoat, he testified before a military tribunal presided over by three Dominican army colonels. Schmidt explained that Trujillo's brother was skimming off large amounts of cash by juggling the books and invoices. After a ten-day hearing, the colonels determined that there was no proof of theft, and ruled that there was merely "suspicion of mishandling of money." Shortly after the hearing ended, an army officer told Schmidt that the dictator's brother wanted to see him immediately. In his office, the dictator's brother put a pistol on the table and said, "You are a troublemaker." He then gave Schmidt forty-eight hours to be on board a Dominican Air Force plane bound for Puerto Rico.

With no passport, he had two days to find a country that would admit him and his wife. Schmidt's wife was sick, and he wanted to go to the United States for her treatment. He took his story to the U.S. Consulate, and the Consul agreed to give the pair temporary visas, but told Schmidt he would need an Affidavit of Support from a U.S. citizen guaranteeing that the American would financially support him if it became necessary. "Then I remembered that I had met somebody in 1949," Schmidt says.

He sent Baker a cable asking him for help. The next morning, the Consul summoned Schmidt to the Consulate, where he showed him a telegram from Baker that the Consul agreed to accept as an Affidavit of Support. The couple left for Puerto Rico that afternoon. From a telephone at the San Juan airport, Schmidt called Baker to thank him. Baker suggested that, after his wife's surgery, they come to Chicago. They did. Schmidt started working at the Firm as an office boy, carrying books to and from the County Law Library, translating documents, and sometimes even taking partners' laundry to the cleaners. "He brought with him a huge desire to succeed, to help, and to become involved," Michel Coccia says.

Although he spoke Hungarian, German, Spanish, and Italian, the thirty-one-year-old Schmidt spoke almost no English. Nevertheless, Baker arranged for him to enroll in the Chicago-Kent College of Law's night school. After he finished work at the Firm, Schmidt went to class until almost nine, caught the train to his South Side apartment, and started studying at eleven. "It was very tough," he remembers. Donald Baker, who tried to help the Hungarian with his studies, says that Schmidt's heavily accented English was "atrocious. I was astounded that someone would come to the U.S. and start law school without knowing the language. That took real brass."

Schmidt graduated from law school, passed the Illinois bar examination, and began working as a lawyer. Russell Baker looked on Schmidt, with his courtly manners, as "Mr. Europe." But he sometimes rubbed his fellow Europeans the wrong way. Hans-Georg Feick, a German who joined the Chicago Foreign Trade Department as a junior associate, says that "Lajos would call you up at any time of the night and ask you to come to the office and do things for him." On some of those occasions when Feick arrived at the office late at night, Schmidt told him that the matter was not really important after all, and that it could wait until the next day.

Although Schmidt could be imperious, at the same time he could be courteous and subservient, particularly in his dealings with Baker. "Russell Baker had a man Friday by the name of Lajos Schmidt," Robert Cox says. "He was sometimes a bit heavy-handed in his handling of partners. Russell was the power behind him, and he used that." After Schmidt had been Chairman for five years, some partners began agitating for a change in the top administrative job. Several younger partners, mostly the Boys of '60, were concerned that Schmidt might become the de facto permanent Chairman.

During the ten years between 1955 and 1965, the Firm had ballooned, adding seventeen offices. Between 1966 and 1975, however, the Firm opened only five new offices. And three of those—Rio de Janeiro, Rome, and Geneva—were in countries where the Firm had existing offices. Firm politics was tainting the growth issue. When a partner proposed opening a new office, one of the first questions asked was "Who will run it?" The question was important because that person normally became the senior partner in the office and gained a slot on the Policy Committee. Because the Policy Committee made most of the important decisions, partners kept a close eye on whether a new office's founding partner would be in Baker's camp.

"There was this anxiety over Russell Baker controlling the Firm and whether he would let it pass to the hands of other people," Haderlein says. "Compared to the Firm's previous growth, we had almost reached an impasse in the late 1960s and early 1970s. We got into a gridlock because Russell Baker developed the view that there were already enough dissenters out there. So it got to be a question of who would rule the roost in a new office."

The struggle over the San Francisco office epitomized the battles during that time. All through the 1960s, a California office had been a formal or informal agenda item at most Firm meetings. Baker wanted one because it was key to his Pacific Basin strategy. He correctly foresaw a tidal wave of business coming to the U.S. from Asia, and he wanted a California office to be there to intercept it. But there was a problem. The California Bar Association's rules prohibited the Firm from using the Baker & McKenzie name. Because law firms could only use the names of lawyers who were qualified in California or who were deceased, John McKenzie's death in 1962 solved half of the problem. To clear the remaining stumbling block, the Firm's founder announced that, at age sixty-seven, he would study for and take the California bar examination. Baker rented a Los Angeles apartment in 1968, enrolled in a bar review course with recent law school graduates in their twenties, and spent hours poring over textbooks. The first two times he took the bar exam, he flunked. Finally, at age sixty-nine, he passed, effectively removing the name issue as a problem.

Still, the partners debated whether to locate an office in Los Angeles or San Francisco. When they settled that issue, the fight over who would head up the San Francisco office turned ugly, driving a wedge between Baker and one of his oldest, staunchest supporters. Gibbons had made it known that he was itching to do something new. He talked to Baker about moving to California, and made a trip to San Francisco to do a feasibility study. When Gibbons pressed the issue, however, his long-time mentor withheld his support.

"We got into a pissing match," Gibbons says. "I don't know how many battles we had fought together. At every Annual Meeting, we were slugging it out on the same side," Gibbons says. "I figured that, if I had asked him to help me rob the First National Bank of Chicago, he would have been down there in the getaway car." Nevertheless, Baker slighted his old friend in favor of a younger Chicago partner, Donald Flynn. Many partners had theories as to why Baker turned his back on Gibbons, including the possibility that Baker thought that Flynn might prove to be more malleable than the sometimes crusty, independent Gibbons.

Whatever the reason, Baker had his way. At its Mexico City meeting in 1970, the Policy Committee reported that the San Francisco office would open in late May "with Donald Flynn and Juan Collas staffing the office, under Russell Baker's guidance." To offset partners' objections that Flynn had a difficult personality and was too junior to open the office, Baker vowed that he would oversee San Francisco himself. But this too caused a problem. Flynn came into conflict with Baker over how fast the San Francisco office should grow. Even though Baker pressured him to bring in more lawyers, Flynn resisted. "Don considered the office to be his own private preserve," Collas says.

Several years passed without San Francisco reaching its potential. Finally, in 1979, Collas and Flynn met Baker in Los Angeles to discuss San Francisco's snail-like growth. "Don and I went to have dinner with Russell, and they really had it out," Collas recalls. "Don was being very belligerent, and Russell was very quiet, but he stood his ground. Don was pounding the table and shouting. Baker just kept eating his food and keeping his composure. Flynn said he wasn't against growth per se. He just wanted the office to grow at a pace that would be manageable. Russell said, 'I think that's too slow.' Don was really upset that Russell was not supporting him."

Chapter Eleven

Rapid Expansion: Amsterdam, Washington, D.C., Brussels & Mexico City

Between 1955 and 1961, Baker & McKenzie opened nine new offices: Caracas, Washington, D.C., Brussels, Amsterdam, Zürich, New York, São Paulo, London, and Mexico City. With that rapid expansion, Russell Baker did not have time to train enough new lawyers to head up each office. Many of the Boys of '60 were still learning the Firm's ways in Chicago, forcing Baker to search for experienced lawyers from the outside. As a result, during that heady six-year period, Baker opened eight of the nine new offices with mature lawyers who had no previous Firm connection.

Amsterdam opened in 1957. Some may have argued that London, Paris, or Frankfurt should have been first, but the Netherlands had been an important trading nation since the 1500s. As a major entrepôt, Holland boasts an infrastructure of traders, bankers, accountants, and lawyers who provide expertise to companies wanting to do business throughout Europe. To make the Netherlands even more attractive, over the years the Dutch Ministry of Finance negotiated tax treaties with most other European countries and the U.S. By using the treaty network and negotiating special tax reductions with the Dutch government, a company could headquarter in the Netherlands, do business in other European countries, and avoid paying double taxes. This combination of tax benefits, geography, and sophisticated professionals made the country a prime location for American companies wanting to expand into Europe.

In 1955, Russell Baker had made a trip to Amsterdam to find a local lawyer to help him with Abbott Laboratories. He began his search on a Saturday, leafing through the telephone book and calling lawyers in alphabetical order.

Johannis "Jimmy" Jacobus Caron was the first to answer his phone. Baker immediately went to Caron's small office in the Stock Exchange Building. A friendship developed, and the two men agreed to work together under a correspondent relationship.

Caron had grown up in the last major remnant of the Netherlands' colonial empire, the Dutch East Indies (now Indonesia). He returned to the mother country for secondary school and university, graduating from the University of Amsterdam Law School in 1935. Caron worked with another Dutch lawyer until the Nazi Security Police arrested his partner for aiding Jews. The two-man partnership dissolved after his colleague died in a concentration camp.

When World War II ended, Caron made himself an expert in Dutch corporate law, and began upgrading his tax skills by attending classes at the University of Amsterdam. As his practice grew, Caron hired Frits LeCoultre, who had spent six years in Java working for a Dutch shipping company. After Indonesia became independent in 1950, LeCoultre joined the other unwelcome Dutch colonials and went home.

During the War, LeCoultre had refused to sign an oath swearing loyalty to the German Occupation Forces. In addition, he was active in an Amsterdam student underground organization. To avoid capture by the Nazis, he assumed a false name and obtained forged identity papers. Then, he moved to the university town of Utrecht, finding refuge in a carpenter's home. During one sweep by the German troops to capture underground members, LeCoultre escaped arrest by hiding in a neighbor's secret basement.

In 1960, LeCoultre transferred to Chicago. He arrived on a Thursday, and spent a lonely weekend by himself in a strange hotel in a strange town. When he saw Russell Baker on Monday, the older man asked him how he was getting along. LeCoultre didn't hold back, telling Baker that he was homesick for the family he had left behind in Holland. Baker invited the young Dutchman to stay in his *casita* in Lake Bluff, where he lived almost as a member of the family. At the office, LeCoultre met the Boys of '60. Over beers after work, they talked excitedly of building a large network of law offices around the world that could compete with the best.

After a year in Chicago, he returned to Amsterdam with ideas of enlarging the office, and battered Caron with talk of growth and mergers with other Dutch firms. But the office's founder wanted to be left alone to practice law his own way, undisturbed by pesky partners with grandiose ideas. "No. No good. We will stay as we are," Caron told LeCoultre. Feeling stifled, LeCoultre left the Firm in 1962.

Getting along with the crusty Caron was difficult for the younger men. Willem van Vliet squabbled with Caron for several years before transferring to Chicago. He wrote, "I have come to the end of my rope. There is a Calvinistic approach to things—either one is damned or not, and when the Judgment Day comes, the Lord has already made up His mind. I have come to the conclusion that I am among the damned."

Having been the son of a high colonial government official in the Dutch East Indies, Caron had learned early about hierarchy. He would "hit his fists on the table if you didn't do something correctly," says Peter Dekker, who witnessed several fist-slamming episodes when he made a novice's mistakes. Caron could also be stubborn. Hating newfangled equipment, he refused to buy a telex machine, even though telexes were faster and more efficient than telegrams for overseas communications. To overcome Caron's resistance, Firm lawyers and clients began deliberately sending telegrams late in the afternoon, U.S. time, so that the Dutch telephone operators would call Caron at home in the middle of the night to read him a five-page cable. Soon afterwards, he installed a telex in the office.

Caron lived modestly. Rather than going to plush restaurants for lunch, he was happy with a sandwich in a corner cafe. He had a passion for American baseball, and could reel off players' batting averages and which teams had played in the World Series as only a fanatic fan could. He loved his work, and would get so wrapped up in his thoughts that "on the street, if you would pass him, he wouldn't see you although he would look you straight in the face," Willem Stevens remembers.

Caron's loyalty to Baker earned him a special friendship with the Firm's founder. He was one of Baker's staunchest allies, normally voting right down the line on Baker's proposals at Annual Meetings. Despite their being of the same mind on many issues, however, they were at opposite poles on the question of how Caron should run the Amsterdam office. The conservative Dutchman didn't want the Amsterdam office to grow, didn't want any interference from the Firm, and wanted to use his own name on the door. When Baker confronted Caron, the Dutchman cited bar rules that prevented him from using the Baker & McKenzie name and from openly becoming a partner with non-Dutch lawyers.

Caron's relationships with Baker and his Amsterdam partners were sometimes testy, but one partner had the political skills to stay on Caron's good side. Willem Stevens joined the office as an associate in 1965. He had attended the State Tax Academy in Rotterdam to train to be a tax inspector. Since the Tax Academy did not carry the same level of prestige as did a full university, Stevens also enrolled in law school at Leiden University, commuting the thirty miles from Rotterdam to Leiden several times a week to take his law school courses.

The young Dutchman did well, and he got a scholarship to study at Harvard for a masters of law degree. There, and at a part-time job with a large Boston law firm, he says, he had "this great exposure to the world." When Stevens looked at the rapidly growing U.S. law firms with fifty or sixty attorneys, he saw exciting possibilities. The American model looked even more attractive when he compared it with the two- and three-man "father and son" Dutch firms.

Back in Holland, Stevens fulfilled his military obligation by becoming an officer in a tank company. With hours to kill, the bored young man began contacting European Harvard Law School graduates to organize an alumni association, and found "in every city at least one guy from Baker & McKenzie." As his military service was ending, Stevens wrote to two Harvard graduates, Wallace Baker in Paris and Klaus Newes in Brussels, asking them for jobs. They wrote back suggesting that Stevens should have lunch with the Policy Committee at its Amsterdam meeting in June 1965, which he did. When he said that he wanted to join the Brussels or Paris office, the partners replied, "You may not know this, but we happen to have an office in Amsterdam. It would be with a certain Mr. Caron."

It must have galled Baker that, for eight years, Caron had so successfully concealed his office's affiliation with Baker & McKenzie. Nevertheless, Baker was interested in the young Dutchman, and jabbed question after question at him. Stevens must have given the right answers; Baker suggested that he interview with Caron. Because Stevens came to him through Baker, Caron was distant at first. With his highly sensitive political antennae, however, Stevens felt the tension and handled himself accordingly. Satisfied that Stevens wasn't Baker's spy, Caron offered the young man a job, which he accepted.

In the mid-1960s, the Amsterdam office grew, but slowly due to Caron's insistence on remaining small. Baker counted Caron as a close friend, but he also saw the Dutchman's conservative nature as a roadblock to the Amsterdam office's growth and its integration into "one Firm." Stevens recalls that "Russell was hitting Jimmy on the head for failing to build up the office. I felt that Russell was disappointed because Jimmy had not really done what he could have done with the assets available."

In the early 1970s, Baker pressured Caron to release the management reins. Although Caron was "very offended," he telexed a London partner: "I confirm that I have decided as senior partner of this office to turn over . . . the administration of the office day-to-day operations, work assignments and financial management to W.F.C. Stevens."

In that same year, 1972, the Dutch Bar Association approved the Amsterdam partners openly becoming full Baker & McKenzie partners. In a letter to Caron and Stevens, Baker enthused: "It gives me exquisite pleasure to enclose for your signatures the Articles of Partnership of Baker & McKenzie." In a separate letter to Stevens, Baker said, "I want you to realize that I understand your role in bringing about this signal result. I know that you will do everything you can to bring the Amsterdam office fully within the orbit of Baker & McKenzie. Our Netherlands office should be considerably larger, more vigorous, and more successful than any other office in the Firm. And I am positive that will be its destiny."

After Stevens took over management, the office concentrated on bringing in more lawyers with combined tax and commercial expertise. Albert van Herk's interests coincided exactly with those of the Amsterdam office. He had dual training, in civil law and as a tax advisor, but, because of bar restrictions in the mid-1970s, van Herk thought he would only be able to practice tax law. He met Stevens, however, and, when van Herk mentioned that there was no place where he could practice civil and tax law simultaneously, Stevens said: "Yes, you can. At Baker & McKenzie you can do both [because the office had official permission to hold itself out as being expert in both tax and civil law]."

The Firm offered him a job, but van Herk, somewhat of a free spirit, had one condition. "I never work on Fridays or weekends. " Amused, Stevens told Caron: "Just wait. He'll find out." The crush of business was so great that, within three months, van Herk was coming into the office on Fridays, and taking work home to do on Saturdays.

In addition to hiring new lawyers locally, the Amsterdam lawyers persuaded Gijsbert Loos to leave the Firm's New York office. When he joined the Amsterdam office in 1972, Loos became its sixth attorney.

Although Caron could be prickly, nobody questioned his interest in fostering international commerce. In recognition of his contributions to the Netherlands economy, Queen Beatrix bestowed a knighthood on him in the early 1980s. Caron's doctors offset that piece of good news when they told him that he had incurable cancer. During his final days, Firm lawyers scurried between the office and the hospital delivering legal documents for him to work on. In 1982, the seventy-one-year-old patriarch of the Amsterdam office died.

Amsterdam is an example of an office that has transitioned through several different management styles. Before 1972, Caron made all the decisions. After that, Stevens served as the Administrative Partner. During his tenure, there were few partners' meetings, but he stopped by partners' offices or chatted with them over lunch about the administrative matters he was considering. In 1978, Loos joined Stevens on a two-man management committee. Stevens gradually phased out of hands-on management, but Loos stayed as the Administrative Partner until 1986, when younger partners took over.

As more associates graduated to partnership, the office began holding regular partners' meetings at a small Amsterdam restaurant once a month. "Sometimes we had lots of drinks, and we had very heavy arguments where we shouted at each other," van Herk says. "Then, we would have another drink, and we would be friends again." Currently, a two-partner Management Committee administers the Amsterdam office, assisted by a staff of professional managers. As an additional administrative tool, the practice groups meet frequently for lunch. And a Consultation Board, composed of secretaries, trainees, staff, notaries, and translators, meets with the Management Committee each month regarding matters that affect them.

Even though Stevens had turned over management responsibilities to other partners years before, he did insert himself into a decision regarding the decoration of the main conference room. Stevens, who collects modern Dutch art, commissioned an artist to prepare a new work. The bas relief piece portrayed three naked women with voluptuous breasts jutting into the otherwise staid conference room. Loos, the son of a Dutch Reform minister, says "we didn't think it was very appropriate." After much debate, the partners reached a compromise; the artist came back and covered the protruding bosoms with decorous robes.

Although the Amsterdam office has made a conscious effort to diversify its areas of expertise, in the early 1980s the lawyers were swamped with its traditional staple—cross-border mergers, acquisitions, and tax work. The office began adding tax lawyers, and, in 1987, it persuaded an eight-lawyer tax firm to join. The next year, it brought in a small civil law notary firm.[1] In 1991, however, the office suffered a setback when its chief banking lawyer took five associates and joined another firm.

In the 1980s, many Dutch law firms were engaged in "merger mania." The Amsterdam office was tempted, and its partners seriously discussed mergers with large Dutch law firms as a way to grow. But, other than the small tax and notarial groups, "we did not really succeed in finding the right merger candidate," Loos says. "We have a particular culture within the office that makes a merger an extremely difficult thing to do. In Dutch law offices, everyone has his own little office and has his door closed. We generally work with open doors." Breaking with the traditional formalism of most Dutch law firms, in the Amsterdam office, Peter Dekker says, "we are very open. We are not required to wear jackets when we walk in the halls. It's always possible for juniors to go to a partner to ask questions. This is unique in Holland." The relaxed informality helps in recruiting young Dutch lawyers, and the romance of international law practice adds to the attraction. "We don't have to sell the Firm to prospective lawyers," Loos says. "People want to work in this Firm because it is an enjoyable environment."

To reinforce the Amsterdam office's culture, it holds two retreats a year. At the spring meeting, only partners go, but associates attend part of the fall meeting. The retreats are intended to get all partners reading from the same page, to let partners and associates air grievances, and to provide a leisurely setting where the lawyers can get to know one another socially. The Amsterdam office also sponsors an annual "cabaret," a dinner at which all new employees must sing, dance, and perform comedy skits, often aimed at partners. They make fun of Stevens's habit of looking over the other person's shoulder at parties to see who else is in the room. And Loos comes under fire for his tendency to sometimes be distracted or forgetful. When the partners have had disagreements over important matters, they have held "mending parties" at an elegant hotel outside Amsterdam. "It was an excellent place. Very quiet, superb food, beautiful rooms," van Herk says. "The relaxed atmosphere helps to create a good atmosphere so that we are able to talk again."

―――――――

Until the late 1970s, the Amsterdam lawyers kept a low profile in the Dutch legal and business communities. Since then, however, many Amsterdam partners have taken prominent roles in the community. They are active in the Civil Bar Association, the Tax Lawyers Association, and the Notarial Professional Organization. In 1991, Stevens was elected to the Dutch Senate, where he chaired the Tax Committee. And Queen Beatrix has awarded him the Royal Order of the Netherlands Lion, putting him in the company of the chief executives of many leading Dutch corporations. With an increased presence in the Dutch legal and business communities, the Amsterdam office has boosted its representation of home-grown clients to more than thirty percent of its business.

The overall collegial atmosphere has helped the Amsterdam office grow from two lawyers in 1957 to more than seventy in the 1990s, and its fee income from $78,000 in 1962 to $25 million in 1995. As the office grew, it expanded its range of expertise from the tax and corporate areas into labor, European Community, environmental, real estate, antitrust, banking, Far East, and intellectual property law.

―――――――

In 1957, the same year the Amsterdam office opened, Baker & McKenzie began operations in Washington, D.C. To start that office, Russell Baker chose Walter Slowinski, a man he first met in the early 1950s when they were both active with the U.S. Chamber of Commerce's Taxation and International Commerce Committees.

At the time he joined the Firm, Slowinski had been practicing law with a prestigious Washington, D.C. firm for almost ten years, and had developed a national reputation as a tax lawyer. In many ways, Slowinski was Baker's kind of man. Like Baker, he came from a humble background. The Polish immigrants' son put himself through school with a combination of scholarships and part-time jobs, graduating from Washington's Catholic University Law School in 1948.

Slowinski was a man with "unbelievable energy," who regularly arrived at the office at 7:30. When he first joined the Firm, Slowinski worked hard at his tax practice and at building up the Washington office. In the 1950s and 1960s, many U.S. corporations were organizing foreign subsidiaries and transferring assets to the non-U.S. entities. "It was not unusual for an American company with an old factory in the United States to bundle up its machinery and send it to Belgium," Jack Janetatos says. Sending the assets abroad was simple, but there was a catch. Unless the IRS approved the transfer, the company would be hit with a substantial tax. Under Slowinski's guidance, the Washington office became expert at getting IRS approvals of the asset transfers.

With his ebullient personality, *The Washingtonian Magazine* said, Slowinski could find a client in the Gobi Desert. Janetatos says "he was very sure of himself. He was always one hundred percent confident that he was giving the right answer. Clients would sense this confidence, and put their trust in it." Slowinski was so successful as a business developer that his Client Credit awards and Fund A points produced enough income so that he did not have to spend hours grinding out legal work. Increasingly, he worked at bringing clients in the door, and then turning them over to someone else.

To broadcast himself and the Firm, Slowinski was involved in public affairs. He served as the international tax counsel for the U.S. Chamber of Commerce, representing the Chamber at Congressional hearings on the 1962 Tax Reform Act. Slowinski's most effective promotional technique, however, was his speech-making. "He was magnificent," Janetatos says. In Washington, he spoke to top executives from across the U.S. about the latest tax developments. In New York, he regularly addressed the American Manufacturers' Association. In Los Angeles, he delivered tax lectures at the University of Southern California Law School. During a question-and-answer session after one of his speeches, an audience member asked Slowinski a complicated tax question. Rather than answer it, he told a story about how he had handled negotiations between General Motors and the Government of Japan. After Slowinski sat down, another tax lawyer on the panel whispered:

"Walter, you didn't really answer that fellow's question. Would you like for me to take a stab at it?"

"That would be a $10,000 answer if a client had asked it in the office," Slowinski snapped. "If you're dumb enough to answer it for free, go ahead." Shaken, the lawyer sat mute.

Always outgoing, Slowinski went almost daily to one of the three prestigious social clubs he belonged to: the Metropolitan Club, the Cosmos Club, and the 1925 F Street Club. In the early 1980s, the Cosmos Club, which boasts a long list of Nobel and Pulitzer Prize winners among its membership, elected Slowinski its president.

While Slowinski was working to build up a client base, he also spent substantial time searching out new lawyers for the Washington office. Michael Waris was one of his early recruits. Like Slowinski, Waris came from a working-class, Eastern European immigrant background. They were both short and pudgy, and both had open, gregarious personalities. Waris too was an excellent student, having won scholarships to the University of Pennsylvania's Wharton School of Commerce and Finance and then to its Law School. After graduation, Waris worked as a clerk for the Chief Judge of the U.S. Tax Court in Washington. About that time, he became friends with Slowinski. After they both married, the two remained in close contact, and Slowinski asked his good friend Waris to be his first son's godfather.

Slowinski continued in private practice and Waris in government at the U.S. Treasury, where he was working many nights and weekends for a modest salary. He confided to Slowinski: "Walter, I'm getting tired of this. Eighteen hours a day, seven days a week." A week later, Slowinski asked Waris to come to the office to discuss a job. Waris had an established reputation as a tax litigator, and part of the reason Slowinski was interested in him was that the Firm was handling a multi-million-dollar tax controversy for one of its most important clients. The Firm had a bright young tax lawyer in Washington, Thomas Haderlein, but he was only two years out of law school in 1962, and Slowinski had almost no tax litigation experience. Slowinski and Baker saw Waris as an experienced tax trial lawyer who could help them settle or try the suit.

"Russell Baker designated Mike to be one of the principal spear carriers in the tax case," William Outman says. Waris and Baker spent hours huddling to plan strategy, and this apparently was the cause of a bizarre estrangement that developed between Waris and Slowinski. In Slowinski's view, the line of communication should have run from Waris to him to Baker. Strangely insecure about his relationship with Baker, Slowinski thought "Mike was a turncoat, and had betrayed him," Haderlein says.

Partners have speculated on other theories as to why the relationship between the two old friends degenerated. But one thing is certain, when Slowinski got mad, he stayed mad. "He was like that joke about Irish Alzheimer's. 'They forget everything but the grudges,'" Outman says. With only rare exceptions, the two never spoke to one another for the next twenty-five years. The wall of silence, Waris says, was "irrational. It was emotional. I've heard of things like this happening to other people, but I never thought they would happen to me."

———

Slowinski recruited three graduates of Georgetown University Law School: John Creed, Thomas Haderlein, and Dennis Meyer, all three of whom later became Chairmen of the Firm. Several other lawyers came through Slowinski's friendship with a Georgetown tax law professor, Philip Ryan, who later became a Firm partner.

In his role as talent scout for the Firm, Ryan channeled Jack Janetatos to Slowinski in the mid-1960s. The son of a Greek immigrant father and a second-generation Polish mother, Janetatos had attended the U.S. Naval Academy. He spent five years in the Navy, most of it on submarines. After leaving the service, Janetatos attended Georgetown Law School. Ryan encouraged Janetatos to consider Baker & McKenzie. Nevertheless, he interviewed with other law firms. At one, he introduced himself to a receptionist. "Yes, you're the one with the funny name," she said. That comment, Janetatos says, led him to decide "that I belonged with Baker & McKenzie, where the senior partner in Washington was named Slowinski."

The year after Janetatos joined Baker & McKenzie, William Outman, who later became one of the office's top customs law experts, signed on as an associate in 1965. To broaden the office's practice into the trademark and patent fields, John J. Byrne joined the five-lawyer office in 1966. At the time, Byrne was already a well-known patent lawyer, and had been the President of the Washington Patent Lawyers' Club. To help Byrne build up the intellectual property practice, the Firm recruited Edward Dyson, a home-grown Washingtonian and a graduate of George Washington University Law School. At the Firm, he first worked for Byrne, and later moved into tax work and then into governmental regulation. Each time the U.S. came up with new laws affecting international trade, Dyson and others were among the country's first lawyers to become proficient in such arcane areas as the anti-boycott laws and the Foreign Corrupt Practices Act.

To expand its experience base further, the Washington office brought in Bruce Clubb to handle customs law and foreign trade regulations. Clubb, who was then a seasoned lawyer, had worked for two prominent Washington law firms and was just finishing a term as a Commissioner on the International Trade Commission. After he left the government, Clubb joined the nine-lawyer office as a partner in 1971.

———————

In the early days, Slowinski was clearly the Washington office's "major-domo," Byrne says. "Walter ran a pretty tight ship as far as wanting to know what everybody was doing." But, like Russell Baker, Slowinski was bored by administrative details. In the 1960s, he began delegating the tedious management duties to more junior men. Meyer was the first to take an active leadership role, with Dyson and Outman joining later. In the early 1970s, the office adopted a three-person management committee and began holding regular partners' meetings. As the Washington office grew larger, the committee, assisted by a full-time management staff, began handling most administrative issues.

When Slowinski retired, Meyer became the office's senior partner. Today, even though the partners treat Meyer, Outman, and Dyson with some deference, "there's a rather strong democratic process around here. Everybody's vote is considered to be important," Dyson says. And, Meyer adds, "nobody ever tries to muscle anybody else."

Strangely, Slowinski and Baker had engaged in a love-hate relationship that their partners found difficult to explain. The two never had direct confrontations. Rather, Slowinski, who instinctively wanted to be everybody's friend, sought Baker's favor, and almost always sided with Baker on Firm issues. There is no consensus as to why there was a certain tension between the two, but some partners conjecture that, because Slowinski had developed such a large client base himself, he may have been too independent for Baker's taste. In any event, Baker reminded him who the real senior partner was by "tweaking Walter's ego occasionally."

In addition to his strained relations with Baker and Waris, two other events adversely impacted Slowinski's personal life during the time when his career was at its zenith. In a widely publicized case, the Securities and Exchange Commission ("SEC") brought an action against an oil and gas tax shelter group, and included Slowinski and Janetatos among the many defendants. The SEC claimed that the pair had written a tax opinion that supported the fraudulent activities of several publicly-traded partnerships. By the time the U.S. Tax Court ruled several years later that the opinion was not fraudulent, the damage had already been done.

The second incident occurred during the Annual Meeting in 1976. A front-page newspaper article detailed how Slowinski had allegedly entangled himself in a conflict of interest by representing an aircraft company that was doing business with the CIA. When the CIA and the company got into an argument, Slowinski supposedly advised the company not to sue the CIA. The company later claimed that Slowinski "was either employed by or in direct communication with the CIA." Even though the company never brought suit, and Slowinski vehemently denied that he was a CIA collaborator, the story hurt. For a man as proud as Slowinski, the attack on his ethics was devastating. In 1986, he retired, and died shortly after that.

In the mid-1980s, the Washington partners had decided to accelerate their growth by hiring lateral partners "in areas that were synergistic to what we do,"

Dyson says. "That was one of the best strategic planning meetings we ever had. The bottom line was that we ought to grow." They brought in Leonard Terr from the Treasury Department, where he had been International Tax Counsel. Daniel Goelzer, the SEC's General Counsel, also joined the office. At the same time, Meyer, who had a national reputation as an international tax lawyer, committed to developing the office's tax practice even further. By the early 1990s, Washington had become the center of the Firm's U.S. tax practice.

In 1957, the year that six European nations signed the Treaty of Rome, the Baker & McKenzie partners voted to open a Firm office in Brussels. Before it became the European Community's capital city, it had been one of Europe's most conservative legal communities, with its monumental Palais de Justice symbolizing its ancient legal tradition. Built in the late 1800s, the Palais projects the law's grandeur and majesty. Under its colossal dome in the central hall, lawyers scurry over marble floors to confer with clients at tables and benches. After dealing with their clients and making their court appearances, the attorneys adjourn to their private preserve, the robing room, to take off their legal garb, long black robes, white bibs, and black scarves tipped with white fur.

Although the Belgian legal profession was steeped in antiquity, the designation of Brussels as the EC's governmental capital brought changes. Foreigners, fearing that the EC might raise trade barriers that would make imported products uncompetitive, raced to get into Europe. In addition to the fact that Brussels would become one of Europe's most important cities, the country had other attractions. Its central location made it a hub for trade and commerce. And the government offered incentives for new investors, including low taxes for foreign corporate executives and interest rate subsidies.

To open an office, Russell Baker found an American lawyer who had been a top U.S. State Department official with the Marshall Plan in Belgium. Thomas Coleman had served in the U.S. Air Force during World War II, and met and married a Belgian woman. The couple returned to the U.S. after the War so that Coleman could finish law school, but his wife didn't like America, so, after graduating, he returned to Brussels to work for the U.S. government. When the Marshall Plan ended in 1954, Coleman opened a law office by himself. Three years later, he met Baker, and agreed to open the office.

Four years after the Brussels office opened, Klaus Newes joined it. An Austrian Jew who escaped to the U.S. before World War II, Newes had spent his formative years in America, but he retained his European heritage. When the opportunity to join the Brussels office arose, he was delighted to be able to put his bicultural background to work. With two American partners, the Brussels office was "a little bit of America in Brussels." The office celebrated Thanksgiving Day, and, at their meetings, the partners often dined in the American style, on sandwiches and soft drinks.

As the office grew, it brought in several more lawyers. One of them was Otto Grolig, a native of the German-speaking region of Czechoslovakia, who became an associate in the late 1960s. When World War II broke out, Grolig's father fought with the German army, and was imprisoned by the Americans after it ended. During the post-War period, the Czechs deported German-speaking citizens and confiscated their property. The five-year-old Grolig, his mother, and four sisters, each with a single rucksack that contained all their possessions, were loaded on a cattle car and shipped to Germany. The itinerant family shuttled from Frankfurt to Bavaria to Vienna, and finally settled in Brussels, which "was the end of the odyssey that started with the deportation and the incredible turmoil," Grolig recalls.

In Brussels, Grolig's immigrant family had no money. His sisters found jobs as secretaries, and, at sixteen, he began waiting tables and singing and playing guitar in dance bands to help support his family. Although he had to work, he managed to get a law degree from the University of Leuven, and then did graduate work at Northwestern University in Chicago. When Grolig, the son of a German solider, returned to Brussels, he joined the office, where his mentor was Klaus Newes, the son of Austrian Jews.

In the early 1970s, the Brussels office suffered a shock. Within a three-month period, Coleman and Newes both died. When Baker received word that Coleman was close to death, he immediately went to Brussels. "Realizing that this visit was probably the last one, it was an emotional event for me," Baker wrote, "and I am sure for Tom as well. As for me, it was an especially sad one. I was there with Tom, both of us helpless in the face of the inevitable. We were in fact saying good-bye to each other. And we both knew it."

Later, Baker made a special trip to Belgium, telling the remaining lawyers that "clients are the most important thing. You have to get out there and don't let them get away." The Brussels partners contacted their local clients and toured the U.S. to assure them that the two deaths would not adversely affect the office's ability to do their work. Baker coordinated with the two remaining partners, Luc Hinnekens and Leon de Keyser, to help the transition go smoothly. And, to make sure that three key senior associates didn't bolt, Baker assured them that they would be made partners at the 1974 Annual Meeting.

By 1975, the Brussels office had six partners and gross revenues exceeding $1 million. With the growth came a need for a more organized administrative structure. Managing lawyers is a difficult enough task, but doing so in Belgium presents an additional twist. Since its creation in 1830, Belgium has had an internal problem stemming from linguistic, cultural, historical, and economic differences, which has sometimes created substantial rivalries between the French and Flemish. As Belgians often do, however, the Firm partners found a compromise. Ignace Maes says that "this cultural and linguistic division has never, ever played a role in the office. We use English at partner and associate meetings because it is the best language for people with different mother tongues." More recently, when the partners adopted a two-member management committee system, they elected Jacques Ghysbrecht, of French descent, and Luc Hinnekens, of Flemish background, to administer the Brussels office.

———————

In 1961, Russell Baker found an attorney to open a Mexico City office. Alberto A. Sepulveda was an established and well-respected Mexico City lawyer when he and two other attorneys joined the Firm. Later, Jorge Sánchez, one of the Boys of '60, moved from Chicago and became the office's fourth lawyer. When Sánchez got there, he soon learned that Sepulveda was in complete charge. The office's accounting department, Sánchez says, was located in the bottom drawer of the senior partner's desk. When he wrote a check, he opened the drawer, got out his account book, and scribbled the amount of the check.

Because Sánchez, a Guatemalan, had spent so much time in Chicago, Sepulveda thought he was one of "Russell's boys," and viewed him as an intruder whose loyalties lay in Chicago. "Alberto resisted my coming down," Sánchez says. "He didn't resist me personally. But just the whole idea of the Firm coming in to take over his practice. I was supposed to be there for a year only. And, at the end of the year, Alberto was hemming and hawing that he didn't know how I could stay on. Russell came down to visit three times during the year, and he squeezed Alberto." Sánchez spent the next thirty years in the Mexico City office.

Even though Sepulveda and Sánchez got off to a rocky start, when the younger man ran afoul of an American client, Sepulveda gave his junior partner his full support. The client, Sánchez says, "was very difficult, very arrogant." Sánchez had written the client a letter advising him on problems related to organizing a Mexican subsidiary, and he wrote back to Sepulveda, saying that he wanted an opinion from an American lawyer, and that he didn't want to deal with a "native" lawyer. "Alberto went through the ceiling," Sánchez says, "and said we wouldn't handle this client in our office." Sepulveda made a special trip to Chicago to tell Baker that he wouldn't represent the client. Baker agreed, and the Firm fired the client.

One reason the Mexico City office could so easily fire a client was that the decade between 1962 and 1973 was "the golden age" of Mexican economic growth. By 1966, the office needed more help, and recruited a Mexican national, Carlos Grimm, to transfer from the Washington office to Mexico City. Grimm became one of three associates who worked for the four partners. The Mexico City office expanded rapidly, representing mostly foreign investors. In the late 1970s and early 1980s, much of its work consisted of preparing loan documents for the surge of bank lending in Mexico. But this glut of lending eventually led to a collapse of Mexico's economic system. The peso plummeted. Many companies defaulted on their loans. Capital fled, and the government imposed exchange controls. Things were so bad that Mexico's Treasury Secretary told the country's foreign lenders that it couldn't pay its $60 billion debt to them.

With the nation virtually bankrupt, many lawyers in the Firm's Mexico City office were short of work. Between 1985 and 1986, revenues slumped fifteen percent. The Mexican economy remained prostrate for several years, during which time the office was also suffering a cultural crisis. In the mid-1980s in Mexico City, six of the lawyers' last names were Sepulveda. Some non-family members believed that Alberto J. Sepulveda[2] thought that, because his father had founded the Mexico City office, the family had additional status. Many Mexico City partners became increasingly insistent that things needed to change. Using the Firm's understated form of communication among partners, which some called "Baker & McKenzie-speak," Sánchez reported to the Executive Committee that Sepulveda's "personal ideas for his professional practice, which includes very importantly the concept of a family firm, are circumscribed by our structure in which decision making is necessarily shared with all partners." More bluntly, Grimm says that Sepulveda's view of giving "certain preference for family members was not workable, and didn't make any sense in the light of a business which was competing with other major institutional firms." Sepulveda resigned in 1985.

While the focus of attention was on Sepulveda for several years, another problem was brewing under the surface. A few senior partners who had each accrued over twenty Fund A points were also reaping the benefit of the Mexico City office having a high ratio of associates to partners. This imbalance generated a large Associate Profit for the Mexico City office. Because the office's partners divided Associate Profit in equal shares, admitting new partners would dilute the amount the existing partners got. With money flowing in from Fund A and Associate Profit, a few senior partners were able to have comfortable incomes without working too hard.

To preserve their sinecures, the older group had violated one of Russell Baker's fundamental principles—that older partners shouldn't exploit their juniors. When associates came up for election to partnership, the older group vetoed them. Although the situation had existed for several years, the Mexico City partners refused to confront the issue. "They let it simmer," says Robert Cox, who was then the Chairman. "As younger people were coming up, it became more focused that some partners weren't carrying their load, and were taking out more money than they should. Then the confrontation became emotional. One day, it just exploded, and people walked out."

Several of the brightest associates, nicknamed the "Golden Boys," left the Firm. "Some of them wanted to stay," Cox says, "but it had gone too far. Words had been spoken in very heated terms." Losing the large group of key young people "kind of gutted the office." But their departures served notice on the global Firm that letting the situation continue would jeopardize the Mexico City office. Several of the senior men who had blocked the associates' upward mobility were long-term partners and had many close friends in the partnership. But the Executive Committee decided that taking no action was too big a price to pay. Cox says he followed a policy of "assuring fair treatment under the Articles and a separation with dignity. I understood that they were not putting their shoulder to the wheel, but it didn't make them bad guys." The Firm negotiated a mutually acceptable settlement, and three Mexico City senior partners retired in the early 1990s.

Despite the troubles in the Mexico City office, it sponsored satellite offices that opened in Juarez and Tijuana in 1986 to service clients operating *maquiladora* plants along the U.S.-Mexican border. In 1992, the Monterrey office opened to service both local and non-Mexican clients operating in that significant industrial city. With the Mexico City office righting its own ship and the resurgence of the Mexican economy, the Mexican offices have been profitable. Although the northern offices in Juarez, Tijuana, and Monterrey are now economically independent from Mexico City under the Formula, the total Mexican office revenues for the four Mexican offices exceeded $16 million in 1995.

Chapter Twelve

The Fight for Control

As the Firm headed into the late 1960s, Russell Baker was in his late sixties, and, William Gibbons says, "he became less sure of himself." At the same time that their leader was aging, the Boys of '60 were developing an appetite for more voice in Firm affairs. Two groups made up the opposition. The majority were seeking changes, but they had no interest in challenging Baker. Rather, they had bought into Baker's dream, and they wanted to add their contributions to it. A second group, however, coveted the throne.

Since 1949, Baker had sat firmly in Baker & McKenzie's first chair. Many elements contributed to his status. The Firm's founder was a generation older than most of the partners. Although he had once told Gibbons that the thing that had decimated other law firms was "the dead hand of an old man," Baker found it difficult to step back from the institution he had created and zealously promoted. In addition to being their elder, Gibbons says, "he was a leader because he was charismatic—a dynamic individual who had the power to convince people of the rightness of his point of view. He led in the sense that people respected and liked him."

There were other reasons for Baker's compelling presence. He had brought in a large percentage of the Firm's clients, and had hired most of the lawyers. More importantly, the partners trusted his judgment. "Of course, he had a bit of an iron hand," Carlos Grimm says. "But I felt confident that Russell wouldn't make too many mistakes. If there is any one man that I felt was the guiding light, the formidable spirit of this law firm from day one, it was Russell Baker."

Even though he had power and prestige, the only official title Baker ever took was Chairman of the Policy Committee, and he was never a "visible dictator, but more of a persuader." That leadership style confused some partners. "The normal control of a law firm would be to set up a hierarchy, where you have your senior partners exercising a degree of control," Terence Lane says. "Russell Baker didn't attempt to do anything like that. He wanted to exercise control by other means."

Even though Baker seldom used overt coercion, as the Firm moved into the late 1960s, its senior partner's control turned from a gnawing background problem into a front-and-center issue. To a degree, Baker had created his own problem. He had enlisted aggressive, entrepreneurial people. He had preached one man, one vote and that the partners should let their ambitions take them as far as they could go. All that said, "having set up the democracy, he still wanted the Firm to dance to his tune," Peter Bentley says. "He was always *primus inter pares*." The political infighting became so highly charged, Thomas Haderlein says, "that many decisions were being made because of who was for it and who was against it, as opposed to whether it was a good idea."

By the year Baker turned seventy, 1971, the young Turks were agitating for more say-so in deciding the Firm's future. The contending parties began drawing lines. One of the opposition's most outspoken members, Ira Wender, had grown up in an affluent New York City suburb. A brilliant student, his elementary and secondary schools double-promoted him three times. He graduated from the University of Chicago Law School at twenty-one, and earned a masters in taxation from New York University Law School. Wender practiced law for a while, and then worked at Harvard Law School's International Program in Taxation, where he co-authored a book on *Foreign Investment and Taxation.* "I decided that I really wasn't an academic guy," Wender says, and he returned to New York to practice law and to teach tax law part-time at NYU.

Wender showed up on Baker's radar screen through his writings and through their having a client in common. At the time, the Firm's Western Hemisphere Trade Corporation and Foreign Base Company business was booming, and it desperately needed all the tax expertise it could get. With no Firm lawyer who had a tax law pedigree that came close to Wender's, Baker invited him to Chicago in 1958 for an interview. He described the Firm's seven offices and forty lawyers around the world, and offered an immediate partnership. Intrigued, Wender accepted.

Wender was a man with a "very high level of intellect," Peter Lederer says. "He had an imaginative, creative mind, and a great deal of personal charm." Gijsbert Loos adds that the New Yorker was "very smart. He was different from many other tax lawyers because he was a very good communicator." And Donald Baker says that "Wender spoke with authority and people listened to him. He was extremely ambitious, and felt like he was a better lawyer than any of the other lawyers. He may have been right." Despite his intellect, Wender carried historical baggage that put him at cross-purposes with Baker. Lederer recalls that "Ira spoke to almost everybody about the story of his life and the fact that he expressly recognized that Russell represented a father figure, and that he didn't much like that."

"Ira and Russell did not hit it off," Gibbons says. "He described Russell as a Midwestern hick and bumbler, a dumb trial lawyer with a big mouth and a small brain. It was a battle of intellectual snobbery." Lederer, one of Wender's supporters, admits that "we probably were, to a degree, snobs. We had come from law schools that were top-tier schools. We were all either law review or had other academic credentials of merit. We had standards for who ought to be a member of the partnership that were radically different from Russell's."

Wender was also quick to criticize and quick to make it known. Not long after he joined the Firm, he says he determined "there was clearly a need for my tax expertise, because, frankly, people there at the Firm weren't particularly good tax lawyers. They were not the top caliber or quality. Russell didn't really have a sense of quality about legal work. He was enamored with the internationalization of law practice. Russell was really more interested in people speaking more foreign languages than focusing on quality. I guess I was young and arrogant enough to believe that I could change that."

The Wender faction had the specialist's disdain for the generalist, and maintained that only highly trained lawyers should work in a particular discipline. They claimed that Baker sent work to lawyers based more on their political correctness than on technical expertise. "If you didn't get juicy things to work on," Wender says, "you didn't make much money and, therefore, it paid to toe the mark." Lane, a close Wender friend, adds: "Because Russell used his ability to allocate work according to his preferences, and in order to exert influence, the person selected to do the work was not always the best lawyer in the Firm."

The Wender group also felt that Baker was not discriminating enough when it came to electing partners. "Russell Baker would make anybody a partner within ten minutes if it served his purpose at the time," Wender says. Thomas Bridgman counters that "the Wender clique didn't want any of Russell's boys in here as partners, or anyone who looked like one of Russell's boys." Wender complained that the Formula encouraged people "to hog good work and precluded matching the best people at the Firm for the project." In essence, the Wender group objected to many of the Firm's most basic philosophical building blocks.

Ironically, Wender had left an authoritarian law firm to join Baker & McKenzie. Despite this background, Wulf Döser says, "the Wender group wanted to organize the Firm along the lines of the typical Wall Street firms. They thought that they were cleverer and smarter than the country boys in Chicago. And they wanted to get rid of super father Russell's divination of how the Firm should grow." Baker, Döser continues, "was fundamentally opposed to the Wall Street system of hierarchy. Of lockstep. Of making it a gamble or lottery of whether the young people would become partners or not."

Baker and Wender also clashed stylistically. Baker had worked his way up from the bottom of the Western social and economic heaps. Wender was born and grew up at or near the top of both—in the East. "Wender was very conversant with the ways and means of East Coast culture," Robert Hudson says. "He had an apartment on the Upper East Side in New York that looked like something out of *Architectural Digest*."

When Baker heard rumors that his detractors were deriding his rural background, his folksy manners, and his earthy language, he became even more combative. During the twelve years that Wender spent at the Firm, the two strong-willed men became embroiled in numerous arguments, many of which were couched in policy or philosophical terms. But the nub of their conflict was that they both wanted the same thing—intellectual control of the Firm. "It was clear that Russell saw Ira Wender as someone who was in competition with him, and not as someone who worked with him," Roger Quinnan says. One of Wender's most vocal supporters, Norman Miller, agrees that "Ira wanted to run Baker & McKenzie. He was a better lawyer than Russell, but he was not better in terms of knowing how to shape and manipulate the Firm."

Because of the bad blood, Wender moved to the New York office in 1961, but the two continued tilting at one another. Wender says he went to New York because he didn't like Chicago and was uncomfortable there. Probably, he says, "Russell was happy to get me out of Chicago." In a letter to Eric Homburger, Baker expressed his frustration: "I would rather have a firm half the size that this one has grown to be, and be associated with friendly, generous, non-aggressive people with whom I want to work, and who want to work with me, than to carry on as in the past." But the past kept repeating itself.

Although the two men were wily politicians, neither of them could kill off the other. If Wender had tried to stage a coup d'état against the much-respected senior partner, he would have had no chance. Because of the "all save four" rule, Baker couldn't expel Wender. Since neither Baker nor Wender could force out the other, the power struggle revolved around who controlled committee appointments, whose policies the Firm adopted, and who became a partner.

The first serious blow-up occurred at the 1961 Annual Meeting over a French lawyer the Firm had hired in 1960. The clear agreement with the Frenchman was that he would initially work in the Chicago office, and, when the partners decided to open a Paris office, he would transfer there. What wasn't clear was whether the Frenchman had entered the Firm as a partner or an associate.

The Frenchman's major problem was that Baker disliked him, perhaps because he had pledged allegiance to the Wender faction. Baker and the Frenchman argued over Baker's giving French work to a lawyer who was not admitted to practice in France. On another occasion, Baker introduced the Frenchman to a client, and told him that they would jointly handle the work. When Baker heard nothing more from the client or the Frenchman, he suspected that the younger man had attempted to exclude him. Baker also criticized the Frenchman's abilities as a lawyer, and claimed that he wouldn't fit into the Firm's family atmosphere.

While Baker and others were berating the French lawyer, Wender's group was extolling his virtues. Finally, Baker let it be known that he believed that the Frenchman was an associate and that he wanted him fired. The Wender faction countered that he was a partner and that he could be ejected only by a super majority partner vote. If the Wender group was right, they could block the dismissal. But, if he was an associate, a simple majority could fire him.

At the 1961 Annual Meeting in the faux-gothic confines of Chicago's University Club, the fight created an "extreme degree of bitterness." The argument was the first public show of Baker's and Wender's mutual aversion, and it was the first time that partners had openly hurled such vitriolic barbs at one another. John McKenzie assembled evidence and prepared a brief arguing that the French lawyer was not a partner. During the debate, a memorandum surfaced that referred to the Frenchman as an associate. Later, the Wender group produced a copy of the same memorandum that referred to him as a partner. Some claimed that Baker himself had perpetrated the forgery, and others alleged that McKenzie had done it. Baker's supporters fired back that he was being "framed," and that the Frenchman himself had altered the memo.

"At that point," Lane says, "everything blew up. Russell Baker was asked to leave the meeting, which he did. The partnership very nearly split at that point. It went on until three or four o'clock in the morning." Finally, the two sides compromised: they agreed to treat the Frenchman as an associate, which meant that he was dismissed, and to give him a generous severance bonus.

Still, the matter wasn't over. Stung by the charges of lying and forgery, Baker asked for a vote of confidence in which each partner would publicly state whether they agreed with the allegations against him. "You had men who were almost in tears," one partner recalls. During the vote, Baker sat pokerfaced. When the overwhelming majority said they thought Baker hadn't lied or forged, he called for an adjournment. "We'll come back this evening, and I'll tell you guys whether or not you still have a Firm," he said. Then he walked out. When the meeting resumed, Baker announced his decision: he would not destroy his own Firm.

The meeting, with its harsh recriminations, started an "era of bad feelings" because so many partners had said things that couldn't be forgotten or forgiven.

"That partnership meeting," Lederer says, "and the feelings that existed in the aftermath, did more to polarize relationships than any other factor that I know of." For the next ten years, a pall of tension covered almost all of the Firm's internal affairs. As a reminder of the mistrust generated at the 1961 meeting, for several years afterward the Firm brought court reporters to Annual Meetings to transcribe every word that was said. "Our meetings were tempestuous. It was very tough," Gibbons recalls. Even though Wender lost the battle over the Frenchman, the fight established him as a man who would stand up to Baker. It also made Wender the lightning rod—the leader of the partners who wanted to break Baker's grip on the Firm.

Just as the first major Baker-versus-Wender conflict erupted over an individual, so did the second. In the mid-1960s, Ramon Diaz was asserting what he viewed as his patrimonial rights over the Caracas office.

A political ultra-conservative, Diaz sent each of his partners a copy of the novel *Atlas Shrugged,* which glorifies anarchic individualism. Due in part to Diaz's "Napoleonistic" bent, another Caracas partner, Malcolm Caplan, was becoming increasingly unhappy. Although he was a junior partner, Caplan had made himself economically independent under the Formula by representing many of the Caracas office's American clients, while Diaz's major client was one of Venezuela's largest industrial groups. Because each lawyer had his own stable of clients, neither could intimidate the other.

Since the Firm had no written rules on who should be the head of an office, Caplan and the office's other partner, Gilberto Delgado, started a campaign to choose the office's leader by vote rather than by fiat. When the Caracas partners voted, Delgado got two of the three votes. Diaz refused to recognize the decision, and appealed it to a special Policy Committee meeting in 1965.

"That was one hell of a meeting," Bridgman says. "It was an oblique challenge to Russell's authority. Diaz wanted to run the Caracas office the way he wanted to run it, and was very upset with Malcolm Caplan, and was not going to let the Firm tell him what to do."

In the past, Diaz had had brushes with Baker. They clashed at one Firm meeting when Baker proposed that, as he had done on several occasions, partners who earned over $100,000 should either leave the excess in the Firm as capital or have it redistributed to partners who were at the low end of the pay scale. Diaz leapt to his feet to oppose Baker's motion, pointing out that the Articles of Partnership and the Formula were a contract that couldn't be broken. "Ramon said that this was pure Communism," Lederer remembers, "and that he had every intention of making $1,000,000 a year, and he intended to keep every penny of it." Being labeled a Communist was not, in Baker's eyes, Diaz's most heinous crime. He had aligned himself with the Wender faction.

At the special Policy Committee meeting, Diaz threatened that, unless the Firm fired Caplan, he would leave. Baker took the floor to deliver a dramatic speech to his partners. He described the Diaz-Caplan conflict as being "just like a Greek tragedy. You can see the actions of the actors. And they are inevitably leading to their own death or destruction—but they nevertheless continue," Michael Waris recalls. After a rancorous debate, with Baker supporting Caplan, the partners ratified the Caracas office's vote, making Delgado head of the office. Diaz resigned.

———

With Diaz gone, Baker and Wender continued their feuds over specific policy questions, but control was always at the core. "Ira was flexing his muscles to have more authority in the Firm. He wanted more opportunity to make management decisions," Patricia Beal says. "He felt that the real decisions were being made by Russell and Lajos [Schmidt]—with some validity."

The final showdown between Baker and Wender grew out of a dispute over yet another individual—a quiet, unassuming Japanese-American lawyer. Jiro Murase was born in the U.S., where his father was a leader in New York's Japanese community. Wanting his son to speak faultless Japanese and to learn Japanese customs, Murase's father sent the boy to school in Japan in the late 1930s. When World War II broke out, Murase stayed in Japan and finished secondary school there. After the War ended, he returned to the U.S., went to college, and got a law degree. As a result of his upbringing in two countries, Murase was not only bilingual but also totally bicultural.

During the late 1950s and early 1960s, Japan was not a significant player in the world economy. Many Westerners scoffed at Japanese products, calling them cheap and shoddy, and Western lawyers paid even less attention to attracting Japanese business. But Murase cultivated a large Japanese clientele. Murase, Thomas Haderlein says, "was one of the most successful promoters of Japanese business in the U.S."

In the early 1960s, Murase left another law firm to join Baker & McKenzie's New York office. Normally, Baker would have been delighted with a lawyer like Murase. He spoke two languages, understood two cultures, and knew the laws of two countries. But Murase had unwittingly taken a desk in the heart of enemy territory. Not only was he in the wrong place, he had inadvertently invaded Baker's Asian domain.

"Before Murase joined the Firm, Russell had taken on Japan as his own pet project," Dennis Meyer says. "Jiro knew more about the inner workings of Japan than Russell did. If they had gotten together and sung the same song, we would have had a hell of a Tokyo office long before we had. He and Russell just did not coordinate in the development of the Japan practice. Murase wanted to be the developer. But Russell had spent so much time on Japan that he was unwilling to give that up and abdicate to Murase." Baker made it clear that the Tokyo office and the Japanese investment flowing to the U.S. were his turf and that Chicago would be the U.S. headquarters of the Firm's Japan practice.

To staff the Japan team in Chicago, Baker hired a young Japanese-American lawyer, Hoken Seki. Beal says that Baker championed Seki as part of his plan "to divert the Japanese practice from New York to Chicago because Jiro was helping to build Ira's empire, and Russell felt threatened by Ira." But, Murase could argue that many more Japanese corporations chose to open branches in New York than Chicago. And, with Murase's years of experience representing major Japanese companies, it appeared logical that the Firm's Japan practice should be located with him in New York.

Murase apparently had a low opinion of the Tokyo office's Japanese lawyers, in part because they hadn't graduated from top universities. He once told John Byrne that, if he tried to convince his Japanese clients to use the Tokyo office's Japanese lawyers, "I'd lose all my face with them. I'd lose my clients." He wanted to staff the Tokyo office with lawyers who were in the Japanese old-boy network, graduates of prestigious institutions like Tokyo University. Murase also objected to the non-Japanese lawyers who worked in the Tokyo office.

Given the antipathy between the Japanese specialist, Murase, and the amateur, Baker, and the astringent Baker-Wender political climate, a clash was inevitable. Eventually, Murase broke one of Baker's cardinal rules. When Baker learned that Murase was flying to Japan, working directly with his Japanese clients, and not involving the Tokyo office, he was furious. Baker had other complaints, including the fact that Murase was sending legal work to an outside lawyer.

Baker was not without a remedy. As the time approached for the partners to vote on whether to elevate Murase from Income to Capital Partner, Baker assembled enough votes to block the promotion at the 1967 Annual Meeting. "We in New York felt a strong loyalty to Jiro, and we were outraged by opposition that we felt was ill-founded," Lederer says

After Murase was voted down, the New York partners retaliated by using the "all save four" rule to stop the election of all the other Capital Partner candidates. Wender and Lederer had proxies from New York partners to give them enough blocking votes. "That was the infamous year when no Capital Partners were elected," Lederer says. "It strikes me as childishly funny now. But it sure as hell didn't feel funny standing up and voting no. It left a lot of people pissed-off at us for a couple of years."

Although Baker held back Murase's advancement, he was still not happy with the Japan practice. In a 1970 letter to Michael Waris, Baker wrote: "The sole purpose of my intense interest in Japan is to establish in that country a practice in Japanese-American law which belongs to our partnership as a whole, and which is in fact and in truth a part of Baker & McKenzie. While that goal is a long distance away, I am, nevertheless, conscious of the fact that we are making progress."

In the winter of 1970–1971, another event further poisoned the atmosphere. As part of the American government's campaign to protect its industry from alleged predatory practices by Japanese corporations, the U.S. filed an antitrust suit against seven Japanese television set manufacturers. Baker represented one of the Japanese companies and Murase another. At first, there was no problem because the seven companies decided to adopt a uniform strategy on the case's major issues. But Baker's client broke ranks with the other six television makers and decided to follow an independent course.

The other six were incensed that Baker's client was going down its own path. "There was warfare," Wender says, "over the fact that Baker & McKenzie couldn't represent both defendants, when one was taking an action which was adverse to the interests of another client. Baker was determined to represent his client, and wanted to drive Murase and his client out." Baker argued that the Firm should represent only his client because it had been with the Firm longer than Murase's client. And, Baker pointed out, he had more antitrust experience, having tried several cases to judgment. When Murase resisted, it reinforced Baker's perception that Murase was not a team player.

Baker was already irate over the antitrust suit when he heard a rumor that Murase had told executives of Baker's Japanese client that some of the Firm lawyers who would be working on the antitrust case were not competent. The allegation that Murase was denigrating Firm lawyers to clients brought Baker to his flash point. Certain Chicago partners said that Murase's actions were "so unpartnerly and outrageous that he should be asked to resign from the Firm. And, if unwilling to resign, he should be expelled." Murase denied making the statements, and the New York partners took his side because "here was our guy being attacked once again."

The partners, at Baker's behest, created a fact-finding committee composed of Baker, John Connor, and Dennis Meyer to go to Tokyo to investigate the charges against Murase. Their report was inconclusive. "We went through the thing and didn't come away with anything," Meyer says. Despite the inability to definitively confirm Murase's guilt, Baker pressed his case. He insisted on bringing charges against Murase at the April 1971 Policy Committee meeting.

The "trial" took place in Paris at the Ritz Hotel, "a fancy venue to have a fancy fight." The meeting broke every Japanese rule related to conducting business in a harmonious way. Robert Cox, then a New York junior partner, recalls that "it was a bewildering experience to watch this take place. It was an attempt by Russell to bring Jiro to his knees." Wender and Lederer acted as Murase's primary defense counsel, and Baker loyalists presented the case that Murase had done things that were harmful and destructive to the Firm.

Baker's faction made a motion that Murase be expelled. It failed. As tempers flared, Gibbons and a New York partner almost got into a fist fight. The wrangling went on for hours. But, with the fact-finding committee's ambivalent report and Murase's categorical denial that he had spoken ill of his partners, the Policy Committee adopted a resolution of full confidence in Murase. The Committee also directed that Murase "be fully consulted and given a meaningful voice in all policy matters dealing with the conduct and staffing of the Tokyo office."

———

Although Murase and the Wender faction had won the day, emotions were too raw. After the meeting ended, Wender told Haderlein that he had decided to resign, and indicated that he planned to take as many of the New York lawyers with him as he could. When the New York partners returned home, the tug-of-war over who would stay and who would leave began.

Wender told Cox that he was departing with several other New York partners, including Murase, to form their own firm. He also indicated that he had been in touch with partners from other offices, including Mexico City and London, and that some of them might defect. Cox felt significant loyalty to Wender because he had hired him. And, he knew, the Wender group would take a large portion of the client work with them, possibly leaving the loyalists without enough work to make themselves profitable under the Formula.

To stem the tide of defections, Baker, Dennis Meyer, and other partners called to lobby the lawyers to stay. Meyer called Cox frequently, pointing out that several of the defectors had difficult personalities. He also reminded Cox that Wender was spending substantial time working for clients in an executive capacity rather than practicing law. Given this, Meyer questioned, how would Wender find time to build up a new law firm? Cox brooded on his decision. "It was a tumultuous, emotional time," he remembers. He concluded that, despite his high regard for Wender, "I had really come to join a firm called Baker & McKenzie."

The Baker & McKenzie loyalists wound up with about two-thirds of the lawyers, but only about one-third of the work. Wender, Bridgman speculates, felt that more lawyers would go with him, but he was "too far down the road and too committed to back off. He didn't have all his ducks in a row. He thought everybody was going to follow him out the door en masse."

Still, the departures were "a heavy blow, and I'm not sure we ever overcame that blow in New York," Döser says. In addition to damaging the New York office, the Murase affair signaled the first real crack in Baker's power. The Policy Committee's refusal to censure Murase emboldened some of the younger partners to consider challenging their septuagenarian leader. Despite his age, however, he was still formidable. Baker nominated every member of every committee, "and they never failed to get elected," Haderlein says. "No one challenged that. He was Russell Baker!" The larger clients and their chief executives still wanted his counsel on important matters. Although his reputation as the godfather of international law solidified his position, his most powerful asset was the respect his partners had for him. Even Lane, who fought him bitterly and openly disliked him, says, "He was not the sort of person I would enjoy having a drink with. Still, I admired him. He was a very, very farsighted man." And Haderlein, who crossed swords with Baker on occasion, adds, "I don't think there was a partner in the Firm who didn't respect him. You might disagree with him, but you surely respected him."

Beginning in the early 1970s, some of the younger partners, almost all veteran Boys of '60, questioned whether Baker's time had come and gone. Many of them were tired of the Wender-Baker and Lane-Baker feuds, and simply wanted the internal strife to go away so they could concentrate on building the Firm. Most of them tried to remain neutral, and did their best to "dampen down the power struggle to keep it from developing into a split," Donald Baker says. They began clamoring for the "old guys to stop hamstringing the Firm's growth," Haderlein recalls. "It was time to take that old bickering generation and move them aside, and to say to both Baker and his opponents: 'A plague on both of your houses.'"

After the trauma of the Murase trial, several Boys of '60 "decided that enough was enough." In the summer of 1971, a group of Chicago partners formed what was eventually called "The Breakfast Club," which usually met once a month at Chicago's University Club.[1] They intended it to be a Shadow Cabinet that would "offset the irrational things" that were going on in the Firm. The most active members were in Chicago, but many partners around the world participated by phone and telex. "We younger partners all grew up together as associates," Haderlein says. "We could all talk to each other. We were in roughly the same age bracket. And we had a lot of career left in this Firm. We wanted to take destiny in our own hands and to keep the old men from running the place into the ground." Club members didn't view themselves as rabble-rousers, but as a corps of younger lawyers who were very interested in the Firm and its approach to management, new offices, and other issues.

In their first move, the Breakfast Club's Chicago members seized control of a bastion of Baker's power, the Chicago Office Committee ("COC"). "We had the majority of votes in the Chicago office," Haderlein says. With their slate of candidates seated on the COC, the Breakfast Club set its sights on deposing Baker's ally, Lajos Schmidt, as the Chairman of the Executive Committee. Their candidate was Michel Coccia. Not wanting to ruffle Baker unnecessarily, they picked a man who had been a Baker stalwart for years, but one they knew would not buckle under Baker's pressure.

The Breakfast Club began a covert lobbying campaign, lining up votes from Frankfurt, São Paulo, and elsewhere. They crafted their argument to replace Schmidt so that even Baker couldn't disagree with them. His surrogate had been in office five years, violating a cherished Baker principle—that managers who had a perpetual lock on their jobs were dangerous. He had preached his suspicion of "empire builders" to his partners for years, and now they used it to box him in. Schmidt's opponents, Bridgman recalls, "were smart enough not to make it an individual or personal thing. Instead, we argued that we might lose the Firm's democratic principle."

The confrontation took place at the New York Policy Committee meeting in September 1971. "The minute that issue became an agenda item, the war had been declared," Patricia Beal says. "Russell scrambled behind the scenes, and tried to fight the good fight." Although Baker had hand-picked many of the Policy Committee members, the Breakfast Club counted on the "enormous amount of unrest in the Firm" as an ally. They were confident they could muster the necessary votes to oust Schmidt, but they still worried that Baker might bring his legendary wrath down on those who voted against him. They engineered the adoption of a resolution "that a secret vote be taken on the question of whether Lajos Schmidt should be asked to serve as a member of the Executive Committee for the ensuing year in light of the fact that he has served for five years." After the secret ballot, Schmidt was out and Coccia was in. "That was the beginning of the realization that change had to come," Beal says. But for those partners who thought that Baker's power was waning, he would remind them that his weight was still considerable.

Coccia, the Breakfast Club's nominee, was the son of immigrants—a French school teacher and a Sicilian tailor who settled in Chicago. When he graduated in 1951 from John Marshall Law School, family friends in Chicago's French community introduced him to the Firm. At the office, he met Russell Baker, John McKenzie, and the four other Firm lawyers. Baker was intrigued by Coccia's French-Italian background and his fluency in French. Baker, in turn, impressed Coccia with "his imagination and perception and belief in a law firm that could do so many things for a client, both domestically and internationally."

Until his election as Chairman, Coccia had been a close Baker ally. But being elected on a "break Russell's control" platform strained the relationship. It became worse when Coccia veered away from Baker. "I wasn't going to be Russell's stooge," Coccia says. Instead of choosing Baker as his chief advisor, Coccia often consulted with other partners. Bridgman suspected that one or more partners told Coccia to "be your own man, and don't listen to the old man. You run it the way you want to run it." Bridgman adds, "I think Mike believed it, and went to the opposite extreme and almost ignored Russell. That was a big mistake."

On one occasion, Baker called Coccia and said he wanted to talk to him. Rather than pay the normal obeisance by going to Baker's office, Coccia told Baker to come to his office. In addition to trivial signs of rebellion, Coccia disagreed with Baker on a number of policy issues. When Bridgman saw Coccia overtly demonstrating his independence, he told him, "You gotta be crazy. The guy is the senior partner of this law firm, the father of this law firm. You have to talk to him." Coccia responded: "He's not going to tell me what to do."

The new Chairman of the Executive Committee went on Baker's "enemies list." Baker laid plans to oust him as Chairman at the 1972 Zürich Annual Meeting. He knew that he could count on his prestige and a storehouse of personal affection to win most partners to his camp. He also knew that many partners who privately disagreed with him would vote his way out of a strong sense of loyalty. One of them, Alberto de Libero, expressed to Baker a sentiment that many partners felt: "I have always regarded you, and I will always regard you, as a second father; I will never forget what you have done for me and the Firm, and my allegiance will always be to you. There might be occasions when I will disagree with you, but it will always be on a specific issue, and I will tell you about it. It will never happen that I will side with your opponents regardless of the issue at stake, only to defeat you."

Knowing that Baker wanted Coccia out as Chairman, the partners did not renominate him. Instead, they elected Haderlein, who was acceptable to both Baker and the Breakfast Club. After the vote, Coccia told Baker, "I don't know why you did this. You son-of-a-bitch, you know I love you, and I could hate you at the same time. You did me in here, and it wasn't right. But let's go have lunch." Baker smiled, and the two old colleagues had lunch.

The Breakfast Club also floor-managed resolutions that allowed the Capital Partners to vote directly for the seven-member Executive Committee by secret ballot. To break the Chicago office's dominance of the Executive Committee, the partners adopted a measure that required that at least six Firm offices be represented on the Committee. And a series of resolutions shifted more power from the Policy Committee, where Baker held sway, to the Executive Committee.

Although the partners had settled the management issue, the pyrotechnics in Zürich were not over. Several Chicago partners wanted to expel a partner and demanded a "trial" at the Annual Meeting. But the partner had precedent and Russell Baker on his side. The Firm had never voted to expel a partner, and Baker, who prided himself on defending the underdog, made an impassioned speech in the partner's defense, saying that he was being "crucified." After a fiery debate, the partners put the issue to a vote, and the motion for involuntary withdrawal failed.

The next fight involved the election of Baker's protégé, Hoken Seki, to Income Partnership. Despite several criticisms of the young lawyer, Baker stood staunchly behind the man he saw as Chicago's hope for developing a Japan practice. Before the meeting, Baker spent hours calling partners to line up support for Seki. In Zürich, "Russell came loaded for bear. He was determined that, however many ballots it took, Seki was going to get elected," Beal says. Seki's opponents persuaded André Saltoun to speak against him. After Saltoun finished, Baker lost his normally cool demeanor. He leveled an attack on Saltoun: "I can't believe what you are doing here. I can't believe this. I helped you." The partners, accustomed to Baker's understated, low-key style, were shocked by his outburst. "It was totally contrary to what I knew of him," Willem Stevens says. Nevertheless, it worked. The partners elected Seki an Income Partner.

Even though he had lost control of the Executive Committee, in his remarks to his partners at the 1972 Annual Meeting banquet, Baker was his usual optimistic self. "Here we are in Zürich—one year wiser and, judging from the financial information on the operation of the Firm, we are all one year richer than a year ago. It takes a strong constitution to withstand repeated attacks of prosperity," Baker told his partners. "I am confident that we can meet that challenge in the future as we have in the past, and that our good fortune will not go to our collective heads."

Then he turned to the issue of the Firm's size. "The bigger this Firm becomes, the more necessary it is that mutual help between partners, departments and offices be increased. In this Firm, the day of the hermit and the loner are gone forever." Next, he talked about his relationships with his partners: "The greatest satisfaction that has come to me as a result of my membership in this Firm is that I have been able to be helpful directly and personally to a number of you, and that all of you have been very helpful to me." His last comment dealt with his ongoing role in the Firm. He told his partners the story of a ninety-eight-year-old rancher friend, José Dolores Romero, from New Mexico. A newspaper reporter from the *Las Vegas Daily Optic* asked:

"Mr. Romero, to what do you attribute your longevity, your long and successful and happy life?"

"I never smoked. I never drank liquor, never fooled around with women, and I always got up at 5:00 in the morning."

The reporter noted the old man's formula, and then asked:

"I had an uncle who did the very same things that you recommend, but he only lived to be eighty. How do you account for that?"

"Simple," said José Dolores, "he didn't keep at it long enough."

"The point of the story," Baker said, "is that I want you to know that I so much enjoy being a partner in this Firm and working with each of you, that I have taken over the old man's formula for living a long life. And I am going to keep at it as long as I can."

The Zürich Annual Meeting ended on September 10, 1972. Two days later, Baker wrote a memorandum to his sons reflecting on the experience. "Very few Annual Meetings have equaled the Zürich meeting in work done, or in drama. In retrospect, I suppose that we will remember the drama." He closed the memo with an admonition to each son to "work like a dog, fight like a fiend, to win, of course, but more importantly, for the sheer joy of battle. Of course, as I always told you when you would ask me: 'Which side of the case were you on, Wussy?' [I told you that] we must be 'on the side of right and justice.' That is why we won so much at this last meeting."

Baker's comment that he "won" at the Annual Meeting is ironic. He prevailed on two personnel issues, but the changes in the management structure hastened the rise of the Boys of '60. In a sense, he may have "won" on the control issues because, after the 1972 Annual Meeting, he fully realized that it was time to start the transition to a new generation. Although he remained a force until he died, he began the process—most of the time with grace.

Chapter Thirteen

The Pacific Rim and the Middle East: Tokyo, Bangkok & Riyadh

In the early 1960s, the investment picture in the Pacific Basin was bleak. In Indochina, dissident groups calling themselves the Vietcong were organizing. The Filipino army was chasing left-wing guerrillas through the jungles. Indonesia's President Sukarno was cozying up to the Communist nations. And Japan was still recovering from World War II's pummeling.

At the time, many Westerners jeered that Japan couldn't produce anything but wood, paper toys, and second-rate knockoffs of Western products. But a few astute observers knew that Japanese corporations were beginning to hum with a dynamism that would eventually make their country the world's second largest economy. When exports of Japanese automobiles and cameras were still a trickle, Russell Baker sensed that the nation would become the Orient's economic engine. Someday, he correctly predicted, Japan would support a Baker & McKenzie office and would provide work to Firm offices around the globe.

Despite opposition from many partners, the Firm opened a Tokyo office in 1963. That same year, enormous typhoons destroyed half of Japan's crops. The next year, though, was better. To evidence its entry onto the world stage, Japan hosted the Olympic Games. Even though the island nation welcomed hordes of sports fans in 1964, its previous centuries of isolation contributed to making the Tokyo office one of the most troublesome in the Firm's history.

For more than twenty years after it opened, the clashing cultures held back the office's development. The nation's suspicion of foreigners made it difficult to locate Japanese lawyers who wanted to work with the *gaijin*. In addition, the Japanese severely limited the number of attorneys who could join the country's Bar Association. Since qualified lawyers were in short supply, they didn't need to enter into dubious ventures with foreigners in order to make excellent incomes. Faced with a shortage of Japanese lawyers who understood the West, Baker decided to initially staff the Tokyo office with Americans. Although they were well-intentioned, the Americans found that peeling back the intricate layers of Japan's homogeneous culture was difficult.

In 1963, Baker shipped Norman Jensen, who spoke fluent Japanese and had lived and studied in Japan, to Tokyo to work with a Japanese trademark firm. To shore up the staff, he also persuaded Chicago's Jack Beem to join the Tokyo office. Beem went to Japan in 1964 for what he thought would be a six-month assignment, but he didn't return home until 1970. During that time, the Tokyo lawyers did almost one hundred percent of their work for Western clients. A parade of Americans and Europeans lined up to enter into joint venture, licensing, and distribution agreements with Japan's rapidly emerging companies. Even though Western companies were anxious to do business with Japanese corporations, "there were serious limitations on what foreign businesses could do in Japan. It was difficult and challenging work to see what kind of approvals we could get from the government," Beem remembers.

With foreigners running the Tokyo office and an often-hostile government making their practice difficult, "Tokyo was a loser for us," Michel Coccia says. "We had individuals working over there under the most difficult set of circumstances." From the outset, the Tokyo office lost money. Several partners claimed that Baker's decision to send Americans to head the office was foolish in light of Japan's well-known xenophobia. "Russell was extremely interested in developing the Japanese practice," Beem says. "He took a particular interest in the office, and in the lawyers in that office. Russell was extremely supportive. The main thing he did was to protect us from others in the Firm who were critical of Tokyo."

By 1975, the Tokyo office had improved from its position of the Firm's least profitable office in 1970 to only the third worst out of twenty-three offices. A sizeable number of partners wanted to shut off the subsidy spigot and to close the office, but Baker always managed to garner enough support to keep it open. To help make the office successful, he worked with organizations that were fostering U.S.-Japanese trade. He served as President of the Japan-America Society of America, participated in trade missions to Japan, and gave frequent speeches to American and Japanese businessmen.

To assuage the Japanese's suspicion of foreigners and to follow the principle of populating offices with nationals, the Tokyo office established a loose relationship with a retired Justice of the Japanese Supreme Court. It also hired several other Japanese lawyers. But, uncomfortable working with foreigners, the Japanese lawyers came and went with depressing regularity. The Firm spent three frustrating years trying to staff the office with nationals before it finally found a Japanese lawyer willing to stake his career on Baker & McKenzie. International law fascinated Masatsugo Suzuki, and he was pleased to join the Tokyo office in 1966. "I was committed to the concept of international practice," Suzuki says. "I believed that we had to promote international law practice in Japan. And I thought that Baker & McKenzie would help develop a worldwide legal practice."

While the legal staff was developing in Tokyo, Baker was implementing his grand design for the Japan practice. During the mid-1960s, he began planning for a California office to intercept the Japanese business that he expected to flow across the Pacific. The Firm recruited Japanese-speaking lawyers to work in the Chicago and New York offices. And Baker encouraged partners around the world who wanted to build a Japanese practice. In the early 1970s, London's Pearce Rood wrote Baker about his interest. "The Japanese banks are bound to be big in London," Baker answered. "There is going to be an immense body of legal work to be done for Japanese companies in London, and it is wonderful business; it is fascinating. Start right away and pour it on, you cannot lose."

The Tokyo office had problems, but an internecine struggle in the U.S. added to them. By the late 1960s, Baker and the New York office's Jiro Murase differed over whether the Tokyo office should have only Japanese lawyers. Evidently, Murase felt that the foreign lawyers' effectiveness was too limited. He called the non-Japanese attorneys the "blind American horses," Suzuki says. "That was a very insulting wording."

Although that problem disappeared when Murase left the Firm in 1971, the Tokyo office was under siege from another source. In the early 1970s, the Japanese Bar Association[1] began exerting pressure to eliminate the foreign taint from the Firm's Tokyo office. It claimed that Baker & McKenzie was illegally practicing Japanese law, and threatened to conduct an investigation. At the same time, it sent letters to the Firm's Japanese lawyers accusing them of selling out to foreigners and being front men for the *gaijin*. With this intense pressure, many Japanese lawyers left the office.

Suzuki stayed, but Japanese Bar coercion forced the office to drop the Baker & McKenzie name and to call itself the more generic Tokyo Aoyama Law Office. The Japanese press picked up on the issue, and referred to the Firm's non-Japanese lawyers as "black ships," a slur that related back to Commodore Matthew Perry's visit to Japan in 1853 with seven black ships. Over the years, "black ships" had come to mean foreigners who wanted to invade the Japanese market.

By 1970, Jensen had resigned and Beem had returned to Chicago. To replace them, the Firm sent another American, Rexford Coleman, whose credentials included a stint teaching Japanese tax law at Harvard before joining Baker & McKenzie. After his arrival in Japan, Coleman began recruiting Japanese lawyers, including tax and patent law specialists. Still, the combination of Bar and cultural pressures prolonged the revolving-door atmosphere of the Tokyo office.

In the mid-1970s, the office brought in a German, Dirk Vaubel, and a Frenchman, Jean-François Bretonnière, to attract European companies wanting to do business in Japan. Shinichi Saito also joined the office during that time. The Firm's multinational practice intrigued Saito. To broaden his international background, he had studied at Columbia University and worked in the Washington office. Even with Saito and Suzuki playing prominent roles, the Tokyo office was still under heavy Bar pressure to make the non-Japanese lawyers leave. As part of its campaign to "decontaminate" the office, the Bar forced it to keep separate financial accounts and to strike all references to Baker & McKenzie from its letterhead and name plate.

The Bar Association problems persisted. In 1986, the Bar adopted a regulation explicitly prohibiting foreign and Japanese lawyers from being partners. A corollary rule banned foreigners from employing Japanese lawyers. The Bar furthered its cultural cleansing by putting intense pressure on the Japanese lawyers in Tokyo. Bretonnière says, "The presence of non-Japanese lawyers was making life for our Japanese colleagues impossible." Finally, the German, French, and two American partners returned to their home countries.

In 1985, the Firm initiated what it called the "Japan Project," the first organized Firm-wide effort to share client information and to coordinate marketing efforts. Saito, John Connor, and Paul Davis were instrumental in shaping the concept and then selling it to the partnership. Their plan envisioned capturing outbound Japanese business at the source—in the same way that Russell Baker had captured American business that was expanding abroad after World War II.

The partners adopted a five-year plan to support the Japan Project because "to work with Japanese companies and get them as clients, you have to invest a lot of time to get acquainted with the person," Bretonnière says. "To just make a trip and to take a little shot at explaining to them that you are the best lawyer in your country will not achieve anything."

The development of Japan's economy after World War II created the framework for the Japan Project. At first, the island nation had set its sights on building up its domestic industry, and most of its capital resources stayed at home. By the 1980s, however, the country had been so successful that it had racked up massive trade surpluses, and countries with unfavorable balances of trade began to demand that the Japanese recirculate their immense profits by investing abroad. The European Community clamored for changes and raised trade barriers to Japanese goods, while American politicians indulged in "Japan bashing." With these threats to Japan's economic lifeline, huge quantities of yen began flowing out of the country to build factories and invest in other projects.

The Firm headquartered the Japan Project in the Tokyo office, and it appointed a Japanese Executive Director to instigate contacts between top-level

Japanese executives and Firm partners. The Japan Project also held seminars for Japanese businessmen and translated promotional materials into Japanese. The fact that Japanese corporations have extremely close ties to their banks helped structure the Japan Project. Typically, when Japanese corporations went to foreign countries, they consulted their bank on which lawyer to use. To establish name recognition and credibility, the Japan Project made contacts at Japanese banks in Tokyo, Yokohama, Nagoya, and other cities.

Under the plan, each Firm office designated a Japan Project Coordinator who was charged with shepherding the incoming Japanese business in his office and advising the other offices of his office's contacts with Japanese companies. The mission statement also encouraged the Coordinators to visit Japan whenever possible, and to join Japanese business associations in their home countries. The Japan Project urged each office to hire a Japanese-speaking lawyer. "The idea was," Connor says, "that, when the Japanese businessmen got off the plane in São Paulo or Brussels, a Baker & McKenzie attorney would understand what the Japanese businessman was talking about, and he would be comfortable with the lawyer because he had the cultural acclimatization."

The multi-year project appeared to be a sound idea, but it was slow to develop. Although it was basically Russell Baker's concepts wrapped in a kimono, there was no Russell Baker to implement it because he had died in 1979. There was no one in the Firm with the tenacity or the political authority to make things happen the way he had. With results slow to materialize, some partners groused that the Japan Project was a "boondoggle" for the scheme's sponsors, who were receiving income supplements out of the Project's hefty budget. In answer to the critics, Connor snapped: "Total lack of imagination." He saw the Japan Project as a milestone "because this was looking for clients institutionally, and not like a bunch of hunters, each out with a rifle in the jungle. That in itself was something new in our Firm."

The Japan Project was successful in channeling Japanese companies to Firm offices, and raised Baker & McKenzie's profile and prestige in the Japanese business community. "That is very important to the Japanese," Connor says, "because they know that they are dealing with a reputable and reliable organization. The executives can't be criticized in choosing us because we are a known commodity."

———

Although it took years for the Tokyo office to become profitable, Bangkok became a financial success almost immediately. Only three years after it opened in 1977, it boasted more than $500,000 in revenues.

Despite the early prosperity, before the Bangkok office opened, Southeast Asia's prospects had been dim. In 1975, South Vietnam's president fled the country, and American helicopters evacuated the last few Marines from the U.S. Embassy. At the same time, Cambodia's government collapsed, and leftist Pol Pot seized power the next year. Laos became a "people's democratic republic," and a military dictatorship ruled Burma (Myanmar). Surrounded on three sides by autocratic regimes, Thailand seemed an unlikely prospect for opening a Firm office. Subscribers to the "domino theory" were forecasting that it was just a matter of time until the country fell to the Communists. The Thai economy, which had gotten a big boost as a U.S. staging and recreation area during the Vietnam War, was faltering after the War ended. Military coups were destabilizing the country and university students were rioting.

Despite that backdrop, John Connor pressed his campaign to expand Baker & McKenzie's reach in the Pacific Basin. Several years before the Bangkok office opened, he had chatted with two young lawyers, one a Thai and the other an Australian, about the country's potential.

John Hancock, a "diminutive, bouncy Australian," had made his first trip to Thailand in pursuit of a Thai girl he met when they were both students at the University of Adelaide. Hancock's sweetheart, Sunissa, had returned home to live with her father, a Thai Air Force Air Chief Marshal. Hancock wrote the girl's father a plaintive letter asking to marry his daughter. "His answer back to me said it was very nice when people loved each other, but mixed marriages were not all that easy. He felt it would be better if I found a nice Australian girl and she found a nice Thai boy," Hancock says.

Hancock pleaded with Sunissa to come to Australia, but her parents had her passport. Three days after Hancock was admitted to the Bar, he cashed in his savings from summer jobs loading wheat and driving taxis. Still short, he borrowed enough money to pay his airfare to Thailand. In Bangkok, Hancock went to see the girl's father to again ask for her hand. He got an unqualified no. "Nevertheless, we went to the registry office and got married," he says. They kept the marriage a secret until Sunissa's sisters could intervene with their parents and get their blessing. After some three months, the pair married again in a Buddhist ceremony.

The Australian found a job at an international law firm in Bangkok, but, after a few years, he told his brother that he wanted to work in another country. Hancock's brother remembered someone he had run across, "a guy named John Connor with a firm called Baker & McKenzie." With that tip, Hancock made a blind call to Connor, and flew to Sydney for an interview. The two Australians talked about whether Hancock could start with the Firm in either Sydney, Hong Kong, or New York, but the long-range plan assumed that he would return to Thailand to open an office.

No concrete job offer came from that first meeting, but, in the spring of 1974, Connor arranged for Hancock to attend a Policy Committee meeting in Brussels to meet more partners. He recalls sitting in an outdoor cafe in Brussels' medieval *Grand Place*, where he and a young partner, John Klotsche, drank beer and ruminated on the possibility of opening a Bangkok office. He joined the Firm in 1975, starting in the New York office.

While the Hancocks were huddled in their New York apartment watching the first snowfall either of them had seen, Suchint Chaimungkalanont was working in the Hong Kong office. Suchint,[2] the son of a textile merchant, had studied law at Chulalongkorn University, and practiced law in Bangkok for a few years. Then, he won a scholarship to study at the University of New South Wales, where, toward the end of his stay, he found a summer job with Baker & McKenzie in Sydney. After that, Suchint returned to his old Bangkok law firm. In 1974, he reestablished his contact with the Firm, and accepted an offer to join the Hong Kong office. Hancock soon followed Suchint to Hong Kong, and the two began working together on the "Bangkok desk." They took turns traveling to Thailand to work on client matters and to study the feasibility of starting an office.

Connor often went with the young lawyers to take soundings on the prospects in Thailand. In 1976, he deemed that the time had come, but he feared that the international partners would not approve it. "I don't think the Firm thought Bangkok was important," Hancock says, "but John Connor thought that we should have offices throughout the region and that Thailand had potential."

"The reason for not troubling the Firm too much with the details was the legacy of the Vietnam War," Connor says. "Attitudes in the U.S. toward Southeast Asia at that time would not have been positive. It seemed that the only thing to do was to start the operation in Bangkok without any official Firm approvals." To mask the new venture, Connor organized a Thai corporation, with the Firm's Hong Kong office as the shareholder. He also sent Hancock and Suchint to Bangkok, but kept them on the Hong Kong office's associate roster.

Operating under the Thai corporation's generic name, it was easy to hide the bootleg Bangkok office. The two lawyers, whom Connor visited monthly, worked in a single room that they furnished with secondhand furniture they bought for about $10. To keep down costs, their secretary doubled as the office's accountant.

In just a year, Connor was satisfied that Bangkok would survive, so he scripted the leaking of the clandestine office's existence to the Firm. After an Executive Committee meeting in Sydney, Connor arranged for Committee member Hubert Stitt to go to Bangkok to "discover" the office. Connor then contacted Hancock and told him that, on Stitt's trip back to Toronto, he would have a layover in Bangkok from 3:00 A.M. until 7:00 A.M., during which time he was to meet with Stitt and disclose the undercover office. "I went to Bert's room, and Bert was advised that there was an office in Bangkok," Hancock recalls. Stitt, one of Connor's fellow Boys of '60, duly reported to the Executive Committee that the Firm had a Bangkok office.

Some partners resented Connor's cover-up and his flouting of the Articles of Partnership. In the understated "Baker & McKenzie-speak" that the Firm uses in its meeting minutes, the European partners adopted a resolution condemning Connor's sleight of hand, expressing "serious concern about the recently adopted method of opening semi-official offices without first obtaining the appropriate approval."

The disclosure forced the Firm to decide whether to close the Bangkok office or to treat it as a *fait accompli*. The partners grudgingly chose the latter, and the Bangkok office formally opened in 1977. Following Buddhist tradition, saffron-robed monks with shaved heads offered blessings for the new office's success. As part of the ritual, the monks smeared the office's front door with a substance that appeared to Westerners to be disgusting. When Dennis Meyer, then the Chairman, arrived to attend the office's opening festivities, he ordered Hancock to "get that stuff off the door!" He relented, however, after Hancock explained, "That is something that the Buddhist priests put on, and you can't touch that. It has to wear off." Connor says, "The blessings seem to have worked because the office prospered from early on."

At first, work trickled in, mostly from the Sydney and Hong Kong offices. Another referral, from Amsterdam, gave Bangkok a major boost. A Dutch-German trading company saw a lucrative business opportunity in barging Thai products through its river system. But the Thai Board of Investment had to grant its permission because Thai law prohibited foreign-owned vessels from plying the nation's territorial waters. Suchint and Hancock convinced the Thai authorities that their client's barges were not "vessels," and got the government's approval for the company to do business.

As the work increased, a few companies asked Baker & McKenzie lawyers to become involved in bribing government officials. Following the Firm's strict policy, the Bangkok lawyers always declined. Shortly after the office opened, it refused to pay a supplier who asked for a bribe to install a telex machine. "We had to wait for a long time to get a telex machine and to get the lines hooked up," Connor says. "But the point to the people in the office was that we were not in the business of paying people off. It is a very slippery slope once you decide to go down it."

Athueck Asvanund joined the office shortly after it opened. Athueck, the fourth son of a family of Chinese descent, chose not to follow his three elder brothers into banking and finance. Instead, he decided to be a lawyer. Athueck graduated from law school in Thailand, and then did graduate work at New York University. He returned to Bangkok, contacted Connor, and joined the office.

After several months in Bangkok, Athueck transferred to Hong Kong for two years. There, under the tutelage of several partners, he learned to untangle the complexities of bank loan agreements and other financing documents. During a trip to Bangkok, the young Thai made contact with an old family friend, the chairman of Thailand's largest commercial bank. When Athueck asked the bank chairman to send him business, he asked, "Why do I need a lawyer? I don't have any problems." Still, because of the family ties, the chairman "got his people and discussed how he could give us work."

The Thai bank dribbled out small domestic assignments at first. Within a year, however, it decided to issue floating rate notes in the London market. Not only was this a major transaction, it gave the Firm a chance to educate the Thai bank in the Western style of doing business. "It was all right to do business on a handshake when you had family companies in Thailand," Hancock says, "but not with companies that are listed on the securities exchange."

Hard bargaining in the gentle Thai culture is usually toxic. But the Firm's negotiations with the London financial institutions caused the Thai bankers to realized that loan agreements addressed important issues and were not useless pieces of paper to be shoved into a desk drawer and forgotten. Later, the bank asked Baker & McKenzie to improve its domestic financing documents. While work for Thai financial institutions was growing, the Bangkok office also developed expertise in handling transactions for non-Thai banks. In the 1980s, the office's Banking and Finance Department accumulated a large stable of non-Thai banking clients that were making loans in Thailand's rapidly expanding economy.

One transaction bootstrapped the Bangkok office into the merger and acquisition field. An old friend called Athueck and asked him to look over some paperwork regarding the purchase of an American company. Because he was busy on other client matters, and was getting ready to leave town for a Chicago Policy Committee meeting, Athueck didn't think he had time to handle the transaction, and tried to beg off. The friend, however, found out that Athueck was leaving town, and booked the seat next to him on the plane. During the flight to Hong Kong, he explained his transaction and why it was so important. It would, he claimed, be the largest buyout of a foreign company in Thailand's history. Still, Athueck was reluctant. The friend got off the plane in Hong Kong, and Athueck continued his flight to Chicago. There, he happened to sit next to David Macdonald at the Policy Committee meeting. In passing, Athueck mentioned that a Thai company wanted to acquire a sizeable U.S. corporation. Macdonald, who specialized in acquisitions and securities work, saw the opportunity and urged Athueck to accept the work.

Athueck contacted his friend and told him that Baker & McKenzie would handle the acquisition. Because the U.S. company had assets in many locations, the Firm fielded a team that included lawyers from Chicago, Washington, Bangkok, and New York. In addition to doing legal work, Athueck spent hours explaining Western business practices to his client. "The client didn't understand about the environmental issues, the American tax law, or just about anything," Athueck recalls. Each day, Athueck, who was working out of New York, phoned and faxed the client in Bangkok. When he checked out of his expensive New York hotel, the fax and phone bills were higher than the room rent.

By the early 1980s, the Bangkok office was rolling. The country's political climate had stabilized, and the economy was growing at more than ten percent per year. The Bangkok office did work for many Thai companies and for the throng of non-Thais who wanted to do business in the Asian nation. To provide full service to clients, the Bangkok office developed substantial litigation expertise.

In one case, a powerful Thai army general borrowed a large sum from a U.S. bank to buy a Thai factory. When the plant went bankrupt, the general refused to pay the foreign bank, figuring that the bank wouldn't dare touch him. Although it was risky, the Bangkok office agreed to represent the U.S. bank in its dispute with the general. As part of the collection process, the Firm's trial lawyers enlisted a team of policemen and took possession of the general's house. While inside, they heard a commotion outside. When they looked out, they saw a detachment of soldiers with guns at the ready. The police drew their guns, and "it was very, very tense." After the armed parties negotiated, they reached a peaceful solution. Later, the general paid his debt, "but our guys were caught in the middle of all of this stuff," Hancock says. Since that incident, "we tell our clients, 'We won't take on a case if our lawyers feel that their personal lives are at stake.'"

In other cases, the Bangkok litigators have carried out "commando" sorties against merchants who sell counterfeit merchandise bearing clients' trademarks. With a court order allowing them to seize the fake products, they enlist squads of motorcycle police to accompany them on raids to confiscate phony Levi jeans and Nina Ricci shirts. A reporter who witnessed one raid wrote: "As soon as the mechanized entourage appears . . . a mild panic ensues as several vendors . . . began tearing down their displayed wares. . . . Another day at the office? Probably not, if you're used to the big-firm practice in New York or Los Angeles or Chicago. But for the. . . . Bangkok office, it's just another scene out of firm founder Russell Baker's vision of a global firm whose native lawyers are steeped in the culture and legal practice of the country in which the office is located."3

In addition to helping their Western clients adapt to the conditions in Thailand, the Bangkok partners trained their Thai associates to deal with Western behavior. The Thais' exchanges of *wais* typify their modest, pacific style. Instead of shaking hands, they greet one another with a bow of the head over hands clasped as if in prayer. In contrast to this gentle approach, Western customs sometimes appear rude to them. Manila's Rafael Evangelista says that most

Asians do not want to appear aggressive and are reluctant to contradict their elders. Also, he says, in many Asian cultures "people who talk too much are considered to be idiots."

The Asians' conciliatory style can sometimes work against them. Early in one young Thai's career, Connor gave him a lesson in how to deal with the aggressive Western style. He and Connor were representing a Thai company that had an American bank as a partner. The bank was insisting on getting out of the partnership, and was "laying down all sorts of silly conditions and demanding various warranties that were totally impractical in the Thai context," Connor recalls. "I decided to be very aggressive with the American bank and to use blunt language. My Thai colleague was shocked that I was so brutal." The negotiations worked out favorably for the Thai client, Connor says, "and the young Thai took the message to heart, because the way he handled transactions with Westerners completely changed."

Today, the Bangkok partners still teach their associates how to deal with cultural differences. Knowing that savvy Westerners sometimes use the Asians' aversion to conflict against them, the Bangkok partners counsel their juniors to be more aggressive. One lesson the Bangkok partners instill in their associates is the importance of which side gets to prepare the first drafts of contracts. In a typical Thai transaction, once the parties agree on a business deal, they instruct their lawyers to write down exactly what the parties agreed to. But, the Bangkok partners warn associates, Western lawyers often grab the opportunity to draft the documents so that they can slip in advantages for their client. When Westerners do this, it puts a traditional Asian lawyer at a disadvantage, because, out of politeness, some of them feel hesitant to point out that the document doesn't reflect what the clients agreed upon.

In addition to on-the-job training, the Bangkok office conducts one of the Firm's most extensive education programs. To become a lawyer in Thailand requires only a four-year university course after secondary school. With the newest lawyers still in their early twenties, and few of them speaking a foreign language, the Bangkok office arranges for its associates to learn both English and the practical side of law practice. The office itself, through its professional development person, organizes seminars on subjects such as banking, intellectual property, and tax. The Firm's Pacific Basin Professional Development Coordinator teaches courses that include business development, negotiating techniques, and drafting documents. Bangkok also makes extensive use of the Firm's many programs for overseas study or work.

By the early 1990s, several international firms had opened Bangkok offices or affiliated with Thai firms. But Baker & McKenzie remained the largest law firm in Thailand, with ten partners and over fifty associates. All of its partners, except Hancock, are Thai. Even though he cofounded the office, Hancock avoids the appearance of being in charge. "In anyone's home country," he says, "the nationals should be the ones running it. If I was in Australia, and there was a guy from another country who was running it and if he was being a bit too aggressive in thinking he was the boss, I wouldn't like it."

Russell Baker's prescription that nationals should run their own offices has worked in Bangkok. In 1980, the office generated some $525,000 in revenue. By 1985, revenue had tripled, and, by 1990, it had tripled again to $5.2 million. In addition to Bangkok's corporate, tax, finance, and other specialties, it has established a Japan Practice Group with two lawyers who speak Japanese. To service the Southeast Asia market, the office has Cambodian and Vietnamese law specialists, and it served as the springboard for opening offices in Hanoi and Ho Chi Minh City.

While Firm partners were exploring the Far East's enormous possibilities, others were pushing to exploit the Middle East oil boom. The sudden spike in oil prices (some six hundred percent in three years) in the early 1970s had created overnight wealth in the region. As petrodollars piled up in the Middle East, American, European, and Japanese companies flocked to the region to sell military hardware, consumer products, and the skills to build airports, highways, and universities.

André Saltoun, a Chicago partner who was born in Baghdad and speaks Arabic, began the Firm's exploration of the Middle East. He considered Beirut an early candidate for a Baker & McKenzie office, but in 1975 Christian and Muslim factions plunged Lebanon into a bloody civil war that wrecked the nation's infrastructure and left more than sixty thousand dead.

Several partners saw Cairo as the best place to locate the Firm's first Middle East office. Politically, Egyptian-Israeli political tensions had eased after the two countries signed a 1974 agreement that put an end to the Yom Kippur War. Another favorable factor was that Baker & McKenzie had three Egyptian lawyers working in the Chicago office. And Egypt, the largest Arab country, was the center of Arab culture. For centuries, its universities had educated young men from other Arab nations, including many lawyers.

With that legal and cultural nexus, opening a Cairo office seemed logical. On the negative side, however, telephone, telex, and air communications to Egypt were substandard. In addition, the government forced companies to exchange Egyptian currency at artificial exchange rates, and made it difficult for companies to send profits out of the country. Worse, Egypt had almost no oil.

Still undecided, several Executive Committee members made trips to the Middle East to determine the best location. One of them, Hubert Stitt, prepared what he called the "EC Mid-East Report," complete with pictures of partners posing with camels and accompanying doggerel:

"Rumor has it that the place to be
For an international firm such as we
Is not England or Spain or Greece
But somewhere in the Middle East.
Clients, we are told, abound
All wondering why we're not around.
What's the city of our pursuit?
Is it Cairo, Jeddah or Beirut?"

To sort out the alternatives, the Firm sent William Gibbons to the Middle East. He recommended a Saudi Arabian office, based on the facts that American companies were working on $22 billion in projects and were selling more than $3 billion a year in products to the desert nation. Despite Gibbons's advice, Saltoun had reservations. Among them were the living conditions and the Saudi cost of living, which was three times higher than that in Chicago. In Cairo, Saltoun argued, the Firm could open an office much more cheaply, and it could be done "in the Baker & McKenzie way, that is, through Egyptian lawyers who have worked with us and are a known entity."

The Saltoun-Gibbons debate continued. Finally, economic reality overcame Saltoun's reasoning. Saudi Arabia had twenty-five percent of the world's known oil reserves. The Kingdom's leadership was determined to transform Saudi Arabia from a medieval society into a modern state. And many of the Firm's natural constituents, multinational companies, were already doing business in Saudi.

At the 1977 Amsterdam Annual Meeting, the partners authorized Gibbons and Robert Cartwright to develop a Saudi Arabian office. During trips to Saudi Arabia, Gibbons had interviewed over ten local lawyers with an eye to forming an alliance. His choice was a two-man Jeddah partnership. They were among King Khalid's principal lawyers, and they "clearly acted as lawyers and not as businessmen—the latter being a common failing among local lawyers in Saudi Arabia," Gibbons said.

The Jeddah law firm provided office space, and, out of Arab hospitality, refused to accept payment for rent, telephone, or telex. Gibbons and Cartwright rotated in and out as client needs required. Soon, Frankfurt's Peter Ficht and Chicago's Samir Hamza began spending substantial time there. The Red Sea port city was giddy with the sudden influx of money. "It was a gold rush atmosphere, awash in petrodollars," Cartwright says. When he first went to Saudi Arabia, "It was stark and undeveloped. The Kandara Palace was the only hotel in

Jeddah worth sneezing at, and it was a broken-down place with peeling paint and stained carpets. During the boom, there were guys sleeping in the lobbies and hallways, and sleeping five to a room."

Taher Helmy, an Egyptian lawyer from the Chicago office, remembers getting off the plane at Jeddah in the mid-1970s. "It was a desert land with one paved two-lane road," he says. On one trip, there was no room at the hotel, and Helmy slept on a couch in the U.S. Commercial Attaché's living room. On another, he and his client bedded down on mattresses on the floor of an un-air-conditioned hotel room. There was little entertainment, and the one television station devoted much of its programming to religious ceremonies. Drinking alcohol was a punishable offense, so the lawyers drank "Jeddah Champagne," a mixture of apple juice and mineral water.

At the office, the lawyers handled work for multinational companies. During his twelve trips to Saudi Arabia, Ficht spent much of his time representing German companies that built desalinization plants in the Persian Gulf to produce fresh water, helping make the desert nation almost self-sufficient in its domestic water needs. Other Firm lawyers negotiated contracts for the sale of F–15 fighter planes and the construction of telecommunications systems and government office buildings.

The Jeddah lawyers continued to be accommodating, and there was occasional talk of their establishing a formal association with the Firm. By 1978, however, the relationship was still ambivalent. The Policy Committee recommended that the Firm either work something out with the Jeddah lawyers or open its own office. But the Saudi attorneys declined because, they said, they were too busy working for the King and wouldn't have time to take care of Firm clients. Baker & McKenzie then opened an office at Al Khobar, where most of the oil companies were headquartered. Although the Firm had some petroleum industry clients, most of its clients were involved in selling weapons and building large infrastructure projects. In the highly centralized Kingdom, almost all of that work happened in the capital, Riyadh.

At the 1979 Paris Annual Meeting, the partners voted to open a Riyadh office, and Helmy managed to get a license for an office there. Following the Firm's tradition of opening offices "on the cheap," Gibbons settled on a villa on a back street. With thousands of foreigners paying large premiums to rent hotel and office space, Gibbons argued that the villa would save money because it could be used as both an office and living quarters. "We wanted to turn a profit," Cartwright says, "and to show the Firm that all the money wasn't going to be sucked out in expenses."

With oil prices skyrocketing, the Kingdom had enough money to convert a country of camels and tents into one of luxury automobiles and high-rises. Countries from around the world, Helmy says, were creating "a metropolis of trees and greenery and cement highways out of desert land." Riyadh, Cartwright adds, had been "a gray, mud-baked, low-rise city. It seemed like it hadn't changed for centuries. By the mid-1980s, the drive in from the new airport on an express-way and the tall buildings impressed on me the dramatic change from the four-teenth century to the twentieth in only ten years."

As oil flowed out and money flowed in, Cartwright says, there was "a boom-town-type environment that attracted characters who might be politely called hucksters. There were guys who claimed to be buddies with a royal prince or to be the King's best friend. And, they'd say, 'If you just sign me up for a ten percent commission, we'll get this contract.' There were a lot of flakes."

To fend off the flakes, and to staff the Riyadh office, Samir Hamza moved to Saudi Arabia. Later, Taher Helmy joined him, and the shuttling in and out by other partners tapered off. In the mid-1980s, however, Hamza and Helmy, both Egyptians, went home to open a Cairo office. To fill the gap, John Xefos moved from the Chicago office to Riyadh. As a young man, he had been fascinated by Islamic culture. At Cornell University, he made friends with a number of Middle Eastern students, and at the University of Pennsylvania Law School, he took courses in Islamic law. When he began looking for a law firm that would be interested in his Middle East background, he ran across Baker & McKenzie. "It was the only law firm that was seriously committed to a long-term presence in the region," he says.

When Xefos first went to Saudi Arabia in the mid-1980s, working conditions were still complicated. The primary communications link was the telex because telephone lines were hard to get. Finding secretaries was even more difficult. Custom prohibited Saudi women from working, and men didn't want the jobs. Imported workers, mostly Indians and Filipinos, were hired, but they had little secretarial experience. "I had to sit down at the telex machine and peck out my own messages," Xefos recalls.

Much of his work related to joint ventures, distributorships, and agency arrangements. In addition to legal tasks, there was "a lot of hand-holding. We had to help clients understand the cultural differences when they came to do business," Xefos says. Saudi work days confounded many Westerners. In keeping with Islamic tradition, Thursdays and Fridays are the weekend. Because most Westerners want to work on those days, "many times, we ended up working seven days a week," Xefos says.

Ramadan was another Muslim custom that bewildered some Westerners. During the holy month, devout Muslims stay at home during the day, fasting until the sun goes down. After dinner, they go to their offices and work as late as 4:00 A.M. Xefos recalls one Saudi businessman who used Ramadan to his advantage. "The foreigners had stayed up during the days," he says, "but the Saudi wouldn't see them until eleven at night. The foreigners were bleary-eyed and jet-lagged by then, and he was nice and fresh. We often tell clients not to plan serious negotiating sessions during Ramadan."

Although differing customs can confuse outsiders, Firm lawyers sometimes find that their most difficult task is explaining Saudi law to newcomers. The *sharia,* the basic body of Islamic law, underpins the Saudi legal system. Because the *sharia's* roots stem directly from the Koran and the prophet Mohammed's statements, devout Arabs believe that the law is divinely inspired. The *sharia's* dual role as an ethical and a legal system sometimes makes it difficult for a lawyer to advise clients. For instance, it outlaws gambling contracts, and a conservative interpretation of the *sharia* would treat insurance contracts as "flirting with the hand of God about what was going to happen in the future," Cartwright says. "And they are seen as a bet on whether a natural disaster will occur or a person will die."

To determine what a client can or cannot do, the Firm's lawyers must look first at the *sharia* and then at the Kingdom's man-made law. Since precedents have no weight, and there is no system for recording previous court decisions, the Firm's lawyers developed rapport with the judges. "When a problem crops up, we go in and chat with them," Xefos says. "You need to have a feel for when they are telling you something accurate, and when the guy is shooting from the hip. It is frustrating at times. Often, you can't give your clients definitive answers." Compounding the problem, the government sometimes issues royal decrees and regulations that aren't distributed to people outside the government.

In a typical case, Xefos reviews the *sharia* and the man-made laws. Then, he visits a contact at the appropriate government agencies. During their talks, Xefos tells the official what he thinks the law means. "Sometimes, he will shake his head no," Xefos says. "We say, 'Why not?' He will say, 'Administrative policy. There is a ruling within the Ministry, and you are not allowed to see it.' Usually, we can reach a compromise, and the government employee gives us some guidance."

In addition to complying with Saudi law, U.S. companies are subject to the Foreign Corrupt Practices Act ("FCPA"), which prohibits Americans from bribing foreign government officials or from making payments to third parties if they know that the payments will be used as bribes. When the U.S. Congress adopted the FCPA in the late 1970s, it created an immediate problem for some Firm clients who were trying to get government contracts. Saudi law required foreigners to have Saudi partners or agents. In some cases, the Saudi had close contacts with government officials. To protect American clients from FCPA exposure, the Firm developed stringent due diligence procedures designed to avoid any illegal payments.

The U.S. Anti-Boycott Regulations presented another stumbling block for American companies. The Arab League had pressured its members to force foreigners to agree in writing that they would not do business with Israel, threatening them with blacklisting if they broke the rule. In reaction, the Anti-Boycott

Regulations prohibited American companies from agreeing to boycott Israel. Although Saudi Arabia was not as hard-line as some Arab countries, the offending language occasionally showed up in a legal document. If, for example, boycott language was buried in a letter of credit, Americans had to refuse to accept payment until the Saudi party excised it.

————————

When oil prices sank in the mid-1980s, the Saudi government's spending cutbacks put many Saudi companies and joint ventures in financial jeopardy, forcing them to restructure their loans from foreign banks. "You had all sorts of people falling by the wayside," Xefos says. The Riyadh office's corporate and commercial work dropped dramatically. But Xefos identified a market niche: the banks that had loaned huge sums for projects in the Kingdom and were worried about their loans. To build the Riyadh office's banking and financial practice, Xefos picked the brains of Firm lawyers in London, Frankfurt, Hong Kong, and New York who represented banks. They sent him forms of financing documents to use as models, and he modified them to comply with Saudi law. "I found a great willingness by my partners to roll up their sleeves and rethink things that had become routine for them in the money centers," Xefos says. "Over time, we developed a set of documents that focus on the Kingdom's unique aspects of doing business."

A major difference between Western concepts and Islamic law is that the *sharia* prohibits charging interest on money, but Xefos has created ways for a bank to be compensated, while at the same time complying with Islamic law. Another troublesome area for Western financiers is that Saudi law has very little to say about how to secure a loan. When the bankers insisted on traditional mortgages and liens, "those were very difficult to put together in the Kingdom. Instead, we learned to piece together a series of practical mechanisms that gave them the same sort of result," Xefos says.

During the mid- and late-1980s, the office continued its work for financial institutions and other commercial clients, and the office grew, but slowly. "I have been accused of being too fussy in terms of who I want to recruit," Xefos says. But he insists that the lawyers who come to the office must commit to stay for the long term. "Other firms," he says, "have tended to take mid-level associates, let them suffer a year or two in the desert, and then send them back home. That isn't our approach."

————————

In 1990, Saudi Arabia became a combat zone. Xefos went to the office on the morning of Saddam Hussein's invasion of Kuwait and found "a bit of nervousness" among the lawyers. He sent one employee out to buy a radio, and another to the bank to get several thousand dollars in cash to buy plane tickets out of Riyadh, if needed.

The shooting war went into a lull after the summer invasion, but Saudi Arabia and its allies began a massive military buildup that temporarily boosted the Saudi economy. Many Saudis made fortunes providing transport for military equipment and renting desert land to the armed forces to set up camps and munitions depots. Defense contractors swamped the office with urgent calls. Some clients said, "Look, there's no time for a written contract. Here is what I am going to do. How much of a risk am I taking?"

By November and December the war winds were blowing. In mid-January 1991, the Geneva peace talks broke down. Saudis rushed to the stores to buy tape and plastic sheets to seal windows and doors against Saddam's threatened use of biological and chemical weapons. Xefos had to decide whether to send his children out of the country, and "concluded that sending them to New York was just as risky as keeping them in Riyadh."

On the night of January 17, Xefos's wife woke him with the news that the allies were on the attack. His house was close to an Air Force base, and he and his family listened while the jet fighters took off. As the war escalated, sirens wailed at the incoming Iraqi Scud missiles. Several Scuds fell close to Xefos's home, one as close as a half-mile. "Like anything else, after it had happened the third or fourth time, we got kind of blasé about it," he says. When the warning sirens went off one night while friends were having dinner at their house, Xefos offered them the option of continuing their meal or hiding in a safer place. The dinner continued.

Executive Committee members called him, saying "Why are you there? Get out!" Xefos also received calls and telefaxes every day from partners from around the world just to say, "Are you okay? Are you sure you should be sitting there in Riyadh?"

Despite the missiles and threats of poisoned gas, Xefos decided to stay, but he wanted the expatriate associates to leave. Two of them who were single refused. Another took his wife out of the country, but flew back by himself. "We had the office fully staffed throughout the War," Xefos says. Although some of his partners saw his remaining in Riyadh as a needless risk, "it meant a lot to the clients that we stayed put," Xefos says. "And it was remarkable how people in the Saudi government knew who had stayed and who had left. That served us well later on."

Baker & McKenzie co-founders (left) Russell Baker, and (right) John McKenzie.

First known photo of Russell Baker, circa 1901, Portage County, Wisconsin.

Russell, at about age 19, shortly after he arrived at the University of Chicago.

(left) Colleagues and opponents alike described Russell as a street fighter. To earn extra money to pay his way through school, he stood in the ring and offered to take on all comers at county fairs.
(right) Elizabeth and Russell Baker, shortly after their marriage in 1925.

Russell, prior to testifying on an international tax issue before the U.S. House of Representatives'
Ways and Means Committee in the early 1960s.

John Creed, 1964-66

Lajos Schmidt, 1966-71

Michel Coccia, 1971–72

Thomas Haderlein, 1972–75

Dennis Meyer, 1975–78

Wulf Döser, 1978–81

Thomas Bridgman, 1981–84　　　　　　　*Robert Cox, 1984–92*

Chairmen of the Firm's Executive Committee

John McGuigan, 1992-95

John Klotsche, 1995-2000

(top) Partners Malcolm Caplan, far left, and Alejandro Alfonzo-Larrain, far right, from the Caracas office, pictured during the signing of oil-service contracts in Venezuela with, from left, Dr. Armand Hammer, Chairman of Occidental Petroleum; J. L. Padron, a Venezuelan official; and Charles Hatfield, Occidental's representative in Venezuela. (bottom) In conjunction with the Firm's 1968 Annual Partners' Meeting in Rome, Pope Paul VI met briefly with, from left, Firm founder Russell Baker, and partners Thomas Coleman and Walter Slowinski.

At a Partners' Meeting in Chicago in 1958, the entire partnership, and even some staff, was able to convene around a single conference table. Pictured clockwise from head of table: Ramon Diaz, Jimmy Caron, Dolores Boyle, Norman Miller, Tony Sarabia, firm co-founder John McKenzie, Peter Achermann, Gilberto Delgado, Donald Baker, Jim Martin, Wallace Baker, Julian Nebreda, Michel Coccia, Frank Morrissey, Dwight Hightower, Frank Jas, Jamie Baker, John Creed, Bill Gibbons, Walter Slowinski, Lajos Schmidt, Norman Jensen, Tom Coleman, and Ingrid Beall.

(top) Twenty-five years later, the partners, some 280 strong, convened in Berlin in 1983. (bottom) Pictured at the Firm's Annual Partners' Meeting in Berlin in 1983, from left Helmut Schmidt, former Chancellor of West Germany; Thomas Bridgman, Chairman of the Executive Committee, 1981-84; Dennis Meyer, Chairman of the Executive Committee, 1975-78; and Alejandro Alfonzo-Larrain, partner from Caracas.

Baker & McKenzie partners take time out for a group photograph during the Annual Partners' Meeting in Paris in September 1979. A few days later, the assembled partners learned of Russell Baker's death and held a memorial service in his honor.

The Firm's unique "One Partner, One Vote" philosophy comes into focus during the Plenary Session at the Annual Partners' Meeting in Vienna in 1991, the year Baker & McKenzie welcomed its 500th partner.

Since 1986, Baker & McKenzie's innovative New Partner Program has provided newly elected partners with an opportunity to forge and develop strong personal relationships within the partnership. Pictured is the Class of 1998, the largest group yet.

Chapter Fourteen

South American Connections: Rio, Buenos Aires & Bogotá

South America was a region that Russell Baker knew well. From his boyhood in Sapello, New Mexico, he had learned to understand the Hispanic culture, and he loved it. He spoke Spanish and some Portuguese. He had married Elizabeth in Mexico City and honeymooned in Cuernavaca. Since the 1930s, he had traveled the continent to work for clients. He even named his dog "Sancho" after Don Quixote's faithful companion.

———

By the mid-1960s, Baker & McKenzie had three Latin American offices: Caracas, Mexico City, and São Paulo. Brazil was a logical place in which to expand, but political and economic turmoil gripped the nation. The country boomed when coffee or raw material prices were high, and busted when they weren't. Leftist President João Goulart permitted Communists to infiltrate the government, and their influence became so strong that one Brazilian Communist boasted that there was no need for a violent revolution. His party, he said, already controlled the government. Goulart's hard left turn produced neither order nor progress, and his economic policies contributed to the near bankruptcy of Latin America's largest nation.

Supported by the conservative oligarchy, the military seized power in 1964. For the next twenty-one years, a succession of stern military men ran Brazil, often overlooking the niceties of constitutional restraints. They imposed a rigid press censorship and suspended due process and habeas corpus. In response, leftist urban guerrillas launched a scorched earth campaign to topple the government. The extremists staged robberies and set off bombs indiscriminately. To rein in the terrorists, the military adopted "a policy of ruthless extermination."

The military's brutal efforts to liquidate the leftists brought an end to the social trauma. The economy righted itself, and grew at an annual rate of ten percent between the late 1960s and early 1970s. With this economic good news and social peace, the Firm's São Paulo partners began considering a Rio de Janeiro office. Even though Brasilia was theoretically the capital city, most of the government agencies were still located in Rio, and the Banco do Brasil, Petrobras, and many foreign banks continued to headquarter there.

In 1967, the partners elected a long-time São Paulo associate to the partnership and sent him to open a Rio office. Almost immediately, Dennis Meyer recalls, it became apparent that Sergio Sardenberg was a very nice man who had little talent for administration. Sardenberg had "very peculiar working habits." He would make early-morning appointments with clients and not show up because he liked to sleep late. Annoyed, some of them found other lawyers.

In 1972, the Firm sent Ronaldo Veirano, a Brazilian, from Chicago to Rio to take charge of the office. Sardenberg felt that surrendering management control would be a loss of face, and resisted the invasion of his province. As word that the two Brazilians were feuding circulated around the Firm, the then-Chairman, Michel Coccia, and Dennis Meyer went to Rio to sort out the muddle. Although they wanted to make it clear to Sardenberg that he was out as the Administrative Partner, they had to handle him with great delicacy. His father was a five-star general, making him one of the most powerful men in Brazil. With the military dictatorship in office, anyone incurring a general's wrath could be clapped in jail and held incommunicado for months or completely disappear.

When Coccia and Meyer left their Rio hotel on a Sunday morning to go to church, General Sardenberg was standing across the street. "We thought he was going to point us out and have some squad gun us down," Meyer recalls. "We had a few moments there where we didn't know whether we were going to get out of Rio or not." The military officer crossed the street and told the Americans, "I understand there is something going on in the office here. That happens sometimes when you need a change in command, and I hope things work out for you." Rather than submit to what he viewed as an embarrassment, Sardenberg negotiated a separation agreement and left the Firm.

With Veirano running the Rio office, many young lawyers joined, including Carlos Castro. To polish his English, Castro went to Chicago in the late 1970s under the Associate Training Program. Working with the other Latin American specialists, he heard Jose Arcila's Castillian Spanish, Marcel Molins' guttural Catalán, and the rhythms of many other Hispanic countries. When Castro returned to Rio in 1979, the seeds of the great port city's decline were germinating. Rio had served as Brazil's capital since 1763, and the *cariocas* had grown accustomed to the prestige of living in Brazil's most important city. In the 1950s, however, the government had decided to re-orient the country toward its unexploited interior. To induce Brazilians to leave the populous coast, the politicians appropriated millions to build Brasilia six hundred miles inland. President Juscelino Kubitshek formally inaugurated Brasilia in 1960, but government officials kept offices in both Rio and Brasilia, and commuted between the two. Gradually, however, the ministries migrated to the splendid new capital, and Rio lost its stature as the "brains, the culture, the power, the authority" in Brazil.

When the government-owned Banco do Brasil moved to Brasilia, it set off a chain reaction, and most financial institutions moved their headquarters. "We had had a flourishing financial practice," Veirano says, "which we lost. All the foreign banks went to São Paulo or left Brazil."

There was more trouble in store. During portions of the 1980s and the early 1990s, Brazil's endemic inflation became virulent. As Rio sagged under the weight of inflation and a teetering economy, poverty and crime became almost uncontrollable. Residents and tourists alike were afraid to walk along Rio's famed beaches for fear of being robbed or beaten. Knowing that the thieves targeted patrons of expensive restaurants, many wealthy *cariocas* refused to go out for dinner unless the cafe had valet parking at the front door. The violence became so widespread that the Executive Committee canceled a scheduled Rio meeting in the early 1990s.

As poverty increased in Rio, socialism lured the population into electing anti-business city and state officials. Many companies fled Rio and moved to São Paulo or other parts of Brazil. The depression in Rio's economy and the Formula's specter sent a chill through the office. "We used to work from 9:00 to 9:00," Castro says, "then, all of a sudden, when the work level dipped substantially we had this sensation, 'Wow, what am I going to do? Switch my specialty? Move to another profession? Open a small business?'"

In 1996, Veirano, Castro, and several other Rio lawyers resigned to start their own law firm. By 1998, however, the two partners who remained, Gabriel Lacerda and Ricardo Salles, had built the office up to sixteen lawyers who generated an acceptable office profit.

The Buenos Aires office's history closely follows that of the Argentine capital's founding. Pedro de Mendoza established the city in 1536, but hostile Indians forced the Spanish to abandon it. In 1580, the Spanish returned, built a town hall and a church, and never left. Following that pattern, the Firm opened a Buenos Aires office in 1968. Instead of populating it with Firm "old boys," it brought in outsiders who knew nothing about Baker & McKenzie or its culture. Three years later, the eleven lawyers resigned en masse to start their own firm, taking with them clients referred by the Firm. It would be a decade before Baker & McKenzie opened another Buenos Aires office.

Despite the Firm's initial pratfall in Argentina, Russell Baker's interest in Latin America's third-largest nation continued. Through his oldest client, Abbott Laboratories, he met a young Argentine lawyer who he thought might fit into his family. During a trip to Argentina in the early 1970s, the President of Abbott's Latin American operations introduced him to his son-in-law, Horacio Soares. Since Soares spoke very poor English at the time, Baker chatted with him in Spanish. "He asked a lot of questions," Soares recalls. Baker liked the young lawyer, but he didn't mention his interest in reestablishing a Buenos Aires office.

Baker and Soares kept in touch by mail, and, eventually, Baker asked the Argentine to come to Chicago for a job interview. Soares scraped the money together and flew to the Windy City where, with his limited English, he struggled through three days of interviews with the Chicago lawyers. The Firm offered him a job in the Chicago office, and, after two years, he returned home to join a well-known law firm. Later, another young lawyer, Miguel Menegazzo-Cané, joined the same law firm and the two became friends.

Meanwhile, Baker & McKenzie partners were making periodic trips to Argentina to keep a finger on the nation's pulse. At times, its pulse throbbed. After almost twenty years in exile, Juan Peron returned to the presidency in 1973. The old dictator died a year later, and his second wife, a former cabaret dancer, succeeded him. She lasted until the military threw her out in 1976.

As the generals and admirals were settling in to run Argentina, Zürich's Peter Achermann went to Buenos Aires to get a first-hand view of the nation's political and economic environment. Over lunch at the exclusive Jockey Club, he and Soares assayed Argentina's inflation, which had jumped to over three hundred percent. They also talked about the military junta's campaign against urban terrorism, which later became known as the "Dirty War."

Even with the uncertainty, Firm partners continued a dialogue with Soares and continued sending clients to him. But the ambitious young man was restless. He contacted Marcel Molins, his mentor when he had worked in the Chicago office, to tell him that he was thinking about leaving his law firm. He also wanted to know whether Baker & McKenzie would refer business to him after he left. Molins assured Soares that the relationship would stay the same, and he and Menegazzo established their own law office in 1978. From the outset, Soares made it clear to Menegazzo that he wanted to turn their firm into a full Baker & McKenzie office. "I didn't know who these guys at Baker & McKenzie were," Menegazzo says. "But, I said 'Why not? Let's give it a try.' So I jumped in without knowing who I was getting into bed with."

Although Soares was pushing for a union with Baker & McKenzie, the Firm's previous Argentine stumble had created a strong prejudice against opening an office with anyone other than home-grown lawyers. The partners moved slowly, but, after three years of discussions, the Firm approved the reopening in Buenos Aires. Even though Menegazzo and Soares were experienced lawyers, they agreed to start as associates. To provide the link with the Firm, Chicago partner Sergio Quattrini was sent to Argentina to open the Buenos Aires office. Quattrini, a Peruvian who had joined Baker & McKenzie in 1974, "was a young, energetic guy," Menegazzo says. "An intelligent person with a lot of interest in developing business."

The office opened in September 1981. As part of the plan to integrate the new lawyers into the Firm culture, Menegazzo went to Chicago in early 1982 under the Associate Training Program. When he, his wife, and two small children arrived in Chicago, Michael Madda had already leased them a house in Evanston. Later, he helped the Argentine battle with car dealers over the price of an auto. And Menegazzo's wife called on other Chicago lawyers' wives to get the names of doctors for her children and tips on where to send them to school.

The Argentine couple's sojourn to the U.S. began smoothly, but one month after they arrived, Argentina's military government ordered its forces to invade the British-controlled Falkland (Malvinas) Islands. The Chicago office had British lawyers, and others visited with some frequency. However, there was no tension, Menegazzo recalls, and the Argentine and British lawyers worked together without problems, but they avoided talking about the two-month-long Falklands War.

Before the invasion, the partners had intended for Menegazzo to work on Argentine business. After the War began, about eighty percent of his work related to other Latin American countries, and, he says, "the other twenty percent were questions like, 'How do we get out of Argentina?'"

When Menegazzo returned home, the military junta had lost power. But the return to civilian government did little to help the economy. By the mid-1980s, the country's foreign debt had skyrocketed to $45 billion and the economy was spinning out of control, with one thousand percent inflation corroding the peso.

The Buenos Aires partners' original business plan had called for rapid growth. But hyper-inflation made it difficult because "you didn't have a chance to budget your results. You didn't have a chance to make a business plan," Menegazzo says. Rather than planning for the future, inflation kept the partners' eyes focused no farther than the next day, week, or month. Instead of using the normal monthly pay period, the office paid employees every two weeks, and gave them raises to compensate for the inflation that, at one point, caused currency readjustments hourly.

Inflation sliced into the office's profits, in part because of the delay between the time the partners sent out bills and the time they were paid. If the office billed fees or expenses in Argentine pesos, when the client paid the statement sixty or ninety days later, the amount billed might have devalued by more than fifty percent. Argentina's exchange control regulations made the problem even worse. The rules limited the office's ability to buy U.S. dollars or other hard currency, forcing it to keep its cash in the ever-eroding pesos. When the office received payments in a foreign currency, the law required it to convert the dollars or deutschmarks into Argentine pesos at an artificial government rate, rather than the more realistic black-market rate available on the street. The office's accounting became so chaotic that it had to hire additional staff to keep track of its financial position.

The Buenos Aires partners tried to reduce the inflation risk by hedging, but that was costly and created its own set of risks. The office reinvested its cash every day in an attempt to keep up with inflation, but the Firm's own system of calculating currency gains and losses worked against Buenos Aires. When the International Financial Department translated pesos into the Firm's currency of record, U.S. dollars, it used a monthly average. "You never knew how much money you had in dollars until you knew what the average was," Menegazzo recalls.

Although the Firm's currency translation formula hurt Buenos Aires, Baker & McKenzie had long had a policy of treating exchange losses as a global expense. With huge exchange losses mounting in Argentina, and in Brazil and several other countries, many partners from hard currency nations such as Germany and Switzerland argued that each office should absorb its own losses. When the partners voted this down, they noted that, if Buenos Aires had been forced to pay its exchange losses, it would have wrecked the office.

With the Argentine economy in shambles, two of the office's major clients went bankrupt and couldn't pay their bills. The ubiquitous Formula intervened to magnify an already serious problem. Because Soares had done much of the work for the two clients, his income slumped to less than $30,000. At the 1986 New York Annual Meeting, he appeared before the Executive Committee to ask for relief, and the Committee agreed to raise his income, but required him to pay back the uplift in three years.

As the decade of the 1980s closed, Argentina found relief from its economic anarchy. In 1989, the country elected a new president, a Peronist, who promptly installed a team of economists to put the nation's house in order. The technocrats curbed inflation, restructured Argentina's massive debts to foreign banks, cut budget deficits, enforced the tax law, and sold off bloated state-owned companies to private industry. With these reforms, Argentina began its recovery, but by then the Buenos Aires office was suffering from internal bickering.

When the office had first opened, Soares, Menegazzo, and Quattrini had been friendly, and had worked together. "Quattrini was wonderful," Soares says. "He is a very intelligent and outstanding lawyer and a hard worker. He had a lot of enthusiasm, and we thought he was a great guy." Later, however, there was a spat over the office's name. After the anti-Americanism of the Falklands War died down, Soares and Menegazzo started pushing to change the name from Quattrini, Soares & Menegazzo-Cané to Baker & McKenzie. "We wanted to be known in the market as what we really were—an international law firm under the name of Baker & McKenzie," Menegazzo says. But Quattrini refused.

The name issue and other irritants bred discontent, but the root cause of the problem was that Quattrini "wanted to be the king." Until Soares had become a partner in 1983 and Menegazzo in 1985, Quattrini had been the only Buenos Aires partner, and, after his seven years in Chicago, he was the old boy in Argentina. Quattrini had developed friendships with many partners around the world, and they remembered him as a charming, outgoing man, so, when they had work to send to Argentina, they directed it to their old friend. With control over much of the work flow, Quattrini had a powerful tool to direct the destinies of the other lawyers.

"There were very tough and strong discussions and arguments," Soares says. Although the Buenos Aires partners tried to contain their problems in the office, several Firm partners knew about the friction long before it became generally known. At first, Baker & McKenzie followed its tradition of staying out of local office disputes unless they were likely to destroy an office. As the office's atmosphere became increasingly acidic, however, the Executive Committee decided it needed to take action. Freddy Paván, the Executive Committee's liaison to the Buenos Aires office, made several trips to Argentina to try to calm the situation. During one visit, he says, "I had long, separate meetings with each side, and then we got together. I said, 'Look, the best way to solve this problem is, instead of talking against the other in the corridors, to sit down face to face, and let everybody tell the other what he thinks is wrong.'"

"Sergio told Horacio that Horacio didn't work hard enough, that Horacio had not invited him to a party at his house, and that Horacio did not say 'hello' one night when they saw each other at Mass. They threw everything out at that meeting, from personal to professional," Paván recalls. Quattrini hammered the point that he worked harder than Soares and Menegazzo. He also felt that Soares and Menegazzo were trying to isolate him. After the outpouring of emotion, "I thought we were going to put things behind us and start all over again," Paván says. "Then, we went out to celebrate, and I felt that the whole problem was solved. Two months after that, Sergio called and said that he was leaving the Firm."

After he announced that he was going to open his own office, the two sides fought over many issues. The arguments became so bitter that neither side would negotiate with the other, forcing the Executive Committee to again ask Paván to intervene. After three difficult trips to Buenos Aires, he got the parties to agree to a separation agreement.

Quattrini's 1992 departure dropped the number of lawyers in the office to fourteen, cutting deeply into its tax and intellectual property capabilities. Over the next three years, however, the remaining Argentine partners managed to fill those gaps by recruiting new lawyers, bringing the total to thirty-five by 1995. The split also caused revenues to decline sharply, but by 1995 they had doubled to almost $6 million.

Part of the reason for the office's post-Quattrini success was that the Argentine government's policy and the economy were working in its favor. Early on, the Argentine partners had identified the nation's privatization program as a major growth area. With some fifty percent of the country's industry in government hands, its decision to sell many state-owned companies created a boon for the office. Baker & McKenzie was one of the first law firms to develop privatization expertise, and its clients included purchasers of the government's gas, electricity, port, telephone, and oil and gas holdings. As other Latin American countries began privatization programs, the Buenos Aires lawyers joined with Frankfurt and New York lawyers to export their skills as advisors to the governments of Uruguay, Paraguay, Bolivia, and Peru. When the Argentine government decided to get out of the business of managing pension funds, the office also leaped on that opportunity. Several Firm lawyers made themselves experts in the area, and brought in huge pension funds as clients.

At about the same time that Baker & McKenzie began negotiations to open an office at the extreme southeastern corner of South America, it was also talking with Colombian lawyers in the extreme northwestern part of the continent. Long before that, however, James Raisbeck, Sr. "made the most important connection that we had ever had," James Raisbeck, Jr. says. "My father was exactly the same age as Russell Baker and they knew each other. My father said, 'Baker & McKenzie is a firm that it would be interesting for us to have a connection with.'"

The senior Raisbeck was a Scotsman who immigrated to America, got a U.S. law degree, and began working in Latin America in the 1920s. Eventually, he moved to Colombia, married, and opened a one-man law office in Bogotá. His son worked for him part-time as a clerk while he studied law at the University of Rosario, the Western Hemisphere's second-oldest university.

Raisbeck, Sr. followed up his idea of making a connection with Baker & McKenzie, and sent his son to Chicago in 1970 to meet Russell Baker. Baker and the other Chicago partners were impressed with the serious young Colombian. Even the Chicago office's demanding trademark partner liked him, and began sending him work. During the next five years, the relationship grew, and the Raisbeck firm became Baker & McKenzie's Colombian correspondent.

As the two law firms grew more comfortable with each other, they began discussing the opening of a Baker & McKenzie office in Bogotá. Baker & McKenzie investigated the ten-man Raisbeck firm extensively. Both the Firm's Chairman, Dennis Meyer, and other partners met with Raisbeck, Jr. at several Miami meetings and made multiple trips to Bogotá. During their visits to Colombia, Meyer says, Firm partners "went out to dinner with their wives, met some of the younger people in the office, and looked at their client list. It wasn't just a short romance."

Meyer also sent the Firm's chief financial officer to Bogotá to review the Raisbeck firm's books. "James Raisbeck was Colombian by birth, but Scottish by heritage, so the books were very tight," Meyer recalls. "He wasn't throwing pesos around, which is one of the things that impressed us. He had as good a billing procedure as any office in the Firm." After an in-depth review of the Raisbeck operation, Meyer concluded that the Colombians were "hard-working, aggressive, resourceful" and that they "could get along on their own and didn't have to have a lot of direction." Many Baker & McKenzie partners, however, were still stinging from the abortive Buenos Aires experience and were skeptical that the Raisbeck lawyers might join the Firm, establish close relationships with clients, and then leave.

Raisbeck partners also had reservations. When Raisbeck, Jr. first proposed the merger, Jorge Lara was concerned that they might have to accept "rules and structures from abroad." Several Raisbeck lawyers worried that they would be submerged in the gigantic Firm and lose their identity in Colombia. But the "international exposure, the integration of cultures, the access to information and clients, the possibility of participating in large multi-jurisdictional transactions" outweighed the Colombians' fears of foreign intervention. Baker & McKenzie partners further eased their anxiety by explaining the Firm's tradition of letting its offices operate independently. And the fact that over half of the Firm's partners were non-U.S. convinced the Colombians that non-Americans could participate fully.

In addition, a practical event spurred the Raisbeck firm to join Baker & McKenzie. At the time, some fifteen percent of Raisbeck's income came from Firm referrals. When Raisbeck, Jr. learned that lawyers from a competing Bogotá law firm had met with Baker & McKenzie, "we realized that the fact that we were correspondents today didn't guarantee that we would be there next year."

In 1978, the two firms worked out an agreement that was subject to approval at Baker & McKenzie Rio de Janeiro Annual Meeting. A significant group of Firm partners voiced misgivings about the merger, waving the bloody shirt of the Argentine experience. Some opponents dug in their heels over the issue of whether to give the Bogotá lawyers Fund A points. It wasn't fair, they argued, to dilute the pool of Fund A money by giving points to lawyers who hadn't earned them under the Firm's rules.

The debate was "acrimonious," Meyer says. "There were a lot of 'nos' on the first go-around." He went to the Firm's seventy-seven-year-old founder for support, telling him: "Russell, I will vouch for the Raisbeck lawyers. I think they are Baker & McKenzie type people, and they will be a good office for the Firm." To support his case, Meyer made two other points: that failure to bring in Raisbeck would set a bad precedent if the Firm might want to join with an existing law firm in the future; and that Baker & McKenzie had to prove that one mistake didn't mean that it couldn't go out and try again. Baker agreed. At the last Annual Meeting he would attend before he died, he summoned his persuasive skills one final time. "We had to have several other votes until he was able to twist enough arms," Meyer says. In understated "Baker & McKenzie-speak," the meeting minutes merely said that "following extensive discussion," the measure passed.

Even though the partners voted in favor of the Bogotá office, as a condition of the merger agreement, the Raisbeck firm agreed that a Baker & McKenzie partner would spend at least two years in Bogotá. "We had no problem with that," Raisbeck, Jr. says, "and actually we very much encouraged it. We knew nothing about the financial accounting aspects and the Formula." Meyer says, "I think that was the main thing that sold it. We were going to have our own person in the office who would bring in the Baker & McKenzie culture." Meyer persuaded Jaime González-Bendiksen, a Mexico City partner, to be the Firm's man on site.

To further ease the transition, Raisbeck, Jr. sent two of his accounting staffers to Chicago to plumb the Formula's mysteries. In anticipation of joining with Baker & McKenzie, Robert Raisbeck, James's young brother, had worked in Chicago before the merger, and, after the amalgamation, Jorge Lara made the pilgrimage.

Lara's father had been a prominent Colombian politician, serving as Secretary to the President and as a Senator during his career. Being a politician in Colombia had always been a dangerous business. Shortly after Simón Bolívar liberated Gran Colombia from Spanish rule in the early 1800s, Colombians divided themselves into Liberal and Conservative parties. During the next one hundred fifty years, bitter hostilities built up and political assassinations were common. In 1948, a decade of unmatched brutality began, and hundreds died in political wars that Colombians call "*La Violencia*."

To protect his family, Lara's father took asylum in neighboring Venezuela. In 1957, the Liberal and Conservative parties reached a compromise, and the *Violencia* epoch ended. Lara's father brought his family back home, and his son enrolled in the University of Rosario law school. There, he met Raisbeck, Jr. The budding lawyers liked each other, and Raisbeck, Jr. arranged for Lara to work in his father's law firm. In the early 1970s, Lara left to take a job with the Colombian government, after which he started a law firm with his father, who had retired from politics. They then joined the Raisbecks in the late 1970s.

Robert Raisbeck also worked at the firm. Early on, Robert's career path had not been promising. He had bounced around various secondary schools with a noted lack of scholastic success. When he finally graduated, he went to the University of Miami, where he flunked out after one semester. Once again an academic failure, Robert returned to Bogotá, where his brother talked him into trying law school. Determined that his brother would join him in the legal profession, James Raisbeck talked the Dean of the Rosario University Law School into admitting Robert in spite of his poor scholastic history. Robert passed the exams and entered law school. Evidently, the experience had a sobering effect. The young man, who had always been somewhat of a playboy, straightened out.

In the early stages of talks between the Raisbeck firm and Baker & McKenzie, Robert went to the Chicago office to spend a year. Working in the Latin American Foreign Trade Department gave him a "full immersion course in how Baker & McKenzie worked and functioned." On occasion, he says, Russell Baker "popped into my office and sat down for a while to talk." Baker, then seventy-six, impressed him because "he cared about people. He cared about what they were doing. He was interested in finding out what you thought, how your family was. You cannot lose that perspective in an office, because, if you do, it just becomes too mechanical, too business oriented. You have to have the human side."

In addition to Baker's friendliness, Robert immediately found a home with the close-knit group of Latin American lawyers in Chicago. They played softball in Grant Park and had lunch together almost religiously every day. There were also outings to William Gibbons's farm, games of backgammon and soccer, and a number of other social events.

———

Even before the Bogotá lawyers had joined Baker & McKenzie, Colombia had experienced economic uncertainty for several years. In reaction to a long-held fear of U.S. dominance of its economy, Colombia had joined the five-nation Andean Common Market, which was designed to keep the "Colossus of the North" and other foreigners at bay. Colombia had adopted laws that prohibited foreigners from owning more than fifty percent of local companies, severely limited the amount of profits foreigners could send home, and required government approval of almost all foreign investment.

The limitations slowed the pace of foreign investment to a crawl, and the nation's lack of domestic capital further bogged down economic expansion. With the restrictive laws chilling most foreign investment, the Bogotá office adjusted to the new economic realities by expanding its intellectual property practice and handling more distributorship and sales representative agreements.

In addition to the problems created by the Andean Common Market, Colombia's external debt, negative trade balances, guerrilla terrorism, and drug trafficking caused economic sluggishness in the 1980s. The guerrilla problem subsided after the USSR, which had been supporting the Marxists through its Cuban satellite, crumbled. In the late 1980s and early 1990s, the government relaxed the restrictions on foreign investment, restructured its foreign debt, and began a privatization program.

The Colombian experience, Robert Raisbeck said, is an example of "how important government policy is in attracting business. When you allow companies the flexibility to make their own decisions, instead of regulating them to exhaustion and putting up hurdles and obstacles, it makes a tremendous difference. Open-market policies brought an economic boom to our office."

With this stimulation, Colombia, and the Bogotá office, began to grow. By 1995, the office had increased the legal staff to almost thirty lawyers and its revenues to $5.3 million. The office's legal specialties included tax, corporate, labor, petroleum and mining, and intellectual property. And, as Colombian companies have expanded and begun looking at foreign markets, the office has brought in local clients, including one of the nation's largest conglomerates.

To further broaden the office's practice, Lara has helped organize a Latin American banking and finance group to facilitate region-wide development of new clients. The Latin American group explored the market for representing commercial and investment bankers. And, as Latin companies became more sophisticated, they began eyeing the London, Tokyo, and New York financial markets as places where they could sell securities to raise capital. The promotional efforts produced work for the Colombian office, among the most notable being a Colombian supermarket chain that sold $60 million of securities in the U.S., and the representation of a consortium of foreign banks that financed the Banco de Colombia's privatization.

Chapter Fifteen

A New Frontier:
China & Hong Kong

In the same year that Baker & McKenzie opened its doors for business, 1949, Mao Zedong led his victorious Communist troops into Beijing. After he consolidated power, Mao announced his Great Leap Forward, designed to industrialize China and transform its small-scale farms into gigantic communes. The Communist leader's first major economic experiment plunged his country into history's worst famine, leaving millions dead from starvation. The Great Helmsman followed that failure with the Great Proletarian Cultural Revolution, which dragged the world's most populous nation through another decade of chaos. Internationally, however, Mao was more successful. In 1971, U.S. Secretary of State Henry Kissinger made a secret trip to Beijing to explore the possibility of resuming diplomatic contacts. He got a positive response, and President Richard Nixon visited the Chinese capital to begin the process of restoring Sino-American relationships.

Shortly after his 1972 China trip, Nixon asked the Majority and Minority Leaders of the U.S. House of Representatives to go to China to assay the political climate. Gerald R. Ford put together a team of Republicans. The Democratic Majority Leader, Hale Boggs, asked an obscure young man he had worked with at the tumultuous 1968 Convention in Chicago to join his entourage. After Eugene Theroux received the telephone call from Congressman Boggs, the four-year associate in Baker & McKenzie's Washington office attended CIA and State Department briefings on the country that few Westerners had penetrated for almost a quarter-century.

In June 1972, the Congressional party flew to Shanghai and Beijing. Everything seemed peaceful, but the Cultural Revolution was at its height. The Congressional party's trip included a carefully scripted excursion to the countryside to acquaint them with the glories of the Cultural Revolution. "The only people we saw were people who were full of enthusiasm for the Revolution and for Chairman Mao," Theroux recalls. But, he knew, if the Red Guards suspected anyone of the slightest taint of Western "capitalist roadism," punishment soon followed. During a guided tour, the group met a man standing in a rice paddy, who told them, "I'm an economics professor, but I discovered that the real truth in life lies with the peasants, so I volunteered to come here and work."

When Theroux returned to the Washington office, he was hooked on the idea of developing a China practice. But, when he tried to proselytize among the partners, he met with disinterest or negativism. Some partners argued that, even though Nixon had signed the Shanghai Communiqué with the Chinese in 1972, the country was still a tightly closed society, and nobody could predict when, if ever, it would open. Now, they said, was not the time to waste money on trying to do business in the People's Republic.

Nevertheless, Theroux made several trips to China, representing clients who were interested in piercing the Bamboo Curtain. But he was still an associate, and he was worried that his somewhat fanciful China specialty might not boost him to election as a partner. In the spring of 1974, he flew to Chicago to discuss his quandary with Russell Baker. Baker fingered his worry beads and told him: "Gene, to become a partner in this Firm is the greatest thing that can happen to a young lawyer. If you have to swim through an ocean of garbage, you've got to hang in there. If you want to do things that interest you, this is the Firm to do it in." At the 1974 Mexico City Annual Meeting, the partners elected him an Income Partner.

Later, Baker invited Theroux to speak to a group of corporate executives in Chicago. Before he spoke on China, Baker addressed them. "It was a Will Rogers-like chat that made them think that they were in the presence of someone who could see around the corner into the future," Theroux remembers. "He had a way of telling the listener, 'You're worth something because you've got something of value. And your companies are great companies that spring right out of the American Midwest. Right out of Chicago. Right out of Moline. Right out of Milwaukee."

Theroux delivered his paean to China, and returned to Washington, where he scraped together enough funding to make trips to the People's Republic. He persuaded a syndicate of clients to pay pro rata parts of his expenses in return for his reporting to them on any interesting developments. If any work for a client came up during his sojourns, Theroux billed that client for the time he worked directly for it. Even though the early trips were not economically fruitful, he says, "the more I went, the more expertise I had. The more contacts I had. The more credibility I had."

The Chinese didn't want foreigners in the country, but for one month each spring and fall the nation held the Canton (now Guangzhou) Export

Commodities Fair to promote the sale of such items as dolls, carbon black, and hog bristles. For Theroux, it was great fishing waters for clients because there were no other lawyers. One of the more exotic clients Theroux snared was Ringling Brothers, Barnum & Bailey Circus, for which he tried unsuccessfully to export a trained panda. "Most of my projects fell flat. I tried to get sporting goods made. I tried to get athletic shoes made. But the Chinese adamantly refused to make anything that had a foreign brand name on it, and they refused to make anything according to foreign specifications."

———

Russell Baker lured Preston Torbert to the Firm with a promise that he could put his Chinese language skills to work. The young man was a kaleidoscope of education and languages. In secondary school, he studied Latin for four years and wedged in a year of Italian. Rather than going to college the year after he graduated, Torbert went to Spain and spent a year mastering Spanish. As a Princeton University undergraduate, he took on Mandarin Chinese, Portuguese, and Russian. To perfect his Russian, he spent six months studying in the Soviet Union.

After Princeton, Torbert enrolled in Stanford University's Chinese language program and moved to Taiwan. Taipei's hot, humid climate and the schooling were tough. Torbert arrived each day for his eight o'clock class. He went into a small cubicle furnished with a table and two chairs, where his Chinese professors drilled him intensively for four hours on sentence patterns and vocabulary. After lunch, Torbert "relaxed" in the language laboratory listening to Chinese tapes. Then he went home to the Chinese-speaking family who housed and fed him. When he finished dinner, he did his homework for two or three hours.

The grueling program lasted for one year; at the end, Torbert's Mandarin was so flawless that, when he spoke to the Chinese on the phone, they thought he was a native. While he was working in the Taipei office a few years later, a Chinese merchant called the office, asking for the lawyer who had represented a sailor the merchant claimed owed him $300. The receptionist told him that Mr. Tao (Torbert's Chinese name) was the right man. Mr. Tao came on the line and, when the merchant asked how he could contact the sailor, Torbert said, "I'm sorry, but I can't disclose information that would be detrimental to his interest."

"Yes, but this guy is a foreigner, and we Chinese have to stick together," the merchant said. "Those damned foreigners, you just can't trust them."

"Well, I don't trust those foreigners either," Mr. Tao agreed. "We Chinese really need to stick together, but I can't help you."

After his sojourn in Taiwan, he returned to the U.S. and got a Master's Degree and a Ph.D. in Chinese history from the University of Chicago. For his Ph.D., he started out reading documents in ancient Chinese, and, in his spare time, studied Japanese. After he completed his classwork at Chicago, Torbert enrolled in Harvard Law School. While he was simultaneously studying law, he finished his doctoral dissertation on a segment of Chinese history in the 1600s and 1700s.

When Torbert interviewed with several New York law firms for a job, his polyglot resume didn't interest them. But, when Baker read his curriculum vitae, he hounded the multi-lingual young man until he agreed to join the Firm. Almost immediately, Baker put Torbert in a position to use his fluent Mandarin Chinese. In 1975, the new associate made his first trip to mainland China with Theroux to attend the Canton Fair.

The trips to the Canton Fair produced a little legal work, but in 1976 everything came to a halt. After Mao's death that fall, the extreme left-wing Gang of Four grabbed power. To keep the revolutionary flame burning, the Gang of Four organized thousands of people to demonstrate in Tiananmen Square, and goaded them to chant slogans against "Arch Unrepentant Capitalist Roaders" and "Harbingers of the Right Deviationist Wind." Other Chinese leaders, seeing that the nation was reeling from the unremitting waves of radical policies, arrested the Gang of Four and set China on a course to bring it out of more than twenty-five years of isolation.

In 1979, several events helped pull back the Chinese screen. The People's Republic adopted a joint venture law (which Torbert translated into English) that allowed foreigners to own equity stakes in manufacturing and other facilities. President Jimmy Carter broke off formal relations with Taiwan, and extended diplomatic recognition to the People's Republic. Meanwhile, Coca-Cola and a few other large corporations legitimized the long-estranged nation's business climate by making major investments in China. Theroux started making frequent trips in and out of the People's Republic with clients, but soon tired of being a "shuttlecock" between Washington and Beijing.

Chinese law prohibited anyone other than citizens from practicing law in China, but Theroux thought he had a possible solution. He proposed to the Ministry of Foreign Trade that the Firm would give lectures on commercial law to the Chinese managers who would be dealing with foreign businessmen. The Ministry recognized the need to train Chinese personnel to handle international business, and agreed to the proposal. The teaching assignment served as a vehicle for Theroux and Torbert to get visas to stay in China for a long period and to develop their profiles as on-site China lawyers.

Before the two began teaching, they persuaded the Executive Committee to fund the China initiative. It agreed to pay for living and travel expenses, Torbert's associate salary, and a $125,000 annual income for Theroux. In 1981, the two began preparing for two months of lectures, which they delivered at the China Council for the Promotion of International Trade Building. Most mornings, they had to walk up seven floors because the elevator was broken. The classes took place in a sparse, undecorated room that had no heat. With the wind blowing through broken windows during the bitterly cold winter, they lectured wearing sweaters, heavy jackets, hats, and gloves.

Weather was not the Americans' only problem. Many of their one hundred students, mostly middle-level bureaucrats from government agencies, knew nothing about the law or legal concepts. During the Cultural Revolution, the Red Guards had branded many law professors and lawyers "leeches and parasites," and banished them to labor camps. To make communication even more difficult, the Chinese students were "very naive about the outside world," Torbert recalls. And there was very little dialogue because, in the Asian fashion, the students were reluctant to ask questions, afraid that they would show ignorance or embarrass themselves.

In addition to cultural differences, the Chinese students used street language to describe legal relationships. When the pupils talked about offer and acceptance of a contract, they used a gambling term, *fapan*, which roughly meant giving something and then taking it back. With his knowledge of Chinese, Torbert prepared a glossary of legal jargon to help the students deal with the lectures on contracts, corporations, and technology transfers. Somehow, he made "retroactive effect" and "limited liability company" understandable to the Chinese.

In the early 1980s, China had opened the door slightly to foreign trade, but it was still closed to social contact with Westerners. The Americans had little personal contact with their students because it "would not have been politically correct," Torbert says. "As long as they were all together in a group where each one could watch over the other, they knew that nothing inappropriate could happen." Even though the two didn't develop close friendships among their students, they did keep in touch with some of them. Several went on to hold high positions in the China International Trust Investment Corporation and the Ministry of Foreign Trade, and one became China's ambassador to the U.S.

During most of their stay, the Baker & McKenzie lawyers lived and worked out of a suite in the Beijing Hotel. Although it was the ultimate luxury the Chinese capital had to offer, living in China for long periods of time "was a hell of a hardship." To break the tedium, on one particularly cold night Theroux and Torbert set out to find what they had been told was "a real hot spot in Beijing." They found it: the unheated cafe at the Peace Hotel, where they sat in their overcoats drinking tea in ten-degree weather until the cafe closed at nine o'clock. Watching television was seldom an option. When the television set wasn't broken, it featured programs on political correctness or the latest technical developments at Number 3 Oxygen Plant.

At the Beijing Hotel, where most of the guests were foreigners, its lobby became a "Grand Central Station." Desperate for diversion, the guests didn't consider it rude to strike up conversations with strangers. Theroux says he met people "you wouldn't meet in the outside world because the Beijing Hotel was really a crossroads of visitors." He ran across several well-known entertainers, politicians, and businessmen, some of whom eventually became clients.

After Theroux and Torbert finished their lectures in 1981, Torbert returned to Chicago. To help deliver a second round of lectures, another Chinese-speaking associate, Charles Conroy, joined Theroux.

Conroy began studying Chinese at age fourteen with a Jesuit priest who had been a missionary in China. At Yale University, he continued his China studies and received a $350 scholarship to spend a summer studying in Taiwan. Conroy had previously met Russell Baker, who told the young man that he might earn extra money by working with the Firm's Taipei correspondent lawyer, Robert Yahng. By the time he got to Taipei, Conroy had consumed $200 of his $350 scholarship in airfare, and needed a job to pay for the rest of his ninety-day trip. He contacted Yahng, who put him to work writing about Taiwanese legal developments. Even with the salary Yahng paid him, Conroy's resources were strained. To save money, he moved into a room on the top floor of a brothel, the cheapest place he could find. "It gave me a great insight into life in Taiwan," Conroy says. He returned home, and later enrolled in Columbia University's law school. When he graduated, he joined the Firm's New York office.

Conroy went to Beijing in 1981 to help Theroux teach the commercial law courses. They arose at six and began classes at eight, teaching until noon. Then, they returned to the hotel, where they checked their messages to see if a client had called. "Gene and I would get very excited if somebody called up and had some business for us to do because we were so desperate to practice law," Conroy remembers. After the lecture series ended, Theroux returned to Washington, leaving Conroy in Beijing by himself with little work to do. When clients did come to Beijing, he worked until late at night because they would be there only for a few days, pushing to get their deals done.

With only sporadic client work, living in China on a daily basis in the early 1980s was difficult. The scarcity of Western food made China feel even more remote. Conroy looked forward to the weekly Lufthansa flights, when a friend, the airline's Beijing representative, wheedled a few bottles of wine and Italian salami from the flight crew. The almost constant feeling that he was under surveillance made the dreary atmosphere even more oppressive. When the janitors cleaned his hotel rooms, they often went through his belongings. He also suspects that agents followed him on occasion, and he is certain that the Chinese opened his mail, read his telexes, and tapped his telephone.

In those early days, one of the hardest things to adjust to, Conroy says, was the psychological hardship of having to function at a very slow pace and of being in a highly regimented society. When he flew back to Hong Kong every few months, getting off the plane was always a shock. In China, Conroy says, most people still wore dull blue Mao jackets that were "colorless masses of clothing. When I'd step off the plane in Hong Kong and see color, see neon, see lights, see automobiles, it was like I'd been in a time warp. It felt like I'd advanced thirty-five years instantaneously."

After almost a year in Beijing's difficult business climate, Conroy moved to the Hong Kong office in 1982. "I was the young kid on the point," Conroy says, "trying to deal with a lot of stuff daily in Hong Kong." From 1982 forward, the British Colony served as the Firm's China practice headquarters. Its lawyers made frequent trips into China, but they found that it was logistically easier to operate out of Hong Kong. Secretarial and word processing support were there, making it easier to draft and translate documents into Chinese. Also, clients preferred to plan their strategy in cosmopolitan Hong Kong, and to fly into China only for the negotiating sessions.

Until the early 1980s, the China practice had required subsidies from both the Firm and the Hong Kong office. By 1983, however, political developments slid the Bamboo Curtain further to the side, allowing foreign investors and their lawyers to enter. Deng Xiaoping's declaration that it was glorious to get rich paved the way for his country's move toward a free-market economy. With the Chinese economy beginning to bubble, "the Firm was there with a good base of clients who were interested in investing in China, and a few smart lawyers who could speak Mandarin and knew their way around China. We were able to put the two together and build a good profile in the China market," Graham Morrison says. Conroy began shuttling between Hong Kong and Beijing almost every week. Torbert and Theroux made trips from the U.S. when necessary. And, in 1983, the Firm recruited Michael Moser, a Harvard Law School product. Having spent several years in Taiwan doing research for a Ph.D. from Columbia University, Moser was fluent in Chinese and had a deep knowledge of China's history and culture. "He was the kind of lawyer that Russell Baker would have grabbed with both hands," Theroux says. "Mike also had the grit to take up long-term residence in Beijing at a time when daily life for a foreign lawyer was no walk in the park."

Conroy became a partner in 1983, and Moser took on more responsibility in Beijing. Every few days, a new client came to Conroy with a Chinese business opportunity, everything, he says, "from port developments to pipelines to aircraft maintenance transactions to building one of the biggest exhibition centers in Beijing—the World Trade Center." Many of these projects involved joint ventures between foreigners and Chinese entities. For the uninitiated, the negotiating sessions could be unsettling. The Chinese side usually packed the conference room with up to twenty people, most of whom smoked so much that even seasoned Western smokers had to occasionally leave the room for air.

Chinese negotiations could drag on for months, sometimes years, requiring stamina and patience. The delays, and the Chinese's ancient mistrust of foreigners, made dealing with them difficult. They still harbored bitter feelings about the 1842 Opium War, when the "foreign devils" conquered them and set up colonies in Hong Kong, Shanghai, Canton, and other cities. The Chinese took the humiliation of foreign domination particularly hard because, Torbert says, "they believe in their hearts that they are the most cultured people in the world. They have five thousand years of unbroken tradition, which no other culture in the world has."

Despite the underlying strain of cultural superiority, some Chinese negotiators were insecure when they dealt with foreign businessmen, whom they believed to have greater business, financial, and technological knowledge. Feeling vulnerable, the Chinese negotiators were often fearful of making decisions, sometimes becoming sidetracked on minor issues or arguing for hours over "boilerplate" contract provisions that Westerners would not have wasted time discussing.

The political element also complicated the bargaining process. At negotiating sessions, it was sometimes impossible to determine which of the persons on the Chinese team played which role. "Based on Western standards of hierarchy," Conroy says, "you would think that the general manager of the factory was the most important person at the table. He might be. But, frequently, it might turn out that his driver was actually the most important person because his driver was the liaison to the Communist Party. So you always had to be careful that you didn't alienate anybody from the other side."

At one point in the mid-1980s, the Chinese cracked down on foreign investment. "What they were desperately afraid of," Conroy says, "was that places like Shanghai and Guangzhou would become separate little city states. If those cities built up their economic power, they could thumb their noses at Beijing." Despite the temporary slowdown, the China practice group continued to grow steadily, adding staff and associates. The group opened Shanghai and Guangzhou presences in the 1980s, but closed them in the early 1990s after the Chinese government adopted regulations allowing foreign law firms to have only one office in China.

In 1985, Conroy left Hong Kong, leaving Moser in charge of the China practice. The next year, the Firm's Chairman visited the People's Republic. During

Robert Cox's visit to Shanghai, Theroux took him to meet the then-mayor of Shanghai. A few years later, the mayor visited the U.S. and insisted on visiting Cox and "his friends at Baker & McKenzie in Chicago. It was a cameo incident," Cox says, "except for the fact that his name was Jiang Zemin, who is Deng Xiaoping's successor as China's leader."

The China practice expanded at a fast pace during the 1980s, but it hit the wall in 1989. In Tiananmen Square, students and citizens had been demanding more democracy and greater freedom. After two months of demonstrations, People's Liberation Army troops entered the Square on June 4. The troops killed or wounded thousands of unarmed protesters, and arrested and executed many more. The Firm pulled most of its lawyers out of China, but, within thirty days, they were back in their offices, and Baker & McKenzie was running advertisements for lawyers to work in the People's Republic.

Moser guided the Firm's China practice through the dark days after Tiananmen. When China reemerged in the early 1990s, Baker & McKenzie was poised to benefit from the country's rapid growth. The number of lawyers involved in the China practice more than doubled and revenues tripled between 1992 and 1997. In addition to business advice, the group developed a dispute resolution practice, and Moser was one of only two foreigners appointed to a Chinese panel of arbitrators that hears international economic disputes.

———

At the same time that Theroux was pioneering the China practice, the Pacific Basin's "pied piper," John Connor, was pushing to open a Hong Kong office. But Hong Kong had problems. In the early 1970s, the Cultural Revolution was "scaring the hell out of everybody." In addition, for an outsider like Baker & McKenzie, the chances of establishing a successful Hong Kong office were not likely. The British controlled the economy, calling their trading companies "hongs," with Swires, Jardines, and Hutchison being among the larger ones. Two banks, the Hong Kong & Shanghai Bank and Standard Chartered Bank, held sway over finances. And two old-line law firms represented most of the hongs and the banks. With a tight linkage that had existed for decades, the prospects for the Firm to break into the inner circle seemed dim.

Hong Kong had drawbacks, but it also had many pluses. The major attraction was that China was routing a large portion of its exports and imports through the colony. Another positive force was the stable and incorruptible British administration. The English legal system provided predictability to business relationships through courts that would enforce contracts and mortgages. With no welfare system, the Hong Kong government ran on a shoestring and kept taxes low. While most industrialized countries were publishing bookshelves full of business regulations, the Hong Kong government let the hongs and banks run their operations almost unfettered.

Although Hong Kong was far from reaching its full potential in the late 1960s and early 1970s, European and American entrepreneurs were beginning to notice the colony, and the Chinese were providing additional vibrancy. The liberal business climate was almost a throwback to freebooting nineteenth-century capitalism. In the industrialized countries, securities, antitrust, and environmental laws slowed down the consummation of deals for months. Hong Kong, however, was "an environment where there was relatively little red tape to get in the way of those business deals," Paul McSweeney says. In the 1970s and 1980s, the British colony hummed with a buzz of commercial activity created by the fountain of money that sprang from its increasingly important stock markets and the glut of banks. Banks had virtually no limits on the amounts they could loan to stock market and real estate speculators. And the risk-takers were more than willing to sign notes and mortgages to get their hands on cash.

Connor sensed that the Easterners' and Westerners' combined commercial flair would bring Hong Kong to a "frenetic level of business activity. It would become a very hyper place, and very competitive. Because the people were transient, and less willing to make a permanent commitment to the place, they wanted to make money fast," he says.

Between 1964, when Connor founded the Sydney office, and 1974, the Firm had not opened a new Pacific Basin office. During those ten years, however, Connor had roamed through the Far East and had gained a unique understanding of the region; which countries were growing and which nations had promising economic and political futures.

After ten years in Sydney, Connor says, his life "was beginning to drag. I guess I was also sick of paying high Australian income taxes that graduated up to 66 2/3 %. Hong Kong had a fifteen percent rate. I think that, more important than any of that, it was an exciting thing to do." Connor had little motivation for leaving Australia. He was in his mid-thirties. He was making an excellent living for his family. And he was the Sydney office's founder and leader. Opening a new Hong Kong office would be a risk. Trying to squeeze out a living in a strange, British-dominated business environment was dicey. And, if he wasn't successful, the Formula would crush him financially.

Nevertheless, by 1972, Connor had formulated a grand scheme to open offices in Hong Kong, Singapore, and Thailand. In 1973, when he went on the Executive Committee, many partners viewed him as the Firm's man with a vision of how to develop its Pacific Basin expansion. The first item on his Asian agenda called for either Hong Kong or Singapore to serve as a regional headquarters. After looking at the two entrepôts, the Executive Committee members saw that Hong Kong was almost twice the size of Singapore, and that it had more bustle.

In addition, the Firm wanted to follow its usual pattern of staffing its offices with lawyers who were qualified to practice in the local jurisdiction. The Singapore Law Society, backed by its government, adamantly prohibited foreign lawyers from practicing there. As a British Colony, however, Hong Kong made it easy for English, Australian, and other Commonwealth lawyers to join its Law Society.

Given these advantages, the Firm quickly settled on Hong Kong. The office opened in 1974 with Connor as the sole partner and Englishman Robert Pick and Australian George Forrai as the associates. "Connor and the two drones," Forrai says of the three-man legal staff. Forrai was the son of Hungarian refugees who escaped their Communist homeland and immigrated to Australia in 1957. He earned his law degree from the University of Sydney, and joined Baker & McKenzie as an associate in 1970. When Connor opened the Hong Kong office, Forrai followed him.

Pick was the other "drone." He was an associate in the London office when Connor told him that the Firm was thinking of opening in Hong Kong and asked Pick if he was interested. Pick read a few books about Hong Kong before he told Connor he would go. When he asked about his salary, "John said, 'You may not get much now. But, of course, things are going to be great, and you'll share in it. If you rock the boat now by asking for a large salary, we won't survive.'" Pick agreed to take $1,000 per month. He later learned that "the normal thing in Hong Kong was that an expatriate was given an apartment, school fees, and six weeks leave pay. But not with Baker & McKenzie."

In 1974, Pick caught a plane for Hong Kong. Forrai, who had already moved up from Sydney, took him to the Firm's bleak office. "It was a little glass cage," Pick says. "It had two small sections inside. One for John and one for George and me." Connor's desk was so low that he couldn't put his knees under it. The thin door separating him from his Chinese neighbor's office conducted the man's loud voice. "He spoke about eight languages—all very badly," Connor recalls. In the other room, Pick and Forrai huddled around a piece of furniture that resembled a coffee table more than a desk.

After several months in the cramped quarters, Connor found space in Hutchison House, which, although it was a marked improvement, had its own peculiar problems. The secretary of another tenant on their floor was certain that she had seen a ghost there. Although exorcists were available, they were expensive, so Connor brought in George, an eight-foot-tall male statue he had bought years before in New Guinea. With glaring seashell eyes and oversized genitals, George was a "fairly ferocious-looking character." Connor placed George just outside his office. After George's intervention, Connor says, the female ghost "decided that she had met a greater spirit and was never seen again."

The competitor law firms were interested in the new boys who were encroaching on their private preserve. Johnson, Stokes & Master and Deacons, the most prominent old-line firms in the colony, dominated the legal market. With Baker & McKenzie lurking on the periphery, the British-style firms continued to practice law in the traditional, slow-moving, gentlemanly fashion. When Connor spotted the weaknesses, he encouraged his lawyers to provide better quality and faster turnaround.

To beat his competitors, Connor was constantly searching for lawyers with skills that Deacons and Johnson, Stokes had overlooked. "John was always on the lookout for bright lawyers he could bring to Hong Kong," Graham Morrison says. "Occasionally, he made mistakes. But he was very much of the view that, if you planted a few seeds around, then a good number of them would grow." Other outside law firms set up Hong Kong offices. As the 1970s drew to a close, three of London's largest firms had opened Hong Kong offices, and American, Australian, Canadian, German, and Swedish firms were eyeing the possibility.

The Hong Kong office's work was not the same as that of most other Baker & McKenzie offices. Typically, when U.S. clients began European or Latin American operations, the Firm's local offices acted as general counsels for the local subsidiaries. In addition to handling major transactions, they had a steady stream of day-to-day legal work that an American in-house lawyer would normally do. In Hong Kong, however, the Firm office got little work from companies wanting to open plants or offices there. The unsettling effects of Mao's death and the arrest of the Gang of Four in 1976 had made Western businessmen reluctant to invest in permanent facilities in a tiny colony that was surrounded on three sides by the world's largest nation. As a result, early on, much of the Firm's legal work was transactional. When the Baker & McKenzie lawyers finished one project, they moved on to the next, forcing them to hunt for work to keep busy.

Connor exhorted the young lawyers to stuff their wallets with business cards and attend conferences and cocktail parties where they should "engage in conversation with people who were likely sources of work." Even though the Hong Kong Law Society put limits on business development, Connor followed the rule that a "first-class lawyer who is a rather dull, gray person who sits in his office will not succeed in Hong Kong." He joined the American Chamber of Commerce, the American Club, the Foreign Correspondents Club, and the Royal Hong Kong Jockey Club.

Robert Pick heeded Connor's advice. He managed to crack into an establishment bastion, the Hong Kong Club. "It was a stuffy, British atmosphere with big armchairs," Forrai says, "full of bookshelves, cigars, and guys with mustaches. It was really plush, and hard to get in." Pick also wrangled a membership in the exclusive Shek-O Club, the only eighteen-hole golf club on

Hong Kong Island. When Pick took other Firm lawyers to the Shek-O to hobnob with Hong Kong's elite, it was almost "the equivalent of going to Buckingham Palace Gardens." In the small expatriate business community in the late 1970s, it was relatively easy to meet people who needed legal services. "You went to clubs for lunch. You went there for evening drinks and dinner," Bruce Porter says. "You were inevitably rubbing shoulders with the business-men and professionals in the city."

While Porter, Pick, and others were concentrating on American and European executives as business sources, much of Forrai's work was coming from the Filipino community. His first major client resulted from a visit to a toilet. One evening in the 1970s, he heard a loud banging on the door of his Sydney apartment. He opened it, and a Filipino neighbor told Forrai that his son was locked in the bathroom. Forrai went to the Filipino's apartment, pried the door open, and freed the man's son.

Shortly after the rescue, the Filipino invited Forrai to have dinner with a group of his fellow countrymen who were visiting Sydney. The Filipinos, execu-tives with a new merchant bank, asked him to help them with some relatively minor legal work. Forrai kept in touch with the Filipinos, and, a few months later, they invited him to attend the grand opening of the Filipinos' new Hong Kong headquarters. Connor, who was just beginning to staff the Firm's Hong Kong office, told him: "George, you've got to hook that merchant bank for the Hong Kong office. Why don't you move up to Hong Kong?" Forrai did, and the Filipino company became a good client.

The next major assignment the Firm got was a complicated piece of litigation for one of Hong Kong's oldest and most respected hongs. In the mid-1970s, Pick got a call from an old Oxford University classmate who was working in Singapore for a Hutchison subsidiary, and was trying to unscramble an Indonesian joint venture that was losing so much money that it had almost "brought the company to its knees." As a partner in the joint venture, Hutchison was liable to an American supplier for millions of dollars worth of earth-moving equipment. Because Hutchison's adversary was a U.S. company, Pick's friend assumed that he could get fast answers to his American law questions, and he was right. Pick called the Chicago office, and quickly got back to the executive. Pleased with the prompt response, Hutchison called in Pick, Connor, and other Firm lawyers, rather than its attorneys of long standing, to defend it in the Hong Kong litigation.

Connor, one of the Boys of '60, understood the American legal system and the American business mentality. He advised Hutchison to counterattack by bringing a U.S. lawsuit. The litigation waxed and waned as the two sides fought their battles in Hong Kong and American courts. Finally, they negotiated a set-tlement, which did not relieve Hutchison of liability, but did give it more time to pay off the debt. Satisfied with the Firm's efforts, Hutchison started sending the office an ever-increasing amount of work. Connor says that "this was a huge break, because it got us into the hongs. Around town, that was the sort of thing that got you a real reputation. We became a serious Hong Kong firm—not just a foreign intruder."

Later in the 1970s, Hutchison, which was still under British management, found itself in financial trouble. One of its major creditors, Hong Kong and Shanghai Bank, gained control of the company, and sold it to a legendary Hong Kong businessman, Li Ka Shing, who replaced many of the old managers. The Firm's Hutchison work dropped off until its lawyers could establish ties with the new executives. Gradually, however, Hutchison began sending increasing amounts of work to the Firm.

Another case that boosted Baker & McKenzie's Hong Kong profile grew out of the massive bankruptcy of the Carrian Group—a media-intense case that rocked the colony's business establishment. Before Carrian's illusive promoter got into trouble, he had approached Connor to do legal work. Connor refused to take him on as a client because, he says, "there was too much about him that was mysterious. There was a lot of paper moving around and companies being formed. All the classic stuff that signals a smelly situation." In just three years, Carrian had bought insurance, shipping, and real estate companies, fast-food restaurants, and many of Hong Kong's travel agencies and taxis.

When Carrian's bubble burst in 1982, the banks that had once grappled with one another for the privilege of loaning money to the high-flying company lost millions in bad loans. In addition to the monetary losses, scandal and bribery charges swirled around the case. One critic said that Carrian's business operations were the "high-water mark of, not just laissez faire, but flagrant cowboy-style, corporate activity." Carrian's creditors forced the company into what was then Hong Kong's largest bankruptcy. Connor's turning down the Carrian representation had been prescient. Because Baker & McKenzie was one of the few law firms that had not done work for the company, it had no conflict of interest to prohibit it from representing the trustee in bankruptcy (liquidator in Hong Kong parlance). The trustee asked the Firm to represent it, and, in the tight little island of Hong Kong, that helped establish the Firm's reputation as having lawyers who could handle high-profile, complex problems.

As the Hong Kong office's work began to grow, several partners decided to leave comfortable practices in their home countries and spend time in the new office. One of the first was Joachim Treeck, who moved from Frankfurt in 1975, to be followed by Wulf Döser and Rainer Stachels in the two successive years.

When Treeck arrived, he and Connor "brainstormed an assault on the German business community." Treeck got lists of the German companies in Hong Kong from his Consul General and from the Lufthansa representative. He told his wife that he would take her to dinner after he got his first client. Within a week, Gabriele Treeck had a meal in one of Hong Kong's finest restaurants.

The London office also supplied two seasoned partners, Malcolm Palmer and Bruce Porter. Part of the rationale for bringing them to Hong Kong was that senior English lawyers could easily relate to the British businessmen and government officials who were running the colony. Connor also lured John Morrow from Chicago to Hong Kong to help expand the banking and finance practice. The Hong Kong office attracted other lawyers from around the world, but, in the early years, Englishmen and Australians were the two largest groups. The Australians set the tone of the Hong Kong office with their energy and entrepreneurial flair. The perception, Englishman Graham Morrison says, was that "the Brits were there to provide nothing more than legal advice." Despite this dour view of the Britisher's role, the melding of the outgoing Australians and the more staid Englishmen made for "a very good combination."

———

Beginning in the late 1970s, and spurred by the 1984 agreement to return the colony to China in 1997, the colony was going through a transition phase that came to be known as "localization." Since the 1840s, the British had dominated trading, banking, shipping, and government. But the Chinese were beginning to emerge as a force. Li Ka Shing's takeover of the sagging old hong, Hutchison, was the most dramatic example of localization. But hundreds of other Chinese entrepreneurs were opening factories that were churning out a cornucopia of products. Some started out making plastic flowers and then moved up to computer components. "They were nimble manufacturers who could arrange low-cost production, and they were very energetic and entrepreneurial," Morrison recalls.

In addition to manufacturing, many Chinese businessmen went into the high-risk real estate market and made fortunes. While the Chinese were increasing their influence in Hong Kong's economy, they were displacing the British in the civil service and police force. The localization process was also taking place in law firms. In the past, many expatriate firms had paid their Chinese lawyers less than the expatriates and treated them as second-class citizens who had little or no chance of becoming a partner. But, with China's upcoming takeover of Hong Kong and the dramatic upswing in China trade, the Chinese lawyers' cultural and language skills gave them strong bargaining power.

Following Baker & McKenzie's traditional pattern of bringing in local lawyers, Connor's original plan for the Hong Kong office had included recruiting and training Chinese lawyers. Nevertheless, some of the Firm's Chinese attorneys feared that the Western law firms would be thrown out of Hong Kong in 1997. Others fretted that the predominance of English, Australian, and American partners might work against them, and a few left to form all-Chinese law firms.

During a Pacific Basin trip in the mid-1980s, then-Chairman Robert Cox stopped in Hong Kong. Although he was not worried that large numbers of Chinese lawyers would bolt, Cox wanted to address their malaise. He reminded them that the Firm's multicultural tradition had eliminated nationality as a factor in electing partners. He also told them that having Chinese and non-Chinese lawyers was consistent with the international city's blend of Eastern and Western traditions. And, he said, the Firm had always followed the rule of promoting local attorneys to leadership roles. Over time, what Cox had said came to be true. By 1995, nine of the twenty-two Hong Kong partners were Chinese, and Lawrence Lee, a University of Hong Kong graduate, was Chairman of the Hong Kong office.

———

Long before the localization process started, the Hong Kong office was beginning to develop practice groups. As Connor looked out his window in the mid-1970s, he saw hundreds of ships moored in Hong Kong harbor, and concluded that a maritime litigation practice would be a natural for the new office. He couldn't find a Hong Kong lawyer with that expertise who was willing to join the Firm, so he ran an advertisement in London for an admiralty lawyer to scoop up what Connor believed would be a profitable business.

Bored at his conventional London law firm, David Fraser was "looking to break the mold." He answered the ad and interviewed with Connor in London. "Connor painted a wonderful picture of opportunity in a new region," Fraser recalls. "He started with a description of the harbor in Hong Kong, one of the most beautiful in the world. It was full of ships, he told me, and it was a place where there was a lot of shipping business, a lot of owners, and a lot of money." Fraser accepted the job, flew to Hong Kong in 1975, and found a house on Victoria Peak with a magnificent view of the harbor.

Not long after Fraser settled into Hong Kong, however, it became clear that Connor's assumption about admiralty work was wrong. Despite the freighters clogging the harbor, London insurance companies controlled the maritime trial work. From their City offices, they decided which lawyers around the world would handle the shipwreck and cargo damage claims. Also, the insurers had established relationships with Hong Kong firms years before. The new boy, Baker & McKenzie, had no chance of cracking into that closed shop. Luckily,

Fraser, who was the only Hong Kong office lawyer with trial experience, was able to survive by handling arbitration and general litigation matters.

Real estate was another practice area that had a troubled start. In the late 1970s, the Hong Kong partners saw owners of jewelry stores and garment factories making overnight fortunes in the colony's exploding property market. Although many investors were placing increasingly chancy bets, the herd instinct wooed financial institutions from around the world. To get business, the banks relaxed their lending standards and channeled easy money into property loans.

When Connor decided to develop a property practice, he approached John Morgans, a Hong Kong government lawyer who had previously practiced real estate law in London. Impressed by Connor's enthusiasm, Morgans joined the Hong Kong office in 1978. He began promoting his practice by writing articles, giving seminars, and having lunches with potential clients. When he looked to the partners for help, however, they were busy developing their own practices. "After about a year or so, I thought we weren't going anywhere. I wasn't a young kid. I had my family, and was in my early forties. Joining the Firm had been a major gamble on my part, and I began to doubt the wisdom of what I had done."

In 1980, Morgans gave notice that he was resigning. "Then the partners woke up and said to themselves that there was more that they should be doing to help me." At one lunch, Morgans was introduced to the head of Hutchison's property department. The crusty Scotsman had been in Hong Kong for many years, and during that time he had built up loyalties to local lawyers. After several glasses of wine, Morgans and the Scotsman replayed their glory days as young men on the rugby pitches. While the two were becoming better friends, Connor was pressing from above, talking to Hutchison executives and directors about sending more real estate work to the Firm. The office also hired several Chinese lawyers to help capture the surging Chinese real estate business. When Morgans saw that the combined efforts were working, he withdrew his resignation. "It was one of those extraordinary things. All of a sudden, the work started coming in great volume," he says. Although there was a major shake-out of real estate prices in the late 1980s, Baker & McKenzie's property practice group grew steadily during the decade. Under the leadership of Morgans and Angela Lee, the group peaked at three partners, ten associates, and some seventy-five paralegals and clerks.

The banking and finance practice was another key element in the office's development. Connor had always preached that, unless the Hong Kong office developed significant banking and finance expertise, it "wouldn't be considered to be an A-grade player." George Forrai had brought in the office's first client, a Filipino bank, but the banking practice was slow to grow at first. The primary stumbling block was that the Firm didn't have a reputation for financial expertise in the world's money centers. In addition, several large banks that had long-established relationships with New York or London law firms nudged them into opening Hong Kong offices to service their business. But the Firm was heavily involved in the boiling property market, and its China practice lawyers had extensive experience in the People's Republic. With this expertise, Baker & McKenzie began representing numerous financial institutions, including Standard and Chartered, one of the colony's premier banks.

Just as this synergystic effect helped the banking and finance practice, a cousin of that practice added to the office's range of talent. When clients wanted to raise money in the Hong Kong stock market, they called on Lawrence Lee, a Hong Kong native who was an important player in the development of the securities law practice. Lee joined the Firm in 1979 as an associate, and, in 1982, transferred to the Sydney office. His timing couldn't have been better. Australia's economy was booming, and the Sydney office was working on many sophisticated corporate matters. John McGuigan liked the young Chinese lawyer, and involved him in financing transactions for publicly and privately held corporations. Lee spent six years in Sydney, perfecting his English and honing his skill in dealing with complicated financing and securities documents.

Then, in 1988, for the second time, his timing was right. Hong Kong's stock market had cratered in October 1987, and was just beginning to stagger back on its feet when Lee returned to his hometown. In a backhanded way, the 1987 crash helped the Hong Kong stock market by exposing a number of evils, such as rampant insider trading and share price manipulation. The government introduced reforms making those practices illegal, and required more public disclosure of corporate information. The reforms brought an added confidence to the stock market, and spurred capital formation through stock offerings.

Lee's old mentor in Sydney, McGuigan, was in charge of both the Hong Kong office and its securities practice. With McGuigan's support, Lee organized a task force to expand the securities practice. His first targets were the Chinese businessmen who had built their own companies. Lee's second target group was another natural constituency. He was one of a cadre of bright young Chinese from modest families who had gotten good educations and were working in Hong Kong. With the "localization" process moving along steadily, Lee's contemporaries were in the vanguard of the Chinese who were rising to prominence in the financial institutions that were underwriting public offerings.

A few expatriates in Hong Kong understood the securities market, but Lee and his colleagues had an advantage. They could explain, in Cantonese and Mandarin, the intricacies of registering and selling stock on the Hong Kong stock exchange. Even though he had a linguistic advantage, Lee ran into a cultural barrier. With their traditional secretiveness, Chinese businessmen were reluctant to disclose the details of their affairs. Lee told them, "Look, if you want to go public, these are the rules. They are designed to protect the minority shareholders. If you want to take their money and put it into your company, you have to tell them what you are going to do with their money."

After defining his market, Lee surveyed the Hong Kong office's partners and associates, and compiled a five-page list of prospective clients. To spread the word that the office had securities law expertise, Lee and his group began taking the prospects to lunch. "Because of the skill level that we had, the merchant banks could see that, at Baker & McKenzie, there was a team of lawyers who could speak the local language and whose work quality was as good as the British City law firms," Lee says.

About a year after Lee launched his securities law blitz, he began to see results. He got assignments from underwriters and from companies that wanted to list their stock on the Hong Kong stock exchange. While this work was growing, Lee predicted that the next surge of activity would come from People's Republic companies that were desperately searching for capital. "They needed the money for survival purposes," Lee says, "to rejuvenate production lines, to build the economy, to get more technology." The Hong Kong office handled the first public offering by a People's Republic company in China and the largest share offering on the Shanghai stock exchange. After successfully issuing stock at home, several People's Republic companies began looking for outside funding. Lee and his colleagues handled the first securities offerings by People's Republic companies in both Hong Kong and New York.

Political events bolstered the Hong Kong office's immigration practice. The 1984 Sino-British agreement to return the colony to Chinese control frightened thousands of Hong Kong citizens. Even though they held British passports, the document did not entitle them to live permanently in England. Worried that the Communists might confiscate their property after 1997, or that they might be arrested as "capitalist roaders," many affluent Hong Kong citizens clambered to secure visas or passports that would allow them to immigrate on a moment's notice to other countries.

William Kuo, a Chinese-American, slipped into the immigration niche. Hong Kong Chinese thronged to his office with visa and passport requests. Kuo also worked with Western companies to arrange safe havens for their key Hong Kong employees. To stave off mass exoduses of Hong Kong citizens, Kuo structured exit strategies that would allow them to go to Canada, Australia, the U.S., and other countries. "The result," Connor says, "was that those people stayed in Hong Kong working at those companies because they knew that, any day they wanted to, they could go out to the airport, get on a plane, and fly off to another country."

Another partner who developed a practice group had grown up in the Australian outback. Until he went to the University of Sydney Law School, David Shannon moved with his family to the farms and ranches that his father managed. He joined the Sydney office straight out of law school in 1972, and, ten years later, he transferred to the Hong Kong office. Over time, he developed an intellectual property practice to service companies that wanted to register, license, and protect their patents, trademarks, and other proprietary information throughout the Far East.

Although the Hong Kong office has had several notable leaders, its founder, John Connor, was the one who made it happen. He had the idea. He lobbied it through the Firm. He recruited the original team. He taught them how to build and to bring in clients. "John was very energetic. He was always looking for opportunity for the Firm," Morrison says. Shannon adds that Connor "had the ability to walk into an office and raise the pulse. Whenever he was around, the office was more vibrant." After he established the office, however, the restive Connor began traveling in order to attend Firm committee meetings, call on clients, recruit new talent, and open the Bangkok and Singapore offices. Then, in 1983, he moved to Singapore. Before he left, he arranged for Sydney's Keith McConnell to fill the Hong Kong leadership slot.

During McConnell's three-year tenure as Managing Partner, he cracked Hong Kong's old boy network. McConnell went to the horse races, one of the focuses of Hong Kong's social and business life, where he put the Firm on many establishment radar screens. The tall, handsome man with a movie star's smile was also a sportsman, playing excellent golf and cricket, favorite sports in the British colony.

After helping to raise the Firm's profile, McConnell returned to Australia. John McGuigan, another young Australian partner, replaced him. While McGuigan had a substantial measure of McConnell's garrulous Irish charm and good looks, the former accountant also had a strong bent toward organizational structure and financial accountability. In addition to his interest in management techniques, McGuigan had a streak of adventure. He had been practicing law in Sydney for just over ten years, and was thinking that "one of the things that really worried me in life was going up and down the same elevator in the same building for the rest of my life."

When McGuigan moved to Hong Kong in 1985, the localization process was transforming it from a British colonial town to a "Hong Kong that was developing its own unique characteristics. The Chinese community in Hong Kong was having an increasingly high profile," McGuigan says.

McGuigan was the office's designated leader, but he made sure that his partners didn't see him as power-hungry. "John was a very cool customer. He didn't immediately just take over," Forrai says. "He consulted with the partners quite a lot." Morgans adds that McGuigan "had a great ability to tread the corridors. He was quite visible. He talked to junior and senior associates. He was always going into offices and asking what was happening. He had a great ability to relate to people."

To prove to his new partners that he was a working lawyer, McGuigan did a great deal of client work. At one point, Morgans told him that he should back off from doing client work and concentrate on looking after the shop as a manager. McGuigan, Morgans recalls, shot back that it was "important that he establish, for everyone to see, his ability to conduct a big deal and to discharge legal work."

In between working on client matters, McGuigan mapped out a management strategy for the Hong Kong office. One basic premise was that law was primarily a business rather than a profession. "He is a bottom-line man," Forrai says. Although he enjoyed rugby, jokes, and a few beers, McGuigan also wanted "to put Baker & McKenzie on the map as the preeminent firm in Hong Kong," he says.

He set the Hong Kong partners to analyzing whether the office had the talent that would attract clients. They concluded that some twenty of the office's forty associates did not have a long-term future with the Firm, and asked them to leave. To replace them, McGuigan recalls, "we combed the globe for nine months, and then, in one six-month period, we hired fifty new associates." The office brought them in from Hong Kong, Canada, Ireland, America, England, Australia, and New Zealand. To persuade young lawyers to pick up stakes and move to the colony, the office paid top salaries and big bonuses. The office also brought in lateral partners to beef up the legal services that it thought that clients wanted.

Another key part of McGuigan's reorganization was to codify a clearly defined practice group concept. Although particular lawyers were recognized for having expertise in particular fields, McGuigan intended for the newly segregated practice groups to instill a sense of teamwork and a sense of accountability. He also brought in more non-lawyer administrators to help run the office, and formed a more potent partner Management Committee. To further the new administrative goals, he introduced what many Hong Kong partners believe was his greatest contribution to the office: systematic business planning as a bedrock tool. "He had a plan for the group, a plan for promotion. Plan this, plan that," Forrai says.

Morrison recalls the partners sitting around a table for two-day planning sessions where they each explained where their practice was and where it was going. "If McGuigan thought you were missing some obvious things, he would make it fairly clear that you'd better get on the stick. You didn't want to annoy John McGuigan. He was a pretty steely character," Morrison says. With McGuigan chairing the meetings, the partners discussed whether they should expand or create new practice areas, how they would fund them, and who they would hire.

During McGuigan's first years in Hong Kong, the partners refined the planning process until it became a well-understood procedure for determining individual partner, practice group, and office objectives. Toward the end of each financial year, the partners met to discuss their business plans for the upcoming year. Then, the practice groups presented their objectives, priorities, and financial targets. When the partners had vetted those plans, they were amalgamated into an overall office plan.

Despite the elaborate planning, "the Hong Kong partners would always begin the financial year convinced that our budget was absolutely crazy and unattainable," Timothy Steadman says. "We would interpret every little blip in the market as a cataclysmic crisis and an end to life as we knew it in Hong Kong. Towards the end of the financial year, we were sure that there was no way we would ever collect enough money to make a healthy profit. So another neurotic frenzy would sweep the office for a few weeks. And, on the last day of the year, we would figure out that actually we'd slightly exceeded our budget. Everyone would relax for a couple of days before starting the cycle of neurosis for the new year."

Although the business plans dealt with all aspects of the office, the designs for business development were among the most important. McGuigan insisted on growth in the numbers of lawyers and clients. When he spotted a company he thought should be a client, "he would be single-minded about finding a way to establish a contact," Morrison recalls. "If you wait behind a desk for the work to come to you, that won't work in Hong Kong. You have to grab the business because someone else will grab it if you don't."

As part of the business development campaign, McGuigan introduced the concept of client care visits. "We would approach our clients in Hong Kong to determine whether we were doing the job they wanted," he says, "which was viewed as a very radical approach to the conduct of the legal business at that time." When McGuigan talked to a client's executives, he told them: "'We'd like to understand your business and to understand where you want to take it so that we can plan our resources to help you get there. We want to know whether we're doing the job that you would like, and whether there are areas where we're falling down on the task.' If clients lodged complaints, and some of them did, we responded, or otherwise it would have been a waste of time."

As part of McGuigan's personal business development efforts, Shannon remembers that "John set about building contacts in the town, and he systematically worked his way through the top bankers and corporate executives. He powered into it—and he didn't go home much." He had little patience with lawyers he thought weren't carrying their share of the promotional load. "There was one partner," he says, "who I found having lunch in his office all the time—and we had a discussion. I saw him going out for lunch one day, but I caught him in the coffee shop of one of the hotels, sitting there by himself. So I went and sat next to him, and we had a good discussion as to why going out and promoting was very difficult with just a newspaper for your luncheon companion."

The associates and partners spent much of their leisure time entertaining clients, often taking them to the Firm's box at the horse races. Because Hong

Kong is "very congested, very noisy, very hot, and very frenetic," and because it can be a claustrophobic place, the office leased a Chinese junk, which it christened *The Bamboozle*. Associates got first call on the junk on weekends, unless a partner had a specific client development need. On promotional cruises, the lawyers and their clients docked at seaside restaurants and dined on seafood, beer, and wine, or sailed to the New Territories to swim in the clean water off the deserted beaches.

The Hong Kong office introduced several new ways of doing things, but the most far-reaching was the junking of the Firm Formula. Connor recollects that the idea of a Hong Kong Formula germinated after he had complained of having trouble attracting partners to Hong Kong. Under the strict Formula, partners who transferred to Hong Kong on temporary tours of duty had a hard time building up a decent income. Wulf Döser's income had plunged by some fifty percent during the year he spent in Hong Kong. Because few partners were willing or able to suffer the financial penalty, one partner suggested to Connor that, instead of forcing the partners to rely on Client and Work Credit, the Hong Kong office should concentrate on maximizing Associate Profit to provide a cushion for partners during their first few years in the new office.

Shortly after McConnell moved to Hong Kong, he and Connor discussed the possibility of performing radical surgery on the traditional Formula. "McConnell correctly saw," Connor says, "that we had to be able to use the partners in much more managerial ways. The way to achieve this was to do away with the Formula." McConnell and Connor presented a new compensation system to the other Hong Kong partners. Under their concept, there would be financial rewards for business promoters, managers, and those who did client work.

The Hong Kong partners implemented the new concept, and, when McGuigan took charge in 1985, they refined the Hong Kong Formula further. Rather than encouraging the "eat what you kill" individualism of the pure Formula, the partners wanted the Hong Kong Formula to promote cooperation and teamwork. They also designed it to free the partners from their time sheets so that they could do things that would benefit the whole office, such as associate training, recruiting, and organizing the office and its practice groups.

A basic philosophical difference between the Hong Kong Formula and the Firm Formula was that it introduced a subjective element into the compensation system. Under the unadulterated Formula, clerks added up columns of numbers, multiplied the results by certain percentages, and that was how much a partner earned. The Hong Kong Formula, however, called for the pooling of all elements that had previously been allocated to individual partners: Work Credit, Client

Credit, Associate Profit, and Fund A. The partners agreed upon a fixed dollar amount that each partner would be paid each year, with only slight adjustments for a lawyer's seniority. The partners, and later a committee, then decided upon the distribution of any additional profits. "It was felt that the fixed portion already provided a decent living salary, and so the extra profits should be awarded on merit," Morrison says.

The partners elected the committee members each year, and to guide them in distributing the subjective portion, the office established criteria for parceling out the money. Among the things that warranted demerits were hogging work instead of giving it to associates, failing to follow up on business development opportunities, failing to carry out a business plan, and not training associates. Most partners thought the system was fair, but Shannon, who was on the committee, says that "some people were unhappy with the committee's decisions. Some people felt that they should have been paid higher. But nobody thought that they were too highly paid."

Critics of the Hong Kong Formula argue that compensating partners on a subjective basis is contrary to the Firm's culture, cutting away at one of Russell Baker's basic principles. Because the Hong Kong Formula relies heavily on Associate Profit, it is also crosswise with Baker's tenet that senior lawyers should not exploit younger attorneys.

Even though partners debate whether the Hong Kong Formula will continue to be successful, there is no doubt that the office grew at a phenomenal pace between 1985 and 1995. During that period, revenues increased from $10 million to $85 million and the number of lawyers trebled. "To have gotten there under the noses of the London and New York firms and the local Hong Kong law firms was a very nice feeling," one attorney says. The Hong Kong lawyers, McGuigan adds, "had a sense that they were privileged to be in this special place at this special time with an opportunity of creating something. We had our sights set on having fun, developing a team, building the office, and making some money."

Chapter Sixteen

Chairmanships:
Haderlein to Bridgman

By the early 1970s, most of Baker & McKenzie's internal struggles and growing pains had ended. The Firm had found itself; its culture was well-defined, a new generation was increasing its influence, and the aging patriarch was easing back from his control position, although not without a few last battles.

At the 1972 Annual Meeting in Zürich, the partners had settled on Thomas Haderlein as the consensus choice for Chairman. Although he was only thirty-seven, he was "one of the brightest intellects in the Firm. He could take a garbled mess and make it come out in a logical, ordered fashion," Michael Waris says. In addition, John Klotsche says, "Tom had a high degree of respect from within the partnership. He was a straight-shooter, very honest, pulled no punches when he thought he was right, and made no special deals for his friends."

Haderlein, a native Chicagoan, had an undergraduate degree in accounting and was a Certified Public Accountant when he enrolled in Georgetown University Law School. He became an honor student and the managing editor of the *Georgetown Law Journal*. With that record, Professor Philip Ryan didn't hesitate to recommend him to Walter Slowinski, who brought him into the Washington office in 1960.

Four years later, Haderlein moved home to Chicago to beef up the tax practice that had been depleted by transfers of several tax lawyers to other offices. His entry into Firm administration came in 1966, when his reputation as a CPA and tax lawyer led to an appointment as the financial advisor to the Executive Committee under Lajos Schmidt's Chairmanship. Haderlein skillfully maneuvered through the political minefields laid by Baker and his opponents during that stormy period and, by 1972, he was a logical choice to succeed Baker's then-nemesis, Michel Coccia, as Chairman.

While Haderlein was in office, he shied away from entanglements with one faction or another. Jorge Sánchez says that "Tom felt that he had to act in such a way that the institution of the Executive Committee would not be tarnished. He worked very hard to make sure that all his decisions had the Firm's benefit in first place. He always advised Russell and kept him in the loop." Still, he and Baker had differences.

In 1973, the last of the tempestuous Annual Meetings took place. Even though the Boys of '60 had ascended to the Firm's intellectual leadership, Baker couldn't resist one final attempt to assert his influence. Before the meeting, he maneuvered to confirm his power over the Policy Committee ("PC") and to reassert its authority to name the Firm committeemen. At the previous Annual Meeting, the partners had circumvented Baker's bastion, the PC, and elected the Executive Committee directly. Still stinging from that loss, Baker launched a two-pronged attack. He wanted to unseat Haderlein as Chairman and he wanted to pack the PC.

On his side, Baker had the Articles of Partnership, which called for the PC to elect the Executive Committee. For years, the PC, which some called the "House of Lords," had been the most powerful body in the Firm. It designated the committee members. It set the Firm's agenda. More importantly, it was Baker & McKenzie's intellectual center, where policies and programs originated. Even though the Boys of '60 had taken over the Executive Committee in 1972, Baker's prestige still permitted him to pick the PC members. Baker planned to put several more of his allies on the PC. To shore up support among the existing PC members, Haderlein suspects that Baker argued that, "if we, the senior guys, lose control of the PC, then we won't count for anything around here. We have to get the nominations and elections back into the PC, and I need your help."

When the PC met just before the 1973 Annual Meeting, rumors had already circulated that Baker was jockeying to reestablish his authority. Upset that the old lion was making yet another charge, one of the Boys of '60 who was also a PC member, David Macdonald, made a motion to clear the room of all non-PC members from the meeting. It passed. Macdonald wanted to exclude them, he says, because he intended lambasting the PC members for their attempt to cling to power, and he didn't want to embarrass them in front of the other partners. Nevertheless, many partners interpreted the banishment as a gross violation of the Firm's rule that all partners can attend all meetings.

Since Haderlein and most of the Executive Committee were not on the PC, they and the other non-members left. At a cocktail party that night at the Mid-America Club, a partner delivered a message from Baker. He told Haderlein that Baker wanted to stack the PC with loyalists, and that he did not want Haderlein to remain as Chairman, although he could stay on the Executive Committee as a member. "I said," Haderlein recalls, "to tell Russell that, if he wants to throw me out, let him do it. But I won't serve on that Committee as anything other than Chairman."

As the partners assembled for the 1973 Annual Meeting's opening session the next morning, Baker approached Haderlein. "I have to talk with you for a minute," Baker said. "This is a very serious matter. The Chicago office has quite a few candidates for partnership, and there is one that I simply cannot support, and he will not be elected at this meeting. That candidate is John Klotsche."

From his bag of trial lawyer's tricks, "Russell followed the old gambit of, if you can't get somebody directly, grab one of his children or his wife and hit them," Haderlein says. "You know it's going to be volatile when he tells you he's going to destroy your number one man in public." Baker well understood that defeating Klotsche's candidacy for partnership would have undercut Haderlein's authority as Chairman. But, knowing that Baker was a master at shocking his opponent to throw him off-guard, Haderlein didn't ruffle. "Russell," Haderlein said, "I hope that you don't have to do that, because, if you do, we're going to have one hell of a fight in public at this meeting." Baker backed off. When Klotsche's name came up, the partners elected him an Income Partner.

Adding to the drama at the Annual Meeting, Peter Achermann "just laid into the PC" for breaking the sacrosanct Firm rule against holding closed-door meetings. Willem Stevens recalls his Swiss partner pounding his fist on the table and saying, "I am a member of this Firm, and I have the right to attend every meeting. You can't throw me out, and if you try, I'm going to stay because it is my right." Haderlein adds that "Peter told the whole partnership how out-raged he was. I called Peter the 'Abraham Lincoln of Baker & McKenzie,' because he freed the slaves when he gave that speech. Holding secret meetings like that could have set a precedent that would have really hurt the Firm's democracy."

After the denunciations, PC members rose to say that they too were dis-gusted with what had happened. One by one they resigned, including Baker. On the spot, the partners elected an Ad Hoc Committee to reconstruct the PC. The proposed reforms expanded the PC's membership from eighteen to thirty-one, and guaranteed each of the Firm's twenty-two offices a seat. Out of defer-ence to their leader, Russell Baker would be the PC's Permanent Chairman for life. Before, the PC had elected its own new members. Now, the Capital Partners would hold that power. The lifetime sinecures would end, and the members' terms be limited to three years, with no re-election for a year after their terms were over. Lastly, the new program called for the PC to elect mem-bers of Firm committees by secret ballot. The entire reform program passed. Although some of the old PC members carried over to the reconstituted PC, all of the newly elected members came from the Boys of '60. "The power of the Policy Committee was dead in terms of it being Russell's," Haderlein says.

Most partners give Haderlein high marks for his handling of the shift in control. Haderlein says, "I didn't want a civil war, and I had too much respect for Russell to attempt to exclude him from continuing as the Firm's sage." With the changing of the guard completed, Haderlein turned to other matters. In the middle of his term, he had to deal with a new issue. The Nixon Administration approached David Macdonald to become an Assistant Secretary of the Treasury. Since no partner had left the Firm with the understanding that he would come back after a few years, Macdonald's opportunity raised the question of how to get him out and then back into the Firm. The Articles of Partnership required a ninety percent partner vote to admit a Capital Partner. With that super majority, Macdonald worried that eleven percent of the partners could block his coming back. Haderlein guided the Macdonald Rule through the partnership, resulting in a 1974 Articles amendment that reduced the ninety percent vote to fifty-one for partners re-entering after government service.

Macdonald went to Washington for an interview with Treasury Secretary George Schultz. "The White House was delighted," Macdonald says, about his lack of political experience. "They didn't want anybody who had ever had anything to do with politics." After Richard Nixon resigned in disgrace over the Watergate Affair, his successor, Gerald Ford, named Macdonald Undersecretary of the Navy. From his time in government, he learned that there was a major difference between public service and private law practice. In government, he says, "If you get six decisions out of ten right, you're doing fine. In the legal milieu, you cannot afford to make one mistake in ten thousand. It is a discipline that is painful to get back into after you've been out making these judgment calls in the government."

When President Ford lost the 1976 election to the Democrats, Macdonald returned to the Chicago office. But his government career hadn't ended. The Republicans returned to power in 1981, and President Ronald Reagan appointed Macdonald Deputy U.S. Trade Representative, the number-two trade negotiator post that carries ambassadorial rank. During his tenure, Macdonald worked in a rarefied atmosphere, negotiating trade pacts with Japan and attending Cabinet meetings at the White House. Although working directly with the President was a heady experience, Macdonald's income had nosedived from around $350,000 a year to $58,000. He left the government in 1983. But, after two stints in Washington, he had a case of "Potomac Fever," and joined the Washington office rather than returning to Chicago.

While Macdonald was serving his first term in the government, the Boys of '60 were adjusting to their new-found role in setting the Firm's course. "By 1974," Haderlein says, "my generation was firmly in control of the Firm. It wasn't one person trying to run things. It was a number of people, because the revolt wasn't a Napoleon kind of thing. It signaled the full democratization of the Firm."

As the Boys of '60 took their seats on Firm committees in the early 1970s, the world was sinking into an ever-deepening global recession. Although the world economy was in disarray, by 1974 the days of tumultuous Annual Meetings were gone. The animosities generated by earlier battles had dissipated. Baker seemed to be happy with the direction the Firm was going, even though he was no longer running it. He still had an office and two secretaries in Chicago, but he was spending more time in Los Angeles. "Russell realized that the essential battle was over," Haderlein says. For the first time, Baker did not have a slate of committee candidates, and he told Haderlein: "Do whatever you want to." After consulting with the Boys of '60, Haderlein came up with candidates for Firm committees.

The younger men were pleased that Baker had stepped aside with dignity, but they began to worry about what life would be like without their founder. He had been their leader for so long that many partners couldn't imagine Baker & McKenzie without him. His personality and his wishes had touched almost everything. As their white-haired senior partner approached seventy-three, the partners saw the need to install additional institutional procedures.

At the fall 1974 Policy Committee meeting, its members adopted a new method of selecting candidates for Firm posts. The men on the newly created Nominating Committee would be required to have been a partner for fifteen or more years and would be chosen by lot. Russell Baker would be a permanent member of the Nominating Committee, and it would consider either partners who volunteered to serve or whose names were put up by other partners. To avoid acrimonious fights over elections to Firm committees, however, it would nominate only one person for each post. By 1974, the Firm's basic committee structure was in place. Over the years since then, some of the committees subdivided or combined, and the names sometimes changed.

During Haderlein's term, the partners also addressed Baker & McKenzie's antiquated retirement plan. The old plan had provided partners with between fifteen and twenty-five years of service with $300 per month, and partners with over twenty-five years with $500. Because the payments were so small, aging partners had no incentive to quit. Senior partners with substantial Fund A, Client Credit, or Associate Profit could skim along with minimal work and still take home handsome incomes. John Creed and Bill Gibbons, along with Haderlein, took the lead in overhauling the retirement benefits by sweetening the financial package for partners who had spent their careers building the Firm.

One provision in the original proposal called for mandatory retirement at sixty-five. But Baker announced "his intention to be carried out of his office feet first," Patricia Beal says. "He made it very clear that, if he took only one dollar a year from the Firm, he would still be in his office every day." To placate his senior partner, Haderlein introduced a provision that didn't require mandatory retirement, but financially penalized partners who didn't retire at sixty-five. The change satisfied Baker, and he did not oppose the new retirement provisions.

In comparison with previous Annual Meetings, the 1975 gathering was tame—with good reason. Despite the recent recession in the world economy, the Firm was growing and prospering. Its revenues more than doubled between 1970 and 1975, from $13 million to $29.5 million, and the number of partners jumped from 103 to 150.

At the Madrid Annual Meeting, the partners voted to set up an evaluation committee to investigate each candidate for partner before his election. They also made it easier to join the club by lowering the Income Partnership voting requirement from ninety percent to seventy-five percent. One minor blip at the Annual Meeting involved whether partners could vote by proxy. The seemingly trivial matter took on another character when put into the Baker & McKenzie context. "This was an example," Willem Stevens says, "of the personal ties that existed among the partners. For them, partnership was a thing you exercised in your personal capacity." Some partners protested that proxy voting was "obnoxious to the democratic process," and that the right to vote could not be transferred to another. Despite the opposition, the partners approved a practical approach to dealing with one hundred fifty partners around the globe by allowing a limited right to vote by proxy.

The only genuine controversy in Madrid arose over the choice of a new accounting firm to represent Baker & McKenzie. The problem had its genesis when Haderlein was putting together a long-term capital and financing package with the Firm's lead bank. Because its borrowings were increasing, and its multi-office structure was becoming more complicated, the bank insisted that it replace its small accounting firm with a Big Eight firm. In the past, the Chicago accounting firm had reviewed only the U.S. offices' financial data, and had looked at information available in America related to the non-U.S. offices. Because the overseas offices were an increasingly important part of the Firm, the American bankers wanted an in-depth review of the offshore financial data.

Treasuring their independence, many non-U.S. offices resisted what they saw as an American incursion into their affairs. "The underlying issue was, we didn't want to be ruled by the Americans, directly or indirectly, and we didn't want them sending over their auditors to us," Stevens says. In addition to objecting to overseas control, partners in the European offices didn't want a Big Eight accounting firm poring over their financial data and client lists because, in Europe, many large accounting houses were direct competitors for tax and legal work. Despite the objections, the partners chose Arthur Andersen & Co. to represent the Firm, but limited it to only financial data available in the U.S.

With the Boys of '60 providing the Firm its moral and intellectual leadership, another of their number, Dennis Meyer, took office after the 1975 Annual Meeting. As a young man, he had earned his law degree from Georgetown University in 1960 and then clerked for the Chief Judge of the U.S. Tax Court in Washington. At the Court, he was exposed to some of the leading international tax law cases, which whetted his appetite to practice in that field. Meyer's law school classmate, Thomas Haderlein, was already with the Firm's Washington office, and he arranged for Meyer to meet Walter Slowinski, Russell Baker, and the other partners. "Tom Haderlein told me that the international tax area was one of the real growth areas," Meyer recalls, "and he was right."

Before taking office as Chairman, Meyer says he "talked to Russell, and I knew that I would have his full support." At thirty-nine, the tall, leonine Washingtonian was the Firm's first non-Chicago Chairman. He commuted to Chicago almost weekly, and spent over sixty percent of his time working on Firm matters. Although Baker & McKenzie compensated him for his service, it didn't make up for the income he would have earned under the Formula.

Meyer's management style—anything but heavy-handed—was exactly what his partners expected. Stevens, who served on the Executive Committee with Meyer, says he was "a man who tried to avoid confrontations. He would go a long way to try to find a solution by diplomatic means." If a Committee member became angry about an issue, Meyer would say, "Let's leave it on the agenda and come back to it later." Soon after he took office, Meyer began focusing on one of his highest priorities. Since 1968, the Firm had opened only two offices, and he was determined to steer it back on an expansionist course. Believing that Baker & McKenzie had reached a watershed, he concluded that "we could sit on what we had or keep moving. I was convinced that we had to get offices opened in strategic places at strategic times."

In Meyer's view, it made no sense to sit on the sidelines in a growing city and send business to an unrelated firm. If the local firm did good work, it would establish a strong relationship with the clients. If the Firm later opened an office, the clients would be locked in to the local firm. Competitor law firms in New York, San Francisco, and London served as another spur, as Meyer saw them gearing up to enter the international marketplace.

In addition to those reasons, a casual conversation cemented Meyer's conviction to follow a growth policy. While he was chatting with the senior partner of a large New York law firm, the partner told Meyer: "'You have a very valuable asset in those foreign offices. We tried to set up something in Paris, and lost several hundred thousand dollars. We're certainly never going to try it again.' That remark convinced me that, once we were in the lead, we ought to lengthen our lead. We had to keep ahead of the pack. But a lot of people were arguing that we had enough offices."

His opponents claimed that the work coming out of some offices was spotty. Instead of expanding, they said, the Firm should concentrate on improving quality. "I was not opposed to improving the quality," Meyer says, "but I also did not think it was a good idea to stop growing." Attuned to his constituents' demands, Meyer hired a Yale University professor in 1978 to develop an education and training program for the Firm.

The slow-growth partners also complained about the cost of new offices. They had a good example to cite. The Minneapolis office had opened in 1976, and was proving to be a financial disaster. The Firm had mistakenly banked on one major client to provide it work during the start-up phase. Shortly after Minneapolis opened, that client hired seven in-house lawyers, cutting the office's fees by seventy percent. The complaints about Tokyo's losses also arose, but, with Baker's assistance, Meyer beat back an attempt to close that office. During his three-year term, the Firm started three new offices, and set in motion evaluations that resulted in new offices in several other cities.

By the mid-1970s, Baker & McKenzie was the largest law firm in the world, with three hundred ninety-six lawyers in twenty-six offices around the globe.[1] Its closest rival, Shearman & Sterling in New York, had two hundred sixty attorneys, almost all of whom were in New York and Washington. To rationalize the Firm's size, and to complement Meyer's expansionist plans, he established new financial and accounting procedures and controls.

He instructed Arthur Andersen "to bring us into the twentieth century in terms of our accounting." He also organized an internal audit staff to visit the local offices to review their financial practices. This met with resistance from some non-U.S. partners who declared that they would not submit to intrusions from abroad. The opposition, Meyer says, arose "because some offices thought that this was a way of getting central management to snoop around like the CIA. It wasn't that they were opposed to financial controls. They just didn't like 'Big Brother' from Chicago digging into their books and records." Nevertheless, practicality carried the day: the Firm's banks wanted to see more data on the multi-million-dollar business before they would extend working-capital credit.

Meyer also made global budgeting a part of the financial planning process. Prior to that, there had never been a Firm-wide budget. "It was $5,000 here and $10,000 there," he says. "Previously, you came in and asked for money, and you got it. Nobody ever looked at how much we were spending on things like the Associate Training Program."

——————

As Meyer's tenure as Chairman was winding to a close, the partners began casting about for his successor. Several members of the Boys of '60 had supporters, but the man whose name came up most often was a lean, six-foot, six-inch German from the Frankfurt office. Russell Baker had identified Wulf Döser early on as a "Firm man," and orchestrated his election to the Executive Committee in 1970 while he was still in his mid-thirties. Döser was well known by U.S. and European partners and highly respected for his intellect and for his legal skills. "But," Jorge Sánchez says, "there were a lot of doubts. I think it was felt that someone in Chicago had to be the Chairman, given the fact that it was the center of gravity, and all the records were there. That was the excuse."

Weighing in favor of a non-U.S. Chairman, Sánchez says, was the idea that "if we were going to be an international Firm, we should have international participation in management." The majority of partners agreed, adding that a European Chairman would also reflect the fact that the balance of power and revenue generation had shifted from U.S. dominance to more equal distribution throughout the world. Specifically, many partners noted, the U.S. share of Firm revenues had drifted down to some thirty-three percent, and only forty percent of the partners resided in America.

The Policy Committee invited Döser to attend its 1977 San Francisco meeting and asked him if he would serve. Döser said he would, and he was elected to a three-year term, beginning in 1978. Many significant Firm issues came up during his tenure, the most important of which arose during the 1979 Paris Annual Meeting: the death of Russell Baker.

——————

In January 1979, Baker had written a memorandum to his three sons detailing their mother's ailments. He ended the memo with as much optimism as the situation allowed. "I am guardedly hopeful . . . . Wouldn't it be wonderful if we both could coast down the remaining course in good health?" But Russell Baker was also failing. As early as 1978, he had sensed that the Rio de Janeiro Annual Meeting would be his last. When Wallace Baker visited his father's Rio hotel room, he found him lying on the bed. In a sad voice, Baker said, "I'm all washed up." Later, when William Outman congratulated Baker on his traditional speech at the dinner dance, he replied: "I just don't have it any more. That was the worst speech I've ever given."

Up to the very end, Baker's compulsion to work never left him. In a letter to Michael Waris, he talked about his weakening heart muscles, and what the doctors were doing for him. Then, he told Waris, "I work at my desk now four or five hours a day. I am hopeful that I will recover and attain the ability to work that I had before the Rio meeting. That meeting just about did me in. If I get back to that point, I would anticipate having a couple of years of mileage and useful work ahead of me."

He never lost his appetite for promoting new business. In the summer of 1979, only a few weeks before he died, Baker had his granddaughter drive him to a Los Angeles hotel to meet with potential Japanese clients. "His body gave up on him, but his mind was there right to the last minute," Beatriz Pessoa says. Baker tried to keep up with his work, but in those final months he wasn't sleeping well. When he did sleep, he had recurring nightmares. In one, he dreamed that he was a college student again, living in the Del Prado Hotel where he had been a janitor. While he was lying in bed at the Hotel, hordes of cockroaches attacked him, but he beat them off.

During bouts of insomnia, he wandered around his Santa Monica apartment. At three o'clock one morning, Baker snapped his light on, and his sister-in-law heard him talking on the phone to his ranch foreman, Susano Ortiz, asking how many bulls were on the ranch and whether the alfalfa crop was high enough to cut. During his last few years, Baker had become almost obsessive about his New Mexico ranch. "He wanted to make sure that all the land was producing something, whether it be grass or some kind of feed for the animals. And no erosion," Ortiz remembers.

Baker hired his grandson, Charles Baker, to work on the ranch during the summer of 1979. He wrote Charles telling him that he would be paid "the going rate for unskilled labor." Despite the low wages, Baker told the boy, the benefits included "a place to sleep, a free horse to ride, beautiful scenery, crystalline air, magnificent clouds, and about two hundred fifty cows, bulls and calves to get very well acquainted with." Then, he advised: "Work like a dog, Charles. Learn all you possibly can. The more you learn, the more fun you can have when you get out of college and start hustling around trying to make a living."

Several partners visited the Firm's patriarch in Santa Monica during his final weeks. "He had become more frail," Robert Deignan says. "He was a little more hunched over and slower moving. For the first time, he appeared to be very vulnerable." Even though Baker knew he was dying, his affection for his wife never waned. "Russ leaned over Elizabeth and said, as he had done all his married life, 'Pucker up, Dibsie,' and they kissed on the mouth. I even detected a gleam of pleasure in his eyes," Janet Ullmann wrote.

About four in the afternoon on September 28, 1979, Baker's nurse found him semi-conscious and called the doctor and the paramedics, who arrived a few minutes later. They attached him to a heart monitor, and determined that he was still alive. Then the paramedics slid Baker onto a gurney and took him to the hospital. Soon after, the doctor telephoned to say that he was dead. Baker had died on the exact day and month his partner John McKenzie had died seventeen years earlier. It was past midnight in Paris, where the partners were holding the 1979 Annual Meeting, and most of them didn't find out about Baker's death until the next morning. Only half-jokingly, some partners claim that Baker willed his death to coincide with the Annual Meeting. "What an appropriate time for him to die—it was symbolic," Waris says.

"Everybody was stunned. We knew Russell was ill, but he had developed an aura of immortality," Bruce Porter recalls. The partners quickly organized a memorial service for Sunday at the Inter-Continental Hotel in Paris. Deignan recalls the scene: "It was very moving. The partners came up and shared a little vignette of something funny or sad about Russell. There was a total unanimity of view, heartfelt by everyone in the room, that the Firm had resulted from what he had done."

Partners and their wives flew from all over the world to attend the founder's funeral at Chicago's North Shore Unitarian Church. "Asians, East Indians, Europeans, South Americans, and Chicago friends came," Ullmann recalls. In his eulogy, the Unitarian minister talked about Baker's "incredible, creative energy," and his "hard-driving work habits, his vision that shaped a law firm that would be referred to . . . as 'the most interesting and exciting law firm in the world.'"

Baker viewed life pragmatically, and he took the same view of death. After the funeral services, the mourners attended a party. Following Baker's written instructions, there was "plenty of grub and champagne." Wallace Baker says his father thought that "you should be happy with the life you had, and you should celebrate your life when you die."

Elizabeth Baker died four months and twenty days after Russell's death, on February 17, 1980.

———

Baker's death left a void. For as long as the Firm had existed, if there were problems, he was there to solve them. If a partner needed advice, he was there to give counsel. If the Firm needed direction, he was there to guide it. Baker, Döser says, was the "*patrón*. He was the last resort. His advice was always sought, even if not always shared. The partners believed that, if anything went wrong, Russell would set it right. To not have the continuity of that super power was unthinkable for some partners." During the remainder of his term as Chairman, Döser spent substantial time "trying to get people used to the idea that we no longer had a papa. I wanted to prove to my partners that the Firm could continue to function, and that it was mature enough to run without Russell Baker."

Even though Baker's absence created a vacuum, Döser did not move to Chicago. Instead, he did most of his work as Chairman from Frankfurt, making trips to Chicago or other offices when necessary. Forced to fly for hours with his basketball-player frame scrunched up in airliner seats, he remembers the constant travel as being "terrible." Nevertheless, during his three years in office, he circled the globe twelve times.

Döser chaired his first Executive Committee meeting in Bogotá. It became tense as Döser used his considerable intellect to question the Committee members. As the day wore on, Committee members made fewer and fewer comments because they "didn't want to be taken apart and skewered." After dinner that night, Cox went to Döser's hotel room and told him that "if he was going to cut the Committee members apart, which I knew was not his intention, these discussions would be very brief." Döser thanked him and "after that, he was more open to people's ideas," Cox says.

Even with this caution, on occasion the German couldn't hold his sharp tongue. He meticulously studied the agenda items for each meeting, and he expected his Committee members to do the same. "He prepared for meetings in a way that would almost scare the hell out of you," Committee member William Outman says. "I remember that, on computerization, things weren't going quite according to target, and he tore into me like a hot knife through butter."

Despite his occasional impatience, the Committee members admired Döser's analytical abilities. Outman recalls a Tokyo Executive Committee meeting where the members were studying a complicated issue that none of them had discussed before. Döser read the proposal for about twenty minutes. "I saw Wulf carve that thing into as many pieces as it needed to be," Outman says. "Then, he queued them all up, and put out the marching orders. It was the most amazing thought display I had ever witnessed. It was just like watching a computer."

Some partners called the Executive Committee the "Wolf Pack," and, during Döser's tenure, he and the "Wolf Pack" confronted a number of thorny issues. They closed the money-losing Minneapolis office, and reshuffled the partners in the Tokyo office. They also presided over office openings in Bogotá, Riyadh,

Singapore, and Buenos Aires. And they started what some partners believe is the first formal international law firm training program by hiring a full-time Director of Professional Development. The Firm also took its first tremulous steps into the computer age. Few partners had any idea as to what computers did or why they were necessary, brushing them off as newfangled gadgets that cost a lot of money.

With his interest in—and understanding of—finances, Döser brought additional fiscal responsibility to the Firm, and introduced more sophisticated planning and budgeting processes. The Executive Committee assigned a staffer, Teresa Townsend, to help implement the program. She reported diplomatically that "in some offices, the planning program was a more fruitful exercise than in others. There were some offices that declined to have my help or hold the planning meetings." Even though many partners were lukewarm about the planning process, it was the first time the Firm had adopted a policy to encourage the offices to examine their futures.

One highly-charged issue that arose during Döser's term was the abolition of the "all save four" rule. Enshrined in the Articles of Partnership since 1961, the rule allowed a small minority of partners to block a partner's expulsion. Even a very troublesome or widely disliked partner could count on his own vote and those of four allies to assure his continuing with the Firm. As a practical matter, no one could be thrown out, and the only way to get rid of a partner was to pay him enough money to induce him to voluntarily withdraw.

Even though the "all save four" rule cut into their pocketbooks, it still had substantial support from those partners who viewed it as the linchpin of the Firm's democracy. With guaranteed lifetime tenure, they argued, each partner could speak his mind and vote his conscience without fear of a "midnight lynch mob." Robert Berner floor-managed an Articles of Partnership amendment that would eliminate the "all save four" rule and replace it with one requiring a ninety percent vote to throw out a Capital Partner and sixty percent for an Income Partner. The partners voted the measure down three times before finally agreeing on the new provision.

Although Döser kept his law practice alive in Frankfurt, he considered the Firm to be his priority client. "What I liked," he says, "was coming to know a lot more partners. And I enjoyed the congeniality on the Executive Committee." But he never became enamored of being a manager. "I did it as a duty, and not because I liked it. Management is a different way of life. I chose to be a lawyer and not a manager."

One of the things Döser did not like was the repetitive annual cycle of the Chairman's job. In 1980, he attended seven Executive Committee meetings in Tokyo, Zürich, Chicago, Milan, and Toronto. He also went to three regional partners meetings, two Policy Committee meetings, and five Financial

Committee meetings. "After you have prepared for an Annual Meeting three times, it is no more fun," Döser says. "Your motivation wears down. There isn't anything strictly new that you can bring to the party."

At the close of the 1981 London Annual Meeting, Döser relinquished the Chairmanship to a rosy-cheeked descendent of Irish immigrants. Thomas Bridgman, an honors graduate of Loyola University Law School, was forty-eight when he became the head of the world's largest law firm.

Before his election, a few partners fretted that Bridgman was merely a litigator who had learned his trade brawling in Chicago's courthouses. With the Firm's size and sprawl, some feared that he wouldn't understand the Firm's international business practice. "People thought that a litigation attorney could not, or should not, run an international trade firm," Sánchez says, because of the different "mind set, focus, way of approaching problems." Some worried that he would handle Firm problems the same way he solved legal problems—in a hard-nosed, adversarial manner. Although he was known as a street fighter in the courtroom, Bridgman was also one of the more gregarious members of the Boys of '60. He genuinely liked his colleagues, and he fully understood the Firm's tradition of collegiality. There was, however, one litigation characteristic in his management style. Bridgman had learned to hold his cards close to his vest, revealing only what he thought the other side should know.

Once, a non-Chicago partner asked Haderlein what Bridgman was doing as Chairman.

"I don't know," Haderlein replied.

"But you are in the Chicago office with him. You should know everything," the partner said.

"Bridgman operates on the principle that he will only disclose what he thinks you need to know. Unfortunately, he doesn't think I need to know anything."

His habit of "hiding the ball" annoyed some of his partners, but they knew they could trust him. "Tom was fair and full of integrity," Robert Cox says. "He could keep his emotions well within him. But he had a wonderful sense of warmth and friendship. Loyalty was very big on his agenda." In addition, Bridgman was seen as having years of history and understanding of the Firm.

Bridgman enjoyed working with his partners, but he didn't enjoy the technical details of financial matters. Nevertheless, he nursed computer technology budgets through the Firm, which resulted in the establishment of the International Systems Department and the appointment of its first director. "Back then," Edward Dyson says, "everybody looked at the expense. How much is this costing? That drove everything." When a proposal to spend some

$300,000 on computer software went before an Annual Meeting, he says, there was "a five-hour discussion on 'Why are we putting this kind of money in software? Why do we have to be linked up?'"

In the early 1980s, the partners had reached the peak of fiscal conservatism. In part, the worldwide economic slowdown drove them in that direction. Investors who were trying to protect themselves against double- and triple-digit inflation drove gold prices to $875 an ounce. Prime rates at U.S. banks soared to over twenty percent, the highest since the American Civil War. British unemployment jumped to more than two and one-half million for the first time since 1935. In West Germany, steep energy costs wiped out the nation's currency surplus, and consumer spending fell.

Economic turmoil continued through 1982 and 1983. In the Firm, as clients' legal budgets fell, so did many partners' incomes. The partners responded with a cost-cutting binge. Although the media was becoming increasingly interested in the Firm, the partners voted down a proposal to devise a plan for dealing with the press. They also crushed an attempt by the Long Range Planning Committee to appropriate funds for a Firm-wide approach to developing business. The partners were stingy on those issues, but they took a different view of a proposal that partners fly tourist, rather than business, class to Firm meetings.

By the time of Bridgman's term, the global partners had reached a consensus as to how the Firm should conduct its business. In the 1960s and 1970s, Annual Meetings often lasted four or five days and went on until late at night, while the partners thrashed out solutions to the unique problems that arose in the world's first multinational law firm. But, by the 1980s, most of the drama of Annual Meetings was lost, and the partners routinely approved office leases, new partners, malpractice insurance, and new office openings. Bridgman determined the success of a meeting by how short it was. His last Annual Meeting as Chairman was scheduled to extend over three full days. Instead, the 1984 San Francisco gathering ended at 11:30 A.M. on the second day. "He was an excellent decision maker," Dyson says. "He could get those agenda items cleaned up."

In his individual dealings with certain partners, Bridgman could be equally abrupt. He sometimes applied the principle of "management by non-management." It was not unusual for partners who thought they had an urgent matter that required Bridgman's personal attention to insist that he immediately jump on a plane and come to their office to fix the problem. "Every partner thinks his problem is the most important in the world," Bridgman says. "I would hear a problem, and, if I didn't think it was that important, I would say, 'I wish I could come, but I can't.' Often, the problems went away by themselves."

During Bridgman's term, Rome partner Peter Alegi called him repeatedly. "The calls would never be short," Bridgman says. "Everything was important to Peter, and every issue that Peter had was life-threatening as far as he was concerned." To screen the calls, Bridgman instructed his secretary to tell Alegi that he was in court. "One day my secretary buzzed me on the intercom and said that Jimmy Caron of Amsterdam was on the phone. I picked up the telephone and said, 'Hello, Jimmy' and I heard Mr. Alegi's voice saying, 'I gotcha, Bridgman!' I had to laugh, and said, 'Peter, that was a good move.'"

As Bridgman's term neared its end, even the parsimonious partners began to see the need for enhanced Firm management. Revenues were well over $100 million, and the number of partners in the thirty-one offices was approaching three hundred. To rationalize global administration, the Policy Committee appointed an Ad Hoc Committee and directed it to analyze the entire management of the Firm. Its recommendations included moving from a part-time to a full-time Chairman.

Chapter Seventeen

The Lateral Partner Experiment: Miami, Los Angeles & Stockholm

In the early 1980s, partner sentiment for accelerated growth was building. During the preceding ten years, Baker & McKenzie had opened only ten offices, and some partners worried about stagnation, even though there had been a small upsurge in the mid and late 1970s. Still, they remembered the heady growth of the 1950s and 1960s, and wanted to put the Firm back on that track.

Years before, Russell Baker had identified Miami as a city where the Firm should have an office. With its large Cuban population, Florida's biggest city was bicultural and bilingual. Superior airline connections and Florida's proximity to Latin America made it the headquarters for several hundred U.S., Japanese, and European companies doing business in Central and South America. In the early 1980s, all logic pointed to opening a Miami office, but there were problems. In 1982, Mexico admitted that it couldn't pay its foreign debt. Soon after, Brazil, Argentina, and almost every other Latin country followed suit. The next year, a Marxist overthrew Grenada's prime minister, and U.S. troops invaded the tiny island nation. These brushfires temporarily slowed the Firm's decision-making process on Miami. But, internally, one partner continued to push for a Florida office. Eugene Rostov, an American who had been in the Firm's São Paulo office for fifteen years, wanted to come home.

Rostov persuaded the Firm to open a Miami office in 1984. To make an impact on the Florida legal market, he believed that he needed to bring in lateral partners, but Firm rules at the time required that a lawyer, no matter how much experience he had, had to go through a purgatory period as an associate so that he could become steeped in the Baker & McKenzie culture. There had been a few exceptions to that rule, but the policy effectively stymied most attempts to recruit outside partners. In early 1985, the Strategic Planning Committee discussed the lateral partner issue. The expansionists argued that the Firm needed to enlist senior lawyers to plug practice area gaps, to help open new offices, and to generate new business. The slow-growth partners countered that latecomers had not paid their dues and shouldn't be given equal status with longtime partners. Also, they said, a bad apple could commit malpractice and create liability for partners around the world. After further debate, the Committee approved the general concept of seeking out lateral partners, but stipulated that the program had to have provisions that assuaged the negative aspects.

Robert Hudson was one of the first partners elected under the new lateral partner provisions. After earning a master's degree in international tax at New York University, Hudson had taken a job with Wender, Murase & White, the firm that had split off from Baker & McKenzie's New York office in 1971. Hudson stayed with them for four years before returning to a law firm in his hometown, Miami. As early as 1982, the Firm had talked to Hudson about opening a Miami office, but he couldn't join as a partner. As a ten-year lawyer, he wasn't prepared to step down the prestige ladder and become an associate. Shortly after the Firm adopted its lateral partner provisions, it again approached him, this time with the prospect of immediate partnership under the new rules.

Even though Hudson was in charge of an eight-lawyer tax department at his firm, he was unhappy with its hierarchic structure. "Everyone who wasn't a name partner was a junior partner," he says. "That made Baker & McKenzie's democratic principles very, very important to me." He also didn't like the fact that a partner's income "was a function of how you got along with the name partners. I got a good dose of how the political process worked, and how subjective considerations played a role in the amount a partner made."

The Firm also satisfied Hudson's hankering to do more international tax work. "Going from what was just a Florida firm to Baker & McKenzie was a move into the big leagues," he says. "I liked the idea of being exposed to clients from different cultures. The fact that I would have partners in cities around the world added another dimension."

Hudson joined the Miami office in 1986, bringing his international tax expertise to complement Rostov's background in international commercial law. To help capture the inbound Latin American work, a young Brazilian partner, Eduardo Leite, transferred from São Paulo. Although the Miami partners planned to emphasize their strong suit—international law—they also wanted to provide a broad spectrum of practice specialties. The office found, however, that, even with the Firm's new lateral partner rules, many senior attorneys in other firms were not interested in joining a start-up operation. When Rostov and Hudson tried to explain the Formula, its complexity frightened many of them. The few who did grasp its nuances still had reservations over the Firm's new lateral partner rules that, they felt, made them second-class citizens because: they did not get a full complement of Fund A shares; during their first two years, the "partners with a fuse" could be easily ousted; and they had no vote for four years.[1]

Many lateral candidates already had good practices, earned excellent incomes, and had their colleagues' respect. Why, they asked themselves, should they leave comfortable situations? Why should they risk the Formula's harshness if they had a bad financial year? "It was a gamble for lawyers to leave where they thought they were doing reasonably well to join this strange bird called Baker & McKenzie," Rostov says. The lateral candidates had seen several out-of-town law firms open offices in Miami, only to shut the doors after a few years. Despite the obstacles, the Miami office met its staffing goals, recruiting real estate and litigation lawyers and bringing in Noel Nation to handle complex corporate matters.

———

During the late 1980s, Miami was one of six offices that the Firm opened and populated primarily with lateral partners. Of the six, Los Angeles was the largest, the most ambitious, the most exciting, and, in the end, the most perplexing. Robert Cox, the Chairman, envisioned Los Angeles as the keystone of his expansionist regime. "Los Angeles was going to be his great accomplishment," Willem Stevens says. But opening in Los Angeles was not the product of one man's ego or enthusiasm. There were many reasons that a southern California office made sense. Years before his death, Russell Baker had said that the Firm needed a Los Angeles office to fully cover the U.S. and to intercept the business that he foresaw would flow in from Asia. And Los Angeles was the nation's largest city in the nation's most populous state.

"Lying right here in our own back yard was a neglected site," Cox says. "Los Angeles was a glaring weakness—a gaping hole—in the Baker & McKenzie map." Over fifty non-California law firms had seen the opportunity and established outposts there. Los Angeles-based companies were pumping out products and selling them around the world. Asian investors were shoveling billions into the booming southern California economy, yet there was no Baker & McKenzie lawyer there to greet them when they got off the planes from Tokyo, Seoul, and Bangkok.

Many partners agreed that a Los Angeles office would neatly round out the Firm's Pacific Basin and American offices. To carry out Baker & McKenzie's manifest destiny, in 1986 the partners charged a five-person search committee with finding the best way for the Firm to open in Los Angeles. It hired a consulting firm to analyze the alternatives. In short order, the consultant inundated the committee with the names of sixty-three groups of lawyers, which the committee narrowed to eighteen.

While the committee was looking at lawyer candidates, it also debated the optimum structure to access the sprawling Los Angeles market. Instead of following the Firm's preferred way of opening new offices—sending a task force of Firm partners to plant the flag and then adding additional lawyers over a long period of time—the committee decided to find a sizable Los Angeles firm with existing clients and an established reputation. To that critical mass, it would graft on a few Baker & McKenzie partners to infuse the newcomers with the Firm's culture and to provide its traditional international expertise.

After sifting through the possibilities, the search committee identified a likely candidate. To validate its conclusion, several partners made trips to Los Angeles and came away favorably impressed. By the time of the 1987 Monte Carlo Annual Meeting, Cox had a solid core of partners who favored the Macdonald, Halsted & Laybourne ("MHL") law firm.

Under various names, MHL had been operating in Los Angeles since 1918. Since then, the venerable firm had expanded to fifty-four lawyers in Los Angeles and eighteen in a San Diego branch. MHL had a solid name as a business litigation firm, but its corporate reputation was tepid and its international was nonexistent. Along with the rest of southern California's economy, MHL was expanding, projecting a $20 million gross income for 1988. The MHL partners were well respected: one had been President of the California Bar Association, another a former Los Angeles County District Attorney. Its senior partner was a courtly, silver-haired lawyer of the highest integrity. And one of its chief rainmakers was a native Angelino who had attended a premier prep school and had contacts in Los Angeles's establishment.

Culturally, the two firms seemed to be a match. Both used a formula compensation system. Both espoused democratic principles. When the two sides discussed dropping MHL's name and using Baker & McKenzie's, there was no problem. And MHL had shown an apparent openness to accepting new partners that would make it easy to send Baker & McKenzie lawyers to Los Angeles and to hire laterals to fill expertise gaps.

From MHL's standpoint, joining forces with Baker & McKenzie solved a major problem. Its partners had watched nervously while large out-of-town law firms invaded their turf and local competitors grew into mega-firms. The MHL partners had heard the law firm consultants' mantra that mid-sized law firms would become extinct. Their choices, some felt, were to downsize and become a specialized boutique, or to merge their way into the company of the mega-firms. Before the MHL partners heard that Baker & McKenzie might be interested in them, they had already talked to a number of law firms about a possible merger. In addition to the practicality of aligning themselves with the ultimate mega-firm, the MHL lawyers were "mesmerized by the status element of going from a local firm to a glitzy international one." It flattered them that one of the "big boys" regarded them so highly, and they were excited about the glamorous prospect of working on worldwide projects. During the wooing period, several MHL partners jetted to Firm offices to attend partners' meetings in Colombia, Hungary, and Australia.

To some MHL partners, Baker & McKenzie appeared to be a savior who would rescue them from a fate of mid-sized mediocrity or being completely snuffed out. The Firm partners they met impressed them as being open, fair-minded people. "Cox, the super-salesman, wowed the hell out of us," Robert Philibosian says. "He had a plan in mind. He had led Baker & McKenzie to phenomenal growth with conservative financial management combined with cutting-edge marketing. We bought into his vision." Intrigued, MHL confidently contemplated the flood tide of business that Firm partners had assured them would wash ashore from the Asian and European offices.

There was much romance and many pluses. But some MHL partners worried that the legal world's Goliath would swallow them up. Cox and others allayed that fear by hammering home the principle that the global Firm did not intervene in local office affairs.

With both MHL and Baker & McKenzie poised for a merger, the Firm partners first debated the issue while they soaked up the beauty of Monte Carlo's Mediterranean setting. A few fretted that all of the thirty-plus MHL partners would not fit into the Baker & McKenzie mold. Some worried that taking on so many lawyers at one time could be a very expensive exercise and could threaten the Firm's culture. Other partners were anxious over the dilution of their Fund A points.

The proponents, however, pointed out that joining with MHL was probably the cheapest way to break into Los Angeles. If the Firm went there on its own, William Gibbons estimated, it might cost between $5 and $10 million. In response to the perceived threat to the Firm's culture, Cox calmed many partners by announcing that John Connor and Gibbons would serve as missionaries to smooth the acculturation process. Connor, the partners knew, had opened more offices than any other current partner. All of those offices had been successful—and Hong Kong and Sydney enormously so. Gibbons had joined the Firm in 1955, six years after it started, and probably knew more about the Formula, Client Credit, and Firm politics than any other partner.

After a luncheon with Prince Rainier's chief deputy, the partners reassembled and approved the general concept of merging with MHL by a vote of one hundred forty nine to eight. Cox reminded them that, if problems arose in the future, they would have another chance to vote for or against the merger agreement once it had been finalized.

The MHL management committee attended the December 1987 Executive Committee meeting to iron out the details. Both sides agreed to jointly develop a business plan and pro forma financial projections. As the merger proposal wended its way through the Firm's approval process, the Strategic Planning Committee studied a Limited Review of MHL prepared by the Firm's accountants, Arthur Andersen & Co. It reported that MHL had had "rapid and dramatic" growth for several years, and that there were a few problems, but nothing major. Although MHL's costs were increasing faster than collections, Andersen said, this was normal when a firm was growing.

By the early spring of 1988, the Baker & McKenzie team had negotiated the parameters of a merger agreement with MHL. Cox called a special Policy Committee meeting in Chicago for March 24. When the Committee members gathered in a Fairmont Hotel ballroom, the proponents gave an upbeat report on why MHL represented an attractive vehicle for entering the Los Angeles and San Diego legal markets. Several partners spoke to the business points. The MHL partners, they said, would join the Firm as either Income or Capital Partners, depending on their years of seniority. There had been talk of "cherry-picking" only the best MHL partners, and leaving out the others, but the MHL partners had objected. As a compromise, for three years after the merger the Firm would have the right to throw out any MHL Capital Partner with only a sixty percent vote, rather than the normal ninety percent.

The projections forecast an operating loss during the first few months after the merger, but MHL's accounts receivable would eventually cover the deficit. The MHL partners would not receive income guarantees, but certain adjustments would permit them to continue taking larger distributions than were allowed under the Formula. The MHL partners would also receive two hundred eighty-two Fund A points. To appease Firm partners who feared Fund A dilution, the new Fund A shares wouldn't be used to compute retirement benefits for MHL partners.

Three Baker & McKenzie associates and four partners would transfer to Los Angeles to flesh out the practice areas that the Firm expected its clients to demand. In addition to Gibbons and Connor, five other partners would shuttle in and out for a few years. To plug other holes, including banking, intellectual property, and Japanese practices, the business plan called for adding a significant number of lawyers in the near term. To cushion any financial risk to the Baker & McKenzie partners who would transfer to Los Angeles, the Firm would guarantee their incomes for three years.

Hong Kong's John McGuigan weighed in with the Pacific Basin partners' support of a Los Angeles office. "The partners should recognize that there will be risks and problems, but this should not deter them," McGuigan said. Tokyo's Shinichi Saito added that, with billions of yen flowing into southern California, a Los Angeles office could capitalize on the Firm's reputation for handling cross-border transactions. A Mexican partner noted that San Diego and Tijuana were almost twin cities, and that the merger would be a major boon to the *maquiladora* (twin plant) practice.

After the laurels came the challenges, the most disturbing of which was a revelation that five MHL partners, who controlled over twenty percent of MHL's business, might be getting cold feet about the merger. John Klotsche was uneasy because MHL financed itself with debt, whereas the Firm used debt and equity. Other partners fired questions about conflicts of interest and whether the southern California offices would take away work from the San Francisco and Palo Alto offices.

Other concerns included a suspicion that all of the MHL lawyers did not meet the Firm's quality standards. Some partners doubted that Baker & McKenzie's referral network would send much business to Los Angeles and San Diego. The network had worked well for non-American offices, they noted, but not for U.S. offices. Connor countered that San Francisco got substantial inbound business, and that the Pacific Basin offices would deliver a solid tranche of work to the southern California offices. Then, several Strategic Planning Committee members said they wanted to see less optimistic financial projections, a more realistic budget, and a scaling back of the anticipated rapid growth. Rather than immediately bringing in a raft of new partners and taking on the high costs of integrating them into the Firm, they argued, Baker & McKenzie should stretch out the growth.

After the two-day debate ended, the Policy Committee voted thirty-seven to five to recommend the merger to the partners. It also required the proponents to use more conservative income and expense figures in the business plan. The merger proposal had weathered the Policy Committee with only a few rocky moments, but, when the "dog and pony show" went to Budapest in May for the European/Middle East Partners Meeting, it ran into a firestorm.

Cox made the case for the merger: "MHL is a fine, outstanding firm with a sound footing in the L.A. community. The review by Arthur Andersen concluded that we had caught MHL on the rise. MHL brings to the table their solid local reputation, a sound financial structure, a solid infrastructure, good associates, and a good client list." When he finished, Amsterdam's Jurriaan Zoetmulder ripped into the merger. The Firm, he said, did not need half of the MHL practice. It did not need San Diego. And the assumption that the Firm could move clients to the Los Angeles office was overly optimistic. Also, the Dutchman said, the office would require much more financial support than was forecast. The proposal was too big, and, "if it was a disaster, it would test the fabric of the Firm."

Other European partners also challenged the plan, claiming that MHL's litigation practice was not compatible with the Firm's traditional international expertise. They also said that Baker & McKenzie's management was already so thinly spread that it couldn't effectively administer the southern California offices. And, they pointed out, some MHL partners were scheduled to be paid more than they had gotten before the merger.

Connor tried to calm the waters. The Los Angeles legal market, he said, was fluid—in the process of gelling. Therefore, there "was still a chance to become a major firm in the short term." Rather than MHL's litigation expertise being a negative, he said, it was one of the best ways of attracting overseas clients. Cox added that the Firm's management could handle the new offices and that the financial risk was a small sum in the context of Baker & McKenzie's overall income.

Despite many European partners' negativism, by written ballot the partnership approved the merger, making it effective on June 1, 1988. The press wrote glowing articles. Over fifteen newspapers, including *The Wall Street Journal*, carried the story. Noting that Baker & McKenzie was one of the last of the large, national law firms to establish a presence in Los Angeles, in early June 1988 the *Los Angeles Times* quoted Cox as saying, "We are a latecomer, but that's given us a bit of a view as to what to do and what not to do." In the same article, an MHL partner rhapsodized that joining the Firm gave him "one-phone-call access to the entire globe. It's very exciting for all of us."

During the office's first year, some good things happened. A lateral partner brought in a Japanese practice with $2.5 million in gross revenues. Several other attractive lateral partner candidates seemed interested. But, Connor believes, some MHL partners threw up roadblocks to outsiders because "they felt it was an intrusion on the MHL entity, and some of them didn't like the level of income guarantees that were being offered to people we wanted to attract." Connor also feels that the Executive Committee was too timid in appropriating sufficient funds to add lawyers with the expertise to service multinational companies.

There were other setbacks. MHL's ten-lawyer corporate department had been a weak spot, but its few clients had supplied both commercial work and a handsome amount of litigation. Not long after the merger, the principal corporate client cut back its business substantially. Shortly after that, three more important corporate clients went bankrupt. Other danger signs flashed. Although southern California's economy was slowing, the Los Angeles office's complement of staff and employees had swelled over fifty percent by late 1988. It had seventy-three lawyers, and the business plan projected hiring another fifty in the next two years. With new attorneys crowding the office's existing space, its leaders started preparing for a move.

To scour the market for suitable premises, the Firm hired a real estate consultant, who turned up space in Citicorp Plaza, a new building under construction in downtown Los Angeles. The Los Angeles partners proposed renting four floors for fifteen years at a cost of $46 million. And, they said, the new landlord would sweeten the deal by agreeing to pay off the existing lease on the old space. The proposal seemed reasonable, and it fit with the expansionist business plan. In April 1989, the global partners approved the lease by a written ballot.

By the end of the first fiscal year, June 30, 1989, the Los Angeles and San Diego offices' gross fees missed their $20 million target by only $200,000. And Connor reported soothingly that the merger had been "remarkably error-free." But there was one hitch. The former MHL partners had received $2.3 million in over-distributions. Eleven MHL partners faced the unpleasant task of paying back overdraws that exceeded $100,000 each, and another eleven each owed between $50,000 and $100,000. At the Singapore Annual Meeting, the Executive Committee reported that the reasons for the over-distributions included an unanticipated associate loss. To ease the problem, the Firm partners approved a plan for the former MHL partners to pay the $2.3 million back, without interest, before December 31, 1990.

The MHL partners were getting their first taste of the Formula's unforgiving harshness. Under MHL's old accrual accounting system, a partner with a big receivable could still have a handsome income because MHL was willing to borrow against future receipts. But the Formula was based solely on cash fees deposited in the bank before June 30 of each year. No collections, no income.

Although there were only a few ripples at the October 1989 Annual Meeting, by the time of the December 1989 Executive Committee meeting, its members were expressing their "disquiet at the continuing lack of regular accounting and related reports" from Los Angeles and San Diego. Not only were the southern California offices' financial reports of dubious value, the offices had millions in uncollected receivables. On occasion, their cash shortages had been so acute they couldn't meet payroll, and had to ask the global Firm for money. To help solve the problems, Gibbons hired a consultant, who promptly reported that accounting and collection procedures were out of control.

In addition to the defective accounting system, another difficulty surfaced. The two men the Firm had assigned to manage the transition, Connor and Gibbons, were plotting different courses for the Los Angeles office. Robert Deignan says that there appeared to be a quiet war between the two Firm veterans over the direction the Los Angeles office should take. "You'd get the Gibbons report, then you'd get the Connor report, and they weren't the same," Deignan recalls.

In general, Connor took a longer-term view of what the office needed and backed a grand design calling for rapid growth. Although Gibbons didn't disagree with that broad strategy, he worried about the more immediate problems. "Bill Gibbons had an extraordinary sense for the daily dynamics of living under the Formula," Deignan says. "He was concerned about the numbers because he knew that the story those numbers were telling was not a happy one. He saw that they were going to work against us."

In addition to their disagreements over the broader picture, Gibbons and Connor differed in style. The tall, craggy Gibbons, who was then in his sixties, often came across as curt and brusque, and he had the peculiar habit of quickly changing his mind on an issue. His longtime colleagues knew of his sudden switches, and teased him about it. But, to the MHL partners, he may have appeared ambivalent.

The other Firm graybeard, Connor, was unfailingly smooth and courteous, but his "drop-in, drop-out" style of management may have confused his new California partners. "Connor flew in, stayed a week at most, stirred the soup until it started boiling, and then he left," Hans-Georg Feick says. In the other offices he had founded, his blueprint had worked. He had followed the classic Baker & McKenzie way—give entrepreneurial lawyers the idea and let them run with it. In each case in the past, they had not disappointed him. Los Angeles, however, was a different set of facts, a different culture, and a different cast of characters.

Gibbons was in the Los Angeles office on a more permanent basis, spending the weekdays on the West Coast and going home to Chicago for the weekends. Although the two were friends, Connor sometimes annoyed Gibbons. "John would come to Los Angeles, and wouldn't announce that he was coming. He would be on his own—going to see people. He would often not tell me what he was doing. He told the L.A. partners that the Firm was going to bring all kinds of work to them from the Far East. I knew that was crap. We had never been able to do that in any U.S. office."

The subdued rift between Connor and Gibbons didn't help, but it was not as damaging as the schism that existed among the old MHL partners. During the merger talks, a basic Firm assumption had been that the MHL lawyers were a harmonious group who would not need precision machine tooling to fit into Baker & McKenzie's culture. But there were wide fissures in the MHL group. Some observers felt that, during the merger negotiations, the MHL group "were on their best behavior when the suitor was in the living room asking for their hand in marriage."

Only a few weeks after the merger, a group of MHL partners staged a palace revolt and threw out the management committee. Gibbons soon learned that many MHL lateral partners felt that the longtime partners treated the laterals as second-class citizens. In addition to the dissension within the Los Angeles office, disgruntled San Diego partners were clamoring to sever all ties with the home office. With the partners wrangling among themselves, Gibbons says, "it was very difficult to get anything done."

Not only did the assumption that the MHL partners were a cohesive group prove to be false, the theory that MHL and Baker & McKenzie were culturally kindred was equally flawed. Only after the merger did the MHL partners fully understand the Firm's tradition of rugged individualism. "We didn't realize just how much it was every man for himself," an MHL partner says. And, Robert Philibosian adds, after the first year under the Formula, "the full impact of each office being a profit center hit us. That, and the 'eat what you kill' approach, came as a shock. I'm not sure that, before then, many MHL partners really understood the Formula."

There was another area of basic miscommunication. From the beginning, Firm partners had repeatedly told the MHL contingent about Baker & McKenzie's tradition of local autonomy. Apparently, some of them hadn't believed it. Their attitude seemed to be that Baker & McKenzie was "the big boy who would run the show." After all, it had established offices all over the world. It was the world's largest law firm. And it was one of the most successful. Rather than taking a strong leadership stance, "the Macdonald Halsted partners truly felt that we would tell them that 'This is how you run a first-class law firm,'" Deignan says. "The Firm's experience was just the opposite. You sign up. You're pretty much on your own. Self-starters are great at Baker & McKenzie. Others don't do as well. We thought that this was just another Baker & McKenzie office, and that they would take care of things themselves."

With no clear sense of direction or leadership, Los Angeles began to drift. In the fall of 1989, however, the mismatch was not as apparent as it later became. "Gibbons told Cox that everything was running fairly smoothly," Feick says, "and he was quite optimistic about the future of the Los Angeles office." Based on this favorable news, Cox invited Gibbons to attend the Executive Committee's next meeting to discuss Los Angeles. In the interim, at a meeting attended only by Gibbons and by Baker & McKenzie lawyers who had transferred to Los Angeles, the Firm lawyers trotted out a list of grievances against the MHL lawyers. As they went through their complaints, Gibbons wrote them down, including a recommendation that four MHL partners should be fired. Gibbons then called Cox to discuss the dissidents' proposals. Cox was furious. "You can't have secret meetings of only the Baker & McKenzie guys," he stormed, "because then it is them against us."

Despite the flare-up, Gibbons went to the February 1990 Executive Committee meeting in Hong Kong, and delivered a gloomy report. He told the Committee that the office's accounting was in disarray, and that the numbers on which the Firm had struck the merger deal were suspect. He also said that, even though the Firm had sent a German partner to Los Angeles to capture the expected influx of European business, it wasn't materializing. After Gibbons presented his somber analysis, Feick, who was on the Committee, remembers that "Gibbons was so pessimistic that Cox blew his top. I've never seen Bob so openly angry. That was a classic example of Gibbons changing his mind all of a sudden."

Even after Gibbons's grim report, no alarm bells went off. Although Los Angeles was somewhat wobbly, many of the Firm's forty offices had had rocky starts. Tokyo had been a financial disaster for more than a decade, and Rio, San Francisco, Singapore, Miami, and Dallas had all been problem children, but they had survived and prospered.

As 1990 wore on, the Los Angeles office appeared to be lurching in the right direction. In a photo that appeared in the May 29, 1990 edition of *California Law Business,* the smiling faces of three Firm lawyers and the office administrator beamed out from the construction site of the new offices at Citicorp Plaza. A longtime Firm partner gushed to the reporter that the Baker & McKenzie lawyers "liked the people and the culture of MHL." The news story spoke glowingly of the tie-in between the Firm's Tijuana and San Diego offices. With southern California on the cusp of Latin America and the Pacific Basin, it said, Baker & McKenzie had arrived just in time to capitalize on its international skills, and MHL's strong trial practice had been a plus. Longtime litigation clients, the article confidently reported, were beginning to call for help in the corporate and international fields. And real estate and banking work were expanding.

In addition to the favorable media attention, at the December 1990 Executive Committee meeting, the Los Angeles/San Diego report showed that their financial performance was strong. But, the Committee cautioned, there were "disturbing reports as to low morale among some of the partners." Part of the morale problem stemmed from an uprising by the San Diego partners, who wanted to cut all ties with their Los Angeles brethren. During its first several years, the San Diego office had had rough economic sledding, and the Los Angeles partners had backed it financially. Now that San Diego was economically viable and was flexing its muscles, some Los Angeles partners saw their colleagues as ingrates. On their part, the San Diegans grumbled that the Los Angeles partners did not send them clients, that they were indecisive, and that they were slackers when it came to marketing. One San Diego partner, Charles Dick, says, "We were almost like our own little firm at the time of the merger. We were entrepreneurial. We had fire in the belly. We felt different from the Los Angeles office, which was drifting along without a mission."[2] Under pressure from the San Diego partners, the Firm eventually approved the unbundling of the two offices in July 1990.

Just before the split, the Los Angeles and San Diego offices had grown to one hundred five lawyers. For the 1990 fiscal year, revenues jumped forty-eight percent, to $30 million. All that was positive. Still, there were blemishes. Profits and revenues missed their budget targets. The MHL partners rang up another $500,000 in over-distributions. When added to the 1989 overdraws, most of them now owed the Firm more than $100,000. And the accounting system remained chaotic. To cure that problem, Los Angeles signed a Service Contract with Arthur Andersen, turning over its internal operations to the accounting giant.

Although the Los Angeles office had problems, in 1990 there was no reason to think it wouldn't survive. But an external force dealt the already rickety office a brutal blow. The 1980s had been a time of breakneck expansion that created "the most tumultuous decade in California since the 1849 Gold Rush." Southern California's ports were America's second busiest, serving as a funnel for the importation of autos, television sets, and other products from Korea, Japan, and Taiwan. Southern Californians had gotten rich making movies and military equipment, including Stealth bombers and Star Wars projects. Foreign capital had flooded in, and Japanese investors bought up some thirty percent of Los Angeles's new office buildings. The state's population swelled to twenty-nine million, making it larger than many nations.

But, in 1990 and 1991, the balloon burst, and southern California's economy shriveled. Deep cuts in military spending hurt, and a devastating freeze and several years of drought punished California's largest industry, agriculture. The unemployment rate jumped almost thirty percent. Housing starts fell thirty-one percent. Bankruptcies skyrocketed. And the banks that had passed out fistfulls of money to finance the speculative bubble felt the pinch. Security Pacific Bank, California's second largest, wrote off $500 million in a single quarter.

When Baker & McKenzie made the decision to open a Los Angeles office, nobody had predicted the economic crunch. With clients closing up, cutting back, or moving elsewhere, many Los Angeles law firms went under, and all of them fired partners and associates. As the economy tumbled, the Los Angeles office sank into its own recession. Inside Baker & McKenzie, some non-Los Angeles partners faulted their southern California colleagues for not spotting the trend soon enough. If they had, the critics argued, the Firm would not have entered into a costly office lease at premium rents and would not have brought in so many lateral partners and associates.

As the economic virus worked its way through southern California, Gibbons retired in mid-1990, and Connor's interest was diverted by problems in the Sydney office. Even if Gibbons and Connor had not phased out, it is doubtful that they could have resolved another festering problem—the ill will and mistrust in the office that created feuding camps.

In January 1991, a longtime Firm partner telephoned Robert Deignan in Chicago and pleaded with him to attend a meeting in Los Angeles with a select group of partners. Deignan, who was on the Executive Committee, had had little to do with Los Angeles before that time, but he flew to the West Coast and met with the group. In their lexicon, they were the "producers" and the MHL old guard—the partners who had spent most of their careers there—were the "non-producers."[3] The producers included the Baker & McKenzie transplants and several MHL partners who felt that the old guard treated them as outsiders. "You were pureblood Macdonald Halsted or you weren't," Deignan says. "Even though you had been there long enough to have had a total transfusion, you still didn't have enough Macdonald Halsted blood in you. On the other side, the producer group seemed to think that they had cornered the market on lawyering skills. There was an arrogance, a condescension toward the Macdonald Halsted group."

Even though the non-producers accounted for a substantial part of the office's business and billable hours, the producers carped that the non-producers didn't have the Baker & McKenzie work ethic and were a drag on the office. The non-producers, they alleged, included a number of mediocre lawyers who didn't measure up to Firm standards. The producers also lashed out at the non-producers for being obstructionists who were blocking the ambitious growth program set out in the business plan. The result of all this, they told Deignan, was that the Los Angeles office had serious financial and morale problems.

Deignan took the issues to the non-producers, and found that they had compiled their own grievance list. They questioned whether the much-talked-about tidal wave of European and Asian business would ever lap on their shores. Several Los Angeles partners had traveled to the Firm's Pacific Basin offices to promote their legal skills. "But," Philibosian says, "the attitude was 'Why do we need to send business to L.A.? Why don't they get their own business?' Under the Formula, there was a disincentive to their sending business to L.A. If another office gave us the business, then they lost the Work Credit. We finally woke up to the fact that the work wasn't coming in like we had expected."

The non-producers' pain only worsened when they realized that the transplanted Baker & McKenzie partners had income guarantees that were unaffected by the office's losses. One bitter MHL partner told a reporter that the Baker & McKenzie transferees "got a huge salary just for showing up, and we are dying under the system." In addition, Kevin Fiore says, the Firm's émigrés "didn't bring any business with them, and they diluted the amount of work that was already here."

In February 1991, the Executive Committee met in Sydney, where Deignan described the "dislike, mistrust, and general unhappiness" in Los Angeles. During breaks in the meeting, the Committee reviewed a stream of "hate mail" from the producer group calling for a meeting with the Executive Committee at the upcoming Pacific Basin partners meeting in Hawaii. If the Committee didn't intervene, they said, the Los Angeles office would collapse.

The Executive Committee agreed to meet, but only with both the producer and the non-producer groups. At the Ritz Carlton hotel on the Big Island, the Executive Committee sat down with the Los Angeles partners. "One by one, the partners around the table began to talk," Deignan recalls. "The entire Executive Committee was present, and this was the first time they really got to see the passion, the dislike, and the severe problems the office was facing from a personality standpoint." Deignan remembers that the two European members on the Committee "were aghast at how the Los Angeles partners talked to one another."

In the "let it all hang out" session, the producers repeated their litany of complaints. The non-producer group shot back that they were hard workers and that they were good lawyers. They also said that the old Baker & McKenzie crowd got all the work referrals from other offices, making the much-vaunted referral network useless to them. Acrimony flooded the room, but neither side put forward a program to solve the problems. After the Los Angeles partners left the room, the Executive Committee members were stunned. "We'd never seen anything like this before," Deignan says. "It was clear that there were deep, deep divisions." Contrary to Firm tradition, the Committee decided to directly involve itself in Los Angeles. It designated Cox and Deignan as the point men to investigate and to meet with the Los Angeles partners and staff members.

In March 1991, Cox and Deignan went to Los Angeles. "Bob Cox was trying to get his arms around it, and I was trying to figure out what the hell was going on," Deignan says. When they delved into the office's problems, they found that it was "almost totally structureless. It was a mish-mash. We decided that we needed to build a skeleton, and then we would begin to put flesh on it." Months earlier, Connor had urged the Los Angeles office to organize itself along departmental lines, but the "resistance levels were quite surprising." He had also suggested that the office begin marketing itself, which, he says, fell on deaf ears.

Following Connor's earlier blueprint, Cox and Deignan decided to organize the office into cohesive practice groups. That, they felt, would permit more logical marketing to bring in new clients. They also put in place a new committee composed of practice group heads to coordinate the attraction and delivery of legal services to clients. A second tier of management, the administrative committee, would continue to exist, but would only make the routine decisions. The reforms did two things: they brought some of the old Baker & McKenzie group into management; and they broadened the base of partners involved in deciding the office's future.

Cox and Deignan also decided to thin the lawyer ranks. "For the first time, the Executive Committee started using the phrase 'partner mix,' the euphemism we'd selected for asking partners to leave the Firm," Deignan says. "We had to face the fact that there were partners who should not have been partners." When Deignan drew up his first list of partners who would stay, it totaled only seven. The severity of the cuts shocked the Executive Committee, which revised the list to include thirteen "keepers."

In addition to the personnel problems, the Los Angeles office's accounting systems were still woefully inadequate. Bills went out only sporadically. Collection efforts were minimal. And operating costs were spiraling. If they could bring order out of chaos, Cox and Deignan believed, profits would come rolling in and the personality issues would ease or vanish.

In May 1991, Cox and Deignan gave the European/Middle East partners an upbeat report at their Stockholm meeting, calling the office a "viable business." The Executive Committee, Deignan reported, was implementing twenty recommendations for cutting costs and increasing revenues. He also noted that the office had moved into its new quarters in Citicorp Plaza in April. Instead of the originally-planned four floors, the office lease covered six floors and would accommodate up to one hundred thirty lawyers.

At the Executive Committee meeting a month later, the members discussed the delicate subject of firing partners. Then, they turned to another touchy issue—firing a client. Before the merger, the Firm had reviewed the MHL client list, and everything seemed to be fine. It was only later that Baker & McKenzie uncovered a client that had been registered under the sobriquet of an affiliate with a totally different name. By the time the Firm discovered that two Los Angeles partners were handling more than $2 million worth of work for the client, a conflict of interest with one of the Firm's oldest clients already existed. The Los Angeles partners objected to the Firm's getting rid of their client, arguing that it would put a huge dent in their already fragile financial situation. Nevertheless, the Executive Committee decided to stay with the Firm's longtime client. As a result, the two partners who controlled the $2 million of work left. Infuriated, some Los Angeles partners viewed firing the client as a stab in the back.

Even with those bad feelings, during the spring and summer of 1991, Deignan and Cox managed to cajole the producers and the non-producers into working together to map out their joint future. When they reached consensus, the Executive Committee announced that it and the Los Angeles partners had approved a comprehensive program to solve the office's problems.

Those efforts were overshadowed, however, by a lackluster 1991 financial year. Following accepted rules, the Firm's accountants allocated Los Angeles a large slice of depreciation on the state-of-the-art computer equipment and new furniture and fixtures it had bought for its Citicorp Plaza premises, exacerbating the struggling office's problems. Other events made the situation even worse, including the failure of several Firm offices to collect Los Angeles fees, the office's inability to collect four major receivables, and the confusion created by a newly implemented billing system.

The office had yet another problem. At the end of 1990, its highest profile trial lawyer, the former California Bar President, left to become a judge. Then, one of MHL's litigation stars and primary business-getters resigned to join another law firm. With the office's two best-known trial lawyers gone, litigation work dwindled. "They were leaders and mainstays in MHL," Philibosian says, "and their departure hurt morale."

Faced with pallid financial statistics, the partner exodus that had begun months before continued. In just over a year, eleven partners left, some of them taking a substantial amount of business with them. And there was another depressant—many Los Angeles partners still owed the Firm their $100,000-plus over-distributions.

As more partners headed for the door, a shrinking number of partners were forced to pay the same amount of overhead costs. "There was concern that, if the lights were going to be turned out, no one wanted to be the last partner," Deignan says. "My goal was to develop a sense of comfort for the Los Angeles partners. I told them that, if they stuck to their business plan, the Firm would not desert them. I pleaded with them not to bail out." But the mismatch of persons and cultures was so pronounced that even an outsider couldn't miss it. "The mistrust and fear on these six floors of the new [Citicorp Plaza building] is almost palpable," a reporter wrote. "Stunned and bitter partners glumly walk the empty halls, so distracted they are unable to pull together and tap the market for business."4

At the 1991 Vienna Annual Meeting, Deignan told the global partners that the most crucial issue was to identify a core group of partners to go forward with. Even with the animosities and the anxiety over whether the office would survive, he said, the Firm was committed to a strong Los Angeles office and to the seventy-three lawyers who were still there. After Deignan spoke, a newly-designated Los Angeles management committee described how it intended to cure the office's ills. They were going to slash costs, they said, including salaries, parking subsidies, entertainment, and rent. Other Los Angeles partners echoed the sanguine view that "things were looking up."

After listening to his Los Angeles partners, San Diego's David Doyle glinted through his horn-rimmed glasses and delivered a withering indictment of the Los Angeles office. More than anything else, he said, his former MHL partners had an attitude problem. The Los Angeles partners wouldn't be able to cure their ills until they confirmed that they were proud to be Baker & McKenzie partners, that they were responsible for their own problems, and that they were willing to work hard to succeed.

After Doyle finished his attack, Deignan addressed the core issue—money. Because defections had depleted the partner ranks, the costs would be so high that the remaining Los Angeles partners would choke on the Formula. Unless the partnership voted in favor of a $1.5 million safety net, he said, the office would collapse. Eventually, the global partners approved the safety net.

During late 1991, Deignan was physically exhausted. After some of his all-day mending sessions in the Los Angeles office, rather than having drinks and dinner with partners, he went back to his hotel room alone. The Los Angeles problems took an emotional toll "because of the loss of people, the loss of jobs.

There were many, many nights when I'd drag my butt back to the hotel after another day of trying to put Humpty Dumpty together again. Every time you turned around, another leg would fall off. I was physically ill from frustration and anger and dismay."

By December 1991, the Firm was publicly admitting its Los Angeles problems. "That office still hasn't jelled yet," Cox told one publication. Both partners and associates felt the tension. Two associates started publishing a bogus newsletter they called the *Rodent*. The *Rodent* lampooned the Los Angeles partners, and decried the two associates' dissatisfaction with law practice in general and with Baker & McKenzie-Los Angeles in particular.

In early 1992, Cox and Deignan announced that they had met with the landlord and Arthur Andersen to restructure the fixed obligations of the Los Angeles office. The landlord had agreed to a $1.4 million rent abatement, and it appeared that Andersen would agree to cut its fees under the Service Contract. Although they had whittled down those and other expenses, the Los Angeles office still had the highest costs per partner in the U.S. By the spring of 1992, the Firm had juggled the "partner mix," and completed severance negotiations with most of the partners who had been asked to withdraw. In the meantime, two Firm partners had transferred to Los Angeles from other offices, a new lateral partner was on board, and a high-profile corporate lawyer appeared to be seriously interested in joining. Executive Committee descriptions of Los Angeles were more hopeful—prospects were "encouraging" and there was reason for "guarded optimism."

When the numbers for fiscal 1992 rolled in, cheers went up. The office had collected $21 million in fees, even though it missed its budget target by $800,000. Local costs remained high, but they were down from $124,000 to $102,000 per partner. The best news of all was that net profits exceeded the budget. Instead of using the entire $1.5 million safety net the global partners had approved the year before, the Los Angeles partners would only need uplifts of $800,000. "We got lucky," Deignan says. "Collections came in, and things were beginning to fall into place. We knew it was going to be a tough go, but we had put a plan in motion and people at the throttle of our little engine who could probably pull this thing off and make it work."

Cox's term as Chairman and Deignan's tenure on the Executive Committee ended in October 1992. At the Executive Committee's next meeting in December 1992, John McGuigan was the new Chairman. When he and the Committee reviewed the Los Angeles numbers since June 30, they were not good. Still, the Committee members supported the ongoing search for more laterals, and gave instructions to seek further relief from expenses. But bad news piled on top of bad news. Gordon Bosserman recalls that "we had one catastrophe after another. There was a continuous discussion of whether we would survive. Living on the edge all the time left us beaten up, tired, and finding it hard to summon the energy to lead the next charge."

In May 1993, the Executive Committee sent out the ominous message that Los Angeles "continues to suffer from a serious cost overhang. The six floors of space occupied by the Los Angeles office are built out for approximately one hundred thirty lawyers and there are presently fifty-four attorneys. The top-heavy fixed cost structure does not, and for the immediately foreseeable future will not, reasonably allow the Los Angeles partners to operate under the Formula at minimally acceptable income levels."

Although the numbers were bad, the Committee hadn't given up. Executive Committee Member John Klotsche resigned from his job as Chairman of the Financial Committee to concentrate solely on nursing Los Angeles back to health, and agreed to move there from Dallas. "We thought Klotsche's coming to L.A. was positive," Philibosian says. "He knew the U.S. market, and he had been successful in leading the Dallas office out of trouble."

At the June 1993 Policy Committee meeting, McGuigan gave a mixed report. The Firm, he said, was "facing the decision of whether it should continue to pro-tect its existing investment in Los Angeles. There is no quick fix, but there is a basis on which to build." Klotsche then outlined his resuscitation plan. He would downsize the lawyer complement and renegotiate the lease to give back three or four floors. And, rather than the ad hoc, year-to-year approach used in the past, the Firm would adopt a five-year business plan. In answer to a partner's question, Klotsche confirmed that the Firm had already "invested" $10 million in Los Angeles, and acknowledged that the Firm had received a poor return on that investment.

Other Policy Committee members spoke. A San Francisco partner was skep-tical that any plan could save Los Angeles. A Palo Alto partner added that his office thought that a survival plan would work, but only if it was radical enough. The words "closing the Los Angeles office" appeared for the first time in Firm meeting minutes. After a blunt debate, the Policy Committee voted unanimously to restructure the Los Angeles office. Shortly after the meeting, Klotsche rene-gotiated the lease to cut three and one-half floors, and McGuigan convinced Arthur Andersen to terminate its Service Contract. Despite these efforts, when the 1993 financials came out, they were a disaster. Fees were $3.6 million under budget, and net profits fell short by $4.5 million.

In October 1993, the Executive Committee again struggled with the Los Angeles issue. Before the meeting, Klotsche had worked through financial mod-els for a five-year plan with three scenarios: no cuts in partners; a few cuts; and severe cuts. Under all three scenarios, Klotsche said, "the office would still be in the tank after five years." The plan forecast an injection of at least $10 million over the five-year period. After the Committee debated the issue for almost two days, Klotsche put the Committee's view into blunt words: "This ain't gonna work. Let's close the doors."

McGuigan and Klotsche called the Los Angeles partners in California to tell them of the decision. Stunned, they hung up the phone to ponder their futures. In the city's shaky economic climate, it might be difficult for them to find work elsewhere. They also worried that the inevitable bad publicity would make their job search even worse. And the Los Angeles partners were not satisfied with the proffered severance packages, which the Firm later increased by $3.5 million.

At the Berlin Annual Meeting, the global partners ratified the recommendation to close Los Angeles, even though Klotsche estimated that the closure would result in an $11.5 million write-off,[5] and that the Firm would be forced to give up some of the $8 million in accounts receivable to settle with the landlord. McGuigan says that the illusive cost of keeping Los Angeles open was the primary reason he decided to shutter the office. But, he says, "I would have gone to the partnership with a request for an appropriation of a substantial amount of money if I felt that the group in L.A., or other partners in the U.S., could realistically have moved the office from Point A to Point B. But I just lost confidence that there was the will and resolve to do what was necessary. To have gone forward, I would have had to put my hand on my heart and sworn to the partnership that I really believed that this was going to work if they put in X million dollars. I was not able to do that."

The Firm's most publicized and most costly failure was the subject of much tooth-gnashing and breast-beating among the partners, but no single cause and no single person was indictable. A September 1994 Executive Committee memorandum noted that the "clash of cultures" was a key reason Los Angeles succumbed. Although the crash of California's economy was a major factor, the Executive Committee's "lessons to be learned" memorandum censured both MHL and Baker & McKenzie for failing to provide leadership. Other culprits included the Firm's network, which only dribbled in work to Los Angeles. The memo found many other faults, all of which led to the conclusion that there was little synergy between the two organizations.

"We were late in the game opening an office there," Willem Stevens says. "We were wrong to think that we could turn a firm like that into a prosperous Baker & McKenzie office by adding all the specialties we needed. We overestimated ourselves." Deignan adds that "we simply picked the wrong firm, and we are to blame for that." Gibbons recalls one of Baker's favorite aphorisms: "Russell used to say that luck is the determining factor in one's life. We didn't have good luck in L.A."

Los Angeles was a high price to pay to learn how to blend an outside group into Baker & McKenzie. So, when Stockholm surfaced as a possible site for a new office, the Firm made certain that it did as much as possible to meld it into the Baker & McKenzie framework.

Although the Nordic nation was highly industrialized, until the late 1980s the Firm had ruled out a Swedish office. Part of the reluctance arose from the socialist governments that had dominated Swedish politics since the 1930s. The leftist politicians had long been hostile to business, and, at some points, they bumped corporate taxes up to seventy percent and personal income taxes to ninety-five percent. But Swedes appeared to be tiring of the socialist policies, and a conservative party was vying to steer the country towards membership in the European Community, reduce taxes, and cut back some of the nation's elaborate social programs.

Even before the political shift in Scandinavia's largest country, a Baker & McKenzie task force went to Stockholm to determine the feasibility of a Swedish office. In the spring of 1989, the Firm sounded out the thirty-lawyer Landahl & Bauer firm, initiating "a two-year-long debate within Landahl & Bauer," Robert Fröman says. "All of us tried to understand the Formula. None of us did." The Landahl lawyers thrashed out the benefits and burdens of joining a global law firm. Some Landahl partners seemed interested, and others didn't. The six bankruptcy lawyers decided that a merger wouldn't help them because most of their work came from Swedish court appointments. In addition, Landahl's older partners didn't want to take on a new venture at a late stage in their careers.

The Landahl partners who favored a merger reasoned that Sweden was a relatively small market, and, Fröman says, "if we didn't get on Baker & McKenzie's international train, it might be a long time before another one stopped at the Stockholm station." The proponents also knew that Sweden had applied for EC membership in 1991, and that the European nations were moving toward integration in 1992. If they remained a local Swedish law firm and weren't part of an international organization, they felt they might be left behind.

The Swedes balanced the negatives and the positives. Finally, six Swedish partners concluded that, if five hundred Baker & McKenzie partners around the world could survive in the Firm, it couldn't be too bad. With the blessing of their remaining Landahl partners, the six began serious discussions with the Firm. Baker & McKenzie formed a three-member team to work with the Swedes: Chicago's Douglas Hoffman, London's Bruce Porter, and Frankfurt's Hans-Georg Feick. The choices were by design. The U.S., Britain, and Germany were Sweden's three major trade and investment partners. At the 1990 Bermuda Annual Meeting, Baker & McKenzie elected the Swedes to the partnership and approved opening the office.

A delegation of Firm partners planned to celebrate the Stockholm office's mid-January 1991 opening. It was inauspicious timing. The Persian Gulf War broke out, causing many travelers to fear that Iraqi terrorists might plant bombs aboard commercial airplanes. Hoffman recalls that, on his flight from London to Stockholm, the British Airways pilot came on the loudspeaker to greet the nine passengers: "Thank you for flying British Airways, and thank you for flying at all." Despite the misgivings, a large contingent of Baker & McKenzie partners attended the inaugural party.

The new Swedish partners worked hard at getting acquainted with Firm partners. Fröman made friends in his capacity as Stockholm's first Administrative Partner. The partners liked the quiet, unassuming Fröman, not knowing that the latter-day administrator had started out life as a musician. When he graduated from secondary school, Fröman received a music scholarship to study at Duke University. Even after returning home and earning a University of Stockholm law degree, Fröman continued his passion for playing the cello and piano. When he wasn't drafting contracts, he composed two operas, both of which were produced in Sweden.

Another Stockholm partner was also interested in music, but his taste was distinctly different from Fröman's. Beginning in his teen years, Claes Cronstedt had played lead guitar in various Stockholm rock bands. A descendant of Sweden's ancient nobility, Cronstedt has the right to use the title of Count, so his fans tagged him the "Rocking Count." After the Rocking Count graduated from Stockholm University Law School, his playing tapered off, although he occasionally plays in a rock band made up of friends in the Stockholm Bar Association.

Before Cronstedt and the other five partners joined, Baker & McKenzie had often struggled with integrating new offices into the Firm. But it was determined that Stockholm would be different. Only a few days after the Swedish office opened, three senior staffers from the International Offices in Chicago went to Stockholm, where they held tutorials in the complexities of Client Credit claims, conflicts of interest, the Formula, and the Baker & McKenzie accounting system.

Before the merger, Porter had worked closely with the Swedes to develop a comprehensive business plan. Afterward, Feick, one of the Firm's best financial minds, helped the Swedes with a cash flow analysis and the transition from accrual accounting to the Firm's cash-based system. The third member of the transition team, Hoffman, worked in Stockholm. During the office's first year, he spent about two weeks a month in Sweden. "It was psychologically important for us to know that Baker & McKenzie was physically there," Cronstedt says, "to have a partner who was experienced enough to be able to guide us. Hoffman told us to beware of the Baker & McKenzie paper shock. We'd never been in an environment where papers were flooding in from the fax every day. He taught us what was important and what was not."

The Stockholm partners did their part to get to know the Firm, taking advantage of Baker & McKenzie's programs that facilitated personal contacts. Some Stockholm partners' children spent summers in the homes of Baker & McKenzie partners in Argentina, the U.S., and other countries. The Swedish partners visited other offices and attended practice group meetings. Only four months after joining the Firm, the Stockholm office hosted the European/Middle East Partners Meeting. At the associate level, the Stockholm office sent several young lawyers to work in other offices under the Associate Training Program, and each Stockholm associate attended the European Associates Meeting every other year.

The primary reason for the merger going so smoothly, Feick says, was that the new Swedish partners were "very enthusiastic about joining Baker & McKenzie. We tried to integrate them immediately so that they had the feeling they had become members of a group rather than being left outside, way up in the north."

Chapter Eighteen

The First Full-Time Chairman: Robert Cox

Robert Cox was born at the tail end of the Depression to a father who raised funds for charitable organizations, and a "very intense Catholic" mother, who wanted him to be a priest. After his first semester at Notre Dame University, he dropped out to become a seminarian at a Benedictine Monastery. Dressed in a brown robe, he obeyed the order's vow of silence, prayed, and studied for nine months before deciding that the monastic life wasn't for him.

He returned to Notre Dame, where he paid his way through school with scholarships, hustling pool, playing cards, and working at university jobs. Just before his graduation in 1959, good fortune came his way. He received a scholarship to attend Notre Dame Law School, and graduated eighth in his class in 1962. After five years with the Securities and Exchange Commission in Washington, a friend he had met there called. Robert Gareis, then a Chicago Baker & McKenzie associate, asked Cox if he would be interested in working in New York. He joined the New York office as an associate in 1967, and became a partner two years later.

During the mid-1970s, the then-Chairman, Dennis Meyer, encouraged Cox to serve on the Executive Committee and he was elected to do so. "It wasn't until my service on the Executive Committee that I began to see the full reach of this Firm." Just before he left the Executive Committee in 1980, Cox took on an assignment that brought his political skills to the attention of a wide group of partners. The San Francisco office was having problems with its senior partner and the Committee asked Cox to find a solution. The partner had invested in outside businesses and, some partners felt, he was not devoting his full time to building the office. In addition, there were strained relationships between him and several of the other San Francisco lawyers, some of whom were threatening to leave. "Our only office in California was coming apart," Cox says. A few partners talked about forcing the partner out, but "the notion of getting rid of a partner in the Firm at that time was something very foreign to us psychologically," Cox says. Practically, it was impossible because the Articles of Partnership required a super majority vote.

Cox flew from New York to San Francisco to meet with the partner. "I asked him whether he wanted to deal with all of the crap that was going to come from people trying to get him out. I asked him whether going through a fight over his withdrawal would be best for him." If he decided to leave without a fight, Cox said, he would arrange an attractive retirement package. The partner agreed, and Cox flew home to New York. "I think that negotiating his departure created a major impression in many partners' minds that I had the political skills to work an issue through the Firm to a conclusion."

After his term on the Executive Committee ended, Cox went back to practicing law full time in New York. But he missed Firm management, having seen "the strength of an organization that took some of the very best lawyers from all parts of the world and put them together in this democratic Firm. Our opportunities were almost exponential."

When he broached development opportunities with one New York partner, he dismissed Cox's ideas with the comment that he preferred "the notion of aesthetic drift." Yet, despite the partners' desire for hands-off management, they were reluctantly realizing that Baker & McKenzie couldn't continue with part-time administration of its twenty-seven offices. By 1980, the Firm's fee collections had exceeded $76 million and it had two hundred eleven partners. Russell Baker's death in 1979 had ended the founder era, and many partners had concluded that the Firm needed a more conventional management structure.

An Ad Hoc Committee on Firm Management issued a report, and the partners approved it at the 1983 Berlin Annual Meeting. The reforms included a call for a full-time Chairman of the Executive Committee who would serve a non-renewable five-year term. Because the Chairman would devote all of his time to management, the new program gave him three years of "re-entry compensation" so that he would have time to readjust to the Formula when he returned to full-time law practice.

Even before the Berlin gathering, an informal nominating process for Chairman had begun, with some twenty-five possible candidates. In the summer of 1983, several influential senior partners met with Cox and told him that they would support his candidacy. Soon after, a consensus began forming that put Cox on almost everyone's list. Just before the Berlin Annual Meeting, the Policy Committee elected him to the Chairmanship for a term beginning in 1984.

Cox's first political issue was a delicate one—how he would be paid. For years, partners who viewed service to the Firm as a duty to be borne with minimal compensation had groused about overpaid and underworked administrators. Tradition was on their side. Russell Baker himself had always been disdainful of careerist managers, and he had never taken a penny for his administrative services. At the local level, almost no office paid its Administrative Partner. Before Cox's term, the Firm had compensated his part-time predecessors with an hourly fee. When the partners proposed paying him by the hour for his new job, he told them, "I'll be working full-time, and then some. If you pay me that way, I'll make a fortune." Knowing his partners' aversion to managers, Cox says, he wanted compensation that didn't appear to make him "a money grubber, but that was high enough to command respect for what I was doing." Cox suggested, and the partners agreed, that his compensation equal the average income of the top fifty partners.

In return for the compensation, however, many partners wanted Cox's personal attention on whatever matter was troubling them. "Most partners wanted a piece of the Chairman," he says. "They didn't accept the authoritarian way corporations work. They thought they had immediate access to me as Chairman." Because he had no vice presidents to whom he could delegate work, Cox worried that he would become too involved in micro problems and lose his focus on the Firm's broader issues. To a degree, Cox's executive assistant compounded the problem. She had come from a corporate background and was accustomed to a hierarchical structure that protected its chief executive from petty details. "It was a little bit of a problem for her, dealing with partners who are used to being equal," Cox says. "But part of her job was to protect, and I can't fault her for that. If I was emotionally down, she would tell partners that I couldn't take a call at that moment. At times, she would mis-execute, and I had to remind her that we were a partnership and not a corporation."

Although the access issue ruffled some partners, Cox's biggest concern was how, and whether, he could lead such a large firm. Russell Baker, who had been dead only five years, had led from a position of strength, based on prestige and force of personality. One partner voiced the feeling of many partners when he told an interviewer that Baker was "the first, last and only real leader this firm ever had. He was an electrifying son-of-a-bitch . . . . Russ was able to lead by example when he wanted to and with brute power when he chose that route. He was never much of an administrator, but when you have that kind of buckshot in your rifle, you don't have to be." The partner continued: "Bob Cox assumes the leadership role minus the client control and minus the deep respect that's paid to the founder. He can't pretend to be Russell Baker, because he's not, and he can't pretend to have unlimited authority, because he doesn't. He's . . . facing the greatest challenge of his career."[1]

Cox's election was part of the Firm's overall attempt to strengthen management so that it could more effectively implement decisions. But the partners, who were suspicious of authority, gave Cox "about as much raw clout as the Vice President of the United States." London's Bruce Porter recalls that "it was very much in Cox's mind that, under our peculiar system, the Chairman had no real authority. The Executive Committee had no real authority. If he wanted to get partners to cooperate and agree to management decisions, then he felt that he needed to create a family feeling—an almost patriarchal feeling—and be able to command support that way."

Recognizing the Firm's cultural limitations, Cox told an interviewer, "My job is not as much to command as to communicate. Once a law firm spills over onto a second floor . . . [it has] to find creative ways to relate, to speak, to share ideas."[2] His critics say that he sometimes let individual partners' problems consume too much of his time. Cox answers that "a lot of our Firm is dealing with personal issues, working with individual partners. Most of what are defined as business issues are truly personal issues." Robert Cartwright adds that "Bob is a very loyal person. It's a weakness and a strength. He tends to hang on too long with people. Sometimes that's good because people can redeem themselves and do great things after more clinical people would have written them off. His first presumption always was that our guys may have foibles, but they're good people."

Cox also saw his job as preserving Russell Baker's principles. He made Baker into an icon, quoting him constantly. He kept the founder's memory alive for "the younger generation that had not known Russell and what he stood for," Willem Stevens says. "Bob instinctively realized that we needed icons," according to Cartwright. "He talked about Russell in a larger-than-life sense."

Cox, the former seminarian who placed compassion and humanism at the forefront, developed a style that was sometimes very emotional. "Bob Cox was a preacher giving sermons. He considered the Firm his parish," Johannes Müller recalls. And, Stevens says, Cox openly conveyed to his partners the feeling that "I'm proud to be a Baker & McKenzie partner. I belong to this family. I love this Firm." Some called Cox "hokey" and dubbed him a "cheerleader." Occasionally, he cried when he spoke about his Firm, and one London partner remembers squirming with discomfort at Cox's "lachrymose outbursts." Former Zürich partner Peter Widmer says, "I absolutely abhorred his style of overwhelming people emotionally. I thought it was totally misplaced and frequently led to mistakes."

Defending his approach, Cox says: "I cared a lot about the Firm, and I believed in it." To convey his message, the Firm's enthusiastic Chairman routinely crossed multiple times zones on planes from Chicago to São Paulo, Milan, and Manila. "To go to the Far East and deal with the heady issues of management, to get to socialize with my partners—the combination to me was exhilarating," he says.

Cox traveled from office to office to "listen to what the lawyers saw and heard and said about where our practice should be going, and what we should be doing as a firm." Many of his partners marveled that he could fly for fifteen hours, get up early the next day, make phone calls around the world, and be ready for a meeting at 9:00 A.M.

Although he didn't have the autocratic powers of a corporate president to force his partners to do things, it didn't frustrate him. "I bought into the way the Firm operated. The partners didn't want dictatorial power. As dispersed as we were around the world, it was important to let partners have their say. I was always asking them where they wanted to go, and what they wanted to do, and then I tried to take them there."

Cox also employed the Firm's full-disclosure doctrine. Knowing that many partners didn't trust the concept of a full-time Chairman, he went out of his way to keep them informed. "The partners wanted to know what I was doing," he says. "I sent out memos telling them what was going on. I didn't believe in management by surprise." He also wanted partners around the world to feel that they were full participants in Firm affairs. "Respecting individuals' rights to participate in the decision-making process," he says, "does not prevent the Firm's leadership from exercising a leadership role. If you ignore or suppress disagreement, you run the risk of alienating a small or large number of the firm's partners."[3]

In addition to the members of the Executive Committee, Cox relied on a coterie of partners around the world to test ideas and to get a sense of how the partnership would react to his proposals. He also depended on his counselors to help frame policy and to act as consensus builders. Once he had that group's support, Cox aggressively lobbied his agenda items. "Democracy," he says, "can be slow and methodical, with consensus-building valued over decisiveness. But we were dealing with sophisticated professionals from all over the world with different views."

Moving his agenda was sometimes difficult. The super majority votes required to get certain things done made it hard to rally enough grassroots support from the hundreds of partners. Another complicating factor, Cox says, was that his partners didn't "come naturally to strategic planning. They, like most lawyers, were issue oriented. It was a tough job to get an idea on the table, to develop it, and to get people thinking longer term."

To get his programs adopted, "the political aspect of the job was fundamental to its success," Cox says. His New York partner, Lawrence Newman, commented that "Robert Cox is an effective politician in the good sense of the word. He loves to negotiate, and he's very good at the political aspects of the Firm." To make a symbolic point, when he moved from New York to Chicago in the summer of 1984, Cox did not become a Chicago partner because he wanted to be seen as an unallied Firm partner.

To maneuver his proposals through the partnership, Cox had an established procedure. After the Annual Meeting each fall, he drew up an agenda of items gleaned from his own thoughts and those he had picked up in discussions with partners. He then took his agenda to the winter Executive Committee meeting for test-marketing. He also sent items that fell within the jurisdiction of another committee, such as finance, to those committees for review. If the appropriate committees backed the proposals, he announced the list to the partners in December or January.

At the spring regional meetings of the Pacific Basin, Western Hemisphere, and European/Middle East partners, Cox, the Executive Committee, and his advisors began selling the plans. They discussed the issues formally at the meeting sessions, and informally over drinks and dinners, making it a point to get the reactions and input of each region's intellectual leaders. Throughout the lobbying process, the proponents massaged and revised the concepts to take into account varying partner views. Once the global partners had given their feedback, Cox and the Executive Committee prepared an agenda for presentation to the Policy Committee in June. If that committee approved the issues, the Executive Committee put them in final form for debate at the Annual Meeting in October.

Even with this careful and time-consuming preparation, some issues still failed. When Cox talked to partners about hiring a Chief of Staff to handle administrative details, he ran into a barrage of criticism. "They didn't want it," Cox says. "They griped that it would cost too much money, and they couldn't figure out what a Chief of Staff would do." The Chief of Staff proposal died, but the Firm did approve the establishment of an International Executive Office. Since Baker & McKenzie's beginning in 1949, the Chicago office staff had handled global accounting and record keeping. Cox and a group of staffers moved to a separate floor in Chicago. After realigning the staff, Cox turned to another top-priority item.

For years, competing law firms had been attacking the Firm by calling it a franchise operation. "The only thing Baker & McKenzie is missing are the golden arches outside the doors," a New York lawyer hooted. "Add that and presto, you've got McDonald's. They're about as much one big law firm as the hamburger giant is one big restaurant." Another competitor jeered that the Firm was "the Kentucky Fried Chicken of law."[4]

When the Firm's name appeared in the press, it was almost always in a negative context; some outsiders characterized it as an amorphous confederation of offices staffed with middling lawyers. Many Firm partners shrank from responding, sticking to the lawyers' traditional view that getting their name in the media was unseemly and unprofessional. "We used to let the other firms define us," Cox says. "The process worked like this: Our competitors would call us a 'franchise' and the media would pick up on that because it made for a good, gossipy story. Because we failed to refute the charges in print, the stories were accepted as gospel."[5]

The prejudice was not limited to the U.S. In 1982, Timothy Steadman was working for an establishment London law firm populated by "upper-middle-class solicitors who viewed all foreigners with suspicion, Americans in particular. They had a pretty dim view of Baker & McKenzie." When Steadman told his colleagues he was leaving to join the Firm, "a look of dismay and pity flitted across their faces."

After Cox became Chairman, he publicly labeled the sniping "total bullshit." He made it his business "to prove that those bastards in the establishment law firms were wrong. Anything we could do to tell people that we were good—better than good—was an intoxicant for me. I liked our story, and I wanted to do something about it." As Cox talked with his partners about the Firm's image, he was surprised to find that some of them had bought into the view that Baker & McKenzie wasn't a first-line firm. "We didn't think well of ourselves," Cox says. "Unless we thought well of ourselves, we couldn't ask anybody else to. We had to develop a sense of ourselves that was respectful."

Cox became a Don Quixote, Johannes Müller says, "fighting against a windmill called franchise. He was offended if somebody told him that the Baker & McKenzie organization was a franchise." Cox decided to use the media to achieve three purposes: to increase partner morale, to blot out the negative image held by many outsiders, and to establish the Firm's identity in the increasingly competitive legal marketplace. Robert Cunningham says that Cox took a "proactive view. If the press called, he wanted us to respond. We shouldn't simply duck. We should try to manage our relationship with the press, rather than to simply hide from it."

Some partners objected to Cox's flirtation with the media. "The culture around the Firm," Cox says, "was to see public relations as something for department stores and discotheques, not distinguished law firms." He viewed his task as making partners "see that there's more to public relations than simply beating your chest louder than the next guy. It was my job to make them see that you can use the media to explain your philosophy, to make a statement about your firm, and, damnit, to set the record straight on that franchise issue."

Cox hired a public relations company to map a campaign. The program centered on his giving interviews to drive home the point that the Firm was the biggest and the best in the international arena. After Cox had been in office for almost a year, a reporter from a legal newspaper interviewed him and two other Chicago partners. When asked several hard questions, the two partners left. Cox took another tack. "It seems to me that you have your mind made up about what we are," he told the reporter. "Maybe you should just go back and write the story the way you want to. This is a waste of time. But, if you're really interested in knowing about this Firm, I'll tell you."

The journalist wanted to explore the charge that the partners were really nothing more than faceless franchisees. Cox told him that the charge was false, and, to prove it, he said he knew all three hundred partners. The reporter tested him by reading off the names of partners and asking him what office they were in. Cox got them all right, and then challenged the journalist to name the partners one by one again, and Cox would give him the spouse's names. The journalist declined, but Cox took the reporter home with him for a drink that evening, and agreed to make himself available for any follow-up questions.

A few weeks later, a highly complimentary story appeared in *The American Lawyer* newspaper. The reporter peppered the article with phrases like "world's largest and most misunderstood law firm," "growing, dynamic firm," and "probably the most stable large law firm anywhere." After the article appeared, other publications bombarded Cox with interview requests. "The word spread that I was a storyteller and that I would give them respect as reporters doing their stories," he says. During one interview, Cox was heaping such effusive praise on the Firm and its partners that the journalist stopped him and asked, "You really believe all this shit, don't you?" "I really do," he answered.

Most partners enjoyed the publicity that painted the Firm in such a favorable light, but some groused that Cox was on an ego trip, granting interviews for his own self-aggrandizement. In response to those charges, Cox went to a Chicago office partners meeting with two clippings that featured large pictures of himself. He held them up and asked: "You know who this is, don't you?" After an uncomfortable silence, he answered his own question: "Yes, it is me, but it is also you. WE are on the cover. That is US. I'm just the spokesperson."

"Bob made a lot of positive contributions," John Klotsche says. "A major one was that he raised the Firm's profile way above what it had been. He saw what was happening in the marketplace, and he understood that the legal industry was going to become transparent, and that we'd better be on the front end of that, rather than the back end."

Cox also expanded Baker & McKenzie's office network. "Bob felt that we had to become an even greater global player than we were because of the competition from the other firms," Jorge Sánchez says. Cox's growth program led to expansion in Mexico, the U.S., China, the Middle East, the former Soviet Union, and Eastern Europe. "We've got a lot of people in the Firm who are pretty good at picking out political and economic trends and acting on them. It is ingrained in our whole psyche," Cartwright says. "Bob foresaw very early on the possibilities that existed, and he seized on them."

When the partners in the Firm's thirty offices elected Cox in 1984, they expected him to take an expansionist tack. Most partners remembered the vigorous growth in the 1950s and 1960s, and lamented the fact that, between 1975 and 1984, the Firm had opened only eight offices. "People were worried about stagnation," Cox says. "They wanted to extend the network of offices. Part of this Firm's ethic is to pioneer its way into the next territory. We had to be looking for that next piece of turf because it is part of our success to go into markets where no one else is." When he stepped down as Chairman after eight years, the Firm had forty-nine offices, a gain of nineteen.

"Bob wanted to leave a legacy," Klotsche says. "Establishing new offices is one of the benchmarks we use to measure our growth and our success. He put more notches on the flagpole than anybody other than Russell." Nevertheless, some partners carped that, under the Formula, new office start-up costs cut into their incomes. Several new offices, including Dallas, lost money when they first opened. "There were a number of people, particularly from Europe, who wanted to close Dallas," Cox recalls. "But we thought it was important strategically, so we stayed with it."

If Cox saw an attractive growth possibility that did not fit within the Firm's rules, he found a way to bend them. To get a new office approved, the Articles of Partnership required a super majority partner vote at an Annual Meeting. In the spring of 1986, the Mexico City partners came to the Executive Committee with a proposal to establish offices in Juarez and Tijuana with two young lawyers—Andrés Ochoa-Bünsow in Juarez and Gonzalo Gomez-Mott in Tijuana—who were unhappy with the traditional Mexican family firm where they were working. They wanted to split off and bring their cross-border *maquiladora* practices to the Firm, and they needed an immediate yes or no. Under the Articles of Partnership, Cox couldn't give them an answer until the fall Annual Meeting. To make the deal, he concocted what came to be called a "presence," rather than an "office."

Under his "presence" concept, Cox entered into a contract with the two Mexican lawyers, providing that they would open offices, but they would not be identified with Baker & McKenzie until the Firm partners voted at the Annual Meeting. Although there was only a slight risk that the partners wouldn't approve the new Mexican offices, before he signed the contract Cox got the Mexico City partners to call every Firm office to tell them what he was doing and to get their informal consent to go forward. Later that year, at the New York Annual Meeting, the partners blessed the new Juarez and Tijuana offices, but several criticized Cox for skirting the Articles of Partnership. Cox responded that the Firm would have lost the Mexican opportunity if he hadn't acted quickly. And, he said, the Articles "cannot be allowed to restrict us to such a degree that we can't conduct our business."

There was another impediment to Cox's expansionist program. For some twenty-five years, the Firm had followed a policy of growing from within; promoting its associates to the partnership. With only the rare exception, if an outsider, no matter how experienced he was, wanted to become a partner, he had to join the Firm as an associate and hope that he would be promoted to partner. This policy effectively chilled Baker & McKenzie's ability to bring in partners laterally. Realizing that the Firm didn't have the internal resources to grow as rapidly as it wanted, Cox convinced the partners to approve a lateral partner program that allowed him to recruit partners without their having to spend time as associates.

In 1986, the Firm instituted the New Partner Program as an acculturation device. Spearheaded by Cox and Bangkok partner John Hancock, it was designed to educate both lateral and up-through-the-ranks partners in the nuances of how the Firm operates. A few weeks after partner elections at the Annual Meeting, the new partners meet for a long weekend to study the Client Credit rules, Articles of Partnership, and the ubiquitous Formula. The Program's informal agenda is to provide a setting for the new partners to build a cadre of friends throughout the Firm. "It is just getting together and getting to know each other," Hancock says. "The new partners go away knowing that in ten or twelve offices around the world there is a person they have met, they have talked with, they have had drinks with, they have played sports with."

Around the globe, the Firm was chalking up successes. But, in the late 1980s and early 1990s, Baker & McKenzie became involved in a spate of discrimination claims in the U.S. The first claim involved an associate whom the New York office had fired in 1986. Before Geoffrey Bowers died in 1987 from Acquired Immune Deficiency Syndrome, he brought an action against the Firm before the New York State Division of Human Rights, charging that the Firm had violated a state law that prohibited employers from dismissing employees because they had AIDS.

At the hearing before an Administrative Law Judge, the Firm said that it had discharged Bowers because his work was unsatisfactory. Fifteen New York partners testified that they did not know that Bowers had AIDS when the office fired him. Nevertheless, the Administrative Law Judge rejected the Firm's evidence, and awarded Bowers's estate $1 million for mental anguish and humiliation plus $68,000 in back pay. Cox told the newspapers that he was "outraged" at the finding. Ultimately, the parties settled the matter in a confidential agreement.

Ingrid Beall, the Firm's first female partner, filed a suit in 1991 asserting that Cox and most of the senior tax partners in Chicago had deprived her of responsibility and income because she was not "one of the boys." The thirty-year tax partner did not directly allege sex or age discrimination because those laws applied only to employees, not to partners. Beall's claims included charges that the defendant partners "sloughed off" her comments at Chicago Tax Department meetings, and that she had been subjected to "derogatory comments" because she was a woman and because she had spoken out in defense of other female attorneys in the Firm. Under Illinois partnership law, she argued, she had been effectively removed from the partnership by male colleagues who had systematically deprived her of meaningful work.[6]

Beall gave interviews that appeared in *The New York Times* on October 13, 1991 and *The Washington Post* on October 14, 1991. She told the *Times*: "This is a firm that has the feeling that women are second-class citizens." When the journalist asked about her decision to sue, Beall responded, "You can't be a wimp and walk away from a bad situation." During an interview at a Chicago public relations firm's office, Beall told the *Post* that she wanted to "teach [Baker & McKenzie] a lesson." She also said that "The young [female lawyers] cannot do it, because then they're a troublemaker. And, if you are a troublemaker, it's hard to move to a new job. I do believe . . . that people shouldn't just stand by and let things happen." Beall also described her suit, in the December 1991 edition of *The American Lawyer*, as a "crusade to improve women's lot at Baker & McKenzie."

A judge ruled that there was no support for three of Beall's claims and that she had no right to recover punitive damages or attorneys fees, but allowed her to continue her suit based upon three other allegations. While the litigation was pending, Beall continued as a partner and went to the office as usual. The two sides reached an out-of-court settlement, and Beall retired in 1995.

In 1994, a sexual harassment case went to trial in California. Rena Weeks, a secretary in the Palo Alto office, claimed that a partner, Martin Greenstein, had put his hands on her shoulders, and, after putting his knee in her back, pulled her shoulders back and said, "Let's see which breast is bigger." She also testified that he put pieces of candy in the breast pocket of her blouse. Although Baker & McKenzie had previously adopted a sexual harassment policy, Weeks named the Firm as a co-defendant. During the trial, several other women testified that they had made complaints against Greenstein in Palo Alto and when he had been in the Chicago office. The case became a *cause célèbre* with the media, and was broadcast nationwide on television. The jury awarded Weeks $50,000 in actual damages and $6.9 million in punitive damages, which the trial judge reduced to $3.5 million.[7] Prior to the Weeks case, the Firm did not have a centralized file that tracked sexual harassment and discrimination complaints. As a result of the lesson learned in the Weeks case, the Firm centralized its personnel files, rather than keeping them in the local offices as in the past.

Perhaps the most embarrassing incident occurred in the late 1980s during a job interview with a black female law student, Linda Golden. Harry O'Kane, a scrappy Chicago tort litigator, made several racially insensitive comments to Golden during her interview. Some five weeks after the interview, Golden sent a letter to Baker & McKenzie, with copies to the University of Chicago Law School Dean and others. Almost immediately, a story appeared in a University of Chicago publication. The Dean called the incident "horrendous" and "completely beyond the bounds of appropriate behavior . . . in any . . . civilized context."

The national media picked up the story, and doused Baker & McKenzie with an acid rain of bad publicity. Chicago newspapers and television featured the incident, and *The New York Times* and *The Wall Street Journal* carried articles. Many law schools, including Yale, Stanford, and the University of Michigan, considered banning the Firm from interviewing on their campuses. An enraged Black Law Students Association called for a prohibition on the Firm's interviewing at every law school in the U.S. The most affected school, the University of Chicago, stopped Baker & McKenzie from recruiting for one year.

On the same day that Golden's letter arrived at Baker & McKenzie's office, Cox and O'Kane sent a written apology by hand-delivery to both her and the University of Chicago. Cox, who had been a Civil Rights activist in the 1960s, also called the University of Chicago Law School Dean. Later, the Dean said that Cox wanted "to know what the Firm could do both strategically and ethically. . . . There was no effort to cover up or minimize the significance of the problem."

Internally, the Chicago office distributed copies of Golden's letter and the Firm's apology to all partners, and told them to frankly explain the situation to clients. Cox and Robert Dilworth met with associates and staff members to explain the incident, and Dilworth and two other partners called the fifty-five law clerks scheduled to work in Chicago in the summer of 1989. Cox released a statement to the press: "This is behavior that we do not excuse and we do not tolerate. Baker & McKenzie finds this conduct inexcusable. . . . We pride ourselves on being a multicultural law firm. . . . I do not believe that Harry O'Kane is a racist. Harry thought he was conducting some sort of stress test for a litigator . . . but whatever his intention was, we find it to be totally unacceptable." Ironically, even though the Firm had not offered Golden a job, O'Kane had wanted to hire the young woman, and gave her a very favorable evaluation.

As the furor spread, O'Kane took a voluntary leave of absence, and then withdrew as a partner. The Firm sent teams of partners to meet with law students around the country to tell them what the Firm was doing to improve its procedures and to apologize. "Some of the responses they gave us were painful truths that we had to accept," Cunningham says. The Firm used the incident as a point of departure for a revision of its interview procedures and as a stimulant to its minority hiring efforts. The U.S. offices formed a task force to develop a comprehensive minority recruiting program, and the Firm established a $500,000 scholarship fund for minority students. In addition, the U.S. offices organized training courses to sensitize their staffs and lawyers to minority issues.

The incident had served as Baker & McKenzie's wake-up call. In an interview with the *American Bar Association Journal*, Dilworth admitted that the Firm had been "complacent" but added that "our new [Equal Opportunity] program represents a recognition of that complacency and establishes a perpetually effective remedy." An American Bar Association official said the Firm "could have chosen to stonewall the media on its recent faux pas. . . . Instead, they chose to bite the bullet and start over by making a sincere effort to root out discrimination."[8] Golden's reaction was that "it's exactly the kind of response I hoped to get when I reported what happened during my interview. Now there seems to be a good ending to what started out as a very unhappy affair."

In addition to handling damage control in the discrimination matters, Cox had to deal with a number of partner disputes. To a large extent, a law firm's success depends upon how it manages the skills, personalities, and egos of its lawyers. In an authoritarian firm, the Executive Committee or Managing Partner can fire an offending partner or slash his income. At Baker & McKenzie, however, where the partners saw themselves as owners of a democratically run business who were shielded by the objective Formula, dealing with a troublesome Capital Partner required considerable diplomacy.

The Articles of Partnership's requirement of a super majority vote to expel a Capital Partner, in effect, stripped management of the power to punish. Because the Firm had spent millions paying recalcitrant partners to voluntarily resign, Cox began nursing a proposal to reduce the ninety percent requirement to seventy-five percent. At the 1990 Bermuda Annual Meeting, however, several partners made impassioned speeches. They warned that Cox's proposal would allow the Firm to put its foot on the neck of each Capital Partner by allowing it to toss out a partner who didn't knuckle under to its demands. When the partners soundly defeated his initiative, Cox says, "It was a shock to me. We had taken so many pains to get those ideas on the table, and then to see them get shot down—I just couldn't believe it."[9]

In dealing with inter-partner problems, Cartwright says, "Bob found it very hard to let go of people." One episode involved the partner who established the Rome office in 1968, and who, by the mid-1980s, had the founding-partner syndrome. He clashed with another Rome partner, Franco Macconi, over office policy, including which partner would occupy which office. "That's how silly it got," Macconi says.

The São Paulo office also suffered from the founding-partner syndrome in the late-1980s. The office's senior partner "was used to being the person who, at the end of the day, made the final decisions," Carlos Rossi says. Several issues created a breach between him and a number of younger lawyers. The atmosphere became so poisoned that the senior partner refused to speak to several of his São Paulo partners. "He became so angry, irritated, and frustrated," Juliana Viegas says, "that he began separating himself from the Firm, and he would not participate in meetings with other partners."

In both cases, the Executive Committee's efforts to calm the animosities failed, so the Firm took two unprecedented steps, each of which violated its policy of non-intervention in local office affairs. In Rome, it gave the Executive Committee management control of the office. In São Paulo, the Executive Committee issued directives on how the office was to operate. Efforts to persuade the two senior partners to voluntarily leave lagged on for months. After difficult, and sometimes emotional, negotiations, one withdrew after twenty-three years with the Firm, and the other retired after thirty-two years.

In Geneva, the Executive Committee found a different remedy for the founding-partner syndrome. Donald Etienne had opened the office in 1968. During the next fifteen years, he recruited, trained, and mentored all of the lawyers who became partners in the Geneva office, and was the office's acknowledged leader. His prestige grew when the Firm asked him to serve on the Executive Committee in 1979, but his duties required him to be out of the office for several months each year. During his absences, Alain Stehlé and others managed the Geneva office. "Sometimes, you cannot wait two weeks to make a decision," Stehlé says. "When Etienne came back from serving on the Executive Committee, he criticized the way we did things. Of course, it was a different way. It wasn't perfect. But it never had been. It became more and more difficult to work together."

Finally, the other Geneva partners asked for outside support. "Bob Cox came two days later, and stayed two or three days in Geneva," Stehlé says. "He was always saying that Baker & McKenzie was a big family, and then I realized that it was true because he came and devoted time just for the people in the office."

The Geneva partners delivered a clear message: if the Firm couldn't work something out, several planned to quit.

"Donald Etienne had started the office," Cox says. "He brought in a number of bright young people who became partners, but Donald still wanted to treat them as if he were the only real partner." Cox held meetings with each Geneva partner, including Etienne, and concluded that "Donald had to get out of that office for a while." At a meeting of all Geneva partners, Cox "encouraged them to tell Donald that, basically, there was a lot of affection in the room for him. But the fact was that he could not run the office like it was his personal fiefdom any more. He had to share responsibility."

Etienne listened while his partners listed their grievances. Then Cox suggested that he leave the Geneva office for a year so that he could "take stock of who he was and where that office was headed."

Shocked, Etienne asked, "Where would I go?"

"Washington," Cox answered.

Before he made the Washington proposal, Cox had cleared the transfer with the Washington partners. Jack Janetatos, then the Washington Administrative Partner, recalls that "Bob Cox called me and asked if they could park Donald in Washington for one year to let him see how a good office was run. Donald stayed with us for a year, saw the democratic process in operation, and went back home." The cooling-off period worked, and, when Etienne returned to Geneva, "the whole thing was solved," Stehlé says.

———

As the Firm grew larger, the partners moved to break it down into smaller components. Baker & McKenzie had long supported the formation of practice groups, made up of lawyers working in the same specialty area, and it later began promoting regional ties. In part because of the European Community's importance, the European partners made the greatest strides in working together. The movement toward regionalization began in 1977 as a practice group of several European partners specializing in EC law. By 1986, this loose structure had evolved into a regional group that was publishing a newsletter and maintaining a library of contract forms and memoranda. As the European nations moved closer together economically, the Firm's EC law practitioners formed a task force and, in 1988, published *The European Single Market Reporter*. The book, which describes EC and national laws, was widely distributed by Firm lawyers and by an independent publisher. "It sounds obvious today, but it wasn't so obvious then," Lynda Martin Alegi says. Eventually, the European partners formalized their relationship in the European Regional Council, a management body, and the European Coordination Center. "This gives us an infrastructure in Europe,"

Willem Stevens says, "and it is a sign that the European partners are willing to spend money on joint projects and not solely on their own offices."

The Coordination Center began operation in Brussels in 1991. One objective was to give Firm lawyers instant access to the latest EC legislation. The Center also maintains a library of European economic information, gathers marketing data, and keeps a client database. Equally important, the Center's full-time staff is charged with knowing who in the European Commission to call to get copies of proposed legislation or to informally discuss EC actions that affect clients' interests. Lynda Martin Alegi recalls one case where the client of a European office needed immediate information on the EC's position on dolphins. "There was this rumor, and we had to verify it," she says. The Firm partner called the Coordination Center with the request, and the staff person "spent half the day on the phone talking to everyone she knew, asking, 'Who in the hell is dealing with dolphin issues?'" After working her way through her network of contacts at the EC, the staffer found the person who was making dolphin policy and got the information the client needed.

Although the Firm appears to be trending towards more regional governance and cooperation, some partners worry that too strong a tilt in that direction could loosen Firm-wide ties. "I think that we must play the European card and work together, but we should not present ourselves as a European law firm," Brussels partner Pierre Sculier says. "The reality is that we are a worldwide firm." Some rival firms have branch offices in several cities, staffed primarily by lawyers from their home countries. Others have loose business referral alliances. What distinguishes Baker & McKenzie from its competitors, Sculier says, is that it has international partners around the globe woven together in a network. If regional groups within the Firm develop separate identities, he adds, that could work against one of the Firm's strongest competitive advantages.

Computerization and telecommunications were a significant factor in knitting the Firm closer together during Cox's term. Baker & McKenzie began experimenting with computers in the 1970s, but its peculiar accounting requirements necessitated many changes to the standard software programs, often resulting in breakdowns and delays. By 1986, the Firm had settled on a more sophisticated accounting software program. Still, there were disruptions.

To unscramble the little-known world of computers, the Executive Committee assigned several partners, including Robert Cartwright, to tackle the problem. It charged them with deciphering the new computer jargon and finding the most efficient way of modernizing the Firm's systems. When Cartwright began work on the project in the mid-1980s, he says, "we were faced with a hodgepodge of individual office approaches. In a horizontal management structure like we have, picking what ought to be the uniform system can be an incredibly difficult process, especially when you have partner egos involved—which we did. In the beginning of our effort to adapt to technology, we had some individual partners who had very strong views, and, in some cases, substantial knowledge. To compound the problem, our staff was weak in the computer area. There were a number of partners who got their oars in, and it was a real nightmare."

Political factions developed over whether Technology A or Technology B was superior. "In the early and middle 1980s, there were lots of options, and lots of new products that were supposedly God's gift to financial systems," Cartwright recalls. In addition to causing debates over technical issues, the choice of computer systems bumped up against the partners' conviction that local offices should operate autonomously, and some offices refused to junk their existing equipment and software to buy something recommended by a Firm staffer or the Executive Committee.

The Firm's international scope created other problems. Not all hardware and software were available in many nations. Most of the new technology companies were undercapitalized, and many couldn't provide maintenance or training globally. This left some local offices with no choice but to buy hardware and software from sellers who could give them on-site support in Rio, Rome, or Taipei. In addition, American tax accounting software was not compatible with most non-U.S. tax systems.

The Executive Committee finally gave up because "it was such a rat's nest." Frustrated, the Committee followed the adage of "When in doubt, hire a consultant." It retained Arthur Andersen & Co. to advise the Firm on how to proceed through the computer jungle, and Andersen concluded that it should write custom software to be used on IBM hardware. Bringing in a third party defanged some of the emotionalism, but, in spite of the recommendation, the Executive Committee left the local offices free to do as they pleased. "The Executive Committee knew that it was being a little irresponsible, but that's what we did," Cartwright says. "We would encourage uniformity in the local offices. But, in terms of real investment in systems for local accounting, the Executive Committee was out of it."

Baker & McKenzie was able to patch together some of the disparate hardware and software, but it still hadn't achieved a seamless system by the mid-1980s. As the decade wore on, some offices began buying Local Area Network ("LAN") software that hooked together all the PCs in an office. When several offices had LAN systems, those offices communicated with each other electronically. By 1992, all U.S. offices had LANs, but many non-U.S. offices still used a variety of stand-alone hardware and software.

At the same time that the Firm was upgrading its data systems, it was also moving to connect the offices for document sharing and electronic mail. In 1988, the Firm developed its first communications network, BakerNet I. Even though it allowed many offices to talk directly to one another, BakerNet I was not user-friendly and, on occasion, messages got lost in its bowels. After several frustrating months of trying to work out the glitches, the Executive Committee instructed the International Systems Department to develop BakerNet II.

By 1992, a working group of systems managers had written a document they called GLUE that set out specifications for implementing common information systems. With these uniform standards, transmission of messages and documents was seamless, eliminating almost all of the old bottlenecks and failure points. By 1997, all offices were linked to BakerNet II, allowing more than 6,500 lawyers and staff to communicate immediately with one another. Baker & McKenzie was also working on BakerWeb, an internal communications system that will operate over the Internet, and was experimenting with video teleconferencing.

In the past, trying to piece together a contract across thirteen time zones had been cumbersome. Now, a Thai partner could transmit a contract to a Mexican client during Thai working hours, and the client would have it when he came to work the next morning. The system also permitted lawyers to send draft documents to several offices simultaneously. If a Swedish client was buying a company with assets in Hong Kong, Canada, and Saudi Arabia, the Swedish partner could immediately put together an acquisition team, send them the purchase agreement, and have their comments back the next day. And a Taiwanese lawyer could write a document in Chinese and send it to New York. Because the New York office has the necessary software, it can print the document in Chinese and give it to a Chinese-speaking client in the U.S.

Although Cox was viewed as more of a "people person" than a "number cruncher," he addressed several financial issues that arose during his term. Among them was the question of whether the Firm should continue using "schedular" billing rates or go instead to market rates in each country. Historically, Baker & McKenzie had approved a schedule of hourly billing rates, based roughly on the seniority level of the lawyer and on how much a U.S. lawyer at that level charged. The system had the advantage of allowing a partner to tell a client that billing rates around the world were generally the same. But, when the U.S. dollar, the Firm's currency of record, lost value, it hurt offices with strong currencies. In those countries, the partners wanted to charge what their local competitors in Zürich or Frankfurt were charging—the market rate. If they used the schedular rate, tied to the U.S. dollar, they argued, the clients were getting too much of a bargain. And, they said, charging the market rate was fair to the client because it would pay the same amount whether it used the Firm or another local law firm. Eventually, the Firm adopted a dual system that allowed local offices to use either the schedular or the market rate system.

———

Cox dealt with many issues during his eight years as Chairman. But perhaps the most interesting one had to do with instigating a breakthrough that, only ten years earlier, no one would have thought possible.

The Wild, Wild East

During the late 1980s and early 1990s, Baker & McKenzie made unprecedented inroads in Eastern Europe. In doing so, the Firm helped ease those countries into the international trade and investment system. After decades of communist rule, the Marxist experiment had failed to generate enough prosperity to give to each according to his need. And Eastern Europeans knew it. In the West, their neighbors were driving sleek automobiles and shopping in grocery stores stuffed with French cheeses, Israeli melons, and New Zealand lamb.

Eastern European freedom movements increased in intensity until the lid finally came off. Lech Walesa's Solidarity Movement swept Poland's parliamentary elections. Lithuania, Latvia, and Estonia clamored for autonomy. A military court convicted and executed Romania's Nicolae Ceausescu for genocide, and the Berlin Wall crumbled. In Hungary, the country's long-time despot, János Kádár, fell, and the nation proclaimed itself a democratic republic.

Even before Hungary freed itself from Kádár's iron-fisted rule, Firm partners were peeking behind the Iron Curtain to see whether there might be an opportunity for Baker & McKenzie. As early as the 1960s, Russell Baker had encouraged a Chicago partner, Lajos Schmidt, to become involved in America's nascent trade with Hungary. Later, in the early 1980s, Schmidt made trips to Washington and Budapest to evaluate the possibility of opening a Baker & McKenzie office in his native Hungary. Although the Firm felt that it was too early for a Hungarian office, when Robert Cox became Chairman, he began listening to Schmidt's arguments as to why Baker & McKenzie should be in Budapest. He authorized Schmidt "to find out if we could build a law firm there that will give us a peephole into what is going on in the rest of Eastern Europe." After Schmidt's investigatory trips, he reported that the Hungarian authorities would welcome a Baker & McKenzie office because it would enhance the nation's ability to participate in international trade.

Several partners objected to investing in a communist country. But Cox saw Hungary as an "opportunity to take advantage of Lajos's expertise and origin. We had a man who spoke Hungarian, and he knew a number of people in the government." The Firm finally approved a Budapest office in 1987. To draw attention to the new office, the European partners held their 1988 regional meeting there. "Lajos put on a show as only Lajos can do," Cox recalls. He staged a reception for over nine hundred at one of Budapest's grandest palaces, with the Deputy Prime Minister as one of the guests. Reporters roamed the banquet hall, and stuck microphones and television cameras in Cox's face to ask about the cornucopia of foreign capital that many believed would follow the world's largest law firm to Budapest.

Not long after the office opened, a young Hungarian-American lawyer working for a London law firm saw a headline in a legal magazine: "Baker & McKenzie Opens Office in Budapest." The two-year associate, the lowest man in a ten-person business law group, was bored with the humdrum work of grinding out corporate documents, and he dreamed of returning to the country that his mother had fled after the anti-communist revolution failed in 1956.

Peter Magyar flew to Budapest to meet with Schmidt, and came away with an offer for part-time work. He went back to London, loaded his belongings in his small car, and drove across Europe in a state of fear, he says, "because I had no idea what was waiting for me. I'd left a great deal of security and certainty at my very structured law firm in London." Magyar had reason to be nervous. In those first years, the Firm was operating in a legal vacuum. Foreign investment and tax laws were almost nonexistent, and getting things done required personal relationships with government officials. "A great deal depended on what sort of deal you could cut with the relevant ministry," Magyar says. He developed contacts in Hungary, in part because of his Hungarian heritage and knowledge of the language, and in part because of his youth. "In the early 1990s Hungary was run by young people," Magyar says. "Nearly everyone who was a decision maker was under forty. The younger people were able to adapt to the new socio-economic and political situation much quicker than the old guard."

Even though Magyar came to know a number of highly-placed officials, Schmidt was the acknowledged master at making government contacts. "That was Lajos's greatest skill," Magyar says. "He could be great friends with an arch-communist and with a former aristocrat who had come back to Hungary. His ability to get to know the right people in the minimum amount of time was unparalleled." Schmidt's talent at finding ways to help foreign corporations through Hungary's bureaucratic labyrinth was remarkable. For one Western automobile company, he convinced the government to pass a law giving it a tax break on its imported vehicles. The other auto companies were outraged when they found out about the special deal, and got the law changed. Still, Schmidt's auto client considered him "a hero who was worth his weight in gold," Magyar says.

When Magyar arrived in 1988, the office had a number of blue-ribbon clients, but it also had a number of exotic entrepreneurs who migrated to Hungary in the late 1980s. Like any boom town, it attracted the fly-by-night as well as the serious businessmen. "It was literally the wild, wild East," Magyar says. "People who would have gone gold-prospecting at the turn of the century were the same kind of people who came to Hungary in '89, '90, and '91. There were a lot of people who thought they could be successful when they'd been failures elsewhere. We quickly learned to weed out the bullshitters."

One of Magyar's first assignments was a joint venture between American and Hungarian automotive companies. "It was pretty heady stuff for a young guy to be involved in," he says. "Negotiating with the government, getting the Deputy Prime Minister to sign a contract, and getting the U.S. ambassador involved. Launching groundbreaking projects was tremendously exciting—it was a once-in-a-lifetime opportunity."

After major automobile, oil, and other large corporations invested huge sums in Hungary, other companies began believing that the nation's democratic changes were permanent. To facilitate the investment gusher, Hungary drafted modern business legislation. "We were living through the rebirth of a nation," says Robert Knuepfer, a Chicago partner who worked for a time in the Budapest office. "People were running around writing the first laws on taxation, immigration, and foreign investment." Even the casual observer could see the glimmerings of entrepreneurship. Restaurants, candy shops, and other businesses popped up throughout Budapest. As small businesses flourished, the Hungarian government began selling its stable of state-owned industries, and, in 1990, the State Property Agency appointed Baker & McKenzie its legal advisor for privatization.

With Hungary leading the way down the capitalist road in Eastern Europe, the work flow into the Budapest office became a torrent. Baker & McKenzie was the only international law firm in the country, and Hungarian lawyers had not yet been trained to deliver Western-style legal services. Much of the office's work involved representing foreign companies doing business in Hungary, including several London merchant banks.

With the huge transfusion of foreign investment into Hungary, about twenty-five foreign law firms followed Baker & McKenzie into the country. Some of them had difficulty integrating themselves into the Hungarian milieu, and some pulled out after only a few months or years. "The thing that differentiated us from the others was that we aimed to become as local as possible, while maintaining a Western outlook," Magyar says. "With the help of our Hungarian lawyers, we were providing Hungarian legal advice, not simply English or U.S. advice in Hungary."

The Budapest office developed a strong reputation in privatizations and cutting-edge financial transactions. Over time, it handled the country's first privatization, the organization of the first foreign-owned Hungarian company, the largest foreign investment in Hungary, the first private placement of shares of a Hungarian company, and the first international financing by a Hungarian company. Although having the deluge of sophisticated business was exciting, Schmidt became less involved in the daily work routine, and the brunt of it fell on the young expatriate and Hungarian lawyers. Overworked, they normally put in twelve- to fifteen-hour days, including many weekends.

Other problems added to the work load. Competent bilingual secretaries were almost nonexistent, so the lawyers often typed their own letters. The outmoded phone system was so bad that the attorneys sometimes spent hours trying to telefax documents to clients. The work flow and the youthful lawyers' inexperience began to take their toll in 1990, when Hans-Georg Feick, the Executive Committee liaison to Budapest, became alarmed. "We were getting a lot of complaints," he says, "from other offices and from clients who said they had written to the office, and never got a response." In addition, several lawyers, frustrated with the unceasing work, quit. To abate the overload, the London office sent associates to Budapest for six- to eight-month tours of duty. To add stability to the office, the Firm made Magyar a partner while he was still in his late twenties. Later, it sent Robert Knuepfer to provide supervision. "The problem was spotted early enough," Magyar says. "Not nipped in the bud, but it was addressed well before there was a major crisis."

Although the Budapest office experienced growing pains, it expanded steadily. By the mid-1990s, the office had fourteen lawyers and ten telephone lines. It was housed in an elegant building that was formerly the headquarters of the People's Patriotic Front, a wing of the Communist Party. "Without this success story in Hungary," Feick says, "we would have faced much more partner resistance to opening an office in Moscow."

———————

In 1985, Mikhail Gorbachev became Secretary General of the Soviet Communist Party and called for sweeping changes, summarized by the slogans *perestroika* (economic reconstruction) and *glasnost* (political openness). He demanded reforms, and blasphemed communist doctrine by proclaiming that central planning was retarding the economy. Gorbachev also relaxed restrictions on foreign investment.

Even though the Soviet Union's attempts to deflate the Cold War did not begin in earnest until the late 1980s, Baker & McKenzie had flirted with opening a Moscow office in the early 1970s. Subsequently, London's David Winter, Chicago's James Hitch, and a handful of other lawyers had handled USSR and Eastern Bloc transactions. In the late 1980s, several events spurred the partners who were interested in opening in Moscow to move quickly. A competitor law firm had opened an office there in 1988. And a new Soviet joint venture law that allowed foreigners to become partners with USSR entities "transformed the East-West Trade Practice from having very little work to being completely swamped," Paul Melling says. Increasingly, it became difficult to service clients by shuttling between Moscow and the U.S. or England.

As the need for a Moscow office became more apparent, the Firm checked with the U.S., UK, Belgian, and other governments to make sure that having an office there would not violate their laws. Not only was there no legal impediment, but the Western governments actively encouraged the Firm to open an office because, they said, Western law firms could help open up trade possibilities. Even before the Firm formally approved the office, Belgian partner Ignace Maes had been working with the Perestroika Joint Venture to smooth the Firm's entry into the USSR. Perestroika, a Soviet-American company that was restoring buildings for use as Western-style offices, was anxious to have the world's largest law firm set up an office. It agreed to serve as the Firm's sponsoring organization, and to steer the attorneys' visa applications through the ponderously slow Soviet bureaucracy. Perestroika also agreed to arrange hard-to-get hotel rooms for the lawyers to live in, and for office space. In return, the Firm paid Perestroika with free legal services.

In addition to arranging residence and office space, Maes also helped bring in the lawyers to staff the Moscow office. Paul Melling, who had been working on Soviet matters for almost eight years, was an obvious choice. In 1982, the London office recruited him out of Oxford University, and one of his first major assignments was to work with Winter on an arbitration case that involved a $300 million claim by a Western company against a Soviet government agency. The case "was fascinating because it was the first time that any Western lawyers had appeared as advocates before a Soviet arbitration tribunal arguing Soviet law," Melling recalls.

From his London base, Melling was spending about three months a year in the USSR, where he learned to speak Russian and obtained a firm foundation in Soviet law. On his trips, he became friends with a few Russians, even though "Soviet citizens were actively discouraged from having any social contacts with foreigners," Melling says. "The people we did business with had to get special permission in order to accept a dinner invitation."

Although Melling's social contact was limited, when he was negotiating agreements with officials at the Ministry of Foreign Trade, the contact was sometimes too close. The Soviets often stacked the negotiating room with large numbers of people in an attempt to intimidate the foreigners, and "there was a very narrow table, so that, sitting opposite each other, your knuckles would be touching," Melling says. The Soviets also used what he calls the "visa panic strategy." Typically, Melling and his client had visas that were valid from Monday through Friday. Knowing this, the Russians would "say 'nyet, nyet, nyet' on every point," Melling recalls. "Then, about an hour before you had to leave for the airport on Friday, they would start negotiating for real." The client was left with the choice of giving in or having to come back to Moscow another time. "Their strategy worked quite regularly," he says.

When the Firm proposed that Melling move to Moscow, he immediately agreed. A second young man, Arthur George, a Washington associate who spoke Russian, also signed on to be part of the new office. After he had graduated from George Washington University Law School, he started work in the Washington office, spending five years there before the opportunity to go to Moscow arose.

In early 1989, Melling and George got on a plane to Moscow, bringing with them a seventy-pound safe in which to store confidential client documents. They also had to import ordinary office supplies such as paper, pens, and pencils from Western Europe or the U.S. and then find a place to store them in their one-room office. They had no secretary, and George spent hours hunched over a cardboard box he used for a table, pecking at a castoff typewriter from the London office. Melling, who couldn't type, either wrote his documents in long-hand or marked up form contracts and sent them by telefax to the London word-processing department for revision.

In their tight quarters, the two lawyers shared one table and an antique and unreliable Soviet telephone. For emergencies, Melling and George used another company's international line until, several months later, they got their own international telephone at a cost of $30,000. Even then, because they assumed that the phones were tapped, they spoke guardedly. Although they did not have to resort to "James Bond-type code words," Melling says, "you just didn't discuss anything sensitive over the telephone." The mail was also a problem. The Soviets routinely opened mail, so, before the international courier services started operating in the USSR, the Moscow lawyers either met their clients in Western Europe, sent messages out with friends, or put confidential documents in diplomatic pouches.

Soon after they arrived, the reality of living in Moscow sank in. One evening, Melling and George joined Baker & McKenzie partners at their hotel to discuss strategy for meetings the next day with government ministries. After deciding on their approach, at about 2:30 A.M. the two young lawyers got a taxi to take them to their hotel. As the cab cruised down a main road, it suddenly swerved off on a side street. Another taxi had followed theirs, and both taxis stopped on the deserted street.

"Arthur and I were sitting in the back of the taxi, and all of a sudden both back doors opened. They were criminals with extremely long knives," Melling says. The thieves dragged Melling and George out of the taxi, took their valuables, and began beating them. When they threatened to kill them, George broke and ran. Startled, the robber who was holding Melling loosened his grip, allowing him to run also. George hid for almost an hour, and then made his way to his hotel. Melling staggered back to the main road and flagged a taxi. With blood running down his face, he explained to the driver that he had been robbed and that all of his money was stolen. "If they took all of your money, how are you going to pay me?" the cabby asked, and then drove off. Another taxi stopped, but Melling didn't tell him that he had no money, and the driver took him back to his hotel.

Despite Moscow's risks, in just a few months the office was so busy that the two associates needed help. John Hewko joined them in December 1989, forcing them to look for more space. After a year in their Spartan office, they moved into larger quarters in a renovated building just off Gorki Street. Robert Cox made a trip to Moscow to inspect the new office, and was appalled at conditions in the Soviet capital. "It was bizarre. Here I was in Moscow, which was one of the great powers militarily. But it looked to me like a Third World country. Shabby. Stores empty of any products."

The police-state atmosphere made the dull, gray city even more oppressive. In his hotel room, the Firm's Chairman found a listening device in the bedroom lamp. At dinner with the office lawyers, Cox recalls, "What came to my mind was that this was a terrible place to live and do business. Food, travel—it was awful. But the genuine excitement that the Moscow lawyers felt for being at the cutting edge was something very special."

The new office space wasn't palatial, but it was a marked improvement over the first one. It had three private offices, a small area for secretaries, and a conference room. It also had a kitchen and a cook. When partners visited from other offices, they often made snide remarks about what they felt was a costly and needless extravagance. What they didn't know was that Moscow had almost no restaurants and, in the few that there were, the service was indifferent. "It was a two-hour proposition anytime you wanted to go have lunch," Hewko says. "To have the entire staff running around Moscow trying to find a place to eat would have been impossible." The Moscow office's cars and drivers were another perquisite that drew sarcastic remarks from Firm partners. "We had a lot of problems with the Firm," Hewko says. "Guys from London saying, 'I take the tube every day. Why do these guys need a car?' People didn't understand. Mail didn't work. Drivers spent all day delivering documents."

Business in the Moscow office was booming. "The pace was torrid," Hewko says. "One joint venture after another." To help, Canadian Carol Patterson joined the office in the early 1990s. With Patterson and others joining, the office again ran out of space. When clients walked in, they were greeted by files stacked on the floor, secretarial and paralegal desks jammed together, cooks in the kitchen, and drivers loitering until their next trip. "Everybody was in a big bullpen," William Atkin says. "It was a mass of humanity." Working in crowded quarters was not the only problem. The Soviets had little understanding of the rule of law. Instead, they had "telephone law," a system by which, Hewko explains, one government official picked up the phone and called a friend in another office to make an agreement or to decide what a law or regulation meant. "Everything was based on personal contacts. It was an almost medieval system," he says.

Adding to the muddle was the fact that, for seventy years, being a capitalist or owning private property had been a crime. As a result, until the early 1990s, Soviet laws governing trade and commerce covered only about seventy-five pages. The brevity made the law easy to learn, but "it was also a curse," Hewko says. "Since the law was so undeveloped, it was impossible to provide clear answers to many of the issues posed by our clients." In an attempt to make up for the shortcoming, the Russians began grafting English, French, German, and other laws onto their existing legal structure. "It was a legislative zoo," Hewko says. "The people drafting it couldn't foresee ninety percent of the problems you face when you attempt to apply the law in a market economy. None of it meshed together. None of it was the product of years of deliberative change like Westerners had." Gorbachev's decentralization measures compounded the problem by giving provincial bureaucrats and legislatures the right to adopt laws and make decisions. For clients doing business in Siberia or St. Petersburg, the lawyers had to parse through two or more layers of frequently conflicting rules and regulations.

Sorting through the ever-shifting USSR law was an exercise in alchemy. There was no *Federal Register* or *Diario Oficial*[1] where a lawyer could find the laws and regulations. Instead, Soviet newspapers published the laws, but haphazardly. After spending several frustrating hours trying to find the law, Firm lawyers sometimes discovered that a ministry had adopted unwritten in-house rules. It was not unusual for a Firm attorney to think that the law was clear on a point, only to find that the bureaucrats put a different spin on its application. Frequently, the bureaucrats didn't have the background to administer the new commercial laws, and there were few guidelines to help them avoid impractical or capricious decisions. This combination sometimes left—at best—gray areas, and—at worst—black holes, where there were no answers to whether a business transaction was legal.

The Moscow lawyers tried to thread their way through the anarchy with their own version of telephone law. "A good lawyer was the one who had contacts in the ministries and could hunt down unpublished legislation or regulations," Hewko says. In addition, the office hired paralegals to make almost daily sweeps of the key ministries to get copies of the latest interpretive letters and regulations.

As late as 1992, the Moscow office library had been a closet "where some things had been thrown together," but the office soon hired a full-time librarian to collate and organize the laws and regulations and enter them into a computer database. Then, rather than combing through stacks of old newspapers to get copies of Russia's legislation, the librarian could find the information on the computer, in both Russian and English. Over time, the Moscow office developed one of the best law libraries in Russia.

While the attorneys were trying to deal with Russia's legal jumble, clients clamored for unequivocal answers to whether they were getting good title to property or whether their loan documents would stand up in court. Instead of concrete answers, they often got a disclaimer or a solid maybe. "It was driving the clients crazy. It was driving us crazy," Hewko says. "At the end of every memo I'd put: 'You should be aware that the Soviet legal system is in a state of tremendous flux. Due to the uncertainty, the advice provided herein should not be viewed as 'ironclad,' but, rather, an attempt to come to reasonable conclusions based on often incoherent, incomplete, and inconsistent legislation and regulations.'"

The need to prepare most agreements in English and Russian made the Moscow lawyers' job even more complex. The office hired a bevy of bilingual staffers to translate between the two languages. Even though the translators were fluent in everyday Russian and English, however, they had been locked into the socialist system for so long that they didn't have the vocabulary for many Western legal concepts, such as "good faith efforts" and "reasonable." Some Russians didn't know what a bank account or a credit card was, and owning stock in a corporation was a completely foreign notion. To fill in the gaps, Firm lawyers taught Western legal and business jargon to the translators.

The language barriers carried over from the office to the negotiating table. For years, the government-sponsored Foreign Trade Organizations ("FTOs") had handled all international business. During that time, the FTO bureaucrats built up an understanding of how Western businessmen and lawyers worked. When Gorbachev dismantled the old centralized system, any Soviet company could negotiate directly with foreigners, but the executives in the newly liberated companies had never dealt with outsiders. Some were so unsophisticated that they didn't know the difference between gross and net profits or what a bank loan was.

"Why would a bank give you money that's not yours?" one Russian executive asked Hewko.

"It's called a loan," he responded.

"How does the bank know you're going to pay it back?"

"It doesn't know," Hewko said. After much discussion, he was able to get the concept of a bank loan across to the Russian.

The inexperienced Soviet executives made negotiations tedious. "It is human nature," Melling says, "that, if you know that the person you are dealing with has more experience than you do, your reaction is to go on the defensive. You are worried that someone is going to use their superior knowledge to take advantage of you." Their fear often led the Soviet businessmen to become inflexible, even on points of secondary importance. The lawyers spent hours explaining contract provisions that, in the West, were standard clauses that warranted no discussion. Instead of negotiating important issues like price and payment terms, Hewko says, the Soviets "lacked the basic understanding of the market mechanism. The boilerplate that you have in contracts was totally new and difficult to translate. So it was really a communications game. One thing we brought to the table was that we could negotiate in Russian and bridge the gap between the Russians and our Western clients."

Although the Moscow office was busy, during its first two-and-a-half years it lost some $1.5 million. Not only were the partners around the world, who were subsidizing the losses, unhappy, the Moscow lawyers were upset. They had blue-ribbon clients, were doing quality work, and were working long hours. Still, the office wasn't profitable. In retrospect, several factors were working against them. Because so many investors were interested in Russia, other Firm offices were asking the Moscow lawyers to devote substantial time to promotional efforts, including speeches in Europe and the U.S. and hand-holding of clients who visited the Russian capital. In addition, there was no on-site business administrator, which forced the Moscow lawyers to stretch their time even thinner in order to perform management functions.

Perhaps the single most difficult problem the office faced was the confusion surrounding its billing procedures. Because the office wasn't formally accredited with the USSR in its early days, the lawyers were forced to send their billing records to other offices for processing and mailing to clients. To many receiving partners, the Moscow fee statements took second place to their own work and billings. The overworked Moscow lawyers, often tardy in forwarding their billing information, also contributed to the difficulty. Some bills became so stale that, by the time clients received them, they had forgotten the amount of work that had been done and complained that the bills were too high. The Moscow lawyers soon began to feel the full impact of the Formula's appetite for cash-only collections. As a stop-gap measure, Ignace Maes agreed to centralize the Moscow billings from his Brussels office.

Another factor that contributed to the Moscow office's early losses was the lawyers' naiveté. In their haste to build the office, Melling says, "one of the mistakes we made was taking on as clients almost anybody who came in the door." Several "flaky" clients with grandiose plans ran up substantial bills and then either disappeared or refused to pay. Not all of the "flakes" were foreigners. A number of Russian "wannabe entrepreneurs" discovered that the Firm had a Moscow office. Many of them didn't know that Baker & McKenzie was a law firm, and made pitches to the Firm to help them sell products that ranged from timber to powdered deer antlers, which some cultures believe is an aphrodisiac.

To drive off the foreign and domestic flakes, the office started demanding written engagement letters and large up-front retainers. Although the office had its share of ersatz promoters, most of its clients were large multinational corporations. A few wanted to make money fast, worrying that Gorbachev's attempt to reform an autocratic system that had existed for centuries created the potential for too much volatility. Most companies, however, viewed the USSR as a large market with potential over the long term.

From 1989 into the early 1990s, Baker & McKenzie was one of only two Western law firms in Moscow, making it one of the few places a stranger could find reliable information. Few clients spoke Russian or had experience in the Soviet Union. To help them, the Moscow office booked hotel and restaurant reservations, arranged visas, and rented cars. After the foreign executives had made the obligatory visits to the Bolshoi Ballet and the circus, there wasn't much to do. While they were waiting for another meeting with a ministry official, bored clients left their substandard hotel rooms and headquartered in the office. "They would grab on to our leg and not let go until they got on the plane and left," George says. "They would use our conference room, our secretaries, and our fax machines because there were no other alternatives. We wanted to be helpful, but at times it got to be a little much."

With little understanding of the cultural complexities of practicing law in Russia, some clients were too demanding, asking for complicated joint venture agreements to be completed in a few days. "The translations alone sometimes took three or four days," Hewko moans. "A guy would come in on the Finnair flight from Helsinki on Tuesday, unannounced, and say, 'I've got to get the deal signed by Friday because my plane leaves at 4:00 P.M. on Friday.' Then, everything stopped. You did nothing but work with him. As soon as that guy took off, another one came in."

———

Life at the office was stressful, but the lawyers' private lives were equally trying. Because the Firm did not want to commit to long-term apartment leases in 1989, Melling and George first lived in the Hotel Budapest, a third-class facility. After work, Melling says he would go back to his bleak room at the Budapest, which was "disgusting. It was dirty. It was infested with roaches, and rodents ran across the floor."

A few months later, the two lawyers moved to the Hotel Ukraine, a building that also housed cadres of mice and bugs, but was a slight upgrade from the

Budapest. Although the Hotel Ukraine had a forbidding exterior, a design one lawyer called "Stalin grotesque," it could be lively on the inside. The hotel security guards were supposed to keep unauthorized persons from entering, "but a lot of black marketers and prostitutes would waltz right into the hotel because the guards had been paid off," George says. One night, while he was waiting for the elevator in the lobby, he looked across a low railing into the cafe area where a cluster of whores and petty criminals were sitting. While he was staring, a brawl broke out. "It was one of those good old saloon fights, like in the western movies, with the chairs flying against the mirrors," George recalls.

Hewko, who arrived in Moscow in the winter of 1989, checked into the Hotel Ukraine with his new wife. He recalls that a "key lady," who reported all comings and goings to the KGB, sat by the elevator on every floor. Security guards screened all visitors, and constantly harassed Hewko's wife, Margarita, claiming that she was a prostitute. On one occasion, a guard blocked her entry, but she walked past him. When the sentry began grabbing at her, she whacked him with an umbrella and escaped to her room, where she called her husband at work. In the meantime, the hotel administration had called the police, who arrived just before Hewko did. When he got off the elevator on his floor, two policeman were breaking down his door with an ax. Hewko managed to explain the situation to the police, and convinced them not to arrest his wife.

Living in the grim hotels could be depressing, and eating in the restaurants was no better. "The caviar was a little bit smelly," Maes recalls. "You ate it at your own risk. The meat was generally overcooked. The potatoes were undercooked. The butter was strong, and the coffee was weak." George recalls that "we got sick on the food about once a month," and, on his trips to the West "stomach-upset medicine was one of the first things you thought of to buy." Good food was not the only thing in short supply. Much-treasured foreign cigarettes were in such great demand that the lawyers often used them as money instead of rubles. The lawyers did so much business in Marlboros that the Moscow office kept petty cash records in dollars, rubles, and cigarettes.

Some partners called the Moscow lawyers' early law practice "pioneering." Others said they were practicing "cowboy law" because they frequently had to shoot from the hip. In either event, they were handling many transactions that plowed new ground. In 1991, the government hired Baker & McKenzie to handle the privatization of Volga Automobile Associated Works, which produced over sixty percent of the Soviet Union's cars. The deal was the largest privatization in Soviet history, and was expected to serve as a prototype for all future transactions. The Firm assembled a team of lawyers from Moscow, Budapest, New York, and London to work on the matter.

In 1991, when Communist Party hardliners arrested Mikhail Gorbachev, many Soviets predicted a glum future for their nation. The Firm's fourteen Soviet employees were certain, Melling says, that "it was the end of *perestroika,* the end of *glasnost*, and the end of Baker & McKenzie in Moscow." But Boris Yeltsin, backed by tank commanders, proclaimed: "We are dealing with a rightist, reactionary, unconstitutional coup." Five days after the rebellion began, its sponsors caved in. Gorbachev continued the process that would end seventy-four years of Communism, but the country was still poised on the brink of collapse. In December, Yeltsin replaced Gorbachev as the country's leader.

With the breakdown of political and economic institutions, crime flourished. "It had all the hallmarks of organized crime in the States back in the twenties and thirties—protection rackets, drug dealing, and prostitution," Melling says. Even with the USSR rapidly disintegrating, foreign investors continued putting money into the tottering state. With more client work than it could handle, the Moscow office's lack of organization and administration came into sharper focus. The four most senior lawyers in the office were still in their thirties, and none of them had management experience. Until 1992, Melling was the only partner, and, as a junior partner, he understood little of the Firm's accounting and financial procedures.

In the San Francisco office, William Atkin heard that Moscow needed administrative help. He flew to Chicago and told Cox he wanted to go. "I thought this was the one time in my life that I would see a major jurisdiction like Russia start from scratch," Atkin says. Cox was skeptical at first because Atkin didn't speak Russian. But he had worked in the Caracas and Taipei offices for several years, and had been active in management in both Taiwan and San Francisco. Within weeks after his chat with Cox, Atkin and his family were headed to Russia. When he arrived in July 1992, his first problem was finding an apartment large enough for his wife and five children. After a three-month search, he rented two adjoining apartments close to Russia's parliament building, the White House.

When Atkin canvassed the office, its shortcomings were obvious. "Everything was strained by just being overwhelmed," he says. "We literally could have worked everybody twenty-four hours a day, and still not gotten all the client work out. We were getting a reputation of not being responsive. With the crush of work, people were getting the work product out too fast. Quality wasn't where it should have been." The native-born Russian lawyers had little experience in handling cross-border transactions. And the Western associates had no background in international commercial law: one had done insurance defense, another had been a U.S. government bureaucrat, and another had specialized in bankruptcy law. They did, however, understand Russian culture and the Russian language.

Atkin instituted immediate changes. He stepped up the office's associate training, sending associates to work in other offices under the Firm's training programs. He laid down a rule that no work could leave the office without a partner's review. He also established what he called the "same-day response rule," which required all client faxes or letters to be answered on the day they arrived. After he had finished issuing edicts, Atkin initiated the networking of the office's computers, connecting the office to BakerNet, and installing the latest billing software. When he had the essentials in place, Atkin supervised the putting of standard form documents and legislative data on computer. Within a year, these innovations made the Moscow office the most computer-sophisticated Baker & McKenzie office in Europe. To beef up the accounting staff, from the San Francisco office Atkin recruited a Ukrainian accountant, who had been educated in Russia and had a U.S. accounting degree, and who understood the Firm's technological systems and reporting requirements.

While the office was organizing internally, Russia moved from crisis to crisis. In March 1993, communists and ultra-nationalists in Parliament voted overwhelmingly to curb Yeltsin's presidential authority. The quick-tempered President responded by assuming almost unlimited power and calling for an April plebiscite. The Russians voted for Yeltsin, and, in September, he disbanded Parliament. In defiance, his opponents gathered arms and barricaded themselves in the White House.

Early on the morning of October 4, 1993, troops loyal to Yeltsin filtered through Moscow to seal off the White House and crush the rebellion. Atkin and his family awoke to the rumbling of tanks and armored personnel carriers that were headed for the White House, about one hundred yards away from their apartment. Loyalist and rebel partisans would kill more than sixty people in street fighting later that day, but when Atkin left for the office, the shooting hadn't started.

At the office, he turned on the television in the conference room, and watched as Yeltsin's police and troops surrounded the White House. Then, he convened an attorneys' meeting to discuss Firm matters, but the lawyers chewed donuts and watched what might have been the beginning of a civil war on television. About 10:30 A.M., Atkin's wife called: "Bill, there are machine guns all around. They are shooting in the street in front of our apartment." Their apartment was so close to the Parliament building that, while they were talking, Atkin could hear canons blasting the White House. He also heard his apartment doorbell ringing furiously. His wife put down the phone and answered the door. When she came back on the line, she said, "Julie has been shot! Please come! She's bleeding to death!"

Earlier, Julie Brooks, a paralegal in the office, had gone to Atkin's apartment, and she and Atkin's seventeen-year-old son, John, decided to climb to their roof to get a better view of the White House action. As they sat on the roof, sniper's bullets ricocheted off other buildings. Suddenly, somebody started firing at them. When they stood up to run, two shells hit Brooks—one in the stomach and the other in the thigh. Brooks shouted that she was hit, and John reversed course, grabbed her, and dragged her to a sheltered place on the other side of the pitched roof. The girl was bleeding profusely, but John couldn't reach the trapdoor that went back into the building because it was on the side of the roof that was being peppered with marksmen's fire. He did find, however, a fire escape ladder in a protected area. Young Atkin tried to help Brooks crawl down the ladder, but she said, "John, I can't do it. I'm too weak," so the boy wrapped his legs around her torso, locked them together, and lowered them both down the ladder, hand over hand, until they reached the ground eight stories below.

After his wife had called, Atkin grabbed his chauffeur and headed home, ducking through back streets to avoid the fighting. When he arrived at his apartment building, Atkin says, "I ran up to our apartment and Julie was lying on the couch. The ambulance people were putting her on a stretcher." At a nearby hospital, the Russian medical team took her straight into surgery. While she was still in the operating room, Atkin went back to his apartment to evacuate his family to the office.[2] When he got them downstairs to the interior courtyard where the Firm car was parked, a gunman was firing into the courtyard. With bullets flying, the chauffeur backed the Volvo station wagon up to the building door. Atkin's family scrambled into the back seat and lay on the floor. As they driver sped away, a bullet slammed into the car.

When he secured his family at the office, Atkin returned to the hospital. There, he discovered that the hospital had critical drug and blood shortages, and called the office for help. Russian and expatriate staffers who had the same blood type risked driving to the hospital. "We were ferrying people back and forth to the hospital to give blood for Julie," Melling says. "We began ringing our drug company clients to find medication."

That evening, Atkin went back to the office. The story of an American paralegal being shot had hit all of the news services. He and the other lawyers kept busy answering telephone calls from journalists and from Firm partners around the world. At about 2:00 A.M., a Russian doctor called the office to ask permission to re-open Brooks to stop internal bleeding. "We asked what chance of survival she had. He said about ten percent," Atkin remembers.

After Melling got word that Brooks might not survive the night, he called her mother in Pennsylvania to arrange for her to fly to Moscow. He also called Firm lawyers in New York and Washington to get Brooks's mother a Russian visa. To secure the travel papers on an expedited basis, the Washington office used its contacts in the U.S. State Department, and New York lawyers asked the Soviet Consulate for help. Ms. Brooks drove from Pennsylvania to New York City, where Baker & McKenzie lawyers met her with a plane ticket and a Russian visa.

Contrary to the dire medical report, Brooks survived the night. Atkin picked up her mother at the Moscow airport and, the next day, a jet ambulance from Helsinki took Brooks back to a Finnish hospital. In what Atkin calls "the best single administrative decision I have ever made," only a few weeks before he had obtained emergency medical evacuation insurance for the expatriates working in Russia. Brooks recovered and returned to the U.S. to recuperate. Two months later, she was back in the Moscow office.

Despite the trauma of Brooks's shooting, the political chaos, and the economic instability, the Moscow office thrived. From a 1991 financial statement that showed red ink, the Moscow office had a handsome profit by 1995. At the outset, the Moscow office lawyers had few local lawyers. By 1997, however, nine of the twenty-three Moscow lawyers were Russian.

As the Moscow office was consolidating its gains, Soviet political developments were opening up new growth opportunities elsewhere. Gorbachev's push for decentralization, and the USSR's collapse, had changed the economic landscape. In the old Soviet Union, Moscow had been the center of everything. "All contracts were negotiated in Moscow," Melling says. "After the Soviet Union's breakup, however, people began doing business in St. Petersburg without ever going near Moscow."

While political events were still unfolding, the Moscow office's two most experienced associates, Hewko and George, began lobbying to open other offices in the Soviet Union. When the two young men began talking about leaving Moscow in 1991, the prospects of their opening new offices were not bright. The Moscow office was grappling with an inefficient billing system and was losing money. Neither George nor Hewko were partners, and the Firm had always shied away from allowing associates to open new offices. Also, with the heavy workload in Moscow, stripping the office of its most experienced lawyers might risk its future.

Nevertheless, George began making plans to return to St. Petersburg, the place where he had been a student in 1980. In 1992, the Firm approved his project and elected him a partner. George found office space on the ground floor of a building next to one of St. Petersburg's famed canals. The office prospered, and grew to nine lawyers, seven of whom were Russian, in its first five years.

Meanwhile, Hewko was planning a Kiev office. His motivation to go to Ukraine was based in part on the romance of being a pioneer who would spread free-market ideas in the socialist nation. He also had an emotional tie, because, during World War II, both sets of his grandparents, well-known Ukrainian nationalists and anti-communists, became targets for Stalin's forces.[3] With the Red Army shooting anyone they thought was an enemy of the Soviet regime, the two families escaped to Western Europe and immigrated to America in the late 1940s. Hewko was born in a Polish-Ukrainian neighborhood in Detroit, and grew up speaking Ukrainian as his first language.

After he got a Harvard law degree, he worked for another firm for a while, but his Ukrainian roots kept tugging at him. When Baker & McKenzie offered Hewko the chance to go to Moscow, he resigned from his old firm and moved there in late 1989. An impatient man, Hewko first floated the idea of opening a Kiev office in November 1990. The two partners he approached said that it was "crazy," noting that all Ukrainian business was channeled through Moscow. Hewko persisted. He began making exploratory trips to Ukraine to visit his relatives there, even though his "whole family got called in for questioning after I left."

In late 1990 and early 1991, Hewko's visits to Kiev increased. It was easy to meet Ukrainians, he says, because they welcomed Americans and Canadians of Ukrainian descent. "There was this euphoria that the Ukrainian émigrés were going to miraculously transform Ukraine into a normal country," he says. When he got wind that a U.S. financier, George Soros, had established a foundation to help Ukraine move toward democracy and a market economy, he was immediately interested.[4] Hewko met a foundation council member on one of his Kiev trips, which led to an offer that he become the foundation's Executive Director. The Firm, however, was concerned that the Russians would view Hewko as helping Ukraine become independent, which might hurt the Moscow office. To allay that worry, Hewko resigned from Baker & McKenzie, although it was understood that he would do what legal work he could for clients in Kiev.

In May 1991, Hewko and his wife bought tickets for the Moscow-Kiev train, and loaded all their belongings and some office equipment in the two compartments they had booked. Because everything had been concentrated in the imperial city of Moscow for over seventy years, Kiev was a backwash. "The Russians brought the Ukrainian people to the brink of poverty," Hewko says. "Moscow sucked everything up. All the talent went there. Ukraine had no army or central bank. No embassies. In a country of fifty-two million people, the Ministry of Foreign Trade was a ten-foot-by-ten-foot room with two telephone lines and four guys. Ukraine had a big learning curve."

In provincial Kiev, while Hewko was busy working, his wife had little to do. With only a few foreigners in the city, social life for an expatriate was limited. When Ms. Hewko went to the market, however, she created a stir with the Geiger counter she carried with her. She used it to scan the tomatoes, potatoes, and other foods to make sure they hadn't been contaminated by the nearby Chernobyl explosion that had spewed nuclear poison over the countryside. When the Ukrainian women figured out what she was doing, they followed her through the market and only bought food where she shopped.

For living quarters, Hewko's Ukrainian friends found him a three-room suite at the Hotel Kiev. Because the hotel was next door to the Parliament Building, many out-of-town deputies also stayed there. In time, Hewko "got to be friends with half of Parliament," Ignace Maes says. "John got to know all the rising new political stars." He spent his days at his Parliament Building office, helping to draft corporate, foreign investment, and other laws. At night, he moonlighted, working on legal matters for clients, including the Canadian government in its purchase of an embassy building and an American elevator company in a joint venture.

In August 1991, a downdraft from Moscow's political upheaval swept through Kiev. Taking advantage of the instability created by the Soviet hardliners' coup against Gorbachev, a group of anti-Soviet deputies, assisted by Hewko, drafted a Declaration of Independence, which Parliament adopted. The deputies also began drafting a constitution. The drafting committee met in a gray granite building that had formerly housed the Communist Party Central Committee. "The room had bare yellow walls that were somewhat paler where recently removed Party icons had hung," a visiting American journalist wrote.[5] "The commission consisted of about a dozen middle-aged men . . . an elderly woman . . . and a young American lawyer, John Hewko . . . from the firm of Baker & McKenzie. . . . His work in Kiev . . . made him, in effect, a founding father of his parents' country."

In December 1991, ninety percent of Ukrainians voted for independence. Hewko took immediate action. Along with the Moscow partners, he put together a business plan for a Kiev office. His plan, however, ran awry of the man the Executive Committee assigned to scrutinize his proposal. Hewko and Richard Davidson were at opposite poles. Where Hewko was brash and excitable, Davidson was an instinctive conservative who carefully mulled over new ideas. "There was the natural tension," Davidson says, "between somebody whose reaction is to go slowly and cautiously, and someone who wants to do it tomorrow."

Davidson worried that the fast-talking thirty-four-year-old had only been with the Firm for three years. And he wanted proof that Hewko's optimistic claims about the potential for business would, in fact, allow the Firm to develop a full-service law office. Aware of the opposition, during his 1991 Christmas vacation in America, Hewko lobbied several U.S. partners, including Michael Waris, who was also the son of Ukrainian immigrants. Although Waris had recently retired, he wrote a lengthy memo to the Executive Committee outlining the rationale for a Kiev office.

As his one-year stint with Soros's foundation was drawing to a close, Hewko became increasingly anxious about his position with the Firm. In his view, the Executive Committee was giving him little support. "All I kept hearing that was opening in Kiev was 'premature, premature, premature.'" The Firm had turned down his requests to hire a Ukrainian-speaking lawyer and to buy supplies and modern equipment. In one phone call with Davidson, Hewko lost it: "I need help! This is bullshit!" he shouted.

In the midst of his efforts to persuade the Firm to commit to a Kiev office, a prominent Cleveland law firm approached him with a tempting offer. The Ohioans would pay him a hefty salary, make him a partner, and bankroll the development of a new office. Hewko debated with himself and talked to his wife and friends, almost all of whom counseled him to stay with Baker & McKenzie.

Despite the advice, Hewko tried to call his contact at the Cleveland firm to tell him that he would join it. With the unreliable Ukrainian telephones, he couldn't make a connection. After he hung up, he placed a call to Cox, which went through immediately. When he told the Firm's Chairman about his other offer, Cox reminded Hewko that Baker & McKenzie had given him the opportunity to go to Moscow and Kiev. "I viewed John as a dynamic individual who was suddenly romanced by someone who said they would do everything for him and pay him more money. He needed to get a perspective on himself," Cox says. "I suggested that John and his wife take a holiday to think over his decision."

In May 1992, the Executive Committee took up the subject of whether to make Hewko a partner and to allow him to open a Kiev office. At first, the Committee voted no. Cox then said, "I guess I presented this wrong. Maybe we need to discuss this again. The risk is not in opening the office. The risk is in not opening the office." The vote switched, and Hewko was back on track. He soon learned that the Executive Committee had approved the Kiev office, with him as a partner at an income level very close to that offered by the Cleveland firm. "Thank God for the lousy Ukrainian phone system," he says. "If that call to the Cleveland firm had gone through, I would have made the biggest mistake of my career."

For the new office, Hewko hired a Ukrainian lawyer, a translator, and an office manager. Because he wouldn't be working with the Ukrainian Parliament any longer, he lost his office in the Parliament Building. Office space was almost impossible to find, and, between June and December, 1992, the office moved to four different locations. "We were like nomads. We could move the whole office in twenty-four hours," Hewko says. In his search for space, he ran across landlords who demanded exorbitant rents, others who asked him to hire their relatives, and others who whispered to him about their Swiss bank accounts where money could be conveniently deposited. "I was determined to play it above board. No bribes, no nothing," he says. Finally, Hewko found permanent office space.

As the client work increased, Hewko needed additional help. One hiring criteria was to have "only young Ukrainians who were completely virgin," because he found the older Ukrainian lawyers "were tainted with the Soviet stuff, and they weren't malleable. They weren't people you could form into Baker & McKenzie associates. So I hired smart young guys so that I could bring them up as Baker & McKenzie lawyers from day one."

To train his new recruits, Hewko had them draft documents directly onto their computers. Then, he and the young lawyers sat side-by-side to edit and critique at the computer. In addition to reviewing their work, he handled the administrative details. "I trained everybody, including the translators. I spent several hours teaching the cleaning lady how to clean the toilets. Those associates whose English wasn't too fluent went to school in the U.S. or England, where they also learned Western concepts." The office that started in 1992 with two attorneys had grown to ten by 1997, eight of whom were Ukrainian.

At the same time the Firm was looking at Kiev and St. Petersburg, it was considering Warsaw as a logical place to open an Eastern European office. Poland had thirty-nine million well-educated and industrious people who had overthrown communism in 1990. Responding to heavy lobbying by Polish-Americans, the U.S. government was channeling aid and encouraging investment in Poland.

To open the Warsaw office, the Firm identified Jur Gruszczynski, the son of a sculptor father and painter mother. He had graduated from Warsaw University Law School in 1981, just as the reformist Solidarity movement was clamoring for liberalization of Polish society. Gruszczynski, a Solidarity partisan, was one of the few Polish lawyers who had business law training, having worked for a state-owned trading company and the Polish Chamber of Commerce. In 1990, when he opened his own law office, he began to get referrals from foreign law firms, including Baker & McKenzie.

Gruszczynski joined the Firm in 1992, and soon learned that, if he had a problem, "it was my problem. At the end of the day I had to make the decision myself, whether it was good or bad." One problem Gruszczynski learned to solve was how to respond quickly to Western clients. In one case, he received an urgent call from a client who needed him to check the title to land in a city about one hundred eighty miles from Warsaw. Knowing that a telephone call to the government Land Registry would not bring the immediate response he needed, Gruszczynski jumped in his car and drove to the town. When he arrived that evening, the Land Registry was closed. Undaunted, he tracked down a Land Registry official in a bar. Gruszczynski persuaded the tipsy official to go with him to the government office, check the title data, and certify the title. Then he drove back to Warsaw that night to deliver the document.

As word spread that the Firm had a Warsaw office, more and more work began flowing to Gruszczynski and the other three lawyers who opened the office. By 1997, the Warsaw office had twenty-three lawyers, twenty of whom were Polish nationals.

———

Between 1987 and 1995, the Firm had spawned the most extensive law office network, seven, in Eastern Europe and the Commonwealth of Independent States ("CIS"), the federation composed of many of the USSR's former republics. Most of the local lawyers, however, had only glimmerings of what a commercial lawyer was supposed to do. Having been nurtured in centrally planned economies, they hadn't learned the skills of trying to find solutions to problems. Instead, they tended to tell clients, "There is a problem here and you can't do what you want to do."

Some of the Eastern Bloc lawyers did not appreciate deadlines and had difficulties meeting the needs of demanding Western clients. Capping the cultural problems that years of communism had created, the Eastern Bloc lawyers were thrown into an arena where there was almost no business law for them to fall back on. "They were being asked to advise on the value added tax which was introduced in Central Europe," Richard Davidson says. "Not only had there not been value added tax before, but there had been very little tax law at all. There was confusion all around."

To solve these common problems, the Firm set up the Central and Eastern European Steering Group in March 1993. The Steering Group, composed of an Executive Committee liaison and a representative of each Eastern Bloc office, coordinates business development efforts, facilitates work product and expertise sharing, publishes a newsletter and promotional materials, and oversees a regional training program.

Many partners see professional training as the Steering Group's most important function. As part of its "missionary school" to teach Western legal techniques, the Steering Group holds seminars for its lawyers. Western European lawyers taught them tax law; London lawyers have gone to Warsaw to instruct on banking and finance law; and the East European and CIS offices provide extensive English language training.

The Eastern Bloc offices have also made extensive use of the Firm's training programs, sending lawyers to other offices to work for extended periods. The Associate Training Program normally requires associates who work in another office to stay there at least one year. Because the training needs were so critical, and because the crush of work was such that the Eastern Bloc offices often could not spare an associate for a full year, a new program permits Eastern Bloc lawyers to go for three months of training in other offices.

———————

While the Eastern Bloc offices were maturing, Baker & McKenzie was also maturing. As it headed toward its fiftieth anniversary, Robert Cox and his successors as Chairman began introducing more sophisticated management and financial techniques and procedures, some of which ran counter to the Firm's historical culture.

Chapter Twenty

The Transition Years: 1989–1994

Toward the end of Robert Cox's first term as Chairman, the partners began casting about for a successor. When the Nominating Committee canvassed for people to stand for the Chairmanship, they found few partners interested in the job, and none who would run against Cox if he wanted a second term.

Even though he tilted toward a second term, and many of his partners had encouraged him to seek it, Cox had some reservations. "You can only stay on the stage so long," he says. "There comes a point when you have exhausted new ideas and your energy level flows downward, not upward." Nevertheless, as Cox weighed the benefits and burdens of remaining in office, he decided that he wanted a second term. There was the practical fact that leaving the Chairmanship would put him face-to-face with the Formula. He told one partner: "I rode that bucking bronco [the Formula] for fifteen years, and getting back on that son of a bitch again wouldn't have been much fun." In addition, he says, "I believed that there were missions to accomplish. My job was not over." Among the unfinished tasks were institutionalizing a management structure, opening more offices, and improving the quality and breadth of the Firm's practice.

As the trial balloons floated through the Firm, several partners came out against Cox's re-election, arguing that the Firm should follow Russell Baker's admonitions against lawyers becoming careerist executives. In addition, the Articles of Partnership specifically said that the Chairman would be elected for a single five-year term, with no re-election. Other partners, however, felt that Cox was doing a good job, and, since there was no clear heir apparent, they wanted him to stay.

At the 1987 Monte Carlo Annual Meeting, the partners organized two debate teams, one in favor of succession and the other against. "Here was a Firm with partners from all over the world who could debate the merits of a business issue in a constitutional context," Cox says. "We didn't do it behind the scenes, and we didn't have back-room politics." Robert Dilworth argued that "extension of an initial term is undesirable because of the multi-cultural nature of the Firm. Rotation is essential. Also, there is the danger of burn-out." Geoffrey Taperell countered that "it is of vital importance to the Firm to be able to [re-elect] the most highly qualified candidate." After the debate, the partners voted for an exception to the Articles of Partnership that allowed Cox to succeed himself. Then, sixty-eight percent of the partners voted in favor of an additional three-year term, beginning in 1989.

During Cox's two terms, several Executive Committee members played prominent roles in Firm management. Brussels partner Ignace Maes shouldered several major responsibilities, including the Firm's expansion into Russia and Eastern Europe. One year, Maes was on the road over sixty percent of the time. With that punishing schedule, he spent only two full weekends with his family. "It was hard," he says.

After his three-year term ended in 1990, Maes's financial and corporate law practice had dwindled, bringing home the reason why many partners are hesitant to serve in management roles. An associate who had worked with Maes's clients left the Firm and took some of them with him. Also, many of his clients had been non-Belgian companies that transferred their employees every few years. When Maes returned to full-time law practice, many of the expatriate executives he had worked with had left Brussels. "In the beginning, there were months with only ten or twenty billable hours. The slump lasted for two and one-half years," he recalls. In addition to losing touch with his clients, he also lost touch with the latest legal developments. It took him several months of hard study, Maes says, to build up his self-confidence to the point that "the fine points of the law were in my head so that I could respond instantly to a judgment call during a meeting."

London partner and Executive Committee member Richard Davidson complains that the Committee's inability to get things done promptly made him an advocate of stronger management. During his four years on the Committee in the early 1990s, Davidson saw the Firm, "warts and all." To some extent, he says, "Committee service can be uplifting or depressing, particularly when a partner overlooks the Firm's interests to pursue his very selfish interests."

Robert Cartwright was another Executive Committee member who weathered the difficulty of transitioning back into law practice. Cartwright had managed to maintain a portion of his practice while he was on the Executive Committee so that "I could still ride the bicycle," he says. "Some other Executive Committee members got so enmeshed in their work that they momentarily forgot how to ride. Still, after I got off the Committee, I had some rough times. If being on the EC doesn't decimate your practice, it can very substantially detract from it." Despite the career risk, Cartwright enjoyed his time on the Committee. "We had a very good bunch of people. Although we had disagreements, there was a lot of camaraderie that went with it. I liked the process of trying to get people to do what you wanted them to do, even if, sometimes, you didn't have their fervent support. All the guys we were managing were busy and successful, and getting them to focus on some of the things was a challenge."

———

Towards the end of Cox's second term, several difficult problems, such as partner disputes and negative headlines in Australia, caused the pressure on him to mount. "There were other issues," Cox says. "They were just sitting there on the desk. My last year began to take a toll. Los Angeles was the worst of all—it was horrific." The crown jewel of his expansionism was falling apart. "He hooked his star to Los Angeles," Jorge Sánchez says. "He felt that it was something that should have been done a long time ago, and he took his best shot at it. Everybody said that we should be in Los Angeles. Nobody could find the way to do it. Bob thought he had it. And it didn't work." Cox, the optimistic deal-maker who thrived on solving problems, found the sepulchral atmosphere in Los Angeles depressing.

Shortly before his term ended, Cox's extraordinary energy level was drained. At about 2:00 P.M. one afternoon, he hung up the phone from a call thanking him for solving partner problems in São Paulo. "I suddenly got up and left. My assistant, Susan Mark, asked me where I was going. I just shook my head. I couldn't talk. I walked home, went to my bedroom, and just sat on the bed. The phone rang and it was Tom Bridgman. Susan had called him because she was concerned. Tom asked if I was okay, and what was wrong. I just gave way. I told him I couldn't do it—the burden was excruciating."

Bridgman told Cox, "Look, kid, it's just a job. Do the best you can and continue on with your life." Cox calmed down, but "at some point, Pat [Cox's wife] walked in. Again, I broke down. Then, I realized I was burned out. The intensity I felt was agonizing. This was never just a job."

Cox finished his term in 1992 and, after he left office, he reflected on whether it had been wise for him to continue in office: "Was it a mistake? I think many people would say that I took one year too many. Some might say two. If I had quit at five years, I would have gotten Caesar's wreath." Although the end of Cox's reign had its ill-starred moments, a large majority of his partners, and the statistics, rank it a success. In his last year, the Firm's four hundred ninety-seven partners divided the profits from over $500 million in gross income, more than quadruple that of 1984, the year he took office. In that year, the Firm had thirty offices with seven hundred fifteen lawyers. When he left eight years later, it had forty-nine offices with 1,604 lawyers who carried some forty-five passports and spoke over sixty languages.

His growth program had taken the Firm into five new U.S. cities and three in Mexico. Baker & McKenzie also established new beachheads in the Middle East, South America, and Western Europe. The Beijing presence prospered, and eventually became a full office. More dramatically, the Firm was the trailblazer in opening offices behind the Iron Curtain. "Bob Cox tried to be more creative in looking at where we should position ourselves. He looked at where he felt that, from a business point of view, we should be, and he did his best to get us there," Bruce Porter says.

Cox also eradicated the sneering media stories that painted Baker & McKenzie as a second-line law firm. Instead, the headlines proclaimed "Baker & McKenzie—Counselors to the World" and "Law Firm Blankets Globe, Getting There First Keeps Baker & McKenzie on Top." His constant reminders that the Firm was a first-class operation helped the partners rid themselves of a nagging insecurity, and instilled a sense of pride in being partners in what Cox calls "one of the most unique social experiments of our time."

As Baker & McKenzie's first full-time Chairman, he had the luxury of being able to plan for the future. Past Chairmen had spent most of their time reacting to the problems that hit their desks. Cox began the process of developing business plans and stronger management, including restructuring the International Executive Office and adding a Chief Financial Officer. During Cox's eight-year term, John McGuigan says, he was "significant in evolving us down the path of running an integrated global law firm."

Cox played out his term against a backdrop in which the worldwide legal profession was undergoing dynamic changes. Perhaps the most profound was that many consultants and lawyers were saying the last rites over law as a profession, claiming that it was a business like any other. Internally, law firms' cost structures were under heavy pressure at the same time that they needed capital to grow. The computer revolution, rising rental rates, and skyrocketing associate salaries soaked up sixty percent or more of the gross revenues of some firms. At the same time, long-established client relationships were cracking. Rather than aligning themselves with one law firm as they had in the past, clients shopped for better quality and lower fees.

In many countries, lateral partners were leaving their old law firms for what they felt were greener pastures, breaking down partner and law firm loyalties. Firms in cities like Sydney and New York dangled signature bonuses and hefty salaries to partners with large stables of clients. To get on the growth path, many firms set strategies to dominate a region or a nation; others chose to merge. Some of the patchwork law firms quickly disintegrated. Finley, Kumble, Wagner, Underberg, Manley, Myerson & Casey was the most dramatic. It had grown from nothing just a few years before to become one of America's largest firms. After its demise, some wags called it "Finley Crumble."

Until the 1980s, Baker & McKenzie had almost no competition for transnational business. A few U.S. law firms had opened Paris or London offices, and some English law firms had experimented with Middle and Far East branches. By the time Cox's term ended in 1992, other law firms were jumping into what had been the Firm's exclusive preserve. The competitor firms, mostly American and English, faced cultural and financial growing pains. Many learned that new offices in strange jurisdictions often run up red ink for several years. Culturally, some had difficulty in admitting partners from multiple countries. And all had to catch up with Baker & McKenzie's almost fifty years of in-depth experience in handling international transactions.

Even though the Firm's background in multinational business was a major advantage, rivals continued to mount challenges to Baker & McKenzie's preeminence. The large international accounting firms presented the fiercest competition. They were both well capitalized and had years of institutional culture that allowed them to operate comfortably in a global framework. In many countries, accounting firms created sister law firms because local law prohibited lawyers and accountants from practicing in the same firm. The law firms did not use the names of their parent accounting firms, but the sponsoring accounting firms controlled them totally. Although they attempted to create an aura of independence, the brother-sister accounting and law firms referred work back and forth on an exclusive basis. Along with the rise of the accounting/law firms, another phenomenon created competition. Many corporate clients began staffing their law departments with international law experts.

―――――――

More than a year before Cox's term was to end, Baker & McKenzie began a search for his successor from a list of thirty-six candidates. "A lot of partners were not prepared to sacrifice their legal careers in exchange for going into a management position," says William Outman, the Nominating Committee Chairman. The Committee pared the original list to four candidates: Robert Cartwright from New York, Robert Dilworth from Chicago, Ronaldo Veirano from Rio de Janeiro, and John McGuigan from Hong Kong.

In June 1991, the Nominating Committee met with each candidate. "The interviews were intense," Outman says. "It was a serious decision, not to be taken lightly." As the scrutiny proceeded, the Committee's consensus, and that of most partners, swung to McGuigan. Before he became a lawyer, McGuigan had worked for five years at an international accounting firm, giving him a strong feel for financial issues. In addition, he had been successful as a Sydney partner before moving to Hong Kong to be the Managing Partner of that office. There, he had presided over the meteoric growth in both numbers of lawyers and profits. "He was the shogun out there," Outman says. "He was dynamic in his outlook. He was young [forty-two]. There was a hope that his fresh approach would bring new ideas to the Firm. Also, he would usher in a new generation to Firm management." In July 1991, Outman called the four candidates, telling three of them that they were not the nominee, and telling McGuigan that he was the choice. At the Vienna Annual Meeting that fall, the partners designated him the Chairman-elect for a five-year term beginning in 1992.

While Cox was still officially the Chairman, McGuigan calculated the Firm's assets and liabilities. "We did well in understanding cultures and creating the environments where people genuinely enjoyed each other's company," McGuigan says. "We had a great capacity to work on a cross-cultural basis, and a sense of being part of one unit. We had a unique infrastructure and a healthy financial capitalization." But he worried that the Firm's spirit of lone-wolf autonomy was a threat. "Part of the success in the Hong Kong office," he says, "was that we said, 'Look, we're going to view this as a business. We want to have an environment that's a lot of fun and plays to the strengths of people. But we're going to get a hell of a lot more out of it if we operate on a collective basis rather than a very individualistic basis.'"

When McGuigan looked at the international accounting firms, banks, and other service companies, he saw them "applying resources on a much more prioritized basis. I was very concerned that, if we didn't move in the direction of channeling resources, and if we didn't view ourselves genuinely as a cohesive business, then the cost of being part of Baker & McKenzie would create some stresses and strains that could be pretty serious."

Compounding the problem, as McGuigan saw it, was the Firm's introduction of lateral partners. To laterals, the camaraderie that Baker & McKenzie partners had developed over decades was of lesser importance, and they would be looking for the Firm to deliver something more tangible. "The partners must perceive that being part of an international firm provides them with benefits," he says. "That includes all sorts of things. It is a brand name, and it is being viewed as a preeminent player in important areas of legal practice. It is having work sent to you from other offices. It is being able, if you're in a capital exporting jurisdiction, to have offices of real quality around the world. As much as the partners like each other, they must be able to say to themselves: 'It makes all the sense in the world to be part of Baker & McKenzie, because, if I wasn't, I wouldn't be able to play in this game.'"

Because law firms were crowding into the marketplace all around the world, McGuigan concluded that the law of supply and demand would affect pricing and, eventually, the survival of law firms. "I was of the view that those very basic market forces were going to impact the legal business in a way that we had been previously sheltered from," he says.

When McGuigan became Chairman in 1992, he set about developing additional Firm-wide expertise in practice areas such as cross-border securities, financing, and technology matters. "At every level of the Firm," he says, "we needed to have a sharper, clearer strategic focus on the practice areas that we were going to be telling people around the globe that we were truly excellent at."

McGuigan also urged the lawyers to listen to their clients, to learn about their industries and businesses, to find out what they wanted from their lawyers and from the Firm, and then to react to the clients' input. The Firm, he believed, could no longer rely solely on its size and the network to woo and keep clients. As the legal business became more sophisticated, McGuigan says, "the mere fact that you were able to hold yourself out as being in fifty to fifty-five locations was not necessarily going to get you cross-jurisdictional work. What you had to be able to say was that we were there and we were also lawyers of quality."

To enhance quality, McGuigan wanted to overcome the Firm's "historical reluctance to saying that we were going to have global quality standards that applied to everybody in the Firm. We had marketplace feedback that Baker & McKenzie was terrific in some places, and a little bit patchy in others. In an environment where you're as strong as your weakest link, and where you're trying to convince clients that they ought to be using you on a global basis, that was obviously something that needed to be addressed."

Baker & McKenzie had always been interested in quality control, but it had not always been effective, in some measure because of the Firm's legacy of individualism and local office independence. Beginning in the 1970s, the Firm had taken steps to improve its lawyers' practice skills. It commissioned a Yale University professor to recommend procedures for supervising associate work, training programs, and follow-up evaluations. In 1980, it hired the first Director of Professional Development. Despite some partner resistance, Edward Dyson, Richard Davidson, and other partners pushed to bring professional development to the top of the Firm's agenda.

A fear of malpractice lawsuits in the 1980s spurred the step-up in lawyer training. Proponents pointed out that well-trained lawyers are much less likely to make mistakes or to venture outside the boundaries of ethical conduct. And, to remain competitive, the Firm had no choice. "The only way we were going to beat the competition," Davidson says, "was by excellence of legal advice." In 1986, David Yates became the Director of Professional Development. Yates agreed that "in order to adjust to the competitive pressures, to counter some of the allegations of patchy quality, and to deal with some of the malpractice issues that we faced, we felt that we needed to be much more systematic in handling the quality issues."

Along with the Firm's Professional Development Committee, Yates began looking into the local offices' procedures for proper assignment of work, encouraging formal training in legal topics, and reviewing the English language lessons in offices where English was a second language. Cox supported Yates's efforts, and, in the early 1990s, the Firm published a *Professional Development Manual* and a *Quality Manual*, which Yates edited. He also beefed up the Associate Training Program and installed controls to assure that young lawyers who transferred to other offices got the maximum benefit. In the past, Davidson says, some of the associates on the ATP had "just sort of wandered for a year and had a wonderful time, and made a lot of friends, but they didn't get that much done professionally."

When McGuigan took office in 1992, professional development fit neatly into his philosophy that the global Firm had to supply the local offices with useful services. McGuigan delivered the budget, and Yates hired Regional Training Officers in North America, South America, the Pacific Basin, and Europe. McGuigan and Yates also installed a quality audit program that provided for teams of partners to review each office's work. The critiques included checking work product such as contracts, conflicts of interest procedures, whether work was given to the most efficient lawyer, client selection procedures, and the extent of budgeting and business planning. As part of the program, each local office designated a Quality Management Partner to monitor and improve his office's quality. Consistent with the concept of greater professionalization, and partly in response to the spate of malpractice claims in the 1980s and 1990s, McGuigan appointed Edward Zulkey, a Chicago litigation partner, as the Firm's first General Counsel. In addition to handling the Firm's legal affairs, he participates in programs for Firm attorneys that emphasize the risks of practice and stress the need for upgrading quality.

To further McGuigan's goal of adding value, International Executive Office staffers made an increasing number of visits to advise on finance, computer systems, and general administrative issues. The visits, Ignace Maes says, make the point that the local offices "are part of a bigger whole than they ever realized. You get real help from experienced people. And you see that it is worthwhile to belong to Baker & McKenzie."

McGuigan initiated other changes, including revising the Client Credit rules to provide incentives to lawyers who bond clients to the Firm. He encouraged the U.S. offices to work together more closely, and suggested that more offices should go off the straight Formula in order to reward behavior that an office wants to foster. Implicit in his approach, McGuigan says, was the idea that "as a Firm, we had shied away from trying to manage the business." McGuigan's activist, sometimes intrusive, agenda suggested that unbridled partner freedom would be curbed. He also felt that a dramatic shift was necessary because "the industry—or profession—was rapidly changing. There were going to clearly be winners and losers, and I didn't want the Firm to be a loser."

Although McGuigan felt that, as Chairman, he should have spent most of his time on strategic planning, tactical issues—including liability questions and partner problems—diverted his attention. The time-consuming process of trying to sell his ideas to the partners was an additional frustration. "You could come up with good ideas. You could work very hard at issues that you felt were very significant. Yet, getting the attention and buy-in of people required an enormous amount of time, energy, and personal effort. There were times when I felt that I had to expend too much energy to achieve very modest changes," he says.

On the plus side, he says, it was exhilarating to go to "Eastern Europe and see what quality work was being performed there, and the sort of clients we acted for up in Beijing. I found exactly the same sense of excitement as we moved into new areas of practice. I enjoyed seeing the enthusiasm of some of the younger partners, some of the associates, who were interacting with some very satisfied clients, which, fortunately, we have a lot of."

After making frequent commutes between Chicago and Sydney to visit his young family, McGuigan let it be known that he wanted to give up the Chairmanship before his term ended. He left office in 1995, and John Klotsche succeeded him.

Afterword

They were headed for Chicago. From sixty-one cities, five hundred sixty-two Baker & McKenzie partners were flying in to attend the Firm's 1999 Annual Meeting. A half century before, the fledgling law firm had taken its first timid steps onto the international playing field. Fifty years later, its partners routinely steered their clients' transactions through a world economy where oil prices can rattle economies from Japan to Europe and speculators can daze Malaysian and Russian stock markets. Although their well-honed skills gave them comfort, their world was changing.

When Russell Baker was bouncing around Europe and Latin America on DC–3s in 1949, the Firm had no competition. By 1999, however, business was global, and other service providers were invading the Firm's once-exclusive international turf. Several large law firms were building global office networks, and well-financed accounting firms were setting up captive law firms. By the 1990s, a generational shift was taking place inside Baker & McKenzie, as the Boys of '60 were retiring and younger partners were rising to leadership positions. Some partners felt that the Firm's sheer bulk was making parts of its old culture anachronistic. And the Firm's high profile meant that it was being held to the most stringent common denominator in all aspects of its practice.

Toward the end of Robert Cox's term as Chairman in 1992, he experimented with change. During John McGuigan's three-year tenure, he sketched out a framework for major cultural and structural innovations. When John Klotsche became Baker & McKenzie's chief executive in 1995, he further defined and implemented the reforms, and added some of his own.

Klotsche, an "old boy," had joined the Firm in 1968. During the first nineteen years of his career, he practiced international tax law at the Firm's office in Chicago. He cherished the old culture. But, even before he had become Chairman, he had decided that, in order to survive in the competitive legal world, Baker & McKenzie would be forced to discard some of its historical ways of doing things. "The Firm is at a crossroads," he said. "We must adapt to the compelling pressure to modify how we do business so that we can keep it in line with the environment we live and work in."

Being steeped in the Firm's traditions, and at the same time seeing the need for reform, gave Klotsche a unique perspective from which to turn the battleship without losing the crew. Change became his mantra. He told his partners that, although he didn't see anything "looming that poses an unconquerable threat to continued prosperity in the short term, our profession and our Firm are in the process of change. It can be forced on us by a major, life-threatening crisis, which seldom brings change in an efficient way. Or we can keep track of our internal and external environments so that we can manage the pace and process of change."

Executing a cultural overhaul of Baker & McKenzie, he felt, would require a delicate political balance. "The acceleration of change in the legal industry will give rise to honest disagreements over the speed of change in the Firm, and will put pressure on unity," Klotsche says. The Firm's democratic tradition, he knew, would slow the process. And, because the partners were equity owners with a say in running the partnership, they had to be persuaded rather than coerced.

Instead of throwing out the Firm's culture, Klotsche elected to preserve some of its most basic tenets. "The key elements in Russell's one firm concept were full disclosure, an entrepreneurial spirit, and democracy," he says. Following Baker's dictates, he continued with the bottom-up, consensus approach to management "because our Athenian democracy is the best way to encourage the formulation of ideas at the grass roots." Although he was sometimes ambivalent about the Firm's entrepreneurial spirit, Klotsche advocated it as being particularly useful in pioneering new offices. During his first four years, Baker & McKenzie started operations in Houston, Munich, Düsseldorf, Bahrain, Baku, Azerbaijan, and Hsinchu, Taiwan.

Klotsche subscribed to another element of the Firm's culture: full disclosure of Firm data via a steady stream of communication with all lawyers. Baker & McKenzie set up Bakerinfo.com, an Internet home page, and a Web site, BakerNet for internal and external client communication, and BakerWeb, an Intranet site which gives lawyers and staff instant access to reams of Firm data. To keep partners and employees current on such matters as significant new legal developments and some of the high-dollar, high-stakes client matters its lawyers handled, Baker & McKenzie started publishing a quarterly newsletter, *Global*.

Another part of the old tradition that Klotsche focused on was the importance of interpersonal relationships among partners. Quoting Russell Baker's maxim, he said that "we want to earn a decent living, have fun, and develop lasting relationships. The Firm is much more than simply a business or place to work; it has that additional, but intangible, element of friendships with people all over the world." In addition, the Firm will "always have a healthy tolerance for diverse partner opinions and a fundamental respect for different mores, people, and beliefs."

Even though Klotsche subscribed to those elements of Baker & McKenzie's culture, he launched an attack on highly individualistic behavior that could create financial risks or embarrass the Firm. "The frontier-like spirit that has so successfully brought us to where we are today has to be balanced against the potential harm," he says. "I evaluate problems and issues based first on what's best for the Firm, then the region, then the office, and, lastly, the individual partner." Klotsche also took aim at the compensation system. However, because there are so many vested interests under the Formula, he dealt with it gingerly. During his term, several offices moved away from the Formula to a more subjective compensation system that, he says, "rewards partner behavior that helps the overall Firm."

Klotsche also set about changing the management style. In the past, most partners had felt that they had direct access to the Chairman at any time. "That perception is not realistic," he insists. Instead, he believes that the Chairman should deal with strategic issues, and should be freed from dealing with "financial bailouts, overly expensive lease commitments, messy lawsuits, adverse publicity, and ugly partner disagreements or defections."

Klotsche's objective was to turn the Executive Committee members into true executives. Their first responsibility was to establish global policy and to ensure that those policies are consistently applied. Rather than being a mere liaison with offices and practice groups as they had been before, the Committee members are now the first, and in most cases, the last, point of contact for solving problems. Another management reform underway forces decision-making down to the level closest to the working partners—the regional and local office managements and practice groups. To train partners to handle the new responsibilities, Baker & McKenzie instituted a Management Training Program at Northwestern University. There, partners attend customized two-week training sessions that cover strategic planning, delivering value to clients at reasonable costs, and implementing change. The training also targets leadership and marketing techniques, and attunes the partners to finding practical business solutions to clients' problems. An unintended benefit is that a bonding takes place during the training sessions, where the partners live in a "boot camp" atmosphere that includes dormitory rooms, cafeteria food, and long hours.

In the new management scheme, practice groups assume increased importance, particularly with regard to meeting client needs. "Our clients," Klotsche says, "are telling us that the relevant business unit of the future will not have an office or geographical focus. Therefore, our view of individual offices as profit centers must be changed. Our clients want to have the best lawyer for the job on their project, irrespective of where his or her office is located." To carry out that idea, the European partners organized the European Law Center ("ELC"). Structurally, the ELC is an economic unit that cuts across office and Formula lines, and all participating partners share the ELC's Associate Profit. The Firm also established a similar venture for the Geneva-based World Trade Organization.

Each region—Latin America, Europe, Asia, and North America—has a functioning Regional Council that receives Firm support and is encouraged to take on management tasks and initiate new programs. The Latin American Regional Council, for example, has opened Latin American Centers in London and Spain, and is taking steps to generate business flow between the Latin American offices and to foster closer cooperation with the Latin American specialists in the U.S.

While the Firm was reforming management, it also began concentrating on issues that would make it clear to partners that they were getting value from being part of the global organization. A primary tool was the Executive Committee's development of a global strategic plan designed to generate more work, revenue, and income. The Committee assessed the competition, the Firm's internal strengths, and the expectations and needs of its client base.

Even before the Firm finalized the strategic plan, it began investing in programs that would complement the anticipated plan. McGuigan had begun several quality programs, and Klotsche further refined them. Baker & McKenzie established a Quality Audit Program, under which partners from other offices review each local office's operations and quality procedures. "It would have been unimaginable just a few years ago for the partners to allow a group of outside partners to descend on their offices to write an unvarnished report on how they practiced law," Klotsche says. "But, under the Quality Audit Program, the local offices have learned from each other, and some significant problems have been identified and dealt with."

The quality programs also include the establishment of the Research and Know-How Center in London, which drafts and updates state-of-the-art contract documents and precedents for practice groups. The Know-How Center also developed a list and description of major transactions and an electronic news clipping service. In addition, it developed a database of information about clients in order to further capitalize on one of the Firm's major assets—its client base.

As part of Baker & McKenzie's overall drive toward market-driven initiatives, in 1998 it launched a formalized Client Service Management Program, appointing Client Service Directors to oversee key clients' needs. "We need to ensure that the right people are managing our important clients, even if this means displacing certain partner-client relationships," Klotsche says.

To remain successful in the twenty-first century, Klotsche believes, the partners must fully exploit the Firm's existing advantages, such as its multi-office network with trained lawyers, its extensive client base, and its strong financial resources. "We have the fundamental business assets, position, and international structure necessary to move us to new levels," he says. "The equation for staying on top is effective management, plus partner support of management, plus product development, plus providing high-quality services to help our clients compete in the world's marketplaces."

A Timeline of Baker & McKenzie

1949

Russell Baker forms Baker & McKenzie as a partnership and establishes the Firm's first office in Chicago.

1955

Baker & McKenzie begins to forge a global law firm with the opening of an office in Caracas.

1957

Baker & McKenzie establishes an office in Washington, D.C., and also enters Europe, opening offices in Amsterdam and Brussels.

1958

The Firm opens offices in New York and Zürich.

1959

The Firm's South American network expands with the opening of the São Paulo office.

1961

London and México City bring the total number of cities where Baker & McKenzie operates to ten.

1962

Baker & McKenzie establishes offices in Frankfurt, Milan, and Toronto.

1963

Baker & McKenzie opens its first Asia Pacific offices in Manila and Tokyo, plus another European office—this one in Paris.

1964

Sydney becomes the 17th city in which Baker & McKenzie opens an office.

1965

The Madrid office opens.

1967

The Firm opens its Rio de Janeiro office.

1968

The Firm establishes offices in Geneva and Rome.

1970

The first West Coast office, San Francisco, opens.

1974

Baker & McKenzie opens in Hong Kong, today the Firm's largest office.

1977

Continuing to develop its resources in the Asia Pacific region, Baker & McKenzie establishes offices in Bangkok and Taipei.

1979

The Firm opens an office in Bogotá.

1980

Baker & McKenzie opens an office in Riyadh, Saudi Arabia, and its 500th attorney joins the Firm.

1981

Reflecting the increasing significance of Singapore and Buenos Aires as financial centres in Asia and Latin America, Baker & McKenzie establishes offices in these cities.

1982

The Firm opens its 30th office—this one in Melbourne.

1984

The Miami office opens.

1985

Baker & McKenzie establishes its second office in the Middle East, in Cairo.

1986

The Firm opens offices in Dallas, Juárez, and Tijuana.

1987

Baker & McKenzie establishes an office in Budapest—*before* the collapse of the Soviet Union. The Firm also establishes operations in Palo Alto and Valencia, Venezuela and hires its 1,000th attorney.

1988

Barcelona and San Diego house the Firm's 39th and 40th offices. The Firm also opens in Los Angeles, only to close that office five years later.

1989

Baker & McKenzie establishes an office in Moscow.

1990

The fall of the Berlin Wall coincides with the opening of a Baker & McKenzie office there. The Firm's 1,500th attorney joins.

1991

The Firm establishes an office in Stockholm.

1992

Continuing its growth in Central Europe and the C.I.S., Baker & McKenzie establishes offices in Kiev, St. Petersburg, and Warsaw.

1993

The Firm opens offices on three continents—in Europe (Prague), Asia (Beijing), and South America (Brasília).

1994

Baker & McKenzie establishes offices in Monterrey, Mexico, Hanoi, and Ho Chi Minh City.

1995

The Almaty, Kazakstan, Santiago de Chile, and Lausanne offices are established.

1997

Baker & McKenzie's 2,000th attorney joins the Firm in the Kiev office and the Firm opens offices in Houston and Munich.

1998

The Firm opens its 58th and 59th offices in Baku, Azerbaijan, and Hsinchu, Taiwan.

1999

Baker & McKenzie marks its 50th anniversary and opens offices in Manama, Bahrain, and Düsseldorf, Germany.

Chairmen of the Executive Committee

1964–1966	John Creed, Chicago
1966–1971	Lajos Schmidt, Chicago
1971–1972	Michel Coccia, Chicago
1972–1975	Thomas Haderlein, Chicago
1975–1978	Dennis Meyer, Washington, D.C.
1978–1981	Wulf Döser, Frankfurt
1981–1984	Thomas Bridgman, Chicago
1984–1992	Robert Cox, New York
1992–1995	John McGuigan, Sydney
1995–2000	John Klotsche, Palo Alto

*From 1962 to 1964, William Gibbons served as Baker & McKenzie's first chief administrative officer, the Secretary of the Firm.

Endnotes

Chapter 1

1. Russell Baker did not use the name Thomas.
2. Howard Bryan, *The Wildest of the Wild West* (Santa Fe: Clear Light Publishers, 1988), p. 3.
3. *Chicago Tribune Magazine*, 28 January 1973, p. 73.

Chapter 2

1. Janet W. Ullmann, *The Brass Bed* (Self-published, 1991). All quotations from Ullmann in the text are from her book.
2. *Chicago Tribune Magazine*, 28 January 1973, p. 73.
3. The University of Chicago gave Baker credit for some of his work done at New Mexico Normal University, which allowed him to begin law school after only two years of undergraduate study.
4. Illinois law did not require Baker to have a law license to practice in the Justice of the Peace courts.
5. Fernando Bermudez, in a February 1, 1980 letter to James Baker.

Chapter 3

1. Before 1992, the EC was called the European Economic Community. In the text, the author uses EC or European Community. The original member countries were Belgium, France, West Germany, Italy, Luxembourg, and the Netherlands.
2. The Firm had three names over the years. In the text, the author uses Baker & McKenzie. Before 1952, the Firm's name was Baker, McKenzie & Hightower. From 1952 to 1955, it was Baker, McKenzie, Hightower & Brainerd. When Andrew Brainerd left in 1955 and Hightower in 1966, their names were taken out of the Firm name.
3. The WHTC law also applied to Canada.
4. Baker co-authored an article, published in 22 *The Tulane Law Review* 229 (December 1947), with Dwight Hightower.
5. These countries were often called "tax havens." Most tax practitioners who used tax havens shied away from using that term.
6. Gibbons wrote a seminal article on FBCs, "Tax Factors in Basing International Business Abroad," which was published in 69 *Harvard Law Review* 1206 (May 1956). Gibbons added chapters that discussed the merits of countries where FBCs could be established and made his article into a book, published in 1957, that bore the same title.

7. There are many versions of the story of how Baker and McKenzie first met. The story in the text comes primarily from John McKenzie, McKenzie's son, and Thomas Bridgman, who worked in the Chicago Trial Department with McKenzie.

Chapter 4

1. There were additional reasons that American companies went abroad, including low wages and tax and financial incentives in some countries. Not all companies elected to use the FBC structure, and chose, for example, to locate in France or Germany and pay the full tax load.
2. *A. P. Green Export Company vs. The United States*, 284 F. 2d 383 (Ct. Cl. 1960), and *Barber-Green Americas Inc. and Barber-Green Overseas Inc. vs. Commissioner of Internal Revenue*, 35 T.C. 365 (1960). The Firm had prepared the documents and organized the WHTC structure in the Barber-Green case. The government appealed both cases, and lost again in the higher courts.
3. In the *A. P. Green Export* case.
4. Even though the government lost the two 1960 cases, it continued its assault on the use of WHTCs to export American products. The Firm's Ira Wender and Roger Quinnan defended two cases the courts decided in 1963 and 1964. In both, the Firm's clients won.
5. Tax practitioners in other law and accounting firms also advised on WHTCs and FBCs.

Chapter 5

1. Over the years, the partners tinkered with the Formula to satisfy changing times and needs. The Formula described in the text comes from the January 1994 Articles of Partnership.

Chapter 6

1. Wallace Baker was in Paris, James in Madrid, and Donald in Chicago.
2. From time to time, the Chicago litigation department's compensation system was modified.
3. Initially, the Foreign Trade and Tax Department was a single entity. In the early 1980s, the tax and trade lawyers divided into two departments. In the text, the author treats the two as separate units.
4. The Firm has had foreign law experts in Chicago from many other countries.
5. The original countries were Chile, Peru, Ecuador, Colombia, and Bolivia. Chile dropped out later and Venezuela joined the Andean Common Market. Decision 24 had many more restrictions on foreign investment than those mentioned in the text.

Chapter 7

1. Mark Stevens, *Power of Attorney* (New York: McGraw-Hill Book Company, 1987), p. 161.

2. Coudert Brothers, a New York law firm that had had a Paris office since 1879, elected its first non-American partner almost a century later, in 1974.
3. Some countries have other legal systems. Saudi Arabia, for example, bases its law primarily on religious texts. Germany also developed a civil law system on which some countries, including Japan, patterned their law.
4. Most common law countries have also adopted legal codes in recent years. For example, the U.S. has the Uniform Commercial Code.
5. The comments in the text about common and civil law lawyers are, by necessity, generalizations. There are, of course, theoretical, indecisive American lawyers, and no-nonsense, pragmatic civil lawyers.
6. In Britain, public schools are, in American terms, private schools.

Chapter 8

1. Not related to Lajos Schmidt.
2. West Germany, in the 1960s, had two bar associations, the German Federal Compulsory Bar Association and the German Federal Voluntary Bar Association. In the text, the references to the German Bar mean the Voluntary Bar and/or the Frankfurt chapter of the Voluntary Bar.

Chapter 9

1. Peter Achermann, *Summary of the History of the Zürich Office of Baker & McKenzie* (Unpublished, 26 February 1996), p. 12.

Chapter 10

1. This quote comes from a 1969 Russell Baker speech to the Policy Committee in which he quoted Waris.

Chapter 11

1. In civil law countries, notaries play an important role in the legal system, preparing wills, real estate documents, and many other important contracts.
2. Alberto J. Sepulveda's father, Alberto A. Sepulveda, retired in 1976.

Chapter 12

1. The Breakfast Club disbanded as an informal policy-making group in the mid-1980s.

Chapter 13

1. Japan has three Bar Associations. At different times, different ones were hostile toward Baker & McKenzie.

2. Thai custom is to address people by their first name. The author has followed that custom.
3. William W. Horne, *The American Lawyer* (May 1991), reprinted by Lexis.

Chapter 16

1. Daniel J. Cantor, *American Bar Association Journal* (February 1978), p. 215.

Chapter 17

1. Over time, the Firm relaxed most of these restrictions.
2. Nancy Rutter, *California Lawyer* (September 1991), p. 34.
3. Deignan says the labels "producers" and "non-producers" were broad generalizations that were not universally correct. The labels are used in the text only to differentiate the two sides.
4. Rutter, *California Lawyer*, p. 34.
5. The final cost was much higher, by several million dollars.

Chapter 18

1. Mark Stevens, *Power of Attorney* (New York: McGraw-Hill Book Company, 1987), p. 169.
2. *Ibid.*, 167.
3. Deborah Graham, *Legal Times*, (25 February 1985), p. 12.
4. Stevens, *Power of Attorney*, p. 156.
5. *Ibid.*, p. 157.
6. Beall's petition contained numerous theories of recovery.
7. Greenstein withdrew from the Firm.
8. *The American Lawyer* (December 1991).
9. In 1994, the Firm lowered the vote to eject a Capital Partner from ninety to seventy-five percent.

Chapter 19

1. These are U.S. and Mexican publications where new laws and regulations are published. Almost all nations have similar publications.
2. Two of Atkin's teenaged sons remained in their apartment and videotaped the loyalist-rebel skirmishes.
3. Western Ukraine had been under Polish control prior to World War II. During most of the War, the USSR dominated the region.
4. Hewko worked for the International Advisory Council to the Ukrainian Parliament, which was funded by the Popper Foundation, which, in turn, was funded by the Soros Foundation.
5. Robert Cullen, *The New Yorker* (27 January 1992), p. 48.

Index